International Marketing

Klaus Backhaus
Joachim Büschken
Markus Voeth

Translated by Brian Bloch

palgrave
macmillan

First published 2005 by
PALGRAVE MACMILLAN
Houndmills, Basingstoke, Hampshire RG21 6XS and
175 Fifth Avenue, New York, N.Y. 10010
Companies and representatives throughout the world

PALGRAVE MACMILLAN is the global academic imprint of the Palgrave Macmillan division of St. Martin's Press, LLC and of Palgrave Macmillan Ltd. Macmillan® is a registered trademark in the United States, United Kingdom and other countries. Palgrave is a registered trademark in the European Union and other countries.

ISBN 0–333–96388–1

This book is printed on paper suitable for recycling and made from fully managed and sustained forest sources.

A catalogue record for this book is available from the British Library.

Library of Congress Cataloging-in-Publication Data
Backhaus, Klaus.
    International marketing / Klaus Backhaus, Joachim Büschken, Markus Voeth.
        p. cm.
    Includes bibliographical references and index.
    ISBN 0–333–96388–1 (paper)
        1. Export marketing. 2. International economic integration. I. Büschken, Joachim, 1964– II. Voeth, Markus, 1968– III. Title
    HF1416.B33 2004
    658.8′4—dc22   2003065841

10   9   8   7   6   5   4   3   2   1
14   13   12   11   10   09   08   07   06   05

Printed and bound in China

Contents

iii

Contents

List of Figures

List of Tables

 # Preface

What Is This Book About?

International marketers face a rapidly changing environment. One of the most fundamental changes is the integration of national or regional markets. The amount of cross-border trade has grown exponentially over the last one hundred years and this trend looks set to continue. Today, industrial buyers and domestic consumers alike practice international sourcing. Industrial buyers employ professionals to reap the benefits of international competition among suppliers, while consumers turn to international websites such as www.ebay.com or www.travelocity.com to do the same. Companies increasingly find themselves needing to internationalize in order to stay competitive.

These are just examples, but at the same time they are what we consider key driving forces behind the *integration* of formerly separated national markets. It happens everywhere and it impacts on virtually every industry. It happened a long time ago in the car industry with the rise of Japanese and German car manufacturers. More recently we have seen national market integration in the pharmaceutical industry, in mobile phones or in the market for steel.

We believe that market integration poses exciting and new challenges to international marketers. No market stands alone. Pricing for cars in Germany today depends heavily on the pricing strategy in Italy or Denmark. Choose the wrong approach and dealers and consumers will turn elsewhere. Senior managers at the Siemens mobile phone division told us that a price differential of 5 per cent is sufficient for the large mobile phone service providers in Europe to buy in Hong Kong instead of Europe.

How do you cope with market integration profitably? What is the arsenal of strategies and instruments to keep market integration at bay? The internationalization process seems to be irreversible. The political and economic benefits are too significant for any liberal economy to ignore.

The time is therefore right to address the significance of market integration in international marketing. This is what this book is about. We are looking at the impact of market integration on international marketing. Its impact is profound. It relates to virtually every national and cross-national marketing activity and all the processes supporting them. It is far reaching and – we think – the most important driving force behind international marketing success at the onset of the twenty-first century.

We do not claim to be the inventors of this concept. However, this is the first comprehensive book on the issue. It stems from our *Internationales Marketing* textbook that we first published in Germany in 1997 and which is now in its fifth edition.

Who Should Read This Book?

This book is targeted at students of international and global marketing at universities, business schools and higher education institutions. It is also targeted at managers of companies concerned with the challenges of market integration. It provides a foundation text on international marketing with the concept of market integration being the backbone of discussion.

This book is authored by three German university professors. We have all been heavily exposed to practical international marketing issues. This book stems from our collective experience and also our frustration with the generic discussion of global marketing. It uses references from many industries and countries to illustrate important issues and provides a rich learning experience. Thus we believe this book is by no means limited to the specifics of marketing in Europe (or elsewhere) or to certain industries. In fact, we consider the very idea of 'marketing in' a certain region as being conceptually obsolete.

The Structure of the Book

The first chapter introduces the idea of market integration. We look at market integration from a macro- as well as micro-economic perspective. From that we develop the concept of international marketing as a mainly *co-ordinative* task. It is concerned with the profitable co-ordination of national and regional marketing activities in integrated markets. This concept deviates significantly from classic textbooks on the issue. They describe in depth the driving forces of market integration on the 'player level' (companies, buyers, intermediaries, consumers) and their impact on international marketing.

The second part of the book addresses the issue of *going international*: the process of internationalization. We discuss market selection and market entry with a strong emphasis on coordination. After all, co-ordination arises from market entry. The third part (*being international*) deals with co-ordination strategies and co-ordinative marketing instruments. It develops a comprehensive framework for identifying and dealing with co-ordination problems including organizational issues.

Thank you

Many people contributed to this book. We owe them considerable gratitude. Dr Brian Bloch of MCM (University of Münster, Germany) translated and edited the German manuscript which was instrumental in making this endeavour possible. Maurice Eschweiler co-ordinated the project and made it much easier for us to keep productive. Basti Mell greatly helped with producing a 'presentable' manuscript to the publisher. We are very grateful for their support.

KLAUS BACKHAUS
JOACHIM BÜSCHKEN
MARKUS VOETH

Acknowledgements

The authors and publishers are grateful to the many individuals and organizations who provided permission for the reproduction of copyright material in this book. Every effort has been made to trace all copyright-holders, but if any have been inadvertently overlooked the publishers will be pleased to make the necessary arrangement at the first opportunity.

The Meaning and Subject Area of International Marketing

1 Internationalization Tendencies in Business

International economic development since the Second World War has been characterized by increasing international linkages and cross-border business activity of firms. This phenomenon is referred to in both theory and practice as 'internationalization' and has:

▸ a general macroeconomic perspective; and
▸ an individual microeconomic perspective.

The Macroeconomic Dimension of Internationalization

In macroeconomic terms, various indicators prove an increasing inter-connection of the global economy with respect to the flow of goods, investments and finances. Figure 1.1 visualizes the development of the world's gross domestic product (GDP) on the one hand, and the development of global exports on the other. While the economic output

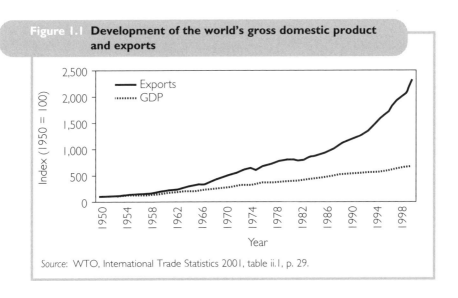

Figure 1.1 Development of the world's gross domestic product and exports

Source: WTO, International Trade Statistics 2001, table ii.1, p. 29.

rose on average by 3.8 per cent during the period 1950 to 2000, world exports, in comparison, rose by an annual average of 6.5 per cent during the same period (WTO, 2001).

The accelerated (macroeconomic) internationalization that has occurred since the 1980s, and which has become apparent with respect to services, has not always been received positively. Among other things, critics argue that:

▸ economic interconnections relate primarily to the industrialized nations; and
▸ internationalization is associated with a number of negative impacts.

Indeed, Figure 1.2 shows clearly that not all countries and regions have participated equally in world trade despite its increasing significance. Rather, trade is concentrated strongly in North America, Europe and South East Asia. The share of world trade enjoyed by these three regions exceeded 85 per cent in 1999. Furthermore, Figure 1.2 also makes it clear that a large share of world trade occurs not only between, but also within the regions mentioned. For example, in 1999,

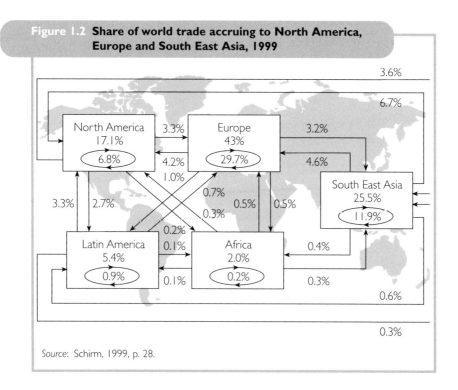

Figure 1.2 Share of world trade accruing to North America, Europe and South East Asia, 1999

Source: Schirm, 1999, p. 28.

more than 29 per cent of world trade took place between the Western European nations.

Apart from the low integration of the developing nations into global trade, the potential economic and societal consequences of an ever-increasing international interweaving of trade has been subject to criticism. For example, Martin and Schumann (1996), who evaluated critically, under the banner of the 'globalization trap', the economic and sociopolitical consequences of ever-increasing international linkages, came to the conclusion that an unrestrained further internationalization would lead to a situation in which the entire global output could be produced by 20 per cent of the globally available work force (see the caricature in Figure 1.3). Furthermore, they argue that the internationalization of the global economy is not the result of inevitable technological or economic changes and developments, but has been brought about deliberately by powerful groups within the industrialized nations. On this basis, they consider it essential to place

Figure 1.3 Caricature of the impact of globalization on employment

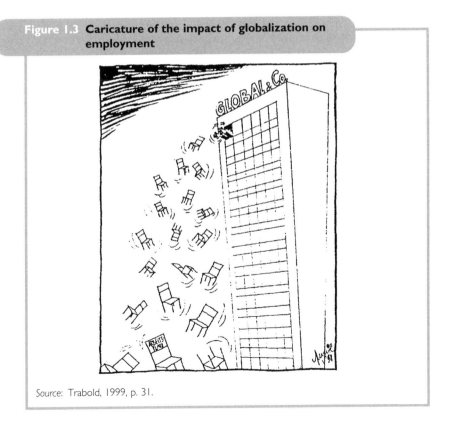

Source: Trabold, 1999, p. 31.

some political restraints on the internationalization of the world economy.

However, Martin and Schumann have no empirical evidence to support their central thesis of 'the end of work' in the globalized economy. The *Institut der deutschen Wirtschaft* (Cologne Institute for Business Research) (1997) analysed the claims of Martin and Schumann and came to precisely the opposite conclusions (see also Stehn, 2000; Kleinert *et al.*, 2000):

▸ Worldwide employment has risen since the beginning of the internationalization of world trade in the 1970s. For example, since 1970, the number of employed people rose by a third in the OECD countries, constituting an annual growth rate of 1.2 per cent. While the number of employed people in Canada rose by 74 per cent during this period and by about 60 per cent in the USA, employment in the European countries increased only marginally.

▸ In order to achieve an increase in employment of 1 per cent, the industrialized nations had to achieve a growth rate of 2.1 per cent, whereas between 1980 and 1995, economic growth of 2.0 per cent was sufficient. For this reason, the decoupling of growth and unemployment supposed by Martin and Schumann (1996) is, according to the *Institut der deutschen Wirtschaft* (1997), not justified.

▸ Since 1970, real income has also developed positively and risen by 2.3 per cent annually in the OECD countries. Thus, in this respect as well, the *Institut der deutschen Wirtschaft* finds no evidence to confirm the view of Martin and Schumann, that the internationalization of the international economy only benefits selected population groups.

▸ Finally, the *Institut der deutschen Wirtschaft* also finds no correlation between internationalization and a decline in social welfare. Between 1970 and 1995, such services have increased substantially in all OECD countries.

Even if it is quite controversial as to whether the increasing internationalization of world trade really does exert a negative impact on employment, for some years protests have been mounting against measures that promote and foster globalization. Since the WTO Ministers' Conference in Seattle in 1999, virtually all meetings of the International Monetary Fund (IMF), the World Bank and the G8 countries, have been accompanied by massive protests by opponents of globalization. Most of all, the non-governmental organizations (NGOs), accuse the WTO, World Bank and IMF of driving globalization for the benefit of the industrial nations at the expense of the developing nations. Therefore these organizations require the WTO to become leaner or to disband – 'shrink or sink'.

The Microeconomic Dimension of Internationalization

Probable microeconomic internationalization tendencies, are, ultimately, the result of intensified cross-border corporate activity. The degree of internationalization of individual economic units (firms) can be depicted on the basis of various indicators:

▸ the ratio of employees working outside the home country in relation to the total population;
▸ the share of foreign turnover in relation to total turnover;
▸ the share of foreign-earned profits in relation to total profit;
▸ the share of foreign production facilities in relation to the total number of production facilities owned or operated by the enterprise;
▸ the share of foreigners in the management organs of the enterprise;
▸ the share of foreign value creation in relation to total value creation; and
▸ the ratio of foreign investment to total investment.

If an increase in these indicators is evident, one can talk of increasing internationalization and thus of that of the firm as well. Figure 1.4 shows the increasing internationalization of the German firm, Henkel, in the second half of the 1990s.

Internationalization and Small and Medium-Sized Enterprises

However, this increase in internationalization can be observed not only in large firms; it also extends to small and medium-sized companies, the so-called SMEs (Hollensen, 2001, p. 3). None the less, many small and medium-sized companies reveal a substantial need for additional internationalization, and thus have considerable internationalization potential. Even if Durnoik (1985) claims to have recognized as early as the 1980s, that, since the beginning of the 1980s, many medium-sized firms were aware that 'they could no longer operate in

Figure 1.4 Development of the number of employees of the German company, Henkel KGaA, working outside Germany

Source: Company annual reports.

secure niches within their domestic markets, untouched and unchallenged by the pressure of international competition', many SME's clearly remain unwilling to become active in the international market. This is a dubious tendency because, in many markets, the internationalization of business activity is by no means a strategic option, but rather a strategic necessity (Hollensen, 2001, p. 5). This phenomenon of 'mandatory' internationalization that can be observed in many sectors of industry characterized by medium-sized firms, is demonstrated well by developments in the German textile and clothing industry in the first half of the 1990s (for a detailed analysis, see Backhaus and Voeth, 1994).

In the 1980s and 1990s, market conditions in the textile and clothing industry changed radically. This highly dynamic development was by no means the result of changes in individual market conditions, but resulted from the interaction of such factors. Changed market conditions and thus new challenges derived from such interdependent factors as:

▸ saturation tendencies;
▸ international trade linkages; and
▸ changes in cost structure.

Saturation Tendencies and International Trade Relations

In the market for textiles and clothing, on the one hand strong saturation tendencies were evident during the 1980s, but on the other, international trade in textiles and clothing grew rapidly, because of, among other factors, an increasingly liberal trade policy in the textile industry. However, foreign markets could not be penetrated to the same extent by German companies, because, in contrast to the German market, foreign competitors were active there. Between 1970 and 1992, the segment-specific trade deficit grew from approximately 1 billion euros (€) to almost 12.5 billion. This deficit resulted predominantly from the disproportionately large competition from Asian businesses. In 1992, exports to these regions amounted to €0.75 billion and imports to 8 billion.

Changes in Cost Structure

Furthermore, the textile and clothing industry was confronted increasingly with changes in cost structure in the 1980s. Even if this 'creeping' substitution of variable for fixed costs is not a phenomenon limited to this industry sector, the substitution process in the textile and clothing industry proved to be particularly problematic. In 1983, it cost €114,000 to establish a job in the textile industry (industry average €87,500), this rose to €375,000 by 1993 (industry average €125,000).

An increased share of fixed costs to total costs forces firms ultimately to strive towards sector-specific increases in turnover, because they can reduce unit-related fixed costs with each additional item sold. With variable costs becoming increasingly less important, the supplier with the largest unit-based cost reduction will achieve competitive pricing advantages which will in turn lead to increased turnover. Fixed costs can be spread over a large quantity of goods, and thus fixed-cost-induced unit costs will be minimized.

The market changes outlined above (saturation tendencies, increasing international trade interconnections and cost structure changes), have meant that, since the end of the 1980s, the industry has fallen into a slow, but steady, decline. Over a time span of over twenty years, the numbers of firms and employees in both sectors have declined by over 50 per cent.

The existence-threatening decline of the entire industry is has thus been accelerated substantially by the fact that the German firms in the textile and clothing industry were unable to undertake appropriate strategic adaptation. For example, the German textile industry attempted to overcome the local structural disadvantages compared with the advantages possessed by the Asian competition, by targeted investment in capital-intensive modes of production. According to the motto 'expensive machines versus cheap labour', tens of billions of DM were invested in the technological upgrading of production facilities during the 1980s and the early 1990s. The aim of this conscious high-tech strategy was to compensate for wage-related cost advantages in the developing and emerging nations, through process-based manufacturing and quality advantages.

In the end, this strategy did not succeed, because it failed to provide German suppliers with sustainable competitive advantages (SCAs) with which they could counter the competition from low-wage Asian nations. Furthermore, contrary to the expectations of the Germans, firms in the East Asian area simultaneously switched *their* production to capital-intensive manufacturing techniques. Figure 1.5 provides a comparative example of costs between Germany and India for the year 1992.

This deliberate strategy to invest in cost-intensive production processes led to marginal, if any, SCAs compared to suppliers from the developing and emerging nations. Instead, an intensification of the

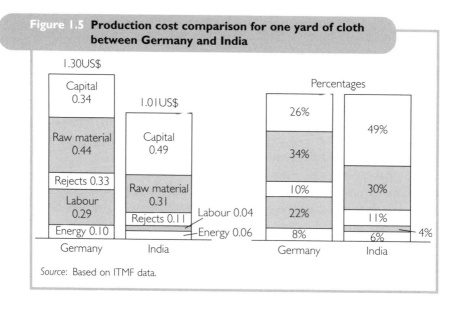

Figure 1.5 Production cost comparison for one yard of cloth between Germany and India

Source: Based on ITMF data.

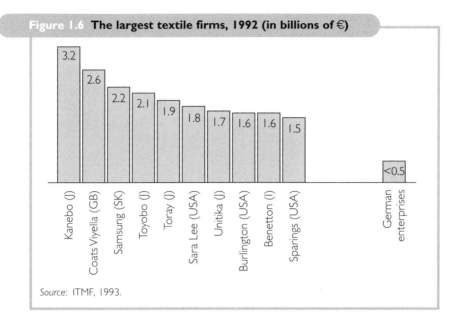

Figure 1.6 The largest textile firms, 1992 (in billions of €)

Kanebo (J): 3.2
Coats Viyella (GB): 2.6
Samsung (SK): 2.2
Toyobo (J): 2.1
Toray (J): 1.9
Sara Lee (USA): 1.8
Unitika (J): 1.7
Burlington (USA): 1.6
Benetton (I): 1.6
Sparings (USA): 1.5
German enterprises: <0.5

Source: ITMF, 1993.

fixed-costs problem had to be taken into account, which later emerged as a 'fixed cost trap' for the German textile firms. Higher production costs in international terms forced firms to sell at prices that, once variable costs were covered, barely contributed to fixed costs. Consequently, the amortization of up-front or pre-production costs could only be achieved through significantly higher turnover. Yet the majority of German textile firms lacked the necessary sector-specific turnover and company size. While international competitors achieved a turnover of between €1,5 and €3 billion through their consistent internationalization strategy, turnover in the predominantly domestic-focused German market hovered around no more than €0,5 billion in 1992 (see Figure 1.6).

In summary, it is clear that the German textile and clothing industry, which is characterized predominantly by medium-sized firms, could only have a real chance of surviving if it recognized that the absolutely vital economies of scale can only be achieved through a consistent globalization of business activity. This internationalization was thus not an option, but a necessity. However, because the German textile and clothing firms had not extended their cross-border activities sufficiently, they lost their competitiveness increasingly and to foreign competitors, and in the German market as well.

Independently of whether firms undertake an internationalization of their business activity voluntarily or, as in the case of the German textile machinery industry, are compelled to do so, there can be no doubt that the significance of international activities has risen sharply. Against this background, the previously national perspective from which business issues were analysed must be supplemented with an international perspective. For the subject of marketing, this means that above and beyond the national level, international considerations must become the central focus.

2 International Marketing as a Co-ordinative Task

Our understanding of marketing, and the managerial tasks associated with it has evolved considerably in recent decades. Initially, marketing was regarded as a managerial function, along with finance, production, or research and development (R&D). This functional perspective was epitomized frequently by equating marketing with advertising or sales. In recent years, marketing is increasingly being interpreted as *interfunctional*. This interfunctional perspective allocates to marketing the task of co-ordinating the value chain activities of a company and its suppliers towards customer requirements, with the objective of achieving sustainable competitive advantages (SCA). In principle, SCAs may be derived from any functional area that yields customer benefits. Customers may prefer the products or services of a company compared to that of its competitors because of quality, speedier delivery/or financial or price advantages.

Against this background, the question arises as to what should be understood by the concept of *international marketing*. An independent analysis of cross-border marketing problems is only necessary if actual decision problems deviate fundamentally from, or are supplementary to, the traditional understanding of marketing. If these conditions do not apply, marketing in the international context is merely a specific application of familiar and generally applicable marketing knowledge.

In the text section, we shall discuss the managerial tasks associated with international marketing. As we shall see, crossing borders is the cornerstone of the dominant or classic understanding of international marketing problems. Our discussion builds on that framework, but at the same time, moves beyond it.

The Classic Understanding of International Marketing

The classical understanding of the concept and content of international marketing is reflected in the definitions given in the literature.

Figure 2.1 Selected definitions of the concept of international marketing

Author/s	Definition of International Marketing
Kahler and Kramer (1977)	Export or international business activity
Albaum, Strandskov, Duerr and Dowd (1989)	Marketing is that segment of business concerned with the planning, promoting, distributing, pricing and servicing of the goods and services desired by intermediate and ultimate consumers. The definition of international marketing is different only in that goods and services are marketed across political boundaries
Bradley (1991)	The orientation of long-term organizational planning for the processing of international markets – in two or more countries
Onkvisit and Shaw (1993)	International marketing is the multinational process of planning and executing the conception, pricing, promotion and distribution of ideas, goods and services to create exchanges that satisfy individual and organizational objectives
Czinkota and Ronkainen (1998)	Planning and execution of (market) transactions beyond country borders
Mühlbacher, Daringer and Leihs (1999)	Transfer of the marketing orientation and marketing techniques to international business activity

Figure 2.1 contains some selected definitions of international marketing.

The definitions of international marketing presented in Figure 2.1, stem from American and European literature. They stress different aspects of international marketing activities. Kahler and Kramer (1977), and Bradley (1991) regard crossing national borders as the central characteristic of international marketing, without an immediate link to the market and consumers. Other writers emphasize, to varying degrees, the significance of the generic understanding of marketing in the international context. Such definitions as those of Onkvisit and Shaw (1993) and Albaum *et al.* (1989) are, in essence, derived from domestic, national approaches which have been expanded by the 'cross-border aspect', without this really permeating the content.

In general, definitions in the international marketing literature are characterized by an emphasis on crossing national borders on the one hand, and run parallel to traditional definitions of marketing on the other. The hazy distinction from familiar (national) marketing which all too often characterizes the classical understanding of international marketing, is clear from the following attempt by Quack (1995, p. 9) to draw a clear dividing line:

> What exactly is the difference between national and international marketing? E.g. with international pricing problems, we first apply our traditional marketing knowledge and we might conduct local pricing experiments. However, an experiment with pricing in Duesseldorf is, *in principle,* the same as one in New York. The basic knowledge found in the literature on such experiments can be applied fully to both cities. But a *precise formulation* of the experiments will be very different. Apart from the different structuring and function of business activities, communication, language and consumer behaviour vary considerably. These differences need to be considered. Also, the comparability of results cannot generally be taken for granted. The development of television shots is even more problematic. There is no shortage of information and knowledge in the literature on how to determine consumer utility or which advertising techniques are the most useful. But the final TV-spot depicting, for example, washing gel for the shower, will look quite different in Germany as opposed to China. In China, showing even a 'naked' shoulder is regarded as pornographic and has indeed been forbidden in a TV-spot. This is very different from the 'generous' depictions of shower gel for various TV-spots in Germany. From these indications, it is already clear that international marketing can only effectively be practiced with a solid basis of knowledge, complemented with many years of experience in national marketing. A sound marketing basis is needed, in order to proceed with the subtleties in the international arena.

This approach raises the question as to why an independent consideration of international marketing issues is necessary, if the crossing of international borders does not constitute a fundamental new challenge. Adapting the marketing instruments of a firm to the market and target groups in question, presented here in the form of an example of communication policy in terms of the extent to which an unclad female body may be shown on TV, is at the core of the marketing concept. Are we dealing with, as Quack's (1995) approach suggests, a mere extrapolation of familiar concepts from the national to the international sphere? Are the questions, approaches and results from the domestic arena just as appropriate to determine activities in the international context? A positive answer to these questions would mean that no in-depth treatment of international marketing was really necessary. Instead, it would be quite sufficient to consider the specific marketing challenges of foreign markets in the form of individual case studies: 'marketing in Japan' or 'marketing in the USA'. International marketing would thus become an appropriately modified replication of national marketing issues and problems. International marketing could then be interpreted as 'multinational marketing', adapted (but no more than that) for regional or country-specific differences.

This multinational approach is particularly common in the Anglo-Saxon literature (for example, as in Czinkota and Ronkainen, 1998). The often substantial cultural differences between various country markets form the basis of this approach. Such cultural differences stem from regionally diverging value systems or communicational artefacts such as language, symbols and customs, impact on the behaviour of customers, agents and dealers, as well as on the degree of internal latitude that can be used in the implementation of marketing programmes (Usunier, 2000). Cultural differences lead to country- or region-specific applications of goods, the nature of procurement processes or the peculiarities of distribution channels. Cultural criteria are thus differentiating factors with respect to buyer behaviour. From this perspective, 'cultural competence' in international business plays a central role and 'must be recognized as a key management skill' (Czinkota and Ronkainen, 1998, p. 64). An understanding of cultural differences and adaptability on the part of marketing managers thus becomes a major determinant of business success.

Characteristics of International Marketing

If international marketing is to justify an independent conceptual treatment, it must relate to a separable class of market-related problems caused by cross-border trade. The following case study provides some indications of the characteristics of international marketing.

'If you ask me, I don't think the idea of expanding our activities into Morocco and Algeria is very promising,' the factory manager, Mr Bresson stated to Miss Dufourcq, as they were leaving the meeting room. The head of the R&D department also shook her head and added: 'Particularly Morocco and Algeria. We know nothing at all about these markets. We don't know if there is any sales potential at all for Corical, neither do we have the faintest idea how the distribution channels are organized there. Anyway, surely it is better to secure our market position in France, before we let ourselves in for an adventure like this. Our company "Medcare" as an international player! That's just ridiculous.'

In the run-up to the monthly meeting that had just been concluded, it was already clear to Mr Fossier, the managing director of Medcare, that his announcement of plans to move into the neighbouring markets in the foreseeable future, would lead to unease. Given that the company had operated purely in the French market since its founding almost fifty years before, it was inevitable that even a modest amount of international activity would meet with scepticism. But when Fossier considered the various difficulties with which he had contended successfully since joining Medcare, he was confident that he could also handle the (partly internal) problems of internationalizing the company.

At the end of the 1980s, after almost four successful decades, the company had run into difficulties. Competitive pressure in the chemical-pharmaceutical industry had forced Medcare's customers either to manufacture for themselves the products they used to buy in, or to compel their suppliers to make ever-greater price concessions. After Mr Louis Gouiffes, Jr. had, for some time, fended off the inevitable decline of the traditional company, he gave up in 1993, and sold out to Roll Inc., a large pharmaceutical company that had been a long-standing customer of Medcare.

At that time, it seemed obvious that Fossier, who, as acting head of the 'corporate development' department, had prepared Roll Inc. for the acquisition of Medcare, would assume a responsible managerial position within Medcare after the takeover. None the less, particularly for the departmental head of the acquired firm, it came as something of surprise that the chairman of Roll had named Fossier as the sole top manager. Accordingly, Fossier was given a reserved and cautious reception at Medcare.

When Fossier looked back over the previous five years, it was clear that 1995 was the decisive turning point. At that time, Roll AG had planned to reduce the workforce of its barely surviving partner radically. That the company eventually gave up this idea was attributable solely to Fossier's resoluteness. Of course, this was much aided by the fact that, in this particular year, Medcare's long-term research project was completed and the consequent named product, 'Corical', was launched successfully in the French market.

Corical is a foodstuff, a calorie-free cellular substance compressed into tablet form using Medcare's cold-compress technology. Because the cellular material swells up when it comes into contact with human stomach acid, Corical provides patients with a feeling of satiety for several hours before it passes naturally through the body. The product is thus an outstanding dietary supplement and slimming pill.

Although from the start Medcare had distributed Corical only through pharmacies, the product had penetrated the market thoroughly after only a few years, because of general appeal to patients, and particularly its natural processes. In 1998, Corical was the market leader in the French market and at the time of writing is still Medcare's most important product.

Even though Fossier was sure that this success story would continue in the Moroccan, Algerian, and indeed any other international market, he had to admit that the sceptical arguments his departmental manager presented, could not simply be ignored. During the afternoon, therefore, he once again looked through the comments his assistant had made during the meeting. Fossier knew that the factory manager, Bresson, who was about to retire, was keen to avoid any stress in the factory. He had pointed out that it was already difficult to produce sufficient quantities of goods for the French market. 'We are just about at the limit of our production capacity. If we have to tap off resources to produce for Morocco and Algeria, we may not be able to provide enough for the French market. I don't need to tell you that our pharmaceutical wholesaler will hardly be willing to build up storage capacity so that we can supply Morocco and Algeria in the future. In fact, he only buys what he can sell within three days. 'Regarding the pharmaceutical wholesaling,' Dufourcq agreed, 'we just don't know anything about distribution in Morocco and Algeria. Does it proceed through wholesalers at all, so that we can sell through our exclusive dealer, Novos Inc., or will we have to sell directly to pharmacies ourselves? And what about consumer behaviour? Are products such as Corical sold mainly through pharmacies in Morocco and Algeria? To be honest, I don't even know how to get that kind of information about these countries.' Fossier did not respond to this, because it was clear to him that this wholesaling issue really did constitute a problem, at least in Morocco. He knew that in Morocco, the distribution channel operated in two phases. Unfortunately, almost the entire Morocco wholesaling system was controlled by Logon, a competitor of Novos in the French market. Fossier was sure that Logon, a company they had decided against using in France because of the unacceptable payment conditions it had stipulated, would only be willing to accept Corical in its product assortment of Morocco if Medcare was willing to give up the exclusive distribution in France through Novos. Fossier had naturally not mentioned this to his departmental managers at this stage, because he felt it would only have increased the scepticism.

However, the critical comments were limited not only to the issues of production capacity and distribution channels. Mr Bon (the financial manager) had expressed doubts as to how the still precarious financial situation could be extended further: 'You know yourself, Mr Fossier, the mother company will not go along with large and risky investments. We can therefore only stick our necks out so far and no further.' And, as if Miss Cathelineau, the sales manager, did not want to be the only person *not* making critical comments, she observed: 'given that we are talking about capacities, we shouldn't be thinking only about production. My sales team already has its hands full. We can't simply take on two more country markets. Of course, Mr Fossier, the problem would disappear if you would finally allow us the new appointments we have been requesting for so long.'

After Fossier had gone through the departmental managers' arguments again, he was no longer so sure if the planned entry into the markets of Morocco and Algeria was such a good idea at this point. After all, it was not only Medcare that had a lot to lose, but himself as well.

The Corical case presents some insights into the challenges of international marketing. It demonstrates that marketing products or services across borders results in:

▸ substantially increased informational needs;
▸ increased operational risk;
▸ the need to co-ordinate marketing activities across borders; and, as a result,
▸ a significant increase in the complexity of the marketing task.

Informational Needs

Given the less (or not at all) familiar market conditions and general business framework, the development of new country markets requires a high level of additional information. In some cases, the information is extremely difficult to obtain (Samli *et al.*, 1993, p. 14).

In the Corical case study, the question arises as to whether consumer behaviour and the distribution structure in Morocco and Algeria can be extrapolated from the French market situation. Furthermore, managers expressed doubt as to how the appropriate information could be obtained.

The cultural specifics of the country markets, and an adequate consideration of their practical implications, constitutes yet another need for information in the context of internationalization. For corporate decision-making purposes, in many instances, only personal experience is really useful (Kobrin, 1984). This requires the immediate presence of management 'on the spot', either through travel or longer-term assignments in the target country. In this sense, cultural knowledge is, most of all, experiential.

Increased Risk

An increased level of business risk is closely associated with the problem of cross-border informational needs. If little information is available, uncertainty rises as to the outcome of business activity.

For example, the manager of the R&D department considered the planned expansion into Morocco and Algeria as an 'adventure', because the company had 'no idea' as to how things worked in those countries. In addition, in his capacity as the head of the financial department, he drew attention to the fact that the mother company would not undertake any risky investments.

Co-ordination Needs

Companies that are active in several interdependent country markets simultaneously, need to co-ordinate their national activities in a reciprocal process (Terpstra and Sarathy, 1997). This includes the problem of allocating scarce resources optimally, with respect to the various relevant countries, financial and management capacity, for example. Management capacity that is allocated to one country is no longer available for another, thus, resource allocation automatically creates reciprocal interdependence in country-specific markets.

The planned entry into Algeria and Morocco confronts Medicare with various co-ordination problems. Firstly, opening up these markets could lead to distribution and supply problems in pharmaceutical wholesaler Novos in France. Secondly, entry into Morocco may mean giving up the exclusive distribution arrangement with Novos. Logon would only be willing to distribute Corical in Morocco, if Medcare distributed in France not only through Novos, but through Logon as well.

Complexity and Managerial Challenges

As a result of the specific characteristics of cross-border marketing, entry into new markets increases the complexity and degree of differentiation of managerial and marketing tasks (Terpstra and Sarathy, 1999; Cateora and Graham, 1999; Keegan, 1999). In this context, the emphasis is placed on the particular significance of meticulous decision-making and preparatory processes, as well as on the unique challenges devolving on managers, and their capabilities.

In the Corical case study, it can be assumed that the negative orientation of the department heads, and thus the second level of the company's management, was largely the result of the lack of international experience on the part of these managers. For this reason, among others, Mr Fossier decided to postpone the internationalization project temporarily.

An observation of the specifics of cross-border marketing as presented in the literature and exemplified in the above case study, highlights this mutual interdependence. Furthermore, an immediate and unambivalent categorization of the phenomenon 'cross-border trade' is not easy.

Not only in the international, but also in the national context, the need for information in new markets can increase significantly the risks associated with product innovations, which may in fact be necessary precisely because of the additional markets to be served. Such a risk exacerbates the already high level of complexity in such marketing situations. This raises the question as to what the root problems of international marketing really are, and how they can be systematized.

With regard to marketing problems related to crossing national borders, we propose differentiating between entry into new regional or national markets and ongoing operation in such markets. From this perspective, it becomes clear that problems of information-seeking and operational risk decline over time to a level typical for the domestic market (see Figure 2.2). All decisions associated with entry into new country markets are characterized in particular by both high information needs and an equally daunting level of risk. New and unfamiliar country markets create high uncertainty, which has to be countered by extensive information-gathering. It is important to bear in mind that some important information on 'if' and 'how' with respect to entry decisions is a priori not available. This includes reactions to the new entry in the country market from competitors who are already operating there. Effects of this kind can only be considered and integrated in decision-making processes in terms of various possible scenarios and their impacts.

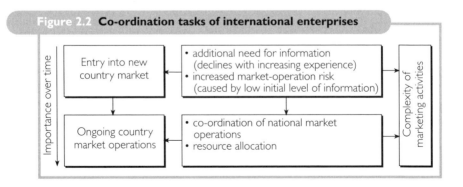

Figure 2.2 Co-ordination tasks of international enterprises

However, market entry decision problems are characterized by the fact that the need for additional information and the level of risk decline to a somewhat 'normal' level for that market. The entering company thus 'learns' how, or through whom, to acquire certain types of relevant information, and what competitive reactions are likely or relevant. Managers responsible for a particular country acquire through a process of maturation, or rites of passage, the ability to evaluate the impact of alternative marketing strategies and instruments. Over the course of this development, firms operate increasingly in a new country market under similar risk and informational conditions as in their home market.

The initial entry and ongoing operation of the individual country markets pose a particular co-ordination challenge, particularly in view of the rapid market dynamics that prevail worldwide. Resource allocation decisions form a major problem area, the magnitude of which remains constant, or even increases over time: 'Indeed decisions made with respect to one market are closely linked to those made with respect to others, and there is a reciprocal impact, often cited as the decisive characteristics of international marketing' (Berekoven, 1985, p. 21). The particular problems of market entry and ongoing co-ordination are primarily responsible for the complexity of international marketing.

In summary, this co-ordinative aspect is the essential feature of international marketing activities. Independent of the phase of internationalization in which a firm finds itself, whether it is planning a new entry or is already active in non-domestic markets, the marketing activities will constantly have to be synchronized with one another. The root cause of this is the increasing linkage between national economies at both the institutional level and that of the individual actors, as well as the increasing networking and interaction between internationally active firms.

Co-ordination in the Context of International Marketing Operations

Co-ordination of national marketing activities becomes necessary in the event of reciprocal dependencies between these markets. This understanding of international marketing departs somewhat from the conventional understanding of the subject. International marketing literature is characterized most of all by either the prevalence of multifaceted regional marketing problems ('local strategies') or as a term referring to a standardized global marketing approach ('standardization strategies') (such as in Takeuchi and Porter, 1989). The 'local strategy' approach emphasizes the significance of national regional market characteristics, and consequentially the need for a regional adaptation of marketing activities: 'Overseas success is very much a function of cultural adaptability: patience, flexibility and tolerance for others' beliefs' (Czinkota and Ronkainen, 1998, p. 63). 'Standardizers', on the other hand, stress the opportunities provided by a unified approach to products and processes, to maximize scale advantages.

As an element of the framework of international marketing, co-ordination is often interpreted differently from these diverging perspectives. Porter (1989) regards co-ordination ultimately as the standardization of country-orientated activities:

> A firm faces an array of options in both configuration and coordination for each activity in the value chain . . . Coordination options range from none to many. For example, a firm producing in three plants could at one extreme allow each plant to operate with full autonomy, including different production steps and/or different part numbers. At the other extreme, the plants could be tightly coordinated by employing the same information system, the same production process, the same parts, specifications, and so forth. . . . In copiers, for example, Xerox has until recently concentrated R&D in the United States, but dispersed other activities, in some cases using joint-venture partners to perform them. On dispersed activities, however coordination has been quite high. The Xerox brand, marketing approach, and services procedures have been quite standardized worldwide (Porter 1989, p. 27; similar views are expressed in Takeuchi and Porter, 1989).

By contrast, in their understanding of co-ordination, Meffert and Bolz (1998, pp. 33 and 255) emphasize the co-operative aspect of the individual corporate activities which are spread over the country markets in order to improve the common implementation of strategies. In this sense, co-ordination is in fact almost synonymous with far-reaching control of the national subsidiaries. Bufka (1998) provides a comparable, but essentially organizational, perspective, in which co-ordination also relates to control placed in the hands of foreign affiliates. For Hünerberg (1994), co-ordination relates additionally to planning and control processes between all participating units (headquarters, branches and so on). The objective of co-ordination is to achieve an overall optimum, a conflict-free balance between the interests of the institutions involved.

What all co-ordination concepts explained here have in common is the objective of coordination to achieve an optimal situation, generally defined as profit maximization for the entire enterprise. However, the need for international co-ordination that is postulated in the literature refers to varying levels. A clear differentiation needs to be made between the internal organizational level and the level of (external) market operations (see Figure 2.3).

Organizational interfaces and, as a result, interdependencies, emerge from the functional, regional or some other form of division of labour (such as regional configuration of production and R&D). These interfaces separate organizational units that are intended to contribute to an optimal performance of the overall task. Attempts to reap the advantages of specialization within these units are associated with the need to synchronize the various activities that they undertake. In turn, this need is based on *informational interfaces*, which link the units and their activities. In this manner, production units are dependent (from a cost perspective), on the development of an optimal production programme, and on information relating to the probable turnover levels in the target markets. Internal organizational information and

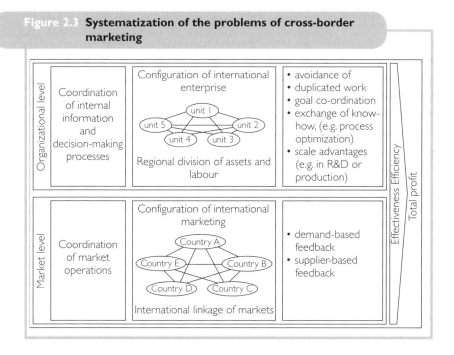

Figure 2.3 Systematization of the problems of cross-border marketing

decision-making processes must be co-ordinated with one another in order to maximize profits. This co-ordination can proceed through a centralized decision-making authority in the form of authority from the top of the organizational hierarchy. Alternatively, similar results can be obtained through formalization (standardized and institution-alized decision-making) and/or through employee socialization (common corporate culture) (Bartlett and Ghoshal, 1990). Thus co-ordinated activities of separate organizational sub-units, targeted at some common goal, can be achieved through different means. However, without the existence of informational interfaces between organizational units, the division of labour and the organizational structure of a company would be of little significance.

An international company operating in various regional markets faces, on the one hand, the need for a regional adaptation of marketing activities to the characteristics and peculiarities of each market, in order to ensure success in terms of a favourable competitive market position. However, the basis of international marketing co-ordination focuses on achieving overall corporate goals. The need for co-ordination arises if interdependency emerges between regional marketing activities. It is here that the real need for co-ordination lies. Interdependency means that marketing activities in one national market affect marketing activities in other national markets, and vice versa.

Operations in one market thus form certain barriers to what can be done in others. However, there does need to be a clear need for synchronization, and this is not the case in every instance. Such a need arises when the feedback (or interdependencies) radiate distinctly and significantly between the markets in which the company is operating or has an interest. These effects then have an impact on the planning and implementation of international marketing strategy.

Interdependencies between Country Markets

The essence of mutual dependence between country markets and their operation can be summed up as follows: 'What we do in the American market depends on what we do in Europe.' There are three main sources of regional market interdependence:

▸ *Supplier-based interdependence*: entering a country market, changing the nature of operations, also alters the general conditions within the supplying firm, changing the degree of freedom of operations in other markets accordingly.

▸ *Demand-based interdependence*: entering a new country market or changing the marketing strategy applied there, may affect demand in other country markets.

▸ *Competitor-based interdependence*: entering a country market, or several new ones, or changing operations through one's own activities or those of competitors, alters the relative competitive situation and thus leads to competition-induced adaptation in other markets as well. In all these cases, the enterprise is confronted with the problem that entering and operating in markets are not isolated marketing issues. Interdependence necessitates a simultaneous approach to planning, because of the types of linkage described above.

Supplier-Based Interdependence

Various internal corporate factors cause interdependence and feedback mechanisms which have an impact on the freedom with which national marketing activities can be executed. In particular:

▸ the configuration of international activities;
▸ the relevant cost functions; and
▸ organizational objectives.

Configuration of International Activities

The configuration of international activities forms a structure of various organizational sub-units and their geographic location (Porter, 1989). This creates feedback between the country markets, if, through the configuration of national units, a reciprocal dependence on resources arises. The structure of internationally active companies is therefore a key research area in international management. Of particular interest is the degree to which corporate activities are spread over the various company markets, the degree of concentration in certain areas, and the extent of centralization of decision-making structures. The importance of the level of centralization has led to the development of distinct forms of international organization (Bartlett and Ghoshal, 1990):

▸ *Multinational enterprises* form strongly decentralized and largely independent national units. The objective of this configuration is to improve on the ability to recognize and exploit different regional or national market opportunities, through adaptation to the specific needs of national markets. This approach is usually accompanied by a strong differentiation of regional or national marketing policies. In this sense, multinational enterprises are characterized through pursuing the marketing advantages of differentiation.

> Typical examples of multinational enterprises can be found in the food industry. In the past, companies such as Unilever or Nestlé attempted used to standardize their activities, but it is now usual to use far more country-specific approaches (see Becker's (1996) discussion of the 'renaissance of multinational corporate strategies'). The chairman of Unilever, Morris Tabaksblat, described his company's attempt at a global strategy and subsequent return to a multinational strategy as follows: 'We gave [the global approach] a good try, particularly with margarine. It worked well in Europe and in the USA. But not in Asia. They don't eat bread there, so why buy margarine? We tried to get the Asians to realize how nice bread tastes, and in the process, learned to sell people what they really want, rather than attempting to persuade them to buy what we want to sell. . . . Eating habits are varied. The Germans eat wurst, potatoes and sauce. The Italians love their pasta, the Chinese noodles, and in Indonesia, rice is the main thing. We sell our products in 160 countries and produce in about 90: but different products, not only with respect to food, but also washing power and hygiene items' (cited in Baron et al., 1997, p. 130).

▶ *Global enterprises* pursue a world-market orientation and the greatest possible degree of decision-making and operational centralization. Marketing operations are largely standardized, so that national units have the character of executive organs in the sense of carrying out strategies developed at headquarters for the global market. Country-specific market characteristics are largely without importance. The objective of this configuration is the maximum exploitation of economies of scale throughout the organization. Thus truly global enterprises strive relentlessly towards efficiency based on standardization.

> Adidas, for example, has its design, development, production and sales outlets centralized at a few locations. All Adidas products are produced in South East Asia and distributed through a

> logistics centre in Hong Kong, to a limited number of sales centres in Europe, and North and South America. Furthermore, overall corporate communication policy is managed centrally from an advertising agency in London.

▸ *International enterprises* constitute mixed forms of the above two extreme types. Certain responsibilities and decisional structures are delegated to national units. Enterprises of this kind strive towards an appropriate balance between (economic) marketing efficiency and a broader effectiveness.

> The formulation of international enterprises is exemplified by the recent market introduction of the 'Palio' model by the car maker, Fiat. The development of this model was guided by an awareness that the demands of customers in the developing countries are distinct from those in the industrialized nations. For this reason, the Italian company did not market the small Fiat Punto, which was developed specially for Europe and North America, in developing countries. By doing, the company distanced itself consciously from a global approach in the minicar segment. On the other hand, the company was not keen to develop, through a multinational approach, a special model for individual markets. They decided, therefore, to offer a product variant tailored to customer preferences in the developing countries. The Fiat Palio was the result, and differed from the Fiat Punto by virtue of a strengthened chassis and body for use on poorly surfaced roads. The wheels were also modified in terms of suspension and design, and the bumpers had greater resistance to flying stones and dirt. The model was produced in various decentralized production locations (see Figure 2.4), although assembly and logistics were controlled centrally in Turin, Italy. For example, flows of materials were registered by satellite and monitored appropriately.

These organizational types (multinational, global and international), differ according to the degree of centralization and emphasis on *either* efficiency *or* effectiveness. However, Bartlett and Ghoshal (1990) found that striving towards effectiveness and efficiency are not mutually exclusive. They suggest an additional organizational type, the 'transnational enterprise', which combines the advantages of market proximity (differentiation) and size (standardization).

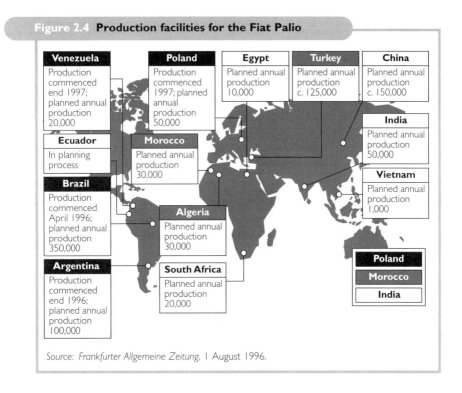

Figure 2.4 Production facilities for the Fiat Palio

Source: *Frankfurter Allgemeine Zeitung*, 1 August 1996.

In the opinion of Bartlett and Ghoshal, the mark of the transnational enterprise is the fact that authority and decisional structures are not allocated through the one-dimensional criterion of the level of centralization. The one-dimensionality arises because, depending on the authority of the head office, all national units are simply allocated the remaining authority, generally in equal measure (nature and extent). In this sense, the national units are equally 'equipped'. By contrast, transnational enterprises allocate authority according to a competitive-orientated selection. Resources, know-how and tasks are allocated selectively, to maximize worldwide competitive advantages. In order to achieve competitive advantages, a degree of resource monopolization can be appropriate (maximizing economies of scale), but this does not necessarily mean that these resources are monopolized by the head office. That is, differentiation advantages are still possible.

This principle is well illustrated by an example (Bartlett and Ghoshal, 1990). For the basic research component of a large enterprise's R&D, strategic organizational planning can also be located effectively at the head office. In order to exploit cost and size advantages on the one hand, the mass-production of standardized production components is generally concentrated in a low-wage country, where the application of advanced technologies, on the other, takes advantage of the innovation-orientated and high-demand markets of the Triad. 'The transnational enterprise concentrates some resources in its headquarters, others overseas and yet others are allocated to numerous national subsidiaries. This leads to a complex configuration of widely spread, but specialized assets and competencies. The widely spread resources are integrated through the strong interdependencies in the firm . . . Such interdependencies are reciprocal rather than sequential . . . Some interdependencies are an inevitable consequence of the specialized and broadly based configuration of production facilities and resources' (Bartlett and Ghoshal, 1990, p. 85).

Such a configuration results in international networks, comprising individual units orientated around a constant, reciprocal exchange of components, products, resources, information and personnel in order to ensure competitiveness. These units may correspond to the individual national subsidiaries, but this need not be the case.

The concept of transnational organizations sometimes provides the stimulus for a 'resurrection' of multinational concerns which were formerly regarded as being superseded: 'The list of large, internationally active firms, which were in dire straits at the end of the 1980s, reads like a Who's who of the major concerns: Boeing, Caterpillar, Du Pont, Salomon Brothers, Texas Instruments, Westinghouse, Xerox' (Anonymous, 1996, p. 3). The particular capabilities of large concerns as networked entities should enable them to capitalize on past success, in particular, 'the ability to combine capabilities and knowledge from various parts of the world. This has most simply been achieved by the sporting goods manufacturer Nike, with its successful mixture of American "heads" and Philippine "hands". In a more sophisticated variant of such an approach, firms get their basic technology from Europe and controlling systems and software from the USA. Electrolux has a research center in Finland, a development centre in Sweden and a designer group in Italy. The leading enterprises back up the process of disseminating skills and knowledge across borders through a constant flow of information' (Anonymous, 1996, p. 22).

If internationally active firms configure their activities as 'transnationals', many additional interdependencies are created. The decision-making processes that were formerly the jurisdiction of headquarters, now need to proceed at the levels of the organization that are relevant for exchange processes. Decisions must now be made directly at the level of the national units, which are mutually dependent on a reciprocal exchange of resources and know-how.

The approach of Bartlett and Ghoshal (1990) highlights the link between international configuration and co-ordination. Depending on the selection of international organizational form, varying needs for co-ordination at various levels of the organization emerge:

> The concept of transnational enterprises is based ultimately on the notion of exploiting the advantages of both a differentiated and a standardized market operation, which is not new. Even in the 1980s, in context of the debate on the advantages and disadvantages of global and multinational enterprises, the point was made that such enterprises need to strive towards market proximity as well as cost efficiency. In the literature, this debate proceeds under such banners as 'bifocal', 'multifocal', 'dual' or 'hybrid' enterprises (Prahalad and Doz, 1987).

Quite apart from the lack of real originality, the concept reveals the following weaknesses (Dähn, 1998, p. 123; Kreikebaum, 1996, p. 115):

▸ neglect of the convergence issue;
▸ no consideration of the rising costs of co-ordination over time; and
▸ lack of empirical proof of the underlying assumptions.

The claim which is generally postulated within the concept of transnational enterprises and refers to all industry sectors (aiming for both market proximity and efficiency), ignores the fact that, in many markets, a cross-border convergence of customer needs can be observed (Levitt, 1983). Such markets reveal increasingly similar preferences and buying behaviour, so that a reformulation from a global to a transnational enterprise seems progressively less productive, with the consequence that the simultaneous pursuit of market proximity and cost efficiency is no longer necessary.

Furthermore, in their concept of transnational enterprises, Bartlett and Ghoshal (1990) place a higher priority on the co-ordination needs of transnational enterprises in comparison with global or multinational forms. In some cases, however, the additional conflict management and co-ordination costs associated with transnational enterprises may reduce the benefits of this organizational form.

Finally, the concept lacks empirical backing. Bartlett and Ghoshal base their analysis purely on a comparison of the least and most successful international enterprises (Matsushita, Kao, NEC, Unilever,

Procter & Gamble, Philips, General Electric, ITT, Ericsson). They thus come to the conclusion that some of these enterprises are only success-ful because they aimed simultaneously at cost efficiency and market proximity. In contrast, the limited success of the remaining enterprises can, in fact, be attributed to the firm pursuing either one goal or the other. Thus, Bartlett and Ghoshal also neglect the many other factors that may be responsible for the success of the firms analysed. A final evaluation of the concept of transnational enterprises – particularly the delineation of the concepts of multinational and global enterprises – seems to be valid only if supported by more empirical evidence.

The Impact of Costs on Marketing Processes

An increasing share of fixed to total costs (fixed-cost intensity) is a phenomenon that characterizes many manufacturing and service industries. According to empirical studies, the proportion of costs that are independent of the production quantity (within a specific time frame), rises continuously (Droege *et al.*, 1993; Backhaus and Funke, 1996). For example, an empirical study by Funke (1995), based on data obtained from 422 medium-sized German companies, produced the following results:

▸ For all the industry sectors investigated, the share of fixed costs rose from 38 per cent in 1972 to over 42 per cent in 1982, and to 47 per cent in 1992. This constitutes an increase of nearly 25 per cent in twenty years.

▸ The increased percentage of firms with fixed-costs shares of at least 50 per cent in 1992 is dramatic: this percentage has more than doubled from 22 per cent in 1972 to 51 per cent in 1992. Furthermore, the greater majority of the responding firms antici-pate additional increases in fixed costs in the future.

The main cause of this increasing fixed-cost intensity lies in personnel costs that become 'more fixed'. This refers to legal restrictions on dismissing staff, and the decreasing use of performance-orientated remuneration systems. An additional reason is the rising share of research and development (R&D) costs, which for the most part have to be spent by a firm before the resulting products or services enter the market (sunk costs). Yet another factor is the increasing capitalization of production, which, at least in the short to longer run, replaces vari-able personnel costs with long-term fixed costs. The hallmark of a fixed-cost-intensive enterprise is a high dependence on production and sales volume, and the resulting costs per unit, because changes in production and turnover do not have much of an impact on variable costs, but have a greater one on unit fixed cost. In the face of volatile production and sales levels, this is accompanied by a relatively low level of overall cost flexibility.

Securing new country markets may exert a significant impact on unit costs if operations there and the necessary production sites are associated with a high share of fixed costs. Additional sales quantities from the new markets affect the allocation of fixed costs, and thus unit costs, all the more radically the larger these quantities are and the larger the share of fixed costs in production. The effect of economies of scale on lowering unit costs and on maintaining competitiveness is therefore a central motivation for internationalizing business activity (Stonehouse *et al.*, 2000, p. 80). Higher production volume because of a new regional market allows unit costs to decline in *all* country markets in which the firm is active. This occurs because the impact of declining units costs prevails simultaneously in all country markets. This creates interdependencies between the country markets and international marketing strategies. The higher the degree of centralization of fixed-cost intensive production, the more the international cost situation changes with sales volume in a single national market. In this sense, the configuration of an international organization influences the extent of unit cost changes.

The aircraft industry is one in which fixed costs traditionally play a major role. Before the first roll-out of a newly-developed aircraft type, there will generally be R&D costs amounting to several billion euros. For example, the development costs of the planned wide-body Airbus A380 are likely to amount to 11 billion euros (Anonymous, 2000). Consequently, the success of aircraft manufacturers depends substantially on the turnover achieved.

If one considers the sales quantities presented in Figure 2.5, which the Airbus company has achieved since the market introduction of the A340 (their largest aircraft so far), the international interdependencies created by high fixed costs are quite clear. If, for example, Airbus were able to market the A340 successfully in North or Latin America, it would also improve its marketing potential in other regions. Because the highest order quantities achieved in North or Latin America would lead to an improved spread of fixed costs, the enterprise would be able to make price concessions in other regions.

Figure 2.5 Regional distribution of A340 orders as of 30 November 2000

Cross-Border Corporate Objectives

The internationalization of enterprises is less a goal of corporate activity than an instrument for achieving corporate objectives. In this sense, internationalization is not a self-serving goal, but must be evaluated in terms of its economic impact. For example, fixed cost depreciation resulting from entering additional country markets should, for example, be regarded as an instrument for achieving overall cost objectives. The same applies to alternative organizational forms. This means that, firstly corporate goals must be defined, forming the basis for country-specific goals and strategies.

At the corporate level, profitability goals (increase in profits, return on investment and return on sales) and its drivers, such as market-related goals (rising sales and market share) and cost-related goals are at the centre of focus. Such goal systems are typically supplemented by financial goals (liquidity, capital structure) and social objectives (security and work satisfaction). Goal definition starts at the corporate level and is then extended to the level of separate divisions and national subsidiaries. This is to ensure that national subsidiaries add to the value of the total enterprise as defined by the corporate goals, and do not follow objectives that are not in the interest of the company.

If degrees of goal achievement at the country or national subsidiary level are dependent on one another, the setting of country-market (sub-)goals will create feedback between the individual country markets. If, on the other hand, the profit contribution of a country is independent of all other country markets, there will be no feedback within the corporate goal system. In the majority of cases, however, this is unlikely, because the degree of goal attainment (level of profit) is to some degree a function of resources invested (financial capacity, management time and so on). Resources are invariably scarce, so that country-specific levels of goal achievement are linked through resource allocation. Expressed formally, the consequence is that the overall profit of international enterprises does not constitute an aggregate function of activities at the national level. That is, country market profit is mutually interdependent.

Demand-based Interdependence

The exchange of information and goods at the level of demand causes demand-based interdependence. Both factors ultimately form the basis of increasing reciprocal linkages between national economies.

Information Exchange between Country Markets

The significance of cross-border information flows is beyond question. The convergence of consumer preferences associated with the global-ization of markets is attributed to a similar process with respect to information (the 'globalization pull' discussed in Levitt's 1983 global-ization theory).

CNN (Cable News Network) can be regarded as the perfect example of a globally present, standardized informational instrument. Since its inception in 1985, CNN established itself as the first truly inter-national TV news programme. As a around-the-clock news provider, it is present in all relevant areas of the world. The programme is produced mainly in Atlanta, Georgia, USA, and partly in London for the world market and is transmitted by satellite.

Global information flows have undoubtedly led to a convergence in consumer preferences. Because the liberalization of information and communications markets has also simplified the access to purchase-relevant information, there are clear co-ordination implications for international marketing. Purchasers can inform themselves about potential suppliers in many countries. Such information extends beyond the goods and services on offer, to include supplier behaviour as well. Such information can influence purchasing behaviour in the home market.

The exchange of information can constitute an independent source of demand-based interdependence. The reasons are manifold:

▸ 'Success stories' of the activities of sellers in particular country markets may exert a positive influence on buyer behaviour in other country markets. The high-speed Transrapid train developed by ThyssenKrupp and Siemens, provides a good example. For a long time, it seemed as though the Transrapid would prove to be a major flop for both companies. In no country in which the need for such a high-speed train had previously been identified, could potential contractors be convinced that it was worth the billions of investment needed to buy the Transrapid. Only when the Chinese government decided, in January 2001, to link the international airport at Pudong in Shanghai with the inner city by means of a Transrapid, was this considered by market observers as a decisive breakthrough in the international market (Anonymous, 2001b), because it was then assumed that this contract would be viewed positively by potential buyers in other countries.

▸ Similarly, the flow of information can also have negative consequences. Information about quality problems in one country may affect buyer behaviour in other countries.

> Coca-Cola suffered this fate in summer 1999. The soft drinks the enterprise had produced and sold in Belgium in June of 1999, accidentally contained hazardous substances and made some Belgian customers sick. Although the firm's products in other countries were not affected at all, the media alerted customers to the Belgian situation and sales elsewhere dropped.

▸ Access to foreign TV programmes and the advertisements they show leads to a possible confrontation with other communication product positioning in the domestic market.
▸ International sources of information on the Internet allow unlimited access to information sources from a number of countries. To an increasing extent, commercial suppliers are using the Internet in two major ways. First, they present their products online in order to inform potential customers about them. Second, they offer

systems where consumers can order the products they are willing to buy. Particularly for firms whose products are sent by mail or though data exchange (for example, software), electronic commerce (e-commerce) has led to completely new distribution channels (this is discussed later in more detail).

According to several experts, the number of Internet users is still growing rapidly, which makes this information, communication and transaction system an important factor in the market place. However, concerning the acquisition of potential buyers, sellers have to realize that they cannot reach every customer via the Internet. On the one hand, there are people with the best access to information technology that our modern society has to offer. They can improve their skills, and, of course, they can earn a lot of money using the Internet. But on the other hand, there is a group of people with no access to the Internet at all, who cannot take advantage of the new medium. For them there is less opportunity to take part in education, electronic transactions, entertainment and communication. The difference between these two groups is called the *digital divide* (compare http://www.digitaldivide.gov/about.htm – accessed 28 October 2000.) Generally speaking, there is a big gap concerning Internet access between industrialized nations and developing countries. In Mexico, for example, only 14 per cent of households have an Internet access via a home PC according to AC-Nielsen.

Exchange of Goods

In order to establish a profitable cross-border exchange of goods, companies need a lot of information about foreign markets. Therefore, having access to sufficient data is a necessary condition to create and to implement a successful international marketing concept. These data have to be transformed into information, which can be used for the exploitation of country-specific price and quality differences (arbitrage). In the area of industrial goods, cross-border purchasing ('global sourcing') has already been important for several decades. Concerning the business-to-consumer market, the emergence of the Internet allows consumers to participate directly in the local, regional, national and international exchange of goods. Consequently, customers are no longer limited in the choice of suppliers in many industries.

Dell, the US computer systems corporation, provides a good example for that situation. Dell assembles computers, which are customized to the individual consumer's needs. The company produces 'ready to start' computers all over the world. Dell's European production facility is based in Limerick, Ireland. From there, the company ships computers to Europe, the Near East and Africa. Dell tries to sell it's hardware in different European countries at different prices. But nowadays, consumers are able to compare the prices quite easily and may buy a product in another country.

If country-specific price and/or quality advantages are known (information as a necessary condition) and outweigh the transaction costs of foreign sourcing (sufficient condition), arbitrage will occur. For suppliers who concentrate on similar target groups in several country markets, but practise price discrimination (different prices for different markets), a major co-ordination problem arises. Arbitrage between the country markets frequently exerts substantial pressure on a differentiated pricing policy.

The exchange of goods forces the affected seller to adapt their international marketing activities. In the past, for many suppliers, the emphasis was on a strategy aimed at reducing the exchange of goods and thus also the need for co-ordination. For example, several automobile manufacturers threatened to cancel contracts with dealers involved in lucrative re-importing. However, this strategy was not possible in the context of the prevailing free cross-border trade and in particular, the harmonization of legal frameworks.

Sellers, who concentrate on similar target groups in various country markets, but use different prices there, can then attempt to reduce the need for coordination through preventing the exchange of goods, but as the example above indicates, the viability of this strategy is contingent upon the legal restrictions the company faces. These should be closely considered. If illegal or impossible to enforce, other options to deal with profit-reducing market feedback should be explored. We will discuss such options in greater detail in the following chapters. Co-ordination problems on the basis of buyer arbitrage processes, can, however, only occur between goods that are potentially exchangeable between country markets. This applies essentially to those goods that are storable and can be transported physically between country markets such as some consumer goods (for example, perfume, entertainment electronics and pharmaceuticals) and to industrial goods, but not to services that can only be used locally (car rental or hospitality services, for example). The physical transportability of a product is, however, not a necessary condition. Thus it is conceivable that foreign dealers or manufacturers' subsidiaries would be selected as contractual partners, but that the product purchased would be delivered in the domestic market (some automobile re-importers operate in this manner). What is decisive is that, in the various country markets for a certain product, contractual partners are available, but the use of the product is independent of this contractual partner (for example, purchasing plane tickets).

Virtual Arbitrage

Information exchange about prevailing price differences between country markets for an internationally standardized product can lead to arbitrage. As early as 1924, Cournot remarked in this context: 'It is clear that goods which are movable, will flow from a market in which they have a lower value, to one in which they have a higher value, until the difference in value no longer exceeds the transport costs.' Arbitrage will therefore occur when market interdependencies are accompanied by regional pricing processes. These arise when the individual country-specific prices are delegated to different decision-making authorities, and marketing interdependencies are not recognized.

If, for example, one considers the online offerings of the firm Nokia, which they advertise in their American and German Internet pages, it is evident that, to some degree, identical products are being sold at radically different prices. In late 2000, the firm was offering head-sets at a price of US$39, whereas the identical products was being sold for €30.17 on the German online page. Because, in late 2000, the exchange rate exceeded 1 €/US$, there were substantial price differences between the American and German online offerings. If one also considers that, for the most part, arbitrage is conducted less by individual buyers and more by commercial re-importers who have comprehensive means at their disposal that enable them to reduce unit arbitrage costs, then it can be assumed that the differential (online) prices charged by Nokia do indeed create a danger of arbitrage processes in the USA and Germany.

Arbitrage may occur either in classical or virtual form. In the case of *classical arbitrage*, a physical transfer of the product in question across country borders is necessary (Barrett, 1996). Because of the resulting additional arbitrage costs, such as travel costs for the arbitrageur and the costs of transporting the goods, the international price difference must be substantially higher in the classical case than for virtual arbitrage. In the case of *virtual arbitrage*, buyers from international enterprises use their information about country-specific pricing differences for an internationally available product, in order to purchase from manufacturers at the lowest possible price worldwide. The result is that there will not be a physical transfer of the goods across country borders, but, because of price negotiations with a domestic seller, the price for the arbitrage product will be adapted to the price in the purchasing market with the lowest price level. In this manner, the arbitrage conditions which proceed from the physical transport of the arbitrage product are irrelevant and necessitate a new approach towards the emergence of integrated markets. The potential for virtual arbitrage is greater for the purchasing institution, the greater their buying power. This is determined, among other things, by enterprise size and market structure, but most of all by the 'value' of the purchasing enterprise for the international seller.

Virtual arbitrage is significant most of all with the marketing of goods and services to organizational (generally corporate) customers. Here, the buying enterprise is characterized, particularly with heavily standardized components, by highly price-sensitive decision-makers, whose aim is to exert downward pressure on sellers through indicating country-market-specific price differentials. If this is successful, there may be major profit declines. Furthermore, such induced price reductions frequently fail to produce additional customer loyalty, because they are not looked upon particularly favourably by buyers. Rather to the contrary, in fact – it is not uncommon for prices agreed upon in the past to damage customer relationships, because they are regarded as having been excessively high.

Competitor-based Interdependence

The interdependence of country markets resulting from measures undertaken by competitors has its root cause in the *relativity of competitive positions* and degree of internationalization of competitors. Competitive advantages in terms of effectiveness (for example, product or process quality) exist only in relation to the performance or actions of certain alternative suppliers. The same applies to the cost situation.

Cost (efficiency) advantages or disadvantages can only be determined in relation to the competition.

Ultimately, the competitive position of an enterprise in a certain market depends on the activities of competitors. Internationalization undertaken by a competitor influences one's own situation in the home market and vice versa, and constitutes another source of increasing interdependence between markets. A firm does not even have to internationalize itself to be affected. The impact of increasing size and an expanded knowledge base which a national competitor derives from its foreign activities, is sufficient to change the relative competitive situation of a purely domestic firm. As Czinkota and Ronkainen (1998, p. 14) put it: 'Those firms and industries that are not participating in the world market have to recognize that in today's trade environment, isolation has become impossible. Willing or unwilling, firms are becoming participants in global business affairs.'

Therefore, feedback between country markets can arise through integration in networks of international competition. The entry of new competitors into a firm's country markets, or a change in the behaviour of established competitors, can force firms to adapt not only in those markets that are affected directly, but also with respect to its other target markets. Figure 2.6 shows the interplay of competitive forces confronting an international enterprise.

As described in Figure 2.6, the international enterprise (S_H) operates in the home market as well as in two additional country markets (Target Countries 1 and 2). In each of the country markets, the seller competes with locally operating firms (C_H, C_{TC1}, C_{TC2}), which also serve other markets in which the firm operates. The firm emerging from Target Country 2 (C_{TC2}) thus also operates in the home market of the firm in question. Furthermore, for the international firm, those competitors which derive from countries in which the firm in question does not operate, are also relevant (C_i).

It is evident that an international firm has to contend with various types of competitors, which comprise an interdependent network of suppliers in terms of competitive position. There are competitors who:

▸ operate only as domestic sellers in individual country markets in which the international firm is active (national competitors);
▸ operate in some or all of the international markets operated by the internationally active firm (international competitors); and
▸ target individual country markets in the context of international marketing (third country competitors).

Figure 2.6 The competitive situation of an international enterprise

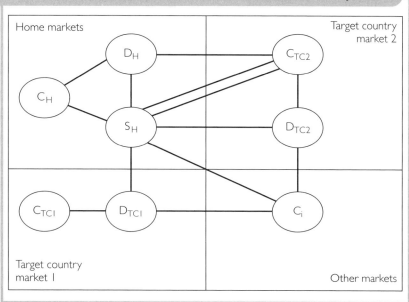

The presence of such a competitive network with reciprocal competitive dependence, constitutes a major restraint on an international enterprise's operational freedom of action in individual country markets. Even if aimed initially only at specific country markets, the actions of a seller or its competitors lead to adaptation not only in these countries, but in others as well. For example, if, in the situation depicted in Figure 2.7, a new (national) competitor enters the home market of firm S_H and sells at a lower price than that which prevailed previously, it may force the firm not only to lower its prices in the domestic market, but in other markets as well. This reaction may be necessary in order to avoid international price differentials that can cause arbitrage.

The competition-based feedback described above applies not just to market entry, but also very substantially to subsequent activity in international markets. Particular difficulties and competition-related feedback must be measured and integrated in the planning of international marketing activities if strategic and/or capital-related links between international competitors arise. These may compete in some areas and co-operate in others. Figure 2.7 shows an example of the automobile industry, in which particularly strong linkages between manufacturers have developed in recent years.

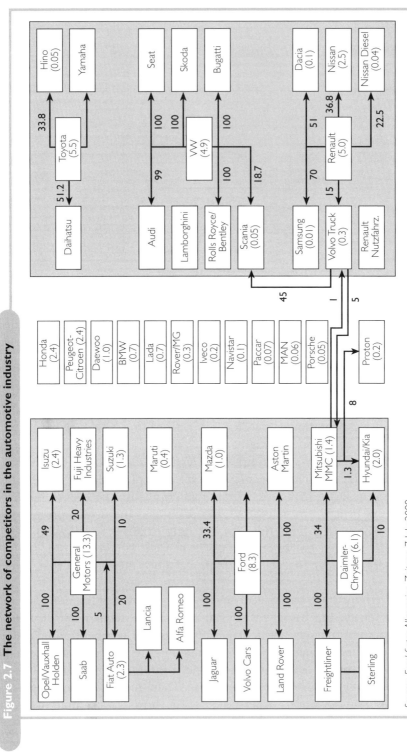

Figure 2.7 The network of competitors in the automotive industry

Source: *Frankfurter Allgemeine Zeitung*, 7 July 2000.
Note: Figures within boxes denote brand's market share; figures with arrows give the share that this company holds of the other company.

In the automobile industry, market experts assume that in the future, it will only be possible to distinguish between 6 strategic groups. Apart from the General Motors group, Ford, Daimler-Chrysler, Toyota, VW and Renault, will constitute the additional 'Group Leaders'. In this context, it is debatable whether the manufacturers which have not previously belonged to any goups, such as Honda, BMW or Porsche, will be able to survive over the longer term, without any group membership.

The following examples show that this is no mere industry-specific phenomenon. Competition-induced interdependence constitutes a fundamental influence on the formulation of marketing activities.

Textile Machines

The example of the textile machinery market, discussed in Chapter 1, demonstrated that, at the beginning of the 1990s, German enterprises could only prevent the decline of the industry if they internationalized their activities consistently. The pressure to internationalize arose through increasing competition from international sellers, who had access to greater economies of scale than did the German manufacturers. The latter could therefore only compete by achieving similar economies. Because the German firms did not recognize the need to internationalize caused by competitor-based interdependencies, and continued to operate largely on a national basis, the decline of the entire industry sector could not be prevented.

The Credit Card Market

In the past, the European credit card market was divided more or less regionally between Visa International and Europay International (Eurocard and Mastercard). While the German-speaking area and Northern Europe were dominated mainly by Europay International, Visa prevailed in Great Britain, France and Southern Europe. However, in 1994, Visa changed strategy and attempted, with aggressive promotion aimed both at customers and traders, to move into the German market. In contrast to Europay, which, between 1994 and 1996 had barely managed to enlarge its retailer network in Germany beyond about 250,000 retailers, during the same period, Visa managed to acquire more than 20,000 new retailers and extend its own network to

256,000 retailers. Because Europay did not counter the threat to its traditional strongholds, it proceeded to lose not only a major share of its German market, but also in the previously secure Danish and Dutch markets.

In view of the changes in the relative competitive situation brought about by Visa's strategy change, Europay found itself also compelled to develop appropriate strategies. The core of the strategy which they had pursued since 1996 was to break up Visa's dominant position in Southern Europe. For example, in the Spanish market in which Visa used to have a share of approximately 90 per cent, at the end of 1996, Europay convinced Sistema 4B, the largest Spanish commercial bank to issue Euro and Mastercards (Burgmaier, 1997).

All in all, it is clear that the strategic change undertaken by Visa in Germany and Northern Europe had implications for the enterprise in the Southern European markets. There were feedback mechanisms between the northern and southern country markets, such that Visa's strategic change in the north led directly to strategic change on the part of Europay in the south.

The Air Transportation Market

After the deregulation of the air transportation market, various airlines (especially the formerly state-owned ones) are facing increasing competition from other companies. In order to provide a worldwide network of flight connections, increased numbers of airlines are creating strategic partnerships with other airlines. With these partnerships, the airlines can operate with lower overhead costs by pooling the scarce resources in many fields of action – for example, in the luggage transportation and boarding areas. In addition to the more efficient use of inputs, the airlines were/are able to offer a more valuable output since they joined global alliances. In May 1997, Lufthansa (German), Air Canada, SAS, Thai Airways and United Airlines got together and institutionalized the so-called 'Star Alliance'. Since several other competitors had already created their own alliances, the members of the Star Alliance were forced to do the same. A lot of market experts think that the airlines that do not yet belong to one of the alliances will fail to exist in the long run. Therefore companies have to join international strategic partnerships if they do not want to become niche operators. Figure 2.8 visualizes the system of alliances in the air transportation market as at April 2002.

Just like the situation in the example from the textile machine industry, firms were impelled towards internationalization through

Figure 2.8 Global airline alliances, April 2002

	Star Alliance		
	Air Canada	Tyrolean Airways	Singapore Airlines
	Air New Zealand	British Midland	Thai Airways
	All Nippon Airways	Lufthanza	United Airlines
STAR ALLIANCE	Austrian Airlines	Mexican Airlines	Varig

	One World Alliance		
	Aer Lingus	British Airways	Finnair
oneworld	American Airlines	Cathay pacific	Iberia
	Qantas	Lan Chile	

	The Qualiflyer Group		
	Swiss	Brussels Airlines	LTU International
	TAP Air Portugal	Volare	Air Europe
The QualiflyerGroup			

	Skystream		
	Aero Mexico	Air France	Alitalia
SKYTEAM	CSA Czech Airlines	Delta	

	KLM-Northwest Global Alliances		
	KLM	Northwest	Air Alps
WORLDWIDE KLM NORTHWEST RELIABILITY	Alaska Airlines	Continental Airlines	Kenya Airlines
	Granada Indonesia	Gulfstream International	Japan Air System
	Malaysia Airlines	Transavia	Air China
	Big Sky Airlines	Hawaiian Airlines	

competitor-based interdependence. The need for airlines to join inter-national networks was created by the simple fact that other carriers had already done so.

Interdependence and Co-ordination

Buyer-, seller- and competitor-based interdependence between country markets create the need to co-ordinate national marketing activities. Only by taking into account linkages in this manner, can the overall profitability of the firm be improved. Feedback mechanisms create informational linkages and reciprocal dependence between decision-making variables (for example, prices in the various markets).

With respect to information, two decisional variables X_1 and X_2 are reciprocally linked, if information about these variables is necessary to make decisions about *other* variables (material interdependence). In this manner, pricing decisions in Country A (X_1) may influence pricing decisions in Country B (X_2). The price level in B constitutes a constraint on pricing decisions in Country A and must therefore be determined a priori. The dependence between the national pricing decisions is then unidirectional, operating only $X_2 \rightarrow X_1$. That is, in our example, the pricing decision in Country A depends on B and not vice versa.

However, reciprocal linkages exist in which $X_1 \rightarrow X_2$ *and* $X_2 \rightarrow X_1$ holds. Reciprocity arises when there is a mutual interdependence of (decisional) variables with respect to a common external goal function. Corporate profit or value maximization is an external goal function creating reciprocal linkages. That is, with international marketing operations, mutual interdependency occurs in the pursuit of cross-border profit-maximization. Feedback between country markets means that profits are not purely a function of national decisions, but of those in other markets as well. The profit maximization objective means that decisions that impact on profits must be made simultaneously with respect to all relevant markets. In our example, the price level in Country B can be set only by determining what price level is needed in Country A in order to achieve this level. Dependencies between decisional variables lead to various co-ordination problems. The resolution of reciprocal dependencies requires simultaneous decision processes.

Figure 2.9 summarizes the feedback mechanisms (interdependencies) that are relevant for international marketing operations.

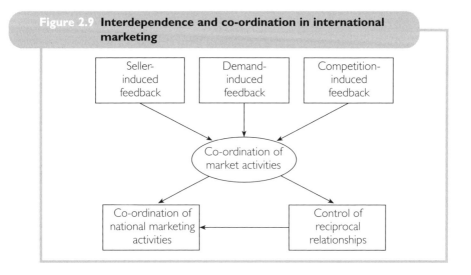

Figure 2.9 **Interdependence and co-ordination in international marketing**

However, the result of these linkages is not only a need for recipro-cal synchronization of national or regional marketing activities specif-ically. What is also necessary is to control the *feedback mechanisms* between the country markets (based on knowing precisely 'what has an impact on what, and how'). This includes the continuous measure-ment and analysis of feedback.

Cultural Distance and the Need for Co-ordination

Cultural distance refers to the extent of cultural discrepancy between two country markets and is regarded, in the literature on international marketing, as a central cause of international marketing problems. The specific managerial problems that arise from cultural disparity include adaptation of marketing measures, decision-making processes and organizational structure. Cultural distance and adaptation do indeed play a major role in the co-ordination of marketing measures. Cultural distance affects customer preferences and buying behaviour which may be exploited profitably.

Up to the time of writing, the often-cited 'global consumer' (Dichter, 1962; Levitt, 1983; Ohmae, 1985) has never really material-ized. In most markets for consumer goods and services, we are still far from the degree of standardization of purchasing behaviour and customer preferences that can be observed in many industrial markets, such as power-generation equipment or engineering services. Furthermore, despite apparent adaptation processes, differences in procurement and use of various goods and services continue to prevail in various regions of the world. The nature and extent of these differ-ences depend of the goods in question, and are generally lower for industrial compared to consumer goods. On closer inspection, the much propagated 'cultural adaptation' reveals itself to be quite super-ficial and to exert a relatively minor impact on the fundamental marketing issues of product procurement and use. Simultaneously, even in politically and economically integrated markets such as the European Union (EU), we observe a strong emphasis of national and cultural characteristics – cultural barriers. Consequently, cultural distance and differences in buyer behaviour remain essential factors in international marketing, and will continue to do so for the foreseeable future.

Cultural differences, and the resulting differential buyer preferences, open up latitude for a profitable differentiation of products and services. This is particularly clear in Europe where, despite high market

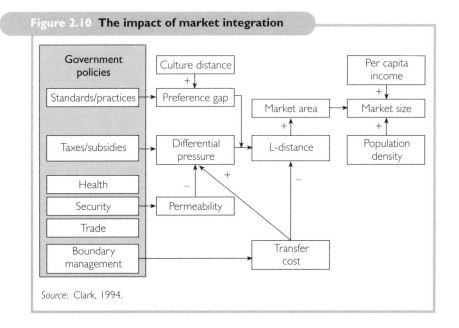

Figure 2.10 The impact of market integration

Source: Clark, 1994.

integration, there is still considerable price differentiation with respect to many standardized consumer goods (automobiles, entertainment electronics, perfume and so on). Integrated markets do, however, put pressure on the degree of latitude for profitable price discrimination.

The model shown in Figure 2.10 (Clark, 1994) demonstrates how differentiation by a seller in terms of quality and/or price, creates international marketing problems via feedback from the demand side in the form of information and goods exchanges.

At the centre of Clark's model is an example of two countries whose territories extend across a common border line on both sides. This border can vary in terms of permeability. Potential buyers on both sides of the border have differing preferences. These can be attributed to the national buyer groups which relate to cultural differences and result from government policies, such as mandated technical product standards or manufacturing processes. An enterprise which operates on both sides of the border will attempt to exploit these differences profitably through a differentiated supply policy.

The permeability of the border, which is also affected by government policy, puts pressure on such attempts at differentiation. The institutional integration of markets promotes the cross-border flow of goods. Consequently, a cross-border market evolves, comprising buyers who switch from the high-price to the low-price market, such that a grey market develops (arbitrage). Clark's model is intended mainly to examine the question of what factors influence the size of this market area. Its size depends on:

▸ *transaction costs*: in the model, these include not only the costs of initiating, developing and controlling contracts, but also logistics – that is, the cost of physical transport;
▸ *the maximum distance (L-distance)* which the rational consumer will travel in order to purchase from a seller in a low-price country. This distance depends on the permeability of the border and the transaction costs incurred by the cross-border purchase;
▸ *price differences (differential pressure)*: the greater the price difference (between standardized or identical goods), the larger the cross border market, because it will be beneficial economically to travel longer distances to acquire the goods. A high degree of border permeability will raise the pressure on differentiation and reduce the average price through increasing arbitrage; and
▸ *per capita income* in the countries in question as well as *population density*.

So far, the Clark model is a fairly generic one, aimed at explaining the development of grey markets. As the criteria of market integration, Clark considers only the physical transport of goods. In fact, the exchange of information (knowledge of prices for the same good in the low-price country) could be sufficient to compel the seller to adapt, because informed clients will threaten to take their business elsewhere unless they receive price reductions. Furthermore, other forms of feedback are not considered by Clark.

The model becomes more relevant if the impact on co-ordination problems by increasingly integrated markets is considered:

▸ institutionally converging markets are accompanied by a harmonization of legal frameworks and the removal of barriers that impede the cross-border flow of goods; the permeability of the border increases;
▸ legally prescribed technical product standards or production processes are harmonized; their influence on the prevalence and intensity of preference differences thus declines; and
▸ transaction costs decline and the size of the cross-border market therefore increases.

In a completely harmonized two-market environment, the size of the cross-border market depends purely on culturally-based preferences, transactions costs, and income and population-density differences. In the extreme, where the cross-border market encompasses both former markets totally, transaction costs are irrelevant (in relation to the value of goods), and cultural differences negligible.

The prevailing price differences reflect, most of all, a differential willingness to pay. If the impact of transaction costs is ignored, the model reduces to one reflecting only cultural distance. The influence of transaction costs may be irrelevant, for two reasons. The first is that local pressure for price adaptation is so large that differences have to be eliminated (without arbitrage occurring). The other reason is that, at least to some extent (such as in electronic commerce (e-commerce) with digitalized goods), certain services and products no longer generate transport costs at all. In converging markets, this means that co-ordination problems are caused by national differences in buyer behaviour, which can in turn be attributed to cultural distance and income differences. If sufficiently large, these differences create profitable differentiation potential for *national* marketing. Market integration places this differentiation under increasing pressure.

Cultural harmonization, which is neither desirable nor to be expected, would thus remove this source of potential profit. After all, the additional costs of product or service differentiation must be more than offset by customers' additional willingness to pay for adapted goods. Failing this, differentiation would not be profitable, and thus makes no sense under conditions of harmonized preferences. In such a situation, there would be no real co-ordination problems and no *inter*national problem. It is quite clear that, to the extent that the relevant markets are characterized by feedback mechanisms, cultural distance leads to co-ordination problems.

Defining and Delineating International Marketing

The analysis thus far has shown that international marketing has inherent peculiarities and problems which can also manifest themselves in a national context (risk, uncertainty, complexity), or in an essentially international context. These include, first and foremost, the problem of co-ordinating national marketing activities in the sense of a reciprocal co-ordination of market-related strategies and their execution.

Against this background, international marketing is defined as:

▶ the *management* (analysis, planning and control) of *market-related interdependence*, and, to the extent that significant interdependence does prevail;

▶ the *reciprocal synchronization of marketing activities* (cross-border problems or entry or operation; and

▶ with the **objective of maximizing the company's value** over *all* country markets.

Figure 2.11 shows the areas of activity of international marketing. International marketing is linked closely to the existence of significant interdependencies which are relevant to decision-making and planning processes. Whether or not an enterprise is generally present in the international market, or only in certain selected markets (general or country-market-specific international abstinence) and depending on the nature of its motivation to enter new markets, a decision-making problem arises with respect to such entry. If the enterprise enters a country market which exhibits feedback to another market in which the firm is already present, the entry decision must be made in the context of co-ordination. This can be termed the '*going* international' problem in international marketing.

Furthermore, if there are changes in the situation in which the original decision was made, the presence of reciprocal relationships can lead to *continuous* co-ordination problems. Such permanent, ongoing

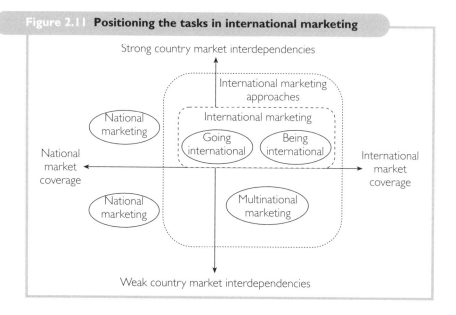

Figure 2.11 Positioning the tasks in international marketing

Figure 2.12 Negotiation training as an example of multinational marketing activities

Source: www.eujapan.com.

country-market co-ordination can be described as a key task of '*being international*'. By contrast, if there are no significant or weak interdependencies, co-ordination of marketing activities will not form the focus of international planning processes. Thus, where planning and activities are relatively independent of one another, the classical, national marketing approaches are far more viable. This can be categorized as 'multinational marketing', which does not differ strongly from national marketing and is quite different from the international marketing problems with which this book is primarily concerned.

In the context of international business activity, enterprises are confronted continually with both international and multinational marketing problems. It is certainly *not* the case that *every* marketing decision is affected by feedback between country markets. For example, if a company enters Japan as a target market, one of the main challenges would be to ensure that relocated employees become familiar with the 'way that market works' and issues such as how to conduct effective negotiations with prospective customers. A multitude of companies offers cross-cultural training services for that purpose (see the example in Figure 2.12). Topics of related seminars and courses range from the language of business, making initial contact, building a relationship, concern about face, communication style, or the role of a contract.

However, an educational and training programme of this nature is essentially a multinational activity that is independent of commitments and activities in other markets. On the other hand, the strategy pursued in Japan may have an impact on the company's overall situation and marketing in other country markets.

The role of purely nationally-orientated goals remains critical to the goal systems of international enterprises. The co-ordination of national marketing policies often reveals that maximizing results in one national market is counter-productive. This will be demonstrated clearly in the discussion on grey markets.

Even if international marketing activities entail both international marketing and multinational marketing, we shall be concerned only with the former, given that the latter does not differ in essence from general (domestic) marketing. We shall therefore concentrate first and foremost on co-ordination problems within the context of international business. The focus will be on market entry (going international) and on subsequent operations (being international).

3 Case Study: Fillkar Electric AG

For a couple of minutes after lunch, Mr Blume savoured the view from the window of his office, looking out across the mountains to the Mosel river, before sitting down at his desk again. Flicking through a copy of *Manager* magazine, he came across an article about Fillkar Electric, and began to read.

> ### The decline of Fillkar Electric
> #### Who is to blame for their plight?
>
> The good years enjoyed for so long by the Belgian electrical giant, Fillkar Electric, are well and truly over, and have been for some time now. With sales in the region of €14 billion in Germany in the last year, an operating loss of €1.6 billion was indeed a bitter pill to swallow for the multinational's German subsidiary.
>
> They were not alone, however, with the entire Belgian parent corporation experiencing similar difficulties. Although the company was able to gloss up the net result for the year by releasing hidden reserves, a dividend cut of 30% was still necessary. After this was announced at a press conference last week, the fallout on the stock exchange the next day was severe.
>
> After all, Fillkar Electric had gained a reputation in recent years for its highly stable dividend policy. Such a drastic dividend cut had not been seen in the entire post-war period. Even insiders had not expected a cut of this proportion.
>
> The question being asked, of course, is why and how this could have happened. One reason that stands out is the wide-scale diversification practised by Fillkar, which meant that hardly any of the company's divisions had the all-important critical mass which is often essential nowadays. Or at least, that is what one well-known management consultant had to say. . . .

Although he was all too familiar with the facts, Mr Blume read the article and its analysis of the troubles. After all, he was head of the A53

Uninterruptible Power Supply (UPS) division of the German subsidiary of Fillkar Electric AG, and had just returned from a major conference of all division heads of the German subsidiary. The board painted a grim picture of the state of the company and appealed to all units to improve the situation. The deficit-ridden units were requested to make a particular effort. Mr Blume sighed – his unit was clearly one of the loss-makers. He was, however, prepared to try to rectify the situation, and attempt to find new approaches. After all, at the conference, the board constantly mentioned the need to be more customer- and market-driven.

The Product

Electrical power has become an indispensable part of today's industrial society, a source of energy that we almost take for granted. Not just in our homes, but also in industry, there are many activities and processes that would no longer be conceivable without electricity. Often, the applications being supplied with power are extremely important and highly sensitive, creating potentially serious repercussions in terms of damage and risk, if power fails for whatever reason. Life-support machines in hospitals, control of vital production processes, accounting systems in banks, etc. are good cases in point. The largest domain, however, is the ever-increasing number of computers on whose reliable operation, the livelihood of many sectors of industry depends. Members of the public simply expect the supply to be constant. Reports from power utilities show, however, that the power supply system is not quite as stable as we would like to believe. Every year, there are numerous disruptions to the power supply for various reasons. Yet, power disruptions to many of the applications mentioned above, could cause severe repercussions within milliseconds.

One possible way of protecting such sensitive power uses against disruptions in the power supply system, is to use a so-called uninterruptible power supply, or UPS for short. A UPS is placed between the consumer and the power supply system. If disruptions should occur, the UPS continues supplying current and voltage to the consumer. The energy required is provided by batteries, with a downstream power inverter.

The maximum level of power that the UPS can support is specified in kilovolt-amperes (kVA). Depending on the application, UPS's can have a power level that extends from 0.5 kVA (e.g. PC back up) to well over 1,000 kVA (e.g. for backup in large computer centres or large production installations). Depending on the number of batteries used, back up can be provided for periods ranging from a few minutes up to several hours.

The capacity of the batteries is the limiting factor in determining how long the UPS will continue supplying power to the application. Communication between the UPS and the user is therefore critical, if battery time should expire before the power supply system becomes active again. Computers today typically have a direct line of communication between the UPS and the computer itself, so that, if necessary, the computer can close down all applications correctly. In addition, a message is sent to the control station or supervisor. The UPS can conceivably be split into two parts, one dealing with energy flow and hardware-specific power supply, and the other with software-specific communication.

UPSs function according to two different technical principles, although there is no standard labelling system for the two concepts. At Fillkar Electric, they are termed 'online' and 'offline'. Figure 3.1 shows a highly simplified circuit diagram of the two procedures.

Offline devices are only available up to a power level of approx. 10 kVA, the restricting factor being the flow of current above this level.

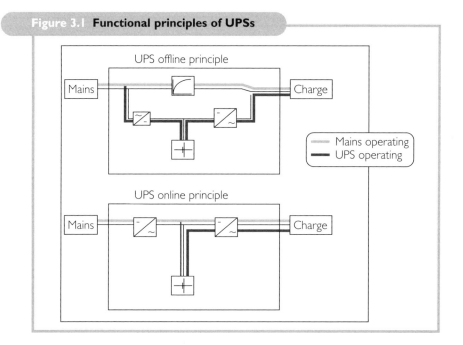

Figure 3.1 Functional principles of UPSs

Online devices, on the other hand, function across the entire power range.

During normal operation, the current in the offline concept flows via a filter from the mains to the consumer. A charge-maintaining current is conducted via a small rectifier to the batteries. Power disruptions are detected by a sensor, which ensures that a relay switches to battery operation within milliseconds, so that direct voltage from the battery is converted by an inverter to a sinusoidal alternating voltage and then made available to the consumer.

In the online concept, the entire current is rectified through the mains supply and adjusted to the battery voltage level. The direct current feeds the battery as well as the inverter, which then sets up a constant and completely new sinusoidal alternating voltage for supplying the consumer. If there is a mains failure, the battery takes over supplying power to the inverter. Consequently, no time is lost through the switch-over.

There are advantages and disadvantages with both procedures. In the case of the offline concept, disadvantages include the 5 ms switchover time and the relatively poor filtering of the mains voltage. Advocates of the offline concept often claim, however, that computer power supply units today can easily cope with interrupts on the scale of 15 ms. The much lower price, facilitated by smaller components, is a clear advantage. An offline UPS costs approx. 30 per cent to 40 per cent less than an online UPS. In terms of the online concept, therefore, the absence of switch-over time and the more effective filtering are advantages, while the higher price is obviously a disadvantage. With regard to the switch-over time, it is often reported that, depending on the length of the phase relationship, even interruptions of less than 5 ms will cause major problems. Whether online or offline devices are used also depends on how the user estimates the risk of a disruption.

A small, battery-driven UPS with 1 kVA, for example, can easily fit under an office desk and costs between €400 and €800 depending on the technology and the particular manufacturer. It is supplied fully wired and is easy to startup. On the other hand, a large installation, with approximately 500 kVA for example, needs its own enclosed space for the batteries alone. It must be commissioned by specialist staff and may cost several hundred thousand euros. See Figure 3.2.

A less costly alternative to the traditional UPS has been available to provide backup for small computers for some time. Based on a built-in solution at direct current level, such devices have not been particularly

Figure 3.2 Different types of large UPSs

popular for various technical and other reasons, so they can be regarded as essentially irrelevant for the future.

Background to Fillkar Electric

Fillkar Electric is a Belgian electrical corporation, whose German subsidiary has an annual turnover of approximately €7 billion. With the wide-scale introduction of the profit-centre concept in the company, the A53 unit now has sole responsibility for worldwide development, production, and sales of UPSs. Despite substantial restructuring, however, Fillkar was, and remains, an essentially large, unwieldy company. The A53 Uninterruptible Power Supply unit has annual sales of roughly €23 million, of which €14.5 million are in Germany. An additional €6 million in sales comes from the rest of Western Europe and the remainder from countries outside Europe. The production facilities are located in Brunswick and Gladbeck, while the German sales headquarters are in Trier.

In order to improve the foreign market position, Fillkar purchased the top Russian manufacturer of UPSs shortly after the dissolution of the Eastern bloc. This move still has not really paid off, though prospects look good. While the Russian UPS market is equivalent to only two-thirds of the German market by volume, massive double-figure growth is anticipated, because Russia is considered to be the key market within the former Soviet Union. Fillkar is the only Western supplier with an insider position in the Russian market. As a result of the new protectionist trend in Russia, it is at the time of writing virtually impossible for other suppliers to gain access to the market.

With a share of 8.6 per cent, Fillkar Electric ranks fifth on the German market, behind competitors such as Siemens, Merlin Gerin and ABB, but ahead of many others. Fillkar is one of the most renowned suppliers of UPSs, having a high profile and a sound reputation with its customers. This is partly because the regular servicing of UPSs systematically maintains close links with the operating companies.

Until four years ago, the unit still made reasonable profits. Since then, however, with internal problems and changing market conditions, the unit has witnessed a dramatic decline in profits, and has incurred losses in recent years. It incurred a deficit of €3.7 million last year. With great difficulty, the company managed to maintain its sales by offering special prices for an older product series. The prevailing price wars are an important contributory factor to Fillkar's current problems. For one thing, production costs for UPSs are very high, although this is necessary in order to maintain quality. Also, order processing costs are high and, despite numerous efforts, the unit has been unable to lower them. Despite the present predicament, there is still a reasonably high level of goodwill towards management, because of earlier market successes. However, as head of the unit with overall responsibility, Mr Blume is well aware that the parent corporation, which has been badly hit itself, will soon look for signs of a turnaround in his unit.

Fillkar Electric is well known for its high-quality, if high-cost, products. In line with its own high-quality expectations, Fillkar Electric only produces and markets online UPSs. Power levels offered currently range from 25 kVA to 1,500 kVA, and are covered by four different product lines. One of the four product lines is no longer state-of-the-art, but the large series (100–1,500 kVA), in particular, is undoubtedly one of the best on the market.

Traditionally, Fillkar Electric's business has been in UPSs for large applications (upwards of 100 kVA), which accounts for over 80 per

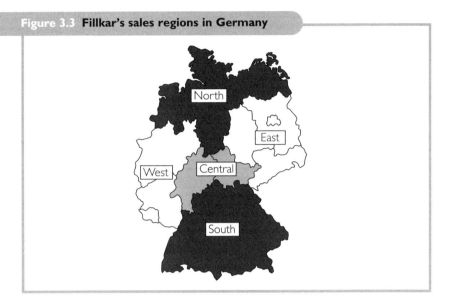

Figure 3.3 Fillkar's sales regions in Germany

cent of its sales. The business is characterized by UPSs that need to be adapted to individual customer requirements. Fillkar has a reputation for meeting even the most demanding customer requirements, as is often the case in power station applications, for example.

Because this business is very intensive in terms of consultancy and customer contact, Fillkar Electric markets its UPSs directly. The company has subsidiaries in the large cities in Germany, where one person is responsible purely for the sale of UPSs. Fillkar has divided Germany into eight sales regions (see Figure 3.3). Customers contact the relevant person (consultant) in the subsidiary directly, and this consultant is responsible for processing the entire order. Depending on the customer, Fillkar is either given a complete product specification, or develops one together with the customer. The consultant in the subsidiary draws up an offer if the required installation is relatively straightforward. If product customisation or a special price are required, the consultant contacts the sales headquarters in Trier.

The Market for UPSs in Germany

According to a study by the highly-rated market-research company, Rost & Pullman, the world market for UPSs is about €1.75 billion. Of this, 40 per cent is located in North America and 30 per cent each in Europe and Asia. The other continents play an insignificant role. The

Table 3.1 Distribution of UPSs by power class

Power class	Market share (in terms of sales) (%)
<4 kVA	29
4 kVA … 25 kVA	41
>25 kVA	30

Source: Rost and Pullman.

study found that the UPS market in Germany in 1993 was worth €120 million. Germany therefore comprises approximately 23 per cent of the European market. Rost & Pullman determined the distribution of UPSs by power class as shown in Table 3.1. These data relate to the German market, but could apply *proportionately* to almost any other market.

After average annual growth of 10 per cent in recent years, lower annual growth of 7 per cent is expected for Germany for the next years. However, this growth is distributed unequally. While the high-end segment is relatively stable and should grow slightly, a decline is expected in the mid-range area as applications move away from this power class, either upwards or downwards. The low end is experiencing the highest levels of growth.

From an analysis of the applications supported by UPSs, Rost & Pullman showed that approximately 70 per cent of all UPSs are used to back up computer systems. After this, the greatest demand comes from telecommunications and processing applications. The trend is for UPSs in the higher power class to be used in less than 70 per cent of cases for backing up computer systems, while small UPSs are used almost exclusively for this purpose; this means that other applications can virtually be disregarded.

The low-end power class of 0–4 kVA is of particular interest. In the early 1990s, there were practically no sales in this range. But for several years now, this market segment has shown by far the strongest growth, and the trend looks set to continue. At the time of writing, it accounts for almost a third of the entire market. The reason for this development is the decentralization of information technology (IT) and the resulting strong growth in the number of local area networks (LANs) with distributed intelligence, as well as the greater penetration of the office world by PCs. This obviously creates a growing need to back up data. UPSs with less than 4 kVA are quite satisfactory for these applications.

Consequently, UPSs with power levels of 0–4 kVA are used mainly to back up network servers. As most PC networks at the start of he twenty-first century are new installations, the demand for upgrading is relatively low.

The online concept has a near monopoly in the high-end power classes (upwards of 25 kVA), while both online and offline compete in the lower classes. The relationship between online and offline is 1:1 in terms of quantities sold.

With respect to the German UPS market, there is still considerable catching-up to be done in the new German states (the former German Democratic Republic). For one thing, the power supply system is still significantly less stable than in the West. On the other hand, many companies are expanding their IT systems. Therefore, while market growth in western Germany is slow, growth in eastern Germany is considerably higher. Many UPS suppliers, including Fillkar, are still under-represented in eastern Germany in terms of staffing. Most business activity is still being handled from the west, which is often problematic in business relationships. Some companies, again including Fillkar, are therefore considering expanding their activities towards the east. However, since it is difficult to estimate how much longer this one-off growth in eastern Germany will last, companies are reluctant to make a major commitment.

Future plans at Fillkar Electric

Just a few years ago, Mr Blume and his colleagues recognized that a completely new market was emerging rapidly for low-end UPSs. They were concerned that Fillkar Electric was not represented in this power class, and decided to attack this high-sales segment with their own small UPS series. Because a number of suppliers were already active in the market, Fillkar would be a relative latecomer. After lengthy discussions, it was also decided to steer away from the mid-range market (4 to 25 kVA), since all forecasts were predicting lower sales in this class.

Fillkar was determined to produce UPSs for this small power class itself, and not buy in from external suppliers and re-label, as many competitors were doing. It was determined not to become a wholesaler and reseller of third-party products. Fillkar planned a series that would cover the range between 0.5 kVA and 5 kVA, to be produced in Gladbeck. There was no question of anything other than the online concept. Specifications had been drawn up two years previously, and these were used for product development. Preliminary costing showed that, with average unit costs, Fillkar could achieve a similar position to that of the large-scale, high-volume, Taiwanese manufacturers. This was a source of pride to the development manager. The same production technology would be used as in the new factory of Taiwan's largest manufacturer. Compared with the costs of other manufacturers, the situation looked promising, with Fillkar hoping to benefit from a 20 per cent learning curve after 10,000 units. The design of the new UPSs was based on the most successful UPSs on the market, as these catered optimally for customer preferences.

The planned quantity was set initially at 5,000 units per year. Even if the plant manager claimed that practically unlimited production capacity could be provided, and even if greater quantities could indeed be produced, the market, and the fact that the company was a newcomer, led Mr Blume to doubt secretly that planned output could be achieved. Above all, it seemed that the cost situation would develop quite unpredictably in the future.

In the meantime, product development was almost complete, and the market launch was to take place within a couple of months. What was missing, however, was a comprehensive overview of the sales and marketing policy for small UPSs.

Customer Relations in the UPS Market

Fillkar had practically no information available on the market for small UPSs. Mr Weiters' investigations were meticulous and thorough, although he did not yet know what information would be needed later for decision-making. He wanted to compare his new findings with the reality of the market for large UPSs. He therefore divided the market into two segments – small UPSs (0–5 kVA) and large UPSs (>100 kVA). Although this did not correspond exactly to what was happening in the market, he believed this polarization to be the most suitable for his investigations, not only because Fillkar is a leading supplier of large UPSs, but also because this might help to differentiate between the various markets for Fillkar's products.

The typical business process in this class of 100 kVA plus, can be described as follows: a large application, such as a computer centre, is at the planning stage. At this point, *an engineering consultant* is often called in. Moreover, a UPS is also included in the design of the complete power supply system. The planner typically produces a work specification and sends an RFQ (request for quote) to various manufacturers.

The supplier then submits an offer. There may be numerous contacts and discussions with the potential customer, both before and after the quote is submitted. The implementation of a project may extend over several months or even years, since large UPSs are tailored closely to the requirements of particular customers. Fillkar has a reputation for being able to implement highly customized solutions.

The planning phase is generally conducted by electrical experts, who are familiar with the difficulties involved in planning a power supply system. As a result, this group (typical Fillkar Electric clients) comprises experts who understand the problems involved and are also interested in how the UPS operates. Depending on the application area, different customers emphasize different criteria. These often include the harmonic content of the sine, overload capacity of the UPS, space requirements, suppression level, system reaction and so on. The UPS sales representatives in the subsidiaries have similar backgrounds to the customers, so are able to 'speak their language' and think on the same level.

Small UPSs, however, are not integrated in planning processes as part of the electrical installation, but are regarded as data-processing peripherals. They are therefore handled by IT specialists who have no electrical training. Like all IT specialists, this customer group is also heavily software-based and software-focused, with little interest in electrical considerations. They have no real awareness of problems relating to the security of power supply, and little interest in how such problems can be solved once detected. These facts were determined by three members of the sales staff, who conducted a telephone survey of users over a period of a week.

It was evident that end-users regarded small UPSs as relatively low-interest products, which demoralized Fillkar employees. Users accept the need for a UPS, but hope they will seldom need to use it, and can thus more or less forget its existence. Much explanation and customer training is also needed, because many users know nothing about UPSs. Furthermore, they do not know the difference between online and offline, and are not interested in such details.

One important result obtained from the telephone survey was that, in spite of the above issues, there was little perceived need for replacing online UPSs with offline UPSs, and vice versa. Since small UPSs are low-interest products, users' opinions and preferences for a particular technology are not particularly well considered, and decisions are made on an essentially *ad hoc* basis. Nor are customers willing to reconsider their preferences at a later date. Consequently, on the one hand, purchasers of *off*line UPSs are unwilling to pay a higher price for online technology, and conversely, *on*line purchasers are not prepared to accept what is perceived as unsatisfactory circuitry, just because of its lower price.

Apart from the difference between online and offline, the perceived price/performance relationship with respect to small UPSs is not as sensitive as that for large UPSs. Thus, beyond a certain price ceiling, customers for small UPSs will even do without the UPS. This applies to purchasers of both online and offline technology. The potential market volume therefore expands considerably as prices decline.

Small UPSs are mainly standardized products, which means that the customer can select or request customization of only a small number of product features. As in many other sectors, standardized UPSs are often bought from the Far East, where they are mass produced. The largest supplier of UPSs in Taiwan is Phoenixtec Ltd. Its factory has an annual output of 25,000 online UPSs in the power class 0.5–5 kVA. In another plant, Phoenixtec makes around the same number of offline units.

In the case of small UPSs, the main selection criterion is not the hardware but the software. There are numerous communication and shut-down software packages for the servers. These provide communication between the UPS and the computer, and ensure the correct shut down of the applications when battery back up time has expired.

As in the case of the price war in the computer market, ruinously low prices have also been the norm in the market for small UPSs in recent years. This has resulted in a far-reaching supplier shake-up, which has hurt the smaller suppliers in particular. Prices for small UPSs have fallen by as much as 35 per cent in the last two years.

We already know, from the Rost & Pullman study, that the main use of small UPSs was to back up servers in PC networks. Mr Weiters therefore began to look in PC magazines for general information about PC networks and how they are purchased. What struck him were the trendy and superficial advertisements of the UPS suppliers, who used phrases such as 'No power, No data. UPSs from XY . . .' These catchy phrases sounded good, but provided little actual information.

In the past, Fillkar rarely used advertising as a means of marketing. Advertisements were run, if at all, in electrical trade journals, where sales information was provided in a very factual and sober manner. In particular, Fillkar advertised prior to major trade fairs, in order to encourage potential customers to visit the Fillkar stand. The advertisements were often accompanied by coupons for a small gift that the visitor could redeem at the stand. In the past, Fillkar was quite pleased with the success of these campaigns.

Meanwhile, Mr Weiters, had noticed that the large trade fairs were also a prominent vehicle for marketing small UPSs. For example, more than 250 suppliers from all over the world were represented at CeBIT alone, and other electronics trade fairs also boasted similar figures. There seemed scarcely a UPS supplier that was not represented at the major electronics fairs. Mr Weiters was amazed, because he considered it an expensive luxury to exhibit at the major fairs. Fillkar typically exhibited at the specialist electronics fairs and plant construction fairs, which were less expensive and therefore seemed better value for money.

During his investigations, Mr Weiters came across the following article in a computer magazine, but was unsure whether it provided the information he needed. The subject of UPSs was not really addressed at all, and only limited information was provided about the customer purchasing processes. Yet the article did seem to give a good overview of the market structure:

> A specific market structure has evolved in the highly opaque PC market. A section of IT dealers has concentrated on private individuals, for example students.
>
> Other dealers, meanwhile, have focused on the industrial sector. It is in this area in particular that PC network installations have come to play a major role. The IT dealers have achieved a key position in the network market since there is scarcely a company left that will install a network without first bringing in IT dealers to provide consulting at the design stage.
>
> The size of the dealers has changed very little. Typically, this type of IT dealer will sell between 20 and 40 PC networks per year. What is interesting is that the dealer always plans and supplies the complete network. It is very rare indeed for an 'unbundled' solution to be purchased from several dealers. The competence of the IT dealer plays a decisive role here, since end customers are mostly unfamiliar with network technology and therefore mainly leave the planning of the entire network to the IT dealer. Many dealers will openly admit that it is they who make the final decision as to which components and peripherals are used.
>
> Furthermore, the IT dealers are either tied to a brand name such as IBM, DEC, etc. or are so-called no-name, free-agent dealers. Both groups are represented more or less equally in PC networks. The IT dealers purchase all computers, components, and peripherals from their contracting partners. It

is worth noting, however, that there is a growing trend in peripherals to move away from this reliance on the components of the contracting partner. The free-agent dealers purchase their goods from IT distributors, such as Computer 2000.

At present major price deterioration is affecting the entire PC sector. Price has therefore become the single largest selling factor. The price war continues to adversely affect not only the margins of the manufacturers, but also the margins of the dealers, which puts them under enormous pressure to reduce costs. The drive for rationalization stretches even to the way information is gathered by the dealers. Generally, the type of information that is sought about offers on the market is not concrete offers from manufacturers, but rather general information on current technological solutions. It is only when the decision is made to purchase a specific component that more detailed information is sought from a few familiar suppliers and a final choice is made.

Despite the present tense situation, representatives of the PC sector are confident about the future. We are hopeful that present difficulties do not herald the end of the PC boom, but are simply a normal phase in a process of structuring and building a market.

In another magazine, Mr Weiters found an article about the IT distributors:

In contrast to the IT dealers, where consulting is a major strength, IT distributors are regarded as pure box movers. Their aim is not to push products, but rather to wait for a pull from the market. To quote one such distributor 'Our products must speak for themselves, this is a golden rule of our business. We also do not advise potential customers, we just ship the goods.' In order to keep the range of offers as simple as possible, and in order to be able to offer good prices, the distributors only list one or two items of a particular product type. The stiff price competition prevalent in the entire IT sector is also being felt by the distributors, who are complaining about drastically reduced margins.

For this reason, of late the distributors have been looking more and more to form long-term business relationships with suppliers. They are working very hard to simplify the entire course of business, and for this reason the process of selecting a supplier is handled very carefully, taking into account factors such as logistics, terms of delivery, market presence, flexibility and so on. In particular, the suppliers located some distance away in the Far East are coming under pressure as a result of this trend:

In the past, the distributors succeeded in forming strong ties with the deal-
ers by offering a very distinctive discount policy on a dealer's total sales.
The IT dealers therefore developed a strong preference for doing as much
business as possible with one distributor.

From the article, the difficulty of approaching users and end buyers was clear to Mr Weiters. In the case of large UPSs, particularly over 500 kVA, there are only a handful of manufacturers on the supply side, and a few large projects on the demand side. This produces a high degree of market transparency, and a well-known supplier such as Fillkar therefore finds out automatically about all potential orders in the entire market.

The situation is somewhat different in the case of the small UPSs, where the quantities being handled are much greater. The idea of having to deal with such large quantities and just as many users, and not finding out about all potential orders is not something Mr Weiters is used to. He is uncertain as to how to identify and approach poten-tial customers. On the one hand, he believes that huge volumes inevitably lead to an anonymity that makes customer contact difficult, but on the other hand, it may be advantageous that every company is a potential customer, which reduces the problem of identifying poten-tial leads. What he does know for certain is that he has substantial sales work ahead of him.

From the analysis of competition, it was clear that the customers came from all sectors, both service business and industry, from small businesses and tax consultants to large corporations. More detailed information was not available, but at least the percentage of UPSs of less than 1 kVA sold to the individual sectors could be taken from the Rost & Pullman reports (see Table 3.2).

As explained above, the main use of UPSs in all power classes is for computer back up. For this reason, some very close relationships have been built up over the years between UPS manufacturers and computer manufacturers. Each computer manufacturer has preferred UPSs from a particular supplier. This means that a different UPS supplier may be considered for each different computer families or size.

As a result of the relatively large quantities sold by computer manu-facturers, very detailed and precise agreements are drawn up for deliv-eries. The decision-makers of the computer manufacturers are electrical specialists and experts in the field of power back up. The computer manufacturers will only accept as partners firms that match them in size and market presence, which reduces considerably the chances of

Table 3.2 Distribution of customers buying small UPSs by sector

Line of business	Market share UPS <1 kVA (%)
Banking, finance and insurance	12.6
Manufacturing	35.6
Government and defence	10.0
Utilities	6.4
Medical and health care	4.6
Retail and distribution	5.0
Transportation	9.2
Communications	3.6
Petrochemicals	10.0
Other end users	3.0

Source: Rost and Pullman.

the small suppliers. In order to avoid becoming dependent on a single supplier, all manufacturers practice multiple sourcing. The question of reliability of suppliers plays a major role, which means that the computer manufacturers have a certain preference for German, or at least European, UPS suppliers, if only for reasons of availability.

Fillkar has neglected the computer manufacturer market for a long time. In fact, it is only quite recently that any effort has been made to establish contact. Initial success was achieved recently, however, by being listed by DEC along with two other suppliers.

The Competition

World manufacturing of UPSs takes place mainly in the USA, Asia and Europe. The large UPS domain is focused heavily on domestic markets, because these UPSs need special on-site configuration, and an extra journey is not really practical. Most Asian suppliers are quite large and belong to diversified major corporations, factors that enable them to offer a complete product range.

Some new suppliers of small UPSs have recently entered the US market, born of the network boom, and have become firmly entrenched. These relatively young companies have a tight hold on the market for small UPSs, but most are only active in the US market.

There are hundreds of suppliers active in the German UPS market. But a differentiation between power classes is necessary when considering the different players. In the field of large UPSs there is only a handful of established suppliers, including Fillkar, of course, and the other companies already mentioned, such as Siemens, ABB and Merlin Gerin, as well as Emerson and Piller. These companies have all been active in the business for decades and traditionally are closely linked with plant construction and engineering offices on the planning side. The marketing and sales structure of all these companies is the same as at Fillkar Electric. Employees are not only familiar with the product lines offered by the competition, but have often known the sales staff personally for a number of years.

Competition in the *small* UPS domain is quite different. First of all, the suppliers of large UPSs have now also entered this market, some having developed a series of UPSs in the past few years, though most import their small UPSs from the Far East. While the majority of suppliers see the future market being dominated by the large UPSs, Merlin Gerin, for example, is very heavily involved in the small UPS market. It makes full use of its powerful branch network to market the UPSs imported from Asia.

Most of these 'major' suppliers find it difficult to repeat the success they achieved in the large UPS market. However, the smaller series are now integrated within their sales programmes and will be promoted and supported alongside the large UPSs.

Despite the vast number of suppliers of small UPSs, only a few still manufacture their own products. The majority buy them in from the Far East. Overall, most small UPSs in local distribution channels come from factories in South East Asia.

Most suppliers of small UPSs sell directly to the end users, which tend to be small companies that focus on a market niche and maintain close, but time-consuming, contact with customers. Convertomatic in Cologne, is representative of the many smaller suppliers in terms of market presence, but has a stronger market standing than the others. Although IT structures in many companies have changed because of downsizing, Convertomatic has succeeded in establishing close contact with the people responsible for distributed computing power. This was achieved through a heavy investment in time and personnel. When necessary, their contacts simply telephone Convertomatic, and the offer is then drafted and faxed back. Of all the suppliers of small UPSs, Convertomatic has by far the most contact with users. With annual sales of €3 million, the company is one of the major suppliers to the German market. The UPSs are bought in from the Far East. Because of some initial quality problems with online devices (from a mid-size Korean company) over the last couple of years, they have only bought offline devices from this firm, and buy their online devices from the largest Taiwanese supplier.

Sola Sinus GmbH, based in Frankfurt, has a different approach. This company operates in the German-speaking countries and in Italy. Sola Sinus does not sell its UPSs directly, but exclusively through IT dealers. These UPSs are bought in from the Taiwanese manufacturer, Phoenixtec, and re-labelled. Through astute warehousing operations, they avoid any delivery bottlenecks from Taiwan and always deliver on time. They have built an excellent reputation for quality through their outstanding service policy. Supported by an aggressive communications and marketing strategy, Sola Sinus has won approximately 11 per cent of the German market for UPSs up to 4 kVA. Sales last year were €3.5 million, of which 80 per cent was in the online sector. This makes Sola Sinus one of the leading suppliers to the German market.

Suppliers from the Far East play a special role. Products from Taiwanese manufacturers are now well established. These manufacturers do not sell under their own label in Europe, but supply exclusively to original equipment manufacturers (OEMs) and intermediaries, which then market the UPSs under their own names. The larger companies among these suppliers have thus secured a strong position in the European market, but just how strong is unclear, because their precise market presence is difficult to determine. Their customers also include, for example, major manufacturers of large UPSs.

American Power Conversion (APC) has been around for 15 years, and is known for its aggressive price strategy. In its brochures, APC boasts of having built and sold more than 700,000 UPSs and of selling the greatest number of UPSs worldwide in the power class up to 3 kVA. With a 15 per cent market share in the USA, this makes APC the market leader in this segment. The company has been expanding rapidly in the past couple of years, and now sells throughout Western Europe and aims to operate eventually on a worldwide scale. APC offers UPSs only up to 5 kVA, and all products are based on the offline principle. Apart from its aggressive pricing policy, the main factor in its success over the last few years has been its good communications software. This company has done particularly well in the USA, and has also been present in the German market for a number of years. It has a market share of 15 per cent and is moving towards the top position in the small UPS segment. APC sells under its own label in Germany. It is listed by the largest IT distributors and is extremely well known among IT dealers.

With its online series, the American firm, Conversion Industries, is another aggressive newcomer in the German market for small UPSs. The company caused a sensation by following the example of some PC suppliers and distributing its products by catalogue only. It is unclear whether Conversion is producing the UPSs itself or outsourcing them. It *is* clear, however, that not long after a brilliant start as a relatively new small company in Germany three years ago, sales began to slip, which it tried to combat by radical price cuts. At present, it is uncertain what strategy the company will follow.

The Tasks Facing Them

The final product descriptions for the new small series went out to sales staff during the last few days. They comprised part of the documentation for the sales conference in three weeks' time. A presentation of the small UPS's by the product manager, Mr Parting, is intended to be a key subject. It is especially important for the sales staff from the subsidiaries to elaborate and agree on a strategy for the marketing of small UPSs. In the run-up to the sales conference, a heated debate has already been taking place about the optimal strategy.

Since his unit depends substantially on the success of the small series, Mr Blume decided to form a group of his most experienced employees in advance of the event. The objective is to develop, as part of a general marketing campaign for the new small series, a proposal for a structured, comprehensive, and well-formulated sales strategy.

The following questions are particularly important in this regard:

1. What do you think of Fillkar's plans for small UPSs? What strategy would you propose?
2. Analyse the international competition network!
3. How succesful would a nationally-orientated strategy be?
4. Should Fillkar try to find a partner for a strategic alliance? If so, what are its requirements for this partner?

Market Entry Strategies in International Marketing: 'Going International'

Introduction

In the context of entering foreign markets, firms either become active for the first time in external markets or increase the number of operational markets. There are two interdependent decisions to be made:

▶ market selection; and
▶ market entry.

Market selection entails choosing the appropriate country markets and *market entry* the appropriate entry strategies. The latter can be divided into temporal (timing the entry) and operational dimensions (choosing the organizational form and determining the marketing instruments).

Interdependencies and the consequent need for co-ordination, play a central role in formulating the initial 'going international' decisions: in terms of market selection, it is necessary to ensure that only those markets are entered, that can be co-ordinated effectively and manageably with current or new markets.

For example, pharmaceutical manufacturers will take care to introduce products only into high-price markets, if there is a danger that parallel re-imports from low-price countries will flood the high price countries. In the early 1990s, such considerations led the pharmaceutical manufacturer Glaxo (now GlaxoSmithKline) to introduce the newly-developed migraine medicine Imigran initially in four high-price European countries at a price of £41 for two injections. However, entry into France, at that time a low-price market, was avoided. Yet, because the medicine generated considerable public interest in France, in order to avoid long-term damage to its image, the company was ultimately forced to negotiate with the French health authorities. In these negotiations, Glaxo insisted on using the price charged in the high-price countries, even though France was regarded as a low-price market. Because no agreement was reached with the health authorities, Glaxo was, in the end, able to avoid introducing Imigran into the French market (Moore, 1997, p. 42; Danzon, 1998, p. 300).

Furthermore, feedback mechanisms can be observed in determining market entry strategies. Both the timing of the market entry as well as the selection of the appropriate organizational form or the formulation of marketing instruments, must take this into account.

With respect to the entry of a firm into a new country market, a decision must be made as to whether the product's packaging, for example, should be given a country-specific adaptation. Seller-related interdependency must be taken into account if the nature of packaging used in other operational markets yields cost savings. Apart from avoiding new design and development costs, using the same packaging will yield further savings because of the larger quantities ordered.

These initial considerations already show that decisions in the context of 'going international' are affected substantially by feedback and the associated need for co-ordination. The extent and structure of these interdependencies depends primarily on whether 'going international' relates to:

▸ one country market or;
▸ several country markets.

If only one country market is to be entered, there is only one set of interdependencies to be taken into account. Conversely, with multiple entry, there are multiple interdependencies. Figure B.1 outlines the interdependencies which relate to one as opposed to several country markets.

Because the 'going international' decision largely determines the interdependencies that have to be considered between the country markets in which a firm wishes to operate, the decision has an impact on the nature of co-ordination instruments. Depending on which

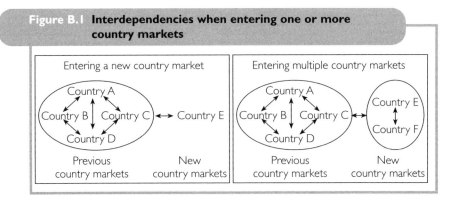

Figure B.1 Interdependencies when entering one or more country markets

country markets are to be operated, the timing and the organizational forms that have been selected for foreign activities, stronger or weaker feedback linkages will have to be considered. Consequently, the decisions relating to 'going international' also have a central significance for subsequent 'being international' activities.

4 The Market Selection Decision

Evaluating Country Markets

In the literature, the evaluation of country markets is considered primarily in terms of risks and opportunities (Doole and Lowe, 2000; Young *et al.*, 1989, p. 26). The main indicators are:

▸ market attractiveness; and
▸ market barriers.

The two pairs of concepts, risk/opportunity and attractiveness/barriers are similar, in the sense that markets that offer substantial opportunities are attractive to firms and country-operation risks, function in a like manner to market barriers. However, because not every market barrier derives from risk, and similarly, market attractiveness is established though analysing the potential for success, establishing the determinants of market attractiveness/barriers constitutes the more comprehensive approach.

The fundamental aim of the market selection process is to analyse country markets in terms of these indicators and thus, ultimately, to identify those that are general (core) markets, future (potential) markets, those that are occasional only, and, finally, those that are best left alone (abstinence markets). Figure 4.1 shows the impact of the indicators discussed above, with respect to the various country market types. In this context, it is important to note that the allocation of country markets to the various categories, can change over time.

In contrast to what is shown in Figures 4.1 and 4.2, it should perhaps not be assumed that the dimensions of 'market attractiveness' and 'market barriers' are independent of one another. Instead, it is quite conceivable that markets characterized by high attractiveness also have high barriers, and vice versa. Competitors will be particularly keen to establish barriers in attractive markets.

Urban (2000), for example, demonstrated how the attractiveness of Asian automobile markets is likely to mutate substantially, between 1997 and 2007. According to this prediction, it can be assumed that

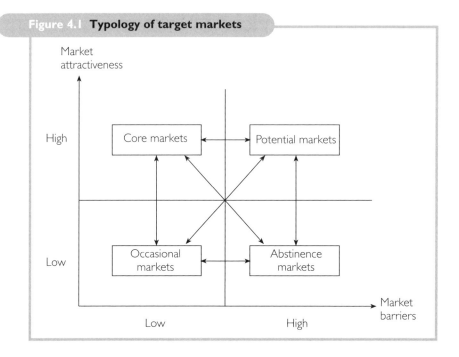

Figure 4.1 Typology of target markets

the market barriers for imports in almost all markets will decline in significance over the coming years.

Determinants of Evaluation

Market Attractiveness

The attractiveness of country markets derives from their potential economic contributions to the company. This potential is, for the most part, multidimensional, so that it can be measured through a combination of criteria (Hill, 1996, p. 58–60). However, empirical studies show that the motives that underlie the evaluation of foreign markets, can frequently be compressed into a few central market-related evaluation criteria.

The attractiveness of country markets can all be determined by cost-related, and thus internal, factors. Through operating in certain country markets, productive capacity can better be exploited, and low-cost sources of labour or raw materials tapped, which would otherwise not

Figure 4.2 **Development of the automobile market in Asia**

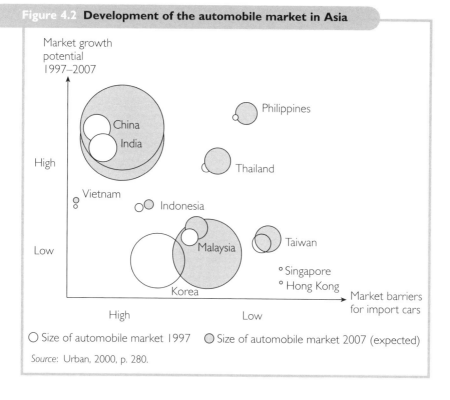

Source: Urban, 2000, p. 280.

be accessible. These are common examples of internal determinants of country attractiveness. (However, certain dangers can also accompany production cost advantages in foreign markets.)

Whether firms pursue internal or market-related objectives in their foreign operations undoubtedly depends both on the industry sector in question and the firm itself. Quite apart from the fact that attractiveness depends in many cases on internal and market-related factors, a study conducted by the Bavarian Metal and Electro Association, suggests that the relative importance of market and (internal) cost-related attractiveness dimensions also depends on the size of the enterprise. From Figure 4.3, it is quite clear from the separately-derived results that market-attractiveness factors (maintenance, creating new markets) is rated considerably lower for small firms than for larger ones.

However, this result is not always confirmed in recent empirical studies on the internationalization motives of medium-sized firms. For example, in the study of Bassen *et al.* (2001) of the 533 responding

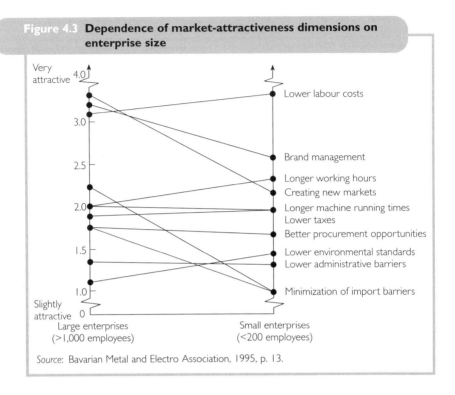

Figure 4.3 Dependence of market-attractiveness dimensions on enterprise size

Very attractive

4.0

3.0

2.5

2.0

1.5

1.0

Slightly attractive 0

Large enterprises (>1,000 employees)

Small enterprises (<200 employees)

Lower labour costs

Brand management

Longer working hours
Creating new markets

Longer machine running times
Lower taxes
Better procurement opportunities

Lower environmental standards
Lower administrative barriers

Minimization of import barriers

Source: Bavarian Metal and Electro Association, 1995, p. 13.

medium-sized German companies, 78 per cent gave the desire to establish new markets as the main reason for internationalization.

Market Barriers

The term *market barriers* refers to all conditions which need to be fulfilled in order to enter and operate effectively in a country market. We can distinguish between *structural* (natural) and *strategic* (established deliberately by other parties) barriers. Bain (1956, p. 3) describes barriers to entry as 'advantages of established sellers, these advantages being reflected in the extent to which established sellers can persistently raise their prices above a competitive level without attracting new firms to enter the industry'. Barriers to entry thus create pricing latitude for established sellers in specific country markets. These barriers can be maintained as long as the costs incurred by new entrants in overcoming the barriers exceed the potential revenue gains which are influenced by the price.

Only when the prices in a barrier-protected market rise to some degree does it pay to invest in overcoming barriers and entering a particular market. In Bain's sense, price differentials between countries for a particular product are an indicator of the existence and magnitude of market barriers.

Barriers to entry may be established for a number of reasons (Simon, 1989, p. 1441) and can be attributed to the following causes:

- economic;
- protectionist; or
- behavioural.

As examples of *economic* barriers to entry, Porter (1986) cites economies of scale in favour of established competitors, capital requirements for market entry or 'switching costs' for buyers. Economies of scale arise if one seller can accumulate sales quantities that provide him or her with a cost advantage over new competitors. These cost disadvantages mean that 'latecomers' receive low contribution margins which can reduce indefinitely the yield on market entry.

High initial investment serves as a market hurdle, if the necessary capital exceeds what is available, or if investment in a particular market is just too risky. The basis of the entry risk is the degree to which the rate of return on market-entry investment depends on, and varies according to, external factors (price level, quantities sold, political developments and so on), and on the extent to which the entering firm's existence is jeopardized by a failed entry.

Furthermore, if it is highly specific, the initial investment can impede entry indirectly. High specificity means that market entry investments in country market A have little or no use for country markets B or C. An enterprise invests with high specificity in entering a new country market if this investment cannot be recovered (equipment or customer relationships have little value in other markets). This characteristic not only makes market exit difficult but, even prior to entry, functions as an inhibiting factor (exit barriers as entry barriers).

Economic entry barriers are predominantly structural in nature (cost disadvantages, capital requirements, specificity). From time to time, however, established competitors create economic barriers to entry by introducing or raising switching costs for clients with respect to moving to other suppliers. Such switching costs can take various forms. For example, technological commitment such as proprietary operating systems which require new investment in the training of computer operators for alternative systems, constitutes just such a barrier. Pricing systems, such as annual turnover bonuses, would also mean substantial losses of accumulated 'points' if switching to another supplier. Switching costs created in this manner force newcomers to offer price- or product-related concessions to potential customers. Such actions in turn have a negative impact on the success and profitability of market entry.

Protectionist barriers to entry are caused by *tariff* and *non-tariff barriers*, which are established to protect local industries or individual sectors. Because of their targeted nature, they are strategic barriers. Despite, or precisely *because of* the many areas in earlier GATT negotiation rounds (Onkvisit and Shaw, 1993, p. 10; OECD, 1996a, 1996b), the dismantling of tariff measures has played a special role. General import bans, quotas, local-content requirements or diverging technical standards limit market-operation potential for foreign sellers in many markets, as the following examples demonstrate.

> ▶ Despite the dismantling of some tariff barriers, Japan is a perfect example in this respect, as in the early 1990s, foreign sellers had no *real* access to this market. An ineffectual law of competition, public procurement processes and purchasing behaviour that favour national sellers, or a state-supported network of relationships between buyers and sellers, were only some of the reasons why in the past, foreign sellers were unable to achieve significant market share in many sectors of Japanese industry. Deysson (1994) cites the examples of the automobile sector, in which, in 1994, foreign sellers had a market share of only 3 per cent, in insurance 2 per cent and paper 3.7 per cent.
>
> Because, on the other hand, Japanese firms were able to export their products in large quantities to European and American markets, Japan incurred substantial trade surpluses. In 1992, the trade surplus with the USA was 49.5 billion dollars (Bauer, p. 1993), and in the following year, even rose to 60 billion dollars.
>
> As a result, in bilateral trade negotiations, the USA attempted to persuade the Japanese to open their market to American firms. At the core of negotiations was the telecommunications sector (for example, electronic appliances), in which Japanese firms had a high market share in the USA, but for which American firms such as Motorola had no equivalent access in the Japanese market. Despite a trade agreement between Japan and the USA from 1989, in which the Japanese government promised to open its mobile-telephone market to Motorola, the

company was not able to gain a significant market share in Japan.

In early 1994, when these discussions threatened to collapse, the US government threatened Japan with appropriate counter measures, because of non-compliance with the trade agreement from 1989. In particular, America's so-called 'Super 301' procedure was applied again. This enabled the USA to introduce a punitive tariff to counter discrimination against American products. Only when the USA announced that such a tariff against Japanese (end-user) telecommunications appliances was pending, did the Japanese government capitulate and facilitate Motorola real and comprehensive access to their market.

Specifically, the two governments arranged a closed agreement, by virtue of which the Japanese government guaranteed the local mobile telephone provider, Idou Tsushin Corp (Ido), credit, so that Ido could re-equip its own mobile telephone network, to enable consumers to use appliances manufactured by Motorola. Prior to that, Motorola had no real chance in Japan, because the Japanese network providers, partly through political pressure, refused to convert to the international standard of 6.5 megahertz frequency, and remained with 8 MHz. As a result of this higher broadcasting frequency, the appliances from foreign manufacturers could not be used in conjunction with the Japanese telecommunication systems.

▸ In January 2001, the US agricultural ministry specified in a decree the maximum permissible holes size in cheese for sale in its domestic market. For Emmental, the holes created by air bubbles were subject to a maximum diameter of 2.06 cm. This led to an outcry from Swiss firms active in the American market, because the typical Swiss Emmental had air holes of up to 4 cm in diameter.

It frequently proved very difficult to eradicate such protectionist measures, because countries persisted in the unilateral promotion of local competitors, and, as a justification, pointed to the same kinds of measures in other countries. The aircraft industry provides an almost perfect example:

Since the 1997 takeover of McDonnell Douglas by Boeing, Airbus is the only real competitor in the global market. If one looks at the order quantities achieved by both enterprises since the market entry

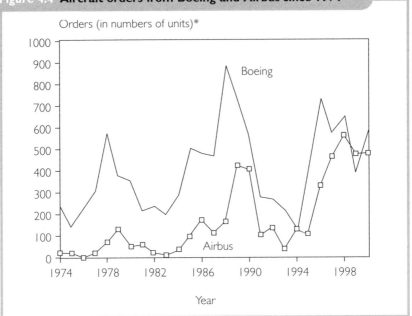

Figure 4.4 Aircraft orders from Boeing and Airbus since 1974

of Airbus in 1974 (see Figure 4.4), it is evident that over time, Airbus has succeeded in reducing the gap between the two quite considerably.

Boeing's remaining market advantage can be attributed to the fact that, at the time of writing, with the 747–400, the company virtually has a monopoly over long-haul aircraft. In order to compete with Boeing in this segment as well, Airbus decided in late 2000 to develop the A380, which would eradicate Boeing's last monopolistic bastion (see the product portfolios of the two companies presented in Figure 4.5).

Because Airbus could only finance its development costs of around US$10 bn, with the aid of favourable loans from participating countries France, Great Britain, Spain and Germany (Pfeiffer, 2000), the USA accused these European states of protectionism at the expense of Boeing. The American president at the time, Bill Clinton, threatened the Europeans with a formal complaint to the World Trade Organization (WTO).

On the other hand, the European states justify their subsidies by claiming that the USA did the same for Boeing, but indirectly rather than directly. The US government invested US$1 bn annually in

Figure 4.5 Product portfolio of Boeing and Airbus after the introduction of the A380

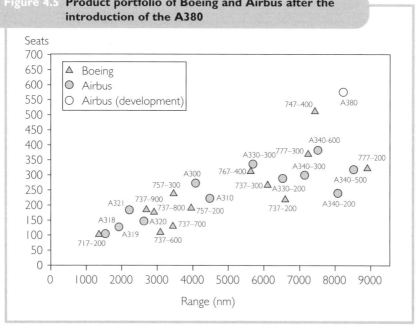

aeronautical research, by awarding contracts to NASA (National Aeronautics and Space Administration). The benefits of this research accrue only to Boeing, so that firms in certain areas and sectors were able to dispense with their own research and thus save 400 million dollars annually (Kläsgen, 2000).

Finally, market barriers can also have a *behavioural* basis. They can originate in customer behaviour, for example, through favouring domestic produce, as in a 'buy British' campaign. Furthermore, behavioural barriers can derive from a subjective orientation towards foreigners (attitude towards foreigners and their products) by the exporting company. Dichtl *et al.* (1983) have demonstrated empirically that the personality criterion 'external orientation' exerts a substantial impact on the market selection by an enterprise. Aversion towards certain potential target countries can thus serve as internal barriers that prevent entry into those markets (Hollensen, 2001, p. 194).

New empirical studies on the personality criterion of 'external orientation' confirm not only its general significance; they also show that the external orientation is closely associated with perceived cultural distance attaching to the particular foreign markets. However, in this context, it is questionable whether German managers rate the cultural distance to many external markets any larger than their 'colleagues' in these markets rate the German market.

For example, Müller and Kornmeier's empirical study (2000) comes to this conclusion. The responding Japanese, Finnish, South Korean and South African managers rated the distance from the German market lower than did the latter for non-German countries (see Figure 4.6).

Figure 4.6 Reciprocal cultural distance of managers from four countries

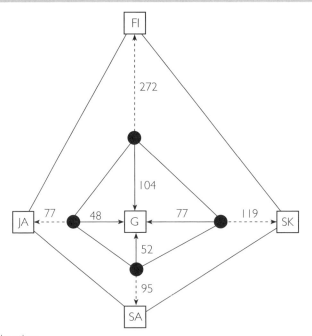

Explanation:
While the distance of South Korean managers from Germany comprises 77% of the objective distance of German managers from South Korea is 119% of the objective distance.
(JA = Japan, G = Germany, SA = South Africa, SK = South Korea, FI = Finland).

Source: Müller and Kornmeier, 2000, p. 35.

The so-called *country risks* constitute a particularly relevant group of market barriers, which reflect criteria from all stated dimensions of economic, protectionist and behaviourally-orientated market barriers. Particularly in connection with the international debt crisis, country risks have been the subject of considerable attention (Kappagoda, 1997).

In many countries, the prevailing limited ability to pay both private and public debts has made risk a core factor in country selection. These risks are regarded as country risks, which can emerge in the context of foreign trade and are not necessarily associated with a specific project. Transfer, payment and expropriation issues are of particular relevance. Figure 4.7 provides an overview of the potential forms and components of country risk.

Because of the structural deterioration of country risk since the second half of the 1970s, many concepts for evaluating country risk have been developed. In terms of structuring the various approaches, Figure 4.8 provides both a qualitative and quantitative differentiation (see Backhaus and Meyer (1986) for an analysis of the basics).

Qualitative evaluation concepts are characterized by an absence of any prescribed catalogue of criteria. From the perspective of the writer or publisher, the relevant concepts are described and, in part, compressed or summarized into overall recommendations. Qualitative evaluations include the country reports from the German Federal Office for Foreign Trade Information (BfAI), the Political Risk Letter (PRL) and the AGEFI Country Index.

Quantitative approaches to evaluation are those based on objective (statistical) data. The objective approaches are thus based either on statistical data such as debt ratios or the net demand for credit, or on econometric models. The World Bank's Two-Gap Model and the US-EXIM Bank Model are examples of econometric models. In addition, the subjective concepts play a large role in the evaluation of country risk. In this context, a differentiation must be made between one-dimensional and multidimensional scoring models.

One-dimensional scoring models are characterized by considering country risk explicitly on the basis of one criterion only, even if there are several risks underlying this single dimension. The Country Rating System of *Institutional Investor Magazine* involves a panel of banking experts who are asked to rate, according to a hundred-point scale, the creditworthiness of individual countries. The IfO (Institute for Economic Research at the University of Munich, see www.ifo.de) Institute's Economic Survey International proceeds in a similar

Figure 4.7 Country risks having an impact on international companies

Country risk components	Brief description
Transfer risks in the broadest sense	Constrains cross-border corporate activities
Inability to pay (transfer risk in the narrower, strict sense)	A country is no longer willing or able to meet its interest and capital payments as well as capital and profit. The debtor country imposes a payment ban or moratorium, thus preventing the conversion or transfer of funds
Exchange rate risks	The exchange relationship of the agreed-upon currency between the two countries can change
Trade barriers	The government creates import barriers and tariffs
Social and political risk	The business activities of the foreign firm are impeded by government measures, social or political unrest, or war
Expropriation in the broadest sense	The government usurps, completely or partially the rights and wealth of individual companies and pays appropriate compensation
Nationalization	There is nationalization of an entire group of companies, which is *usually* associated with compensatory payment
Confiscation	This affects an entire national economy and usually occurs after a revolution. There is generally no compensation

Source: Backhaus and Siepert, 1987.

manner, with its ESI Concept. Although the ESI concept measures various criteria, a country comparison proceeds according to one dimension only.

In contrast, multidimensional scoring models divide country risk into various components that are considered country-by-country by a panel of experts. The partial evaluations are frequently weighted and summarized into a total point score. The information system of the BERI (Business Environment Risk Index, see www.beri.com) Institute is

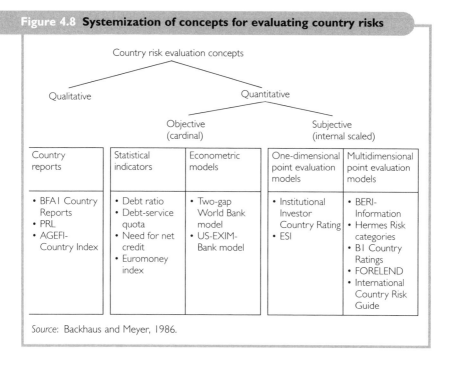

Figure 4.8 Systemization of concepts for evaluating country risks

Country risk evaluation concepts

Qualitative — Quantitative

Objective (cardinal) — Subjective (internal scaled)

Country reports	Statistical indicators	Econometric models	One-dimensional point evaluation models	Multidimensional point evaluation models
• BFAI Country Reports • PRL • AGEFI-Country Index	• Debt ratio • Debt-service quota • Need for net credit • Euromoney index	• Two-gap World Bank model • US-EXIM-Bank model	• Institutional Investor Country Rating • ESI	• BERI-Information • Hermes Risk categories • BI Country Ratings • FORELEND • International Country Risk Guide

Source: Backhaus and Meyer, 1986.

one of the best-known multidimensional scoring models (Doole and Lowe, 2000, p. 124).

Empirical studies have established that all types of market barriers (economic, protectionist and behavioural, as well as country risk) are monitored by firms in the context of an internationalization process. For example, in a survey carried out by Bassen *et al.* (2001), medium-sized firms were presented with possible internationalization barriers. Figure 4.9 shows the proportions of respondents rating the various barriers from 'strong' to 'very strong'.

The empirical study indicated that all types of barriers are highly significant for at least a proportion of the respondents. Economic (such as quality of local components) as well as protectionist (such as trade barriers) or behavioural causes (such as insufficient qualifications or linguistic skills) are significant. Furthermore, the country risk 'political stability' is regarded by most respondents as significant.

Interdependence and Country Market Evaluation

Market attractiveness and market barriers can seldom be considered in a valid way with respect to one country independently of other others

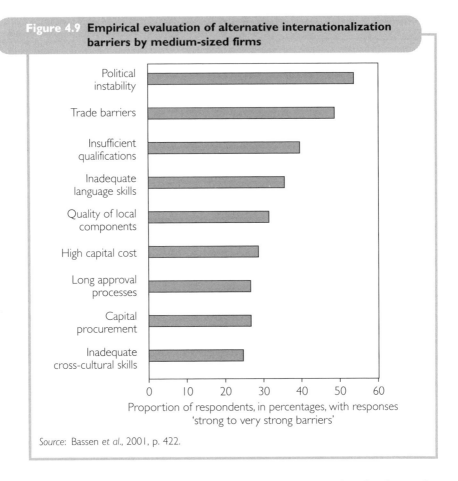

Figure 4.9 Empirical evaluation of alternative internationalization barriers by medium-sized firms

Proportion of respondents, in percentages, with responses 'strong to very strong barriers'

Source: Bassen et al., 2001, p. 422.

in which it operates or plans to operate. The reasons for this lie in the interdependencies or linkages between the markets. Using selected examples, Figure 4.10 demonstrates how the buyer (demand), seller (supply) and competition-related dependencies may be relevant in either raising or lowering the attractiveness of a market.

These interdependencies may also have a bearing on the risks associated with processing foreign markets. For the internationally operating enterprise, it is the *total risk arising from the entire portfolio* of country markets that counts. This may not be influenced much by the addition of a particularly risky market, if, at the same time, a change in the overall portfolio is undertaken to compensate for this (individual) risk. Operating according to single country-market risk is thus only appropriate where there are no interdependencies and such compensation is thus impossible.

Figure 4.10 Examples of the influence of interdependency on market attractiveness and market barriers

	Raises market attractiveness	*Increases market barriers*
Supplier-based interdependency	The attractiveness of country markets can be increased if operating there, yields economies of scale, which have a favourable impact on opportunities in other markets. For example, the profit contribution of the American market may be small for a firm. However, the quantities sold there may yield economies of scale that allow the firm to sell at more competitive prices in other markets. In such a case, operating in the American market does make sense In addition to the cost effects, entering a demanding country market, such as the German luxury-automobile market, can increase the level of corporate know-how, which can lead to a general international improvement of the competitive position	A firm that operates consistently and effectively through its own capabilities in a French-speaking and cultural area, creates internal market barriers with respect to other country markets with different cultures, if its internal know-how becomes too strongly focused. Because the entire internal communication of this firm is orientated towards the French-speaking language and culture, activities and operations in other countries would demand, at the very least, a change in this aspect of corporate culture
Demand-related interdependence	A country may be attractive because it serves as a bridgehead or reference market for entering other countries. For example, France serves as a reference market for the French-speaking countries of North Africa. Similarly, the USA serves this	A country market can have high barriers for a firm, because its presence in certain other markets would be regarded by buyers as negative and undesirable. For example, some Mexican buyers reject products partly because the manufacturing

Figure 4.10 *continued*

	Raises market attractiveness	*Increases market barriers*
	purpose for South America. Thus, even if France and the USA do not offer any direct potential benefits, there can still be 'spillover' benefits with respect to other markets.	company is active in the USA. Because of conflicts between these countries in the past, American products, or those that are strongly represented in the USA, may be rejected.
		During the height of the anti-apartheid campaign, firms that were present or active in South Africa, jeopardized their chances seriously with countries that were particularly opposed to the apartheid system
Competition-related interdependence	Developments in the credit market, outlined earlier, showed that firms regard certain markets as particularly attractive, because of competition-related interdependence. The attractiveness of the Southern European country markets for the credit-card provider Europay, derives mainly from the fact that these are countries in which their arch-rival, Visa, has a traditionally strong market position. Because Visa was increasing its activities in countries in which Europay was particularly active in the past, Europay reacted by intensifying its own operations in Visa's core markets in *Southern Europe*	A country market can create high market barriers for a firm, if its activities there might result in 'retaliatory actions' in other markets that are relevant to the firm. In the example given on the left, Visa could have considered avoiding intensified activity in Northern Europe in order to avoid a massive attack by Europay in its traditional core markets.

The main difficulty in evaluating country markets lies in analysing attractiveness and barriers in the context of possible interdependencies with other markets. While the feedback to individual country markets in relation to markets that are already operational is relatively easy if several additional new country markets are to be entered. In this case, feedback between the new markets is also relevant. Furthermore, the interdependencies now depend on the specific combination of existing and new markets.

Selection of Country Markets

Procedure for Country Market Selection

Because market attractiveness and market barriers in terms of individual countries cannot be determined in a straightforward manner in view of the interdependencies described above, the question arises as to what methodological approaches can be used in this context.

With respect to the methodological procedures, two basic methods can be identified:

▸ grouping; and
▸ filtering.

For *grouping processes*, all potential country markets are grouped according to their similarities, so as to select the appropriate combination of target country markets. Sub-optimal evaluation of individual criteria can, in effect, be compensated by above-average evaluations on other criteria. Subsequently, credibility considerations must be undertaken in order to select the appropriate groups. This occurs frequently through a comparison of segmentation issues in terms of the strengths and weaknesses profile of the company.

In contrast to grouping processes for which all relevant determinants are considered simultaneously, *filtering processes* operate in several phases (Schneider, 1984; Köhler and Hüttemann, 1989). For filtering processes, it is not the formation of market segments, but rather the market selection itself that forms the focus of attention. For each filtering stage, the total number of potential countries is reduced by those that do not meet the criteria of the particular filtering stage. Thus, with each filtering stage, specific criteria come into play, and in the first phases 'go'/'no-go' factors are used, whose non-fulfilment will immediately exclude the country from any further consideration. At

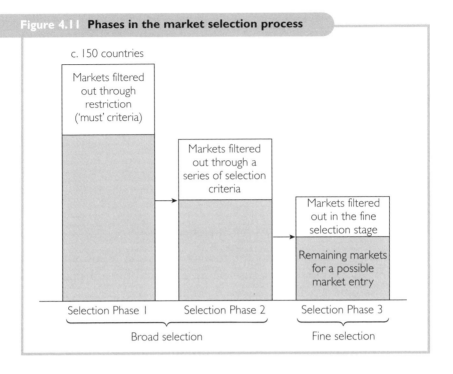

Figure 4.11 Phases in the market selection process

the conclusion of the process, all countries remain, that have met the various demands, and are thus real operational targets (see Figure 4.11).

Grouping and filtering processes differ substantially from one another in terms of methodology, and thus reveal quite different advantages and disadvantages:

▸ The main advantage of grouping procedures lies in their potential for revealing feedback to other country markets. Feedback can occur on various market attractiveness dimensions (cost position, pricing etc.). Taking all dimensions into account simultaneously increases the chances of improving the quality of the selection process. Schneider and Müller (1989, p. 7) none the less argue, convincingly and relevantly, that grouping procedures are beset with some fundamental methodological and application-related problems. The methodological limits of the procedure lie mainly in the absence of statements about the country segments that are to be selected by the firm. Furthermore, the nature and number of criteria that are analysed parallel to one another are determined mainly by the quantitative and qualitative data available to the firm. Apart from this essentially methodological problem, a further shortcoming of grouping procedures is that they are relatively laborious and expensive to implement. For small firms which only plan to operate in a few selected country markets, this grouping procedure is often impractical due to the need for comprehensive data gathering.

▸ In contrast, filtering processes do not require any special primary information, at least not in the early stages. The widespread use of filtering processes in practice is thus largely attributable to their ease of operation. However, these filtering procedures can also be methodologically problematical, because of the subjectivity of evaluations, and with respect to compensatory (feedback) criteria. The results obtained from filtering processes depend largely on the selection of filtering variables and the evaluation of qualitative criteria by analysts. Furthermore, the successive procedures imply that country markets will sometimes be excluded from further analysis, because of their failure to fulfil compensatory criteria, even though market operations in that country would in fact be advantageous.

Problems may occur with respect to establishing feedback between country markets, such as when a country market seems unattractive viewed in isolation and is thus eliminated from early filtering phases, although an entry into this market is necessary in order to enter another, clearly attractive market. Demand-based interdependence through the bridgehead function (see Figure 4.12) between these markets is thus not considered when using filtering processes. The consequence is a sub-optimal country-market selection.

In general, both filtering and grouping procedures reveal some central weaknesses which imply that their isolated use is of questionable benefit. Consequently, a combination of procedures seems advisable. If the market selection process is divided into a rough analysis followed by a fine one, as suggested in the literature (Hollensen, 2001; Lilien and Kotler, 1983, p. 311), a first step can reduce the number of country markets to be analysed with the aid of filtering. If the selection is carried out purely through go/no-go criteria, the stated methodological problems of filtering processes will be overcome. By thus reducing the quantity, the subsequent fine selection can be undertaken on the basis of grouping procedures. The following example illustrates such a combined approach of filtering and grouping procedures.

Brown Ltd

Brown Ltd is a medium-sized pharmaceutical company, which specializes in manufacturing generic and other medical products. After selling its products exclusively in the British market, its managers decided to market the company's most successful 'pride and joy', a medicinal diet pill, outside Great Britain. Although the managing directors, Michael and John Brown, were in agreement on limiting their sales to EU countries, there was some uncertainty as to which EU country markets could be operated successfully.

The management gave a working group the task of discussing the issue. Led by Miss Elisabeth Hughes, the working group was to make some suggestions by January of the following year, as to the appropriate country markets for Brown Ltd's slimming pills.

In January, as agreed, the working group presented the company's management with the results of their discussions. Miss Hughes first elaborated the procedures undertaken by the working group: 'Our procedures were based on the following series of steps:

▸ The first thing we did was agree on the criteria for evaluating the country markets. We decided that one criterion *had* to be met for a particular market to be considered at all. This was the ability to sell the product not only through pharmacies. Thus, some markets could be eliminated from the outset, because, distribution of our product through pharmacies only is mandatary in those countries.

▸ The next step was to get some internal and external experts to evaluate the criteria for each of the remaining country markets. The evaluation was done on a scale from *0 = very bad* to *10 = very good*, and this was to be rated as much as possible from the perspective of the company.

▸ From these individual evaluations, we then calculated the average evaluations (see Figure 4.12), which served as the basis for grouping the remaining country markets. With the aid of cluster analysis (for details, see Backhaus *et al.*, 2000, p. 328), we have established various groups that were evaluated as being similar.

▸ For the cluster analysis we used, a hierarchical procedure. With that, the individual country markets were grouped (stepwise) in terms of their similarities, until – in the last step – all country markets formed a single cluster. With each clustering step, the 'dissimilarity' between the groups so established, is determined.

Figure 4.12 Example of evaluating the country markets

Country markets in the European Union

Criterion	Austria (AUS)	Belgium (BEL)	Denmark (DEN)	Finland (FIN)	France (FRA)	United Kingdom (UK)	Greece (GRE)	Republic of Ireland (IRE)	Italy (ITA)	Luxembourg (LUX)	Netherlands (NET)	Portugal (POR)	Spain (SPA)	Sweden (SWE)	Germany (GER)
Distribution beyond pharmacies possible?	no	yes	no	yes	yes	yes	yes	no	yes	no	no	yes	yes	no	yes
Market volume		3.2		3.9	9.2	9.4	3.6		8.4			4.8	5.1		7.9
Competition intensity		7.3		8.1	4.1	3.2	9.5		2.9			8.4	7.1		3.6
Retailing structure		3.9		2.1	8.6	6.1	7.1		6.9			5.1	5.8		8.0
Future market development		8.5		7.9	4.1	5.0	1.2		4.8			2.9	3.9		3.8
Ability to implement proven marketing concepts		8.7		7.1	2.3	10	5.4		2.9			4.9	6.1		3.4

In order to derive understandable and usable results from the procedure, we shall introduce the individual steps of the cluster analysis separately in the following section.

▸ Within the cluster analysis, we determined initially the similarities between the country markets, by defining the quadratic Euclidean distances between the markets. The following applies for the quadratic Euclidean distance:

$$d_{A,B} = \sum_{j=1}^{j} (x_{Aj} - x_{Bj})^2$$

where:

$d_{A,B}$ = distance between country markets A and B

x_{Aj}, x_{Bj} = value of the criterion j for country A or B.

▸ For example, the quadratic Euclidean distance for the country pair Belgium/Finland, yields the following value:

$$d_{BEL,FIN} = (3.2 - 3.9)^2 + (7.3 - 8.1)^2 + \ldots + (8.7 - 7.1)^2 = 7.29$$

▸ Figure 4.13 shows the quadratic Euclidean distances revealed by the country markets in relation to one another. It is evident that the largest similarity (because of the smallest deviation) exists between Italy (ITA) and Germany (GER). These countries are thus compressed into one of the first stages.

▸ In order to determine which country markets should be combined on the next clustering step, e.g. the distance between Italy and Germany after the grouping must be determined. The literature offers a number of clustering procedures (Backhaus *et al.*, 2000, p. 348), which reveal all advantages and disadvantages. Here, we have applied a single-linkage procedure. This means that the distance between the grouped object bundle and an individual object has precisely the minimum distance between *both* individual grouped objects and the individual object itself. Let's assume you want to establish the distance between Belgium (BEL) and the cluster Germany/Italy. The distance between Belgium and Italy is 102.73 the distance between Belgium and Germany is 102.77. Thus, with this approach, the distance between BEL and the group GER/ITA is 102.73 (see Figure 4.14: '8-cluster solution').

▸ Conversely, for the next step, the objects that have the smallest distance from one another are fused. These are clearly the country

Figure 4.13 Example of quadratic Euclidean distances

	BEL	FIN	FRA	UK	GRE	ITA	POR	SPA	GER
BEL	0	7.29	128.65	74.03	79.42	102.73	51.01	35.18	102.77
FIN		0	123.82	87.08	74.83	97.58	39.74	33.13	101.56
FRA			0	67.2	80.79	5.82	58.3	48.13	3.6
UK				0	109.93	52.18	79.62	50.21	51.02
GRE					0	85.85	9.79	17.48	64.87
ITA						0	54.06	40.79	3.2
POR							0	4.71	44.12
SPA								0	32.23
GER									0

Figure 4.14 Remaining process of merger

After 1st merger phase

	BEL	FIN	FRA	UK	GRE	POR	SPA	ITA/GER
BEL	0	7.29	128.65	74.03	79.42	51.01	35.18	102.73
FIN		0	123.82	87.08	74.83	39.74	33.13	97.58
FRA			0	67.2	80.79	58.3	48.13	3.6
UK				0	109.93	79.62	50.21	21.02
GRE					0	9.79	17.48	64.87
POR						0	4.71	44.12
SPA							0	32.23
ITA/GER								0

'8 cluster solution'

After 2nd merger phase

	BEL	FIN	UK	GRE	POR	SPA	ITA/GER/FRA
BEL	0	7.29	74.03	79.42	51.01	35.18	102.73
FIN		0	87.08	74.83	39.74	33.13	97.58
UK			0	109.93	79.62	50.21	21.02
GRE				0	9.79	17.48	64.87
POR					0	4.71	44.12
SPA						0	32.23
ITA/GER/FRA							0

'7 cluster solution'

After 3rd merger phase

	BEL	FIN	UK	GRE	SPA/POR	ITA/GER/FRA
BEL	0	7.29	74.03	79.42	35.18	102.73
FIN		0	87.08	74.83	33.13	97.58
UK			0	109.93	50.21	51.02
GRE				0	9.79	64.87
SPA/POR					0	32.23
ITA/GER/FRA						0

'6 cluster solution'

After 4th merger phase

	BEL/FIN	UK	GRE	SPA/POR	ITA/GER/FRA
BEL/FIN	0	74.03	74.83	33.13	97.58
UK		0	109.93	50.21	51.02
GRE			0	9.79	64.87
SPA/POR				0	32.23
ITA/GER/FRA					0

'5 cluster solution'

After 5th merger phase

	BEL/FIN	UK	GRE	SPA/POR	ITA/GER/FRA
BEL/FIN	0	74.03	74.83	33.13	97.58
UK		0	109.93	50.21	51.02
GRE			0	9.79	64.87
SPA/POR				0	32.23
ITA/GER/FRA					0

'4 cluster solution'

After 6th merger phase

	BEL/FIN	UK	ITA/GER/FRA/SPA/POR/GRE
BEL/FIN	0	74.03	33.13
UK		0	50.21
ITA/GER/FRA/SPA/POR/GRE			0

'3 cluster solution'

After 7th merger phase

	UK	ITA/GER/FRA/SPA/POR/GRE/BEL/FIN
UK	0	50.21
ITA/GER/FRA/SPA/POR/GRE/BEL/FIN		0

'2 cluster solution'

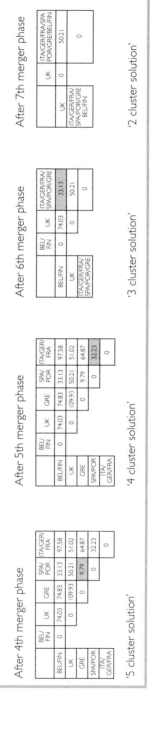

markets Italy/Germany on the one hand, and France on the other.

- This process is continued until all country markets are located in one cluster. This is achieved after seven clustering steps.
- As mentioned earlier, the development of the respective distances in the individual cluster stages are analysed not (Figure 4.15). Where a greater than proportional rise in distances arises, the process is generally 'cut of'. In our example, such 'elbows' arise within the distances at two points. Consequently, a 2-cluster as well as a 4-cluster solution is feasible. A 4-cluster solution seems more likely and credible to us, otherwise all foreign country markets would be allocated to one cluster.
- If the company proceeds according to this suggested solution, then the following differentiation between market segments can be made:
  - *Belgium and Finland*: These are markets with no attractive volume to offer. However, the market is likely to develop very positively. It is advantageous that the competitive situation is weak and that, in addition, our proven marketing concepts can be used there.
  - *Spain, Portugal and Greece*: These markets have an above-average volume, low competitive intensity and thus a rather poor overall market development.

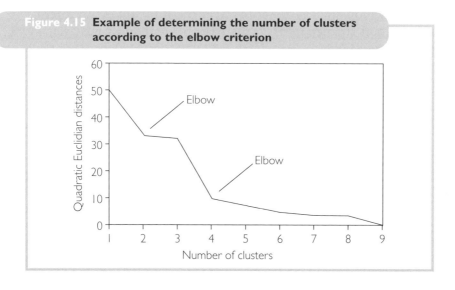

Figure 4.15 Example of determining the number of clusters according to the elbow criterion

> ▸ *Italy, Germany and France*: These are the currently high-volume markets, which, however, are thus attracting the attention of our competitors. Furthermore, we can do little there with the marketing concepts we have developed for the German market.

In the above example, the firm uses a combination of filtering and grouping procedures. Initially, there is a two-stage filtering. Only EU counries are considered (first filtering). Secondly, only those countries within this group are considered, in which distribution through non-pharmacy outlets is legally permissible (second filtering). The remaining country markets are grouped on the basis of their similarity cluster analysis.

Also unavoidable for such a combined procedure however, is that ultimately the segment selection proceeds on the basis of perceived credibility. In the example discussed above, the enterprise must determine whether, or what, clusters should in future be operationalized. The exact size and number of selected segments depends substantially on the internationalization strategy followed by the enterprise.

Selection of Country Markets and Internationalization Strategy

The selection of country markets indicates not only process-related problem formulations, but is also influenced substantially by the internationalization strategy towards which the firm strives. An internationalization strategy refers to the basic orientation of management towards cross-border activity (Onkvisit and Shaw, 1993, p. 21). A basic and standard differentiation is made in the literature between the following three orientations:

▸ ethnocentric
▸ polycentric
▸ geocentric.

An *ethnocentric* orientation refers to operating in external country markets in a manner characterized strongly by the domestic market and only a few, selected country markets are operated (Hollensen, 2001, p. 293). There is therefore an ethnocentric orientation when sellers focus their marketing activities on the domestic market, and when only isolated and often opportunistic use is made of foreign markets

(Hennan and Perlmutter, 1979). In this context, the focus of internationalization is on using elsewhere, and to the maximum advantage, marketing knowledge gained in the home market. The target markets for the ethnocentric approach are those in which existing knowledge is relevant. This relevance is a high degree of *similarity* to the domestic market. The hallmark of ethnocentrism is the principle of 'looking for similarity', which can be interpreted as a form of seller-based interdependency, because the superordinate goal of the firm is purely that of selling in markets similar to those back home.

A *polycentric* (or multinational) *orientation* is one where, apart from its home market, an enterprise covers additional foreign markets. In contrast to the ethnocentric orientation, the seller is in this case willing to consider the particular characteristics of the foreign market, and to develop and implement country-specific strategies. In general, the organizational anchoring proceeds through the formation of separate subsidiaries. These subsidiaries have sufficient decision-making autonomy to pursue their chosen strategy and marketing measures, so that they appear almost as national companies in the home market and are in fact integral components of the host country's economy.

Against the background of the model of 'management by interdependency' presented in Section A, the polycentric strategy applies the principle of multinational marketing and far less so the international approach. To the extent that the polycentric strategy determines that foreign markets should be operated by completely autonomous subsidiaries linked to one another only by weak buyer, seller and competitive feedback, market operations are characterized by national marketing problems. In such a case, there are, from the perspective of the company as a whole, a number of national marketing perspectives 'marketing in Country A and so on', so that cross-border problem formulations to international marketing problems recede into the background.

In the case of a *geocentric* (global market) *orientation*, all individual country markets will ultimately be considered from the perspective of the seller, who serves the market with standardized products and does not take national needs into account. The main indicator of this internationalization strategy is the consistent search for cost and price advantages based on large quantities of sales. Firms that pursue a geocentric orientation build their activities quite deliberately (certainly in the case of sellers) on demand and competitor-based feedback between the various country markets in which they operate.

Depending on which internationalization strategy an enterprise pursues at the time of making its market selection decisions, or on what type of internationalization process the enterprise is using, different results emerge within the decision making process:

▸ For a firm with an ethnocentric orientation, operations are only undertaken in foreign markets if, in the short run, opportunities exceed risks. For such sporadic foreign activity, firms are generally only active in country markets, when low exit barriers enable them to terminate their activities as soon as the opportunity-risk constellation changes, or turns out to be less advantageous than expected. It can be assumed that firms working on this basis will select a single or only few country markets.

▸ As a characteristic element of polycentric firms, an intensive consideration of country-specific conditions means that similarity between country markets and the home market plays only a minor role, in comparison to the situation with ethnocentric firms. While, for ethnocentric firms, the transfer of familiar and successful concepts from the home market to new country markets plays a central role, polycentric firms see adaptation to national preferences as being the key to success. The selection of country markets will therefore be focused more on factors such as an additional need for capital, the necessary personnel (including staff available locally), technological resources for achieving country-specific products, and the capability of co-ordinating individual country market activities. Because the polycentric orientation that is typical of multinational enterprises focuses heavily on country-specific characteristics, all countries where there is a demand for the products themselves are potential markets. Enterprises with a polycentric orientation thus typically select more country markets than do ethnocentric firms.

▸ The objective of a geocentric marketing orientation is to integrate all corporate activities into an overall system, so as to increase international competitiveness through economies of scale and economies of scope. Striving for economies of scale, however, limits activities to those countries in which there is a demand for the company's standardized products. For this reason, enterprises with a geocentric orientation concentrate frequently on countries with relatively similar demand preferences and competitive structure. In terms of the market selection process, such enterprises generally choose more country markets than do ethnocentric firms, but fewer than polycentric firms.

Market Entry Strategies

Timing the Entry

Once the market entry decision has been made, firms need to decide on the appropriate point in time to enter the various markets. Two basic alternative market entry timing-strategies have been identified in the literature: the successive 'waterfall strategy' and the simultaneous 'shower strategy' (for further aspects of timing in international marketing, see Keegan, 1999).

The Waterfall Strategy

For firms that are characterized by an ethnocentric orientation, there will generally be only a stepwise extension of the operational country markets, because the number of country markets is limited to those with similarities to the home market and there are many cases in which the necessary resources for the simultaneous entry of country markets is lacking because of the size of the firm. The stepwise extension of cross-border operations is determined by the order in which the individual country markets can be approached (Ohmae, 1985; Ayal and Zif, 1985; Hollensen, 2001, 204).

Figure 5.1 illustrates the basic principle behind the waterfall strategy, where the number of markets is extended successively. After an introductory stage, during which experience with the product (to be sold externally) is gained in the home market, the seller proceeds with the second stage, introducing the product into selected foreign markets. These markets can be chosen in such a manner as to provide the greatest possible similarity to the domestic market. Only by doing this can the seller take full advantage of domestic experience. Each further stage of the model raises the level of heterogeneity of the additional markets.

The fundamental principle thus translates into an attempt to increase the number of operational markets systematically, in the context of which different planning procedures are possible. On the one hand, at the end of each introductory phase, the firm can rethink

Figure 5.1 The waterfall strategy

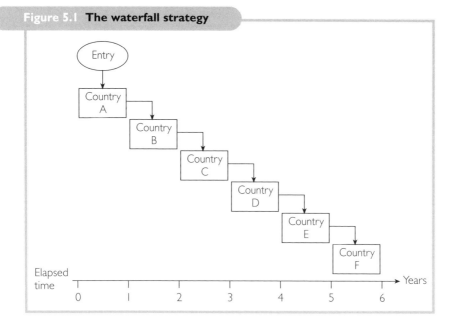

the markets that should be entered next. In this case, the firm can consider a possibly changed data situation at each stage. On the other hand, it may be advisable for a firm, before the first foreign entry (and before commencing the waterfall model at all) to decide not only on the markets which are to be operated *initially,* but also which countries will be entered in the future.

In comparison to a simultaneous approach, the waterfall strategy offers a number of advantages (Kalish *et al.*, 1995).

▸ The fact that one can probe the foreign market tentatively, and thus not serve all intended markets immediately (but only at the end of the process), is significant, because firms frequently do not have sufficient resources at the beginning of the internationalization process to operate in parallel in a large number of markets. The enterprise is thus able to grow along with its available resources, and extend its foreign business.

▸ Similarly, the level of risk is limited. The firm tests the desired markets step by step, so it can terminate its efforts at any stage if it becomes clear that sales of the product are unlikely to be as successful as originally expected.

▸ The stepwise introduction of products offers an added, and less obvious, advantage that the product life cycle can be extended, if

Table 5.1 Sample data illustrating the waterfall strategy

Year (t)	Turnover Country A	Turnover Country B	Turnover Country C	Total turnover according to waterfall strategy	Total turnover with simultaneous introduction
0	0	–	–	0	0
1	50	–	–	50	120
2	80	0	–	80	192
3	90	40	–	130	216
4	80	64	0	144	192
5	50	72	30	152	120
6	–	64	48	112	–
7	–	40	54	94	–
8	–	–	48	48	–
9	–	–	30	30	–

products that have matured on the domestic market can be introduced successfully in foreign markets. This requires lower capacities in all branches of the enterprise.

Table 5.1 demonstrates how a firm introduces a product innovation successively according to the waterfall strategy, in country markets A, B and C. The introduction is completed at t_0 at home (Country A), t_2 in Country B and t_4 in Country C. The firm pursues this strategy so that products can be eliminated if turnover declines for two successive years.

The graphs in Figure 5.2 also make clear that the firm should assume that the market success of the product in country markets B and C which are only entered later, will be weaker than in the original home market. Figure 5.3 compares the overall development from the waterfall strategy with those of simultaneous entry in all three countries.

Although a simultaneous introduction of the product in all three country markets would seem to mean that between t_1 and t_4, higher turnover will be achieved in comparison to the introduction through the waterfall strategy, closer observation reveals that, ultimately, the reverse will occur. On the one hand, the higher turnover in the years indicated has been achieved through a market exit four years earlier than with the alternative strategy. What appears more important, however, is that higher production quantities are concealed behind the higher turnover. Consequently, the

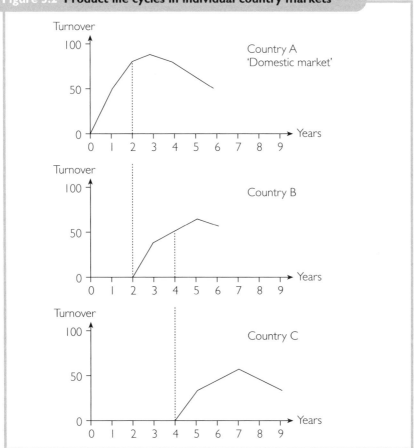

Figure 5.2 Product life cycles in individual country markets

production capacity of the enterprise will have to be expanded for a short period of time in order to achieve maximum output orientated around year t_3. Because this capacity is significantly higher than that necessary for the waterfall strategy, it can be assumed that the latter leads to lower productive capacity through lengthening the product life cycle, and simultaneously to an improved exploitation of this capacity.

▸ Also in terms of co-ordination, the waterfall strategy may prove advantageous. First, the relatively long period of decision making opens up the possibility of adapting to prevailing market conditions, and to new developments. Co-ordination mechanisms do not need to be developed under pressure, but only stepwise

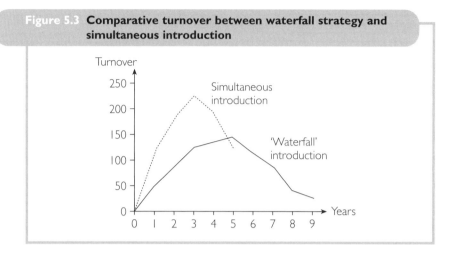

Figure 5.3 **Comparative turnover between waterfall strategy and simultaneous introduction**

according to need. Second, the waterfall strategy is sometimes necessary if demand-based interdependencies mean that certain country markets evolve into reference markets for buyers in other countries. In such a case, the country serving as a reference market needs to be entered before other markets. Third, and finally, a declining price level may reduce willingness to pay in some countries, so a delayed market entry can be exploited more comprehensively through eliminating the danger of arbitrage.

When the optimal pricing policy for each country *in isolation* is on a declining path (skimming strategy), delaying the market entry becomes a profitable marketing instrument, because the delayed market entry in the low-price country market narrows the price difference (see Figure 5.4). A delayed introduction would then entail correspondingly lower price differences.

The result of such a delayed introduction would be a convergence of prices in both observed markets. This convergence would be greater, the more sharply the prices decline over time, and the greater the length of delay prior to market entry. If substantial price reductions have already been planned for the individual country markets, small delays in the timing of market introductions may be sufficient to achieve a given reduction in price differences. The positive effects of a delayed introduction (lower revenue loss), must be contrasted with possible negative effects. These include lower turnover potential

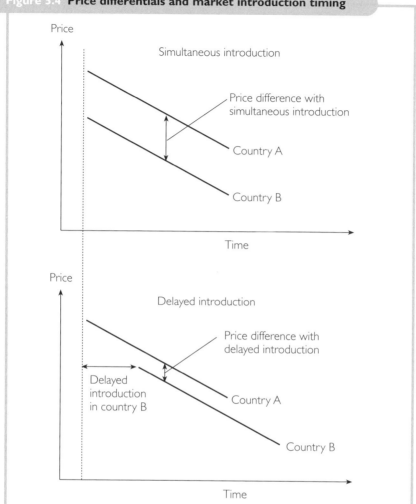

Figure 5.4 Price differentials and market introduction timing

because of competition who entered the market earlier. The following simple example should illustrate the above point:

A washing machine manufacturer based in the Netherlands was active only within the EU. In 1997, the firm introduced a new 'eco machine' to the market, which did the same job as conventional machines, but used considerably less water, washing powder and electricity. Because the product had been marketed successfully in the EU, at the end of 1998 the company's management decided to sell the machine in the economically up-and-coming eastern European countries. Hungary and Poland seemed particularly attractive, because the economic development in these countries over the 1990s had provided a broad section of the population with sufficient purchasing power to buy high-quality goods from the West.

The initial investigations by the washing machine manufacturer's market research department with respect to the market situation in Poland and Hungary yielded the following information:

▸ In both countries, there are variable units costs (production, transport and distribution) of €800.
▸ In Poland, an introductory price of approximately €1,800 is optimal. At this price, an annual quantity of 10,000 machines can be sold.
▸ In Hungary, the optimal introductory price is €900. At this price, 9,000 machines can be sold each year.
▸ It can be assumed that, in the markets during the years after the introduction of the product, the first domestic competition will lead to a price reduction. Independently of when the individual country markets are entered, and of the introductory price, it will be necessary to reduce the price annually by €50 from the original level. This should be done in both countries over the following years, in order to maintain the profit-maximizing level.
▸ For the above mentioned prices, however, grey imports between the country markets cannot be excluded. The cost of reimporting amounts to €500. It can be expected that 20 per cent of the above-mentioned buyers in the high-price country will be covered by re-imports.
▸ In contrast, arbitrage processes between the European countries and the already operational EU country markets are not significant.
▸ Finally, it must be assumed that the product will have a short life cycle in both country markets. After about four years, it can be expected that strong local competitors will also offer an eco washing machine, competition may force western European competitors out of the market.

In view of the data obtained by the market research department, a simultaneous entry into Poland and Hungary would result in re-imports from the low-price country Poland into Hungary, because the price difference between the markets would exceed the arbitrage costs. The arbitrageur could earn a maximum profit of €100 per machine. If one assumes that, in fact, 20 per cent of the 9,000 buyers (1,800) who are willing to buy such an eco machine, would re-import, the firm would obtain the contribution margin (DB) shown in Figure 5.5, over the ensuing four years.

This contribution to revenue of €41.98 could, however, only be increased if the negative effects caused by re-imports can be avoided. For each Hungarian customer who re-imports, additional revenue of €600 is lost, because the re-importer has purchased machines at the lower price in Poland. During the four years of market presence, the entire revenue loss is thus €4.32 million.

Precisely this additional contribution can be earned by the firm if the market introduction in the low-price country, Poland, is delayed by two years. In this case, the price in the more expensive country, Hungary, will already have declined from €1,800 to €1,700, so that the price differential between Hungary and Poland would now be €500. Because this price difference corresponds exactly with the costs of arbitrage, there will be no re-imports, so that the firm (assuming unchanged competitive conditions and ignoring interest-rate differences) will achieve additional revenue of €4.32 million within a total period of six years' market/presence in Hungary and Poland.

Figure 5.5 Example of determining the marginal revenue with a parallel marketing introduction

Year	Hungary	Poland	Total
2000	$DB = (1.800 - 800) \cdot (9000 - 1.800)$ $= 7.2$ m	$DB = (1.200 - 800) \cdot (10.000 + 1.800)$ $= 4.72$ m	11.92 m
2001	$DB = (1.750 - 800) \cdot (9.000 - 1.800)$ $= 6.84$ m	$DB = (1.150 - 800) \cdot (10.000 + 1.800)$ $= 4.13$ m	10.97 m
2002	$DB = (1.700 - 800) \cdot (9.000 - 1.800)$ $= 6.48$ m	$DB = (1.100 - 800) \cdot (10.000 + 1.800)$ $= 3.54$ m	10.02 m
2003	$DB = (1.650 - 800) \cdot (9.000 - 1.800)$ $= 6.12$ m	$DB = (1.050 - 800) \cdot (10.000 + 1.800)$ $= 2.95$ m	9.07 m
		Total	41.98 m

Note: DB = Contribution margin.

Apart from stated advantages, however, the waterfall strategy can, also lead to problems. For example, difficulties can always arise when, even in the first stage of the model (that is, when operating with only a few country markets) if there is a low level of success and thus further or alternative operations in other countries are not undertaken. It may well then be the case that, despite only moderate success in the initial country markets, the product would be received far more positively in other countries.

A commitment to international markets according to the waterfall strategy, may also not succeed particularly well, when the introduced product innovation creates an incentive to imitate. In such a case, there is the danger that, within a certain time span in which one concentrates purely on the domestic market or on a few foreign ones, competitors may imitate the product, and sell it in countries in which, according to the waterfall strategy, entry was only to be effected at a later stage.

Apart from these advantages and disadvantages of the waterfall strategy, a number of external background conditions also influence a firm's choice of strategy. As factors influencing the selection of a water-fall versus a shower strategy, Kalish *et al.*, (1995), identify the following theoretical considerations:

▸ A long product life cycle must be expected with which market entry can be completed. The longer the cycle, the greater the opportunities for lead users to benefit from the experiences of those already operating in the relevant country markets. This flow of communication exerts a positive influence on production adoption in the target markets. The longer the time span between the entry in two country markets, the greater the impact of this 'lead effect'. Such delays in entering new markets exert a positive influence on market development for the product in question.

▸ Conditions are unattractive for a market entry. If the target country markets or potential turnover there is small, growth slow, the level of innovation low and/or (fixed) entry costs high, a delayed market entry is preferable to a simultaneous one.

▸ There is a low level of competitiveness in the target markets. If the prospective competitors in the target markets are weak, the danger of a loss in potential turnover in the interim, through the activities of rivals, is lower. This is particularly the case where a monopolistic situation is likely.

Shower Strategy

In the context of the shower strategy, the individual country markets are not entered successively, but (more or less) simultaneously within a relatively short time span. Some individual countries or country groups can, none the less, be entered before others. In contrast to the waterfall strategy, the time frame up to entry into another market or group is considerably shorter, and is frequently no longer than one or two years until the last of the selected countries becomes operational. Therefore, in practice, the fact that can be observed for the polycentric strategy as well, applies – namely, that different points in time for entry do not play a significant role. Differentiated entry timing arises more from operative problems, such as those arising from founding subsidiaries. Figure 5.6 demonstrates the fundamental principle of the shower strategy.

For an extension of corporate activities in terms of the shower strategy, the following reasons are relevant (Keegan, 1999):

▸ In many industry sectors, a tendency towards *shortening product and technology cycles* can be observed. In such sectors (semiconductors, computers and so on), firms are compelled to introduce their products simultaneously in all targeted country markets, because new product generation can be expected so soon that it is impossible to enter foreign markets successively. Any attempt at a stepwise entry carries the danger that the next technological generation will already be ready for the market, and will be offered by competitiors, before the planned entry has been carried out.

Figure 5.6 The shower strategy

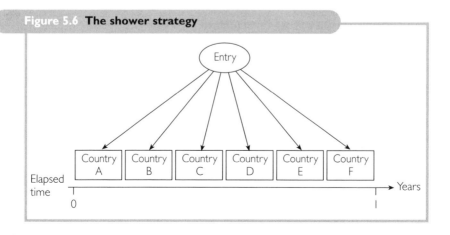

▸ The shortening of product and technology cycles is often accompanied by *an extension of research and development times*. This extension also increases the amount of money that must be invested in R&D. In conjunction with the outlined shortening of product and technology cycles, this has the consequence that the firm has less time to amortize these outlays. The greatest opportunity to amortize R&D expenses completely occurs when the firm is present in all selected markets as early as possible.

▸ Through an early entry into all selected country markets, it may also be also possible for a firm to create market barriers for competitors who plan to enter the market at a later point. This earlier commitment can thus *establish an image profile*, with the help of which the efforts at market entry made by rival firms, can be prevented.

The simultaneous entry of the targeted country markets, however, leads to the disadvantages of the shower strategy already outlined above. The need for co-ordination emerges as particularly problematic, because of the interdependencies between the country markets in which there is a simultaneous presence. For a seller, a maximum co-ordination problem prevails. Furthermore, the necessary co-ordination instruments need to be developed relatively rapidly, because the adaptation time offered by the waterfall strategy is not available here.

Selection of an Appropriate Organizational Structure for Foreign Business Activity

Classical Organizational Structures for the Internationalization of Marketing Activities

A number of alternative organizational forms or types of business type can be used for entering foreign target markets. The classical forms include indirect export, direct export, licensing, joint ventures, subsidiaries and contract production (Jeannet and Hennessey, 1998, p. 307–30). Because these organizational forms are encountered in many variants – subsidiaries, for example, can be differentiated in terms of how the relationship with the parent company is structured – some systemization is necessary in order to gain an overview of these variants. Various criteria can be used for such a systemization (Jeannet and Hennessey,1998; Perlitz and Seger, 2000):

▸ *Control*: what degree of influence does the enterprise exert over the activities of intermediaries and business partners in the target market?
▸ *Capital transfer and participation*: to what degree will capital be transferred to the country market?
▸ *Value creation focus*: is the spatial focus of value-creating activities at home or elsewhere?
▸ *Transaction costs*: a more recent approach differentiates according to transactions costs, between alternative means of entering markets. The objective is to provide an aid to market selection processes through considering the costs of the various available alternatives.

The key feature of this approach is the assumption that different market-entry strategies lead to different levels of transaction cost. Transaction costs should be understood in this context as all costs entailed in initiating, securing and controlling transactions for a market entry (Williamson, 1991; Backhaus *et al.*, 1994). A company can thus choose between various entry designs, which differ in terms of the proportion of ownership or the level of integration. While on the one hand it is possible to enter markets though totally dependent institutions (integration), on the other it is possible to operate through institutions that are foreign to the company (external partners).

The entry design will then be selected which minimizes the sum of production and transaction costs (all costs entailed in achieving the desired market presence in the target market). If these transactions can be achieved more 'cheaply' internally than through the market, there will be internalization (subsidiary, direct export through a general representative). Otherwise, recourse can be made to a partner (indirect export or licence). Various intermediate forms, where there is a partial integration of transaction costs, are also possible. A joint venture is a good example, where the mutual capital participation provides elements of both extremes.

Because the decision-making criteria listed above overlap to some degree, they are frequently used in combination. The system presented in Figure 5.7, for example, uses the criteria of 'capital transfer' and 'value creation focus' in parallel with one another.

As part of such a scheme, organizational forms for foreign business can be divided up in terms of whether or not the company manufactures in the foreign market. To the extent that the former applies, a differentiation between direct and indirect export is also possible. For indirect exporting, the initiation of contact with customers, securing

Figure 5.7 Systematization of alternative organizational forms for foreign business

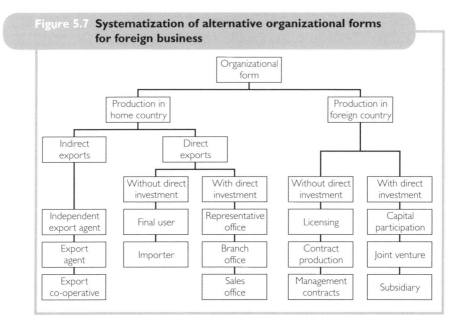

orders and delivery proceeds through a legally and economically autonomous third party, which is normally in the foreign country. The organs which serve this purpose (Bradley, 1991, p. 290) include:

▸ *Export traders* market the products of manufacturers on their own account and generally in their own name in foreign markets. Export traders normally specialize in particular types of goods or country markets.

> The French wine trader, Boisen-Anders, for example, exports French wine to almost every continent of the world. In order to lower transportation costs, Boisen-Anders buys pooled quantities of bottles, coming from several regions of France. After pooling the wine, the company exports the bottles to Canada, Europe, Asia and the USA.

▸ *Export agencies* operate under their own direction, but not on their own account. Product ownership and the associated risks remain with the manufacturer.

> The export agency Bananor, which is located in Machala, Ecuador, distributes bananas for small and medium-sized plantations in the

region. The enterprise, which was founded in 1993, ships approximately 2 million kilograms of bananas to Hamburg, which are then distributed and marketed in Germany.

▸ *Export co-operatives* are collectives formed by exporting firms, which transfer some or all export functions to a central exporting organ. This trades in its own name or that of the members.

In November 2001, for example, the Czech Republic-based meat producers, Masna Studena, Maso Plana, Kostelecke Uzeniny and Masny Prumysl Krasno, announced their intention of banding together as an export group. Next to the purpose of forming a co-operation to promote and sell Czech meat successfully in the international arena, the group wants to dominate the local market. Together, the four members already control 50 per cent of the local market, and since there is a meat surplus in the Czech Republic, it is necessary to sell abroad. By forming the export co-operative, the group wants to resolve the situation by selling their products in the EU and Eastern Europe (Kuchar, 2001, p. 13).

In contrast, there is direct export, where the exporting company serves a foreign market without the aid of any intermediaries. It is important to note the difference between a company investing in the foreign market or not. There is direct export *without direct investment* in the following cases:

▸ *Final users in the foreign market* are served directly by the company.

Just like the wine export trading company, Boisen-Anders, discussed above, there are many wine producers who are selling their products directly to consumers in foreign countries. These companies acquire most of their customers when they are travelling through the wine territories of France, Italy and Spain and in many cases the Business-to-Consumer relationships between these sellers and buyers last for a long time.

▸ The company delivers to a *foreign importer*, who resells the products to the foreign final users.

In 1988, the US home textile dealer, Hellenic Rug Imports Inc., was established to service its mother company, Mazarakis Flokati of Greece. In order to revitalize the premium quality Flokati Rug market in the United States, which had deteriorated in the late 1980s, Hellenic Rug imports home textiles from countries around the globe. In March 2002, the company announced the formation of a new import division that receives rugs from India. Hellenic Rug also imports textiles from Belgium, Egypt and Brazil (Corral, 2002, p. 8)

If, on the other hand, direct exports are to be made through *direct investment*, this can be achieved via the following organizational forms:

▸ *Representative offices* generally require a low level of direct investment in foreign markets. A few individual employees of the company represent its interests 'on the spot', observe the market, make and maintain business contact, and undertake such activities as acquisitions.

The Goldmann GmbH & Co. KG, Germany, manufacturers special chemicals, thermoplastics, dyes and candle dyes. In 1977, the family business decided to extend its activities into the Asian region, and for this reason, established a representative office in Chengdu.

▸ *Branch offices* frequently evolve out of representative offices and are characterized by considerable decision-making powers.

The State Bank of India (SBI) has evolved from the banks of the British East India Company (the first was founded in 1806). For a long time (since about 1935), the SBI was also India's central bank. The enterprise has branches in major international financial centres such as Chicago, London, Los Angeles, New York, Frankfurt, Osaka, Paris and Tokyo.

▸ *Sales agencies* are the most capital-intensive form of direct export, because of the high level of service that is transferred to the foreign country, as well as maintenance and supplementary services.

The Leadman Electronic Co. Ltd, Taiwan, was founded in 1979 and manufactures computer housings, power adapters, uninterrupted power suppliers, soundcards and multimedia loudspeakers. In 1989, the company founded a sales agency in

> Hannover-Langenhagen, which serves customers in the whole of Europe. It has its own storage facility, to enable it to provide goods rapidly and reliably.

The common characteristic of all organizational forms so far introduced, is the fact that the goods sold abroad are manufactured at home. Where *production occurs in the foreign country*, fundamentally different forms of organization are used. In such cases as well, however, it is possible to differentiate in terms of whether there is direct investment or not. Where this is not the case, the following organizational forms are possible:

▸ A *licence* can be issued to other firms, enabling them to operate in the foreign market. An international enterprise can give a foreign licensee the right to use patents, processes, know-how, logos and so on in return for payment (Stonehouse *et al.*, 2000, p. 154).

> In July 2000, Qualcomm Inc. announced the conclusion of a licensing agreement for Code Division Multiple Access technology with the Taiwanese First International Computer Group (FIC). For a payment of several million US$, a comprehensive licensing agreement gave FIC the right to produce cordless appliances according to CFMA standards and to market them in certain parts of Asia. [see http://www.qualcomm.com/press/pr/realises2000/press251.html

▸ *Contract production* occurs where an international enterprise contracts out to a foreign partner certain parts of the overall production process and makes available to this partner, information as to the nature, quality and technical standards of the product and associated processes. In general, the international enterprise retains responsibility for the subsequent marketing of the goods.

> Korea's leading consumer product manufacturers are thinking about plans that would move their production of several items abroad. By doing this, the companies hope to cut costs by producing the goods in countries with a low wage level. Samsung Electronics, for example, is producing TVs, LCD monitors, DVD players VCRs and refrigerators in China, Mexico and Hungary. Similarly, LG Electronics Inc. started to make PDP TVs

> in China in 2001 and plans to raise its overseas production continuously (Anonymous, 2002).

▸ For *management contracts* as well, production takes place in the respective foreign market. In this case, the international enterprise provides only know-how, while the necessary investment is generally provided by local partner enterprises.

Finally, the international enterprise may be willing to undertake direct investment in a foreign market. In this context as well, there are various possible forms of organization:

> Particularly in the example given of the clothing industry, it is customary with a production contract intended to exploit wage-rate differentials in a foreign country, that there is also a parallel management contract. Employees of the relevant clothing enterprise from the home country perform managerial activities in the firms producing under contract. The aim here is to ensure that the goods have the necessary quality and are manufactured at the lowest possible cost

▸ One possibility is that the international enterprise acquires a *capital participation* in the foreign enterprise. In comparison to the alternatives of contract production and management contracts, the enterprise acquires greater influence on the foreign company, and thus greater control.

> The example of the electricity (power) industry demonstrates that former monopolistic enterprises tend to increase their international presence with the aid of capital participation. Accordingly, the French power supplier Electricité de France (EdF), has acquired several participatory agreements with other European power suppliers and distributors (see Figure 5.8).

▸ A second possibility is that of entering into a *joint venture* with a foreign company. In contrast to a capital participation, where the international company invests in an existing foreign company, a joint venture generally entails a new economic entity. The following examples demonstrate that, in many industry sectors, joint ventures are a popular organizational form for foreign business.

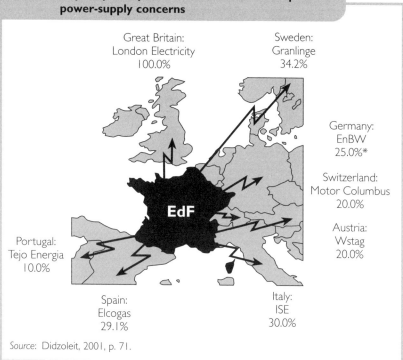

Figure 5.8 Capital participation of EdF in other European power-supply concerns

Great Britain:
London Electricity
100.0%

Sweden:
Granlinge
34.2%

Germany:
EnBW
25.0%*

Switzerland:
Motor Columbus
20.0%

Austria:
Wstag
20.0%

EdF

Portugal:
Tejo Energia
10.0%

Spain:
Elcogas
29.1%

Italy:
ISE
30.0%

Source: Didzoleit, 2001, p. 71.

▸ In the 1990s, Coca-Cola (USA) and Nestlé (Switzerland) created BPW (Beverage Partners Worldwide), a joint venture focussing on the fast-growing, ready-to-drink tea and coffee categories. BPW operates autonomously but uses the capabilities of Nestlé and Coca-Cola.

▸ Procter & Gamble used joint ventures to enter several markets in Asia. In the Philippines, for example, the company started up a joint venture with the Manila Refining Company, a producer of candles and fertilizers. After some years, the joint venture was incorporated as the Philippine Manufacturing Company. Similarly, Procter & Gamble filed a joint venture with the Phuong Dong Company in Vietnam to enter the emerging Vietnam market. By doing this, the American industrial giant was able to launch international products such as Safeguard, Tide, Pantene, Rejoice, Ariel and Camay in a short period of time on to a foreign market.

> ▸ Maxxium Worldwide recently became one of the big international marketers in the alcoholic beverage industry. Maxxium Worldwide is a joint venture created by Jim Beam Brands (USA), Highland Distillers (Scotland) and Rèmy-Cointreau (France) in August 1999. The Swedish Vine & AB company joined the partnership as an equal member on 20 March 2001. Maxxium Worldwide focuses on the creation of an international sales and distribution network. This network enables the members to offer their products worldwide. Each company would not be able to fulfil this task as successfully as the joint venture can.
>
> ▸ The Dutch Philips company and Whirlpool (USA) formed a joint venture to market laundry equipment in 1989. The companies got together to launch a dual branding system – the so-called Philips-Whirlpool. Since then, Philips has used its resources in a more productive way and Whirlpool benefits from becoming more popular in Western Europe.

A significant reason for the large number of market entries via joint ventures in the international arena is that many countries only tolerate and support foreign firms when they operate in this form.

However, the use of joint ventures creates the additional problem that success in a foreign market depends substantially on the behaviour and various managerial characteristics of the participating firms. Also, or perhaps particularly with equity joint ventures (the partners have equal shares), disagreement as to strategic thrust and orientation are not uncommon.

In contrast to many of its international competitors, German Telekom AG (DTAG) was prevented legally for many years from becoming active in international markets. Yet international presence is always an important condition if a firm is to be considered at all by large global clients. On the one hand, these clients generally prefer worldwide support from a single source, and on the other hand, to generate sufficient 'traffic' in their own network. Consequently, after its privatization, DTAG saw itself being compelled to become active as quickly as possible, not only in the most important foreign markets, but also worldwide. Because internal growth (developing a companys own networks in foreign markets) was impossible for reasons of time and cost, DTAG pursued a strategy of operating in foreign markets through participating in their local telecommunication enterprises. As Figure 5.9 shows for the mobile telephone area, the enterprise achieved this objective by the beginning of 2001, in the major northern European markets, at least. Conversely, DTAG is not, at the time of writing, present in the southern European markets. However, because market experts agree that ultimately, only those firms in the European mobile telephone markets that are present throughout Europe will be successful, in early 2001, DTAG felt obliged to seek a strategic partner. Telecom Italia was regarded as the ideal partner, because it had precisely the opposite strength–weakness profile to that of DTAG – while Telecom Italia was not involved in any participatory projects in the northern European markets, it was active in the south, precisely where DTAG was under-represented.

Figure 5.9 Equity participation of DTAG and Telecom Italia in Europe

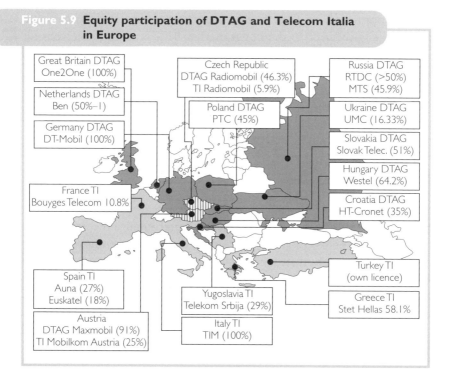

Great Britain DTAG
One2One (100%)

Netherlands DTAG
Ben (50%–1)

Germany DTAG
DT-Mobil (100%)

Czech Republic
DTAG Radiomobil (46.3%)
TI Radiomobil (5.9%)

Poland DTAG
PTC (45%)

Russia DTAG
RTDC (>50%)
MTS (45.9%)

Ukraine DTAG
UMC (16.33%)

Slovakia DTAG
Slovak Telec. (51%)

Hungary DTAG
Westel (64.2%)

Croatia DTAG
HT-Cronet (35%)

France TI
Bouyges Telecom 10.8%

Spain TI
Auna (27%)
Euskatel (18%)

Austria
DTAG Maxmobil (91%)
TI Mobilkom Austria (25%)

Yugoslavia TI
Telekom Srbija (29%)

Italy TI
TIM (100%)

Turkey TI
(own licence)

Greece TI
Stet Hellas 58.1%

▸ Finally, there is a third possibility, that of establishing independent *subsidiaries*. The main characteristic of subsidiaries in this context is that they are legally autonomous and liable for the capital invested in foreign countries. Conversely, one talks of *branches* when the parent company is liable (Berndt *et al.*, 1999, p. 36).

Because firms do not always have sufficient time available to them to establish their own subsidiaries in foreign markets as part of their attempts to internationalize, they attempt increasingly to take over established local competitors.

Considering the number of alternative forms of market entry available to international enterprises, the question arises as to which form should be selected. The literature indicates that the *appropriate* organizational form depends most of all on the size of the enterprise (Moen, 2000). The situational context must also be taken into account, and this relates to a number of influence factors. Figure 5.10 provides an overview (see also Hollensen, 2001, p. 236).

It should be noted that the selection of organizational form is not a static 'once only' decision. The way in which an enterprise operates in a foreign market generally changes over time. In the early phase of internationalization, low-risk approaches (such as direct or indirect export) dominate, and, as experience grows, more and more value creation is transferred to the target market. This is attributable, among other factors, to the fact that increasing competition over time demands greater market proximity on the part of all decision-making units.

Furthermore, the selection of organizational form is affected substantially by feedback, particularly supply-related, and determines the need for co-ordination in subsequent market operations.

Recent Organizational Forms of Market Internationalization

Newer organizational forms for the internationalization of market operations diverge form the previously dominant emphasis on the degree of participation in local distribution or in the transfer of capital. In essence, they focus on the reduction of capital commitment in the context of internationalization, and at the same time on making the process easier and faster. The new forms include:

▸ co-operation and networks; and
▸ electronic commerce (e-commerce).

Figure 5.10 Forms of market entry and the situational context

Enterprise-related factors			Market-related factors				
Strategy	*Cost situation*	*Product-related factors*	*Legal situation*	*Economic situation*	*Competitive situation*	*Retailing situation*	*Consumer situation*
• internationalization strategy	• technology	• nature of product	• export and import restrictions	• market volume	• number strength of competitors	• number and power position of sales intermediaries	• income
• targeted market segments	• locations	• phase of PLC	• dumping regulations	• market structure	• substitute goods	• condition structure	• price elasticity
• competitive situation	• factor costs	• level of innovation	• taxes	• exchange rates			• demand behaviour
• market position achieved (degree of familiarity, image etc.)	• productivity	• extent of product differentiation	• price controls	• inflation			• market transparency
	• economies of scale and experience curve effects		• local content regulations				
	• distribution costs						
	• capacity utilization						

Source: Meffert and Bolz, 1998, p. 144.

Co-operation and Networks

The discussion on classical organizational forms assumes (implicitly) that an enterprise possesses the necessary resources for international-ization (capital, know-how, managerial capacity). However, this is not always the case. Small and medium-sized firms, in particular, can rapidly reach the limits of their capabilities when attempting to inter-nationalize. Consequently, new organizational forms focus on co-oper-ation: foreign markets are entered and operated with one or more partners. The co-operative components of this form of entry, serves to *gain resources through co-operation*. In this sense, co-operation is not just a means of entry, but an approach to acquiring the resources needed to internationalize. It is thus an instrument for making market entry easier and quicker.

> The concept of 'cooperation', which has recently increased in signif-icance for medium-sized companies, is also confirmed by empirical studies. For example, Bassen *et al.*, (2001) found that 64 per cent of the responding medium-sized companies indicate that they use co-operative agreements in order to enter foreign markets.

Various types of co-operation serve as instruments of international-ization and can be categorized according to the number of partners and their origin (Johnsen and Johnsen, 1999):

▸ Two enterprises (a dyadic relationship) co-operate in order to enter a foreign market, in which they combine their financial means, know-how and managerial capacity. The pooled resources enable, for example, distribution intermediaries to be acquired in the foreign market. In this sense, co-operation provides a critical mass. Such partners can come from the same industry sector (horizontal co-operation), different stages in the value chain (vertical co-opera-tion), or from different sectors (lateral co-operation). Complementarity between the various skills and common strategic goal-setting, are decisive.

▸ Several enterprises from the same or different sectors of industry and value chain stages form strategic networks as 'long-term, purposeful arrangements amongst distinct but related-for-profit organisations that allow those firms in them to gain or sustain a competitive advantages *vis-à-vis* their competitors outside the network' (Jarillo, 1988, p. 32).

Firms extend their strategic focus through co-operative entry into foreign markets. Apart from the situation of the individual partner ('my company'), the *positioning of the network* ('us'), becomes an issue as well. At first, the competitive situation of the cooperation is critical to its success, and less so the role of individual network members. If the co-operation fails, the objectives of the individual members will not be achieved either.

Certain conditions must be fulfilled in order to ensure successful internationalization through co-operation:

▸ *Confidence in the network partners* (Thorelli, 1990; Ring and van de Veen, 1992; Håkansson and Snehota, 1995): numerous empirical and theoretical investigations show unanimously that confidence in network partners is a necessary condition for successful co-operation. But first, confidence must be established, which is a time-consuming process. The cultural peculiarities of partners are particularly important (Kanter, 1996).

In September 1996, a number of medium-sized Scottish textile producers formed at a textiles trade fair in Paris, the 'Ayrshire Knotwork Network Initiative' (Johnsen and Johnsen, 1999). The network was intended to promote the internationalization process of the individual partners. An awareness that each individual partner was too small to compete with the more cost-efficient South East Asian producers was decisive for the formation of the network. A total of 27 firms are involved in the network, many of which had been competing with one other for a long time. The internationalization of the various partners was intended to provide an incentive to remain in the network. The members were committed to providing each other with additional benefits from common marketing activities. A common brand (MAC) was established, in order to create a framework for end-user-related marketing activities. However, the partnership has, at the time of writing, not achieved its objectives. The basic problem is the reluctance of network members to contribute the work needed to ensure the success of the venture. In fact, the focus was shifted to the network itself, to prove that it was 'worth the effort'. A fundamental problem was the difficulty encountered in overcoming mistrust between former competitors. The partners did not trust each other to pursue the long-term interests of the network, so that failure became a self-fulfilling prophecy.

▶ *Incentive-contribution equilibrium* (Thorelli, 1990): each partner will be constantly aware of the balance between its monetary and non-monetary contributions and, similarly, the monetary and non-monetary returns. Only if a subjectively perceived medium- and long-term equilibrium of inputs and outputs is expected, will partners co-operate or remain in the network. The danger of opportunistic exploitation by another member of the network may influence such perceptions.

▶ *The existence of promoters in the network* (Thorelli, 1990; Johnsen and Johnsen, 1999): networks have an inherent tendency to disintegrate if they are not well maintained on an ongoing basis. In this respect, the role of a co-ordinator or 'facilitator', who serves as the central contact and clearing house, is of great significance. The co-ordinator is responsible for communication in the network, ensuring a balance between the interests of the participants, adaptation to changing conditions and generally countering the tendency for decline.

Companies seeking co-operation or hoping to establish networks in foreign markets, must first pose the question as to what special capabilities their companies have to offer to interested parties. This generally relates to other enterprises whose resource gaps can be filled through internationalization, so that the process is mutually beneficial. The incentive-contribution relationship must be balanced for all partners. The path to the network thus begins with the individual company: with no special capabilities or distinctive resources that are of use to the other party, one cannot be an appealing partner (Kanter, 1996).

Electronic Commerce

With the explosive growth of the Internet in the 1990s and its opening to commercial use, many firms have been able to develop an organizational structure for internationalization which has turned the former rules of the game in international marketing upside down (see Figure 5.11).

Products and services that are suitable for electronic commerce (e-commerce) can be marketed worldwide without the aid of partners or distributors. There are no longer resource gaps, because the Internet has no distance-dependent transport costs, and the set-up costs for international trade are no different from those for domestic business.

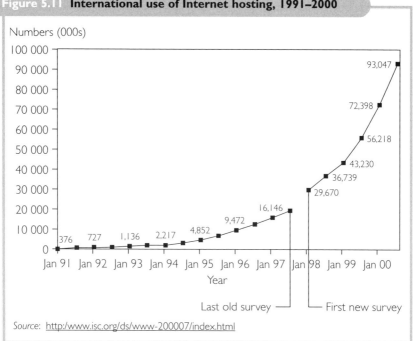

Figure 5.11 International use of Internet hosting, 1991–2000

Numbers (000s)

Source: http://www.isc.org/ds/www-200007/index.html

In international markets, e-commerce also has the advantage that all distribution activities are in the hands of the seller (control advantages). There are therefore no conflicts of interest with partners.

In the context of international marketing, the Internet serves two distinct functions (see Figure 5.12). For one thing, it is a *marketing instrument*, which opens up new means of communication and interaction with customers. In this respect, it can be used for approaching and communicating directly with customers – provided they have access to the medium. The Internet thus becomes a means of initiating transactions which subsequently can also be processed in the traditional manner.

The American computer company, Dell, provides a good example (http://www.dell.com). The company was founded in 1984 by Michael Dell and specialized in direct PC sales. From the start, the business operated by excluding dealers and other intermediaries. Two years after the introduction of the first Dell PCs (still with the Intel 8088 processor), a 'next-day-on-site' service was introduced in

Figure 5.12 Applying the Internet in international marketing

	The internet as a medium		The internet as a medium and market
Basic functions	Storage of/access to information	Transport of information	Environment
Business use	Information gathering	Business communication/information management	Marketing
Focus	Internal	Internal/external	External
Affected divisions	All divisions, especially market research and R&D	All divisions, especially data processing	Marketing, sales, customer service
Applied Internet services	WWW, E-mail, FTP, Telnet	E-mail, WWW, News, FTP	WWW, E-mail
Potential impacts	Completion/substitution of traditional information sources	Completion/substitution of traditional communication paths	Completion/substitution of traditional markets, distribution and communication paths
Benefits	Efficient information gathering, time savings, cost reductions	Efficient information management, time savings, cost reductions	Reduction of transaction costs, creation and management of customer proximity and loyalty
Examples	Online-search for suppliers, online desk research	Data warehouse, online information-integration, co-operation management	Online promotion and PR online ordering/delivery/payment, online customer services (hotlines, teleservices, teleconsulting)

Source: Lampe, 1999, p. 366.

1985. In 1996, the possibility of ordering a PC through a British web site was offered for the first time. At the time of writing, Dell has several million 'hits' on its website and sells both hardware and software worth more than 40 million US$ every day through this medium. For larger clients, special websites are constructed. The internet thus provides efficient service individualization. IBM recognized the Internet-sales trend far later and announced an appropriate initiative only in April 1999.

As in the case of the Internet bookseller Amazon.com, orders that have been initiated through the Internet proceed along traditional channels. The products are sent by airmail, with the usual impact on time and cost. Buyback services are also offered, of necessity, through partner enterprises in various (physical) locations.

For those goods or services that can be delivered directly through the Internet, it serves as an independent *virtual marketplace*. The Internet is thus a kind of 'marketspace' in which supply and demand meet. The physical mailing of goods or 'real' provision of services thus becomes superfluous. Products and services that can be delivered through the Internet include software, insurance or financial services, and information/advisory services of various kinds.

The increasing influence of the Internet for interaction between buyer and seller is of great significance for international marketing. The global orientation of the Internet becomes an instrument which offers small and medium-sized enterprises in particular highly efficient access to almost all country markets *simultaneously*.

Skin Trade is a small company on the Isle of Wight (UK). Dorian and Simon Holmes are running this retail shoe shop on their own. They do not employ any other workers. However, the company sells variety of fashion boots worldwide worth £600,000. Half of this amount is earned in the USA and there is a growing demand in other regions including Eastern Europe. Only the Internet enables the company to sell the shoes worldwide. Dorian Holmes accidentally realized the potential of the new medium. After he launched the website for Skin Trade in 1999, he saw an e-mailed invitation to tender for a £40,000 order for shoes for the Kuwaiti army. At that time, the two brothers started thinking about the possibilities of selling their new surf-style shoes and clothing in foreign countries (Bradley, 2002, p. 271).

Access alone, however, is not synonymous with establishing a global client base (Samiee, 1998). None the less, it remains a fascinating perspective. The availability of cost-effective international packet and courier services, but most of all the digitalization of services, eliminates the need for establishing a complete international distribution and service-partner network.

On closer examination, as an instrument of internationalization, the Internet is by no means *the* future in the sense of being overwhelmingly positive. Samiee (1998), for example, points out that mail order businesses have not replaced classical distribution channels. The successful application of the Internet in international marketing is thus linked to a series of critical influence factors, which are listed below.

Access

Use of the medium assumes the ability to access target customers as well as their ability to use the Internet. Access (connectivity) is by no means shared equally throughout the world. While North America and Western Europe are well 'networked', the number of PCs with Internet linkages in other parts of the world remains low. Thus access from the perspective of a globally-orientated enterprise remains selective. The inadequate telecommunications infrastructure in Africa, Eastern Europe and parts of Asia remains a major impediment to customer access. Figure 5.13 clarifies this point, using the example of Internet hosts available in various regions of the world in summer 2000 (per million inhabitants). The table shows that the distribution of Internet structure (per capita here) in the countries indicated, is highly varied.

Acceptance

The use of the Internet as a procurement instrument assumes appropriate buyer motivation. Samiee (1998) indicates that cultural aspects play an important role in acceptance of the Internet:

The single most important factor that influences international marketing on the Internet is culture. The influence of the internet increases with the faster adoption of a generally impersonal internet buying culture (as opposed to patronizing shopping centres or favourite stores). The prime consumer shoppers for the internet are likely to be catalogue customers followed by teleshoppers. It is worthwhile to

Figure 5.13 Geographical distribution of Internet hosts in various country markets (per million inhabitants)

North America		Central Europe		Africa/Arabia	
USA	130,204	Great Britain	35,209	Tunisia	11
Canada	51,717	Germany	23,372	Morocco	33
Mexico	5,441	Netherlands	68,486	Egypt	86
		France	16,640	Israel	26,627
Latin America		Austria	43,163	South Africa	4,719
Colombia	1,112				
Brazil	4,161	**Southern Europe**		**Asia**	
Argentina	5,037	Italy	27,332	Japan	27,219
Chile	3,618	Spain	13,668	Thailand	870
		Portugal	11,737	India	33
Northern Europe		Turkey	1,686	Pakistan	40
Finland	138,030	Greece	10,094	China	73
Norway	111,912				
Denmark	69,751	**Eastern Europe**		**Australia/Oceania**	
		Russia	1,758	Australia	69,025
		Poland	6,705	New Zealand	83,654
		Bulgaria	1,872		
		Hungary	12,830		

consider that just as catalogue shopping did not replace store patron-
age, the internet will eventually find a similar niche among some
consumers in some, but not all markets. (Samiee, 1998, p. 18)

Cultural influences on the acceptance of the Internet should not therefore be under-estimated. The differing popularity of teleshopping and
mail order, according to cultural circles and population groups, shows
that the Internet also has its limits.

Apart from cultural influences, the Internet fails at a decisive point
in the procurement process. It allows only limited product demonstra-
tion and evaluation of a seller thus far unknown to the buyer, and
limited perspectives for conveying utility-creating purchasing experiences. If the central product criteria are not standardized and the seller
is not already personally known, the Internet does not allow for a
complete evaluation of alternatives. Familiar brands and standardized
good are thus the most likely candidates to be shifted to internationalization through the Internet. Consequently, the most successful electronic commerce enterprises (by turnover) derive from these sectors.
The Internet is therefore regarded as particularly promising for highly
standardized industrial goods (Nairn, 1997), an area in which procurement efficiency is very significant and the buying experience as an
autonomous component of utility is irrelevant.

Feedback to the Distribution System

Using the Internet can lead to negative reactions, if the foreign distribution partners feel in danger of being replaced by this medium. Feedback of this kind occurs if the Internet is used in parallel with a traditional distribution system, so that the areas of impact (target groups, products and so on) overlap. This becomes problematic if a transitional phase is planned between traditional and virtual business. Such a phase is appropriate provided not all current and potential customers from the old system have access to the Internet, it is not seen as a medium with equivalent performance, and not all the firm's services are digitalized or can be distributed through mail order.

During this transitional phase, the overlap between distribution channels is necessary, because otherwise the Internet would lead to massive revenue losses. The situation is quite different for set-ups, new enterprises which from the beginning forgo traditional co-operation with independent partners for the purposes of internationalization. The introduction of an Internet-based distribution system endangers the specific investments made by partners. Investments are specific where their returns depend on the business relationship with a particular supplier. If the relationship with this partner terminates, the investment is lost. These possibilities can be compared with the advantages of using the Internet. One way out of this dilemma could be to use the Internet only for new foreign markets, and to refer orders from other regions to the 'old' partners. A parallel application of the Internet would also be possible for new product ranges or supplementary services (finance, delivery of software releases and so on). The parallel use of the internet is unproblematic if the core business of foreign partners is not affected.

Market Transparency

The profitable use of regional or national preferences constitutes a central challenge in international marketing. In this context, using the Internet can lead to serious problems. A high level of freedom to access information is characteristic of the Internet. To the extent that access is unregulated, price and product information that would otherwise be available only with considerable effort, and possible expense, is readily accessible across borders, on what are, in fact, *national* websites. National or regional quality and price differences thus become 'public'. Firms therefore risk becoming sources of information which release feedback. Not only with respect to a particular enterprise, the Internet can raise market transparency substantially. This rapid and inexpensive medium creates access to information about many alternative suppliers and raises the level of information at the disposal of buyers. This, in turn, increases the pressure to adapt to external price differentials.

This formulation of information on a company's own web page, in conjunction with the information offered by competitors, is thus a truly critical factor in international marketing. Where there are international price differences, an unfettered and excessively liberal dissemination of corporate pricing information can therefore lead to massive problems. Companies must find a compromise between the legitimate need for information from the Internet by potential customers, and the optimization of differential marketing in different countries. Also, with the Internet, it is necessary to ensure the differentiated treatment of customers from regions with different preferences and willingness to pay. If this is not possible, the application of the medium must be considered critically.

Costs

When compared to the cost of establishing a classical distribution network with comparable market coverage, these Internet costs are marginal. They none the less indicate that it is necessary to plan, implement and control the Internet presence just as systematically as any other marketing instrument. Furthermore, the fact that many companies who have been praised for their exemplary websites are still waiting for positive financial results, indicates the problems associated with Internet business.

Despite these limitations, the Internet will change international marketing permanently. This is inevitable through startups alone, where there is no danger of feedback within the distribution system. Under certain circumstances, the Internet reduces considerably the need for resources. This is particularly advantageous for small and medium-sized enterprises, whose access to country markets was formerly extremely difficult, or even impossible. For established enterprises, this means an increase in competitive intensity. The impact of 'critical mass' (size, number of employees, capital base and so on), will decline substantially. Furthermore, as a strategic factor, location may become quite irrelevant, which means a complete change in strategic framework conditions. This will be particularly important in the area of standardized consumer goods (internationally branded products) and industrial goods. The development of those goods that can be digitalized or dispatched at low cost with simple logistical systems will be accelerated most of all.

The Internet presents a simultaneous challenge in terms of a nationally differentiated market presence, because it increases transparency and reduces profitable market differences. The potential results from a simple and rapid internationalization must be compared and contrasted with these disadvantages. Young and non-established small enterprises in particular, will decide in favour of a rapid entry into foreign markets through the Internet. However, merely being present on the Internet no longer constitutes a competitive advantage. It could in future, however, constitute *a necessary condition for competitiveness.* The changes in buying behaviour as a result of the permeation of the Internet into all industry sectors, may turn an internet presence into a 'must', without in itself providing any marginal revenue benefits. The opposite may well prove to be the case.

The Influence of Feedback on the Selection of Organizational Form

Apart from situative influence factors, the choice of organizational form is influenced by interdependencies between country markets. Interdependent country markets force enterprises to co-ordinate their marketing efforts, to the extent that it becomes necessary to consider which organizational form will provide sufficient integration.

Integrated marketing activity in independent markets requires control of local distributors and partners. From this perspective, the question as to the selection of an organizational form for internationalization divides into the following issues:

▸ In country markets with a high degree of independence, organizational forms with *high control potential* (traditionally high capital participation) are appropriate. The close integration of local sales agents to the company's own enterprise, enables the 'pushing' of the company's interests through, for example, simple directives. Conflicts of interest between partners can thus be 'resolved' quickly, although probably at the cost of demotivating local management. Electronic commerce thus offers high control potential, because all activities are in the hands of one seller. To the extent that the products of an enterprise are suited to e-commerce, there is therefore an alternative to classical organizational forms.

▸ In country markets with a low level of interdependence, organizational forms with *low control potential* are sufficient. The pursuit of purely national interests thus does not come into conflict with the interests of the company.

This very simple observation assumes that conflicts of interest will inevitably arise between an internationalizing company and its local partner. The causes of such conflicts can be viewed from various perspectives: the enterprise must optimize internationally, whereas the local partner generally deals with an essentially local situation. These conflicts of interest disappear when a partner is selected that also has an international presence, and thus similar co-ordination problems. These can be triggered partly by demand-related interdependencies, which have as much of an impact on a multinational sales agent as on the manufacturer. An organizational form with low control potential would thus be sufficient, because the need for control, in the sense of intervening in the marketing decisions of the sales agent, is reduced.

Internationalization through the formation of partner networks can intensify coordination problems considerably, particularly if the network of operational country markets has different degrees of interdependence for the individual partners. Co-ordination interests can thus be highly varied, and consequently, conflicts of interest are likely to occur in the co-ordination process. Such co-ordination and harmonization problems must also be taken into account in selecting co-ordination partners.

Changes in the degree of interdependence of markets require adaptation in the selection of organizational form. Increasing interdependency between markets determines the transition to alternatives with higher control potential. The increasing transfer of capital and value-creating activities, typical of the internationalization process, is thus not only an indicator of the increasing significance of foreign markets for many enterprises, but also of the rising degree of interconnection.

Furthermore, for international enterprises, only those organizational forms are advisable that can be integrated into the international organizational network established in the past. For example, if an enterprise has already been active in a number of markets, and if all country markets up to that point have been served through subsidiaries on the spot (direct export), it can be assumed that the enterprise will also use this organizational form for new markets. Any other form would not conform to this concept. Conversely, it is equally conceivable that the firm discussed above would use the entry into new markets as an opportunity to change the organizational concept that has so far been used. For example, the enterprise could establish subsidiaries for the first time in the new markets, and subsequently move step-by-step towards this organizational form in the existing markets.

In each of the cases observed, the organizational form selected in each individual country market cannot be independent of the other country markets. Because the particular organizational form depends rather on the international configuration of activities, there are seller-related interdependencies between the new and already-operational markets.

In this context, it also becomes clear that the degree of freedom in selecting the organizational form for new country markets depends on the level of internationalization that has already been achieved within an enterprise. An enterprise that is only just starting the process has considerably more latitude on entering new country markets than does an enterprise already active in a number of markets. Against this background, the situational factors depicted in Figure 5.10 on page 131, are particularly helpful for a firm at the beginning of its internationalization process, and that has either no, or only weak, seller-related interdependencies impacting on the selection of organizational form in new country markets.

The Marketing Instruments

Determining how the various marketing instruments (product, price, distribution, communication policy) are to be applied in the new country markets is part of the 'going international' decision-making process. The firm that is internationalizing has to make a fundamental decision in terms of the extent to which the instruments are to be adapted to the peculiarities of a particular market, or whether to proceed essentially as elsewhere. In other words, the enterprise has to consider the classic standardization versus differentiation issue in all instrumental areas.

These decisions must be made in the context of buyer, seller and competitive interdependencies between the new markets and the old ones:

▸ *Seller-related feedback*: economies of scale effects suggest standard-ization in product, communication and distribution policy. For example, if a country-specific product formulation is dispensed with, costs can be reduced, which may improve the competitive situation in *both* new and existing markets.

▸ *Demand-related feedback* can work against an international price differentiation. The danger of revenue-reducing reimports caused by demand-related feedback on the buyer side is caused by interna-tional price differentiation and intensified by an internationally unitary product and communications policy. For this reason, the potential for a standardized product and communications policy is always limited, if there are demand-related interdependencies and, at the same time, price differentiation is profitable.

▸ Finally, the standardization/differentiation decision depends on *competitive feedback* between the various instruments. The more closely linked the enterprise's network of international competi-tors, the more the standardization/differentiation decision is inter-related with competition.

Because, in terms of co-ordination, there are arguments both for and against using similar marketing instruments for new markets, it is necessary to evaluate the level of standardization/differentiation that is appropriate in terms of 'going international'. What matters is the profit achieved over all country markets. In the case of interdependent country markets, the pursuit of national profit maximization is detri-mental to the enterprise as a whole. This is well illustrated by the following example:

In the EU, Volkswagen has a differentiated pricing policy with a high level of standardization for its various automobile models. This differentiated policy makes sense, because the willingness to pay for vehicles in Europe varies. This variability derives from different levels of income and utility weightings (transport, fun, prestige). Price reductions in relatively low-price markets can lead to substan-tial market share, and thus profitability growth. However, such actions lead simultaneously to profit-reducing feedback in (rela-tively) high-price markets.

Profit or turnover maximization at the level of national sales organizations or subsidiaries, generally intensifies this problem. The co-ordination of national market entry through different co-ordina-tion instruments tends to signal a move away from national or regional goal systems. This means that firms need to look more at their total operations and less at the specific contributions to profitability of national subsidiaries.

The Product

The optimal degree of product standardization/differentiation can be defined as a revenue-optimizing reaction to the impact, most of all, of demand- and supplier-related feedback:

▸ With respect to demand-related feedback, a low degree of product standardization is a possible instrument for avoiding or reducing arbitrage.

▸ Furthermore, product standardization leads to substantial cost savings which extend far beyond country markets and can have a positive impact on the entire enterprise (seller-related feedback).

Therefore, a decision needs to be made in the context of product policy, as to which elements of the product mix should be standardized.

Core Areas of Product Policy

The potential need for various degrees of product–policy standardization caused by interdependency is a multidimensional problem. A number of elements of product policy can be differentiated with respect to time (product introduction, variation, differentiation and elimination) as well as in pure product-characteristic terms (specifications, packaging, labelling, associated services) (see Figure 5.14).

For the instrumental formulation that is at the centre of interest here, the product characteristics form the initial focus. In terms of this decision it is necessary to bear in mind that the various elements do not exert an equal impact on product performance in the market. Figure 5.15 provides a categorization.

Product Core

The product core relates to the part that provides the user with the fundamental or basic utility (Czepiel, 1992, p. 74). The main task of the product core is to fulfil a function required by buyers, because the buyer purchases the entire product with the objective of using it to

Figure 5.14 Temporal and product structure elements of product policy

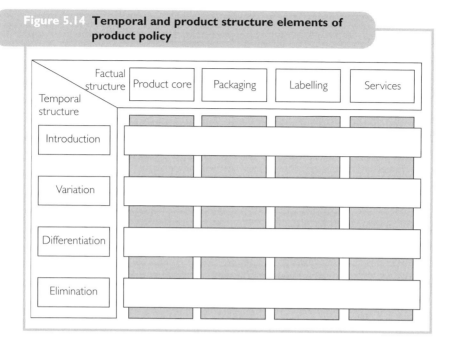

Figure 5.15 Product components

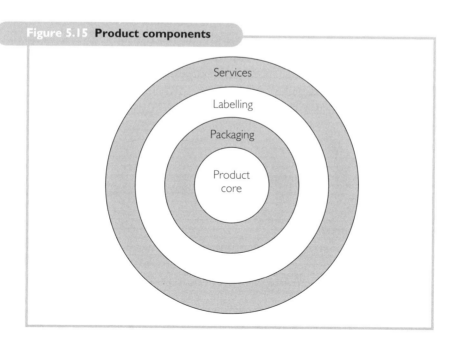

satisfy some particular need (communication – telephone; mobility – automobile). With respect to the potential for standardization, it can be assumed that this depends on the level of homogeneity of consumer needs. The more similar the needs and preferences of consumers in both new and established markets, the more viable a standardization of the product core becomes.

It can make just as much sense for a firm to offer standardized products, despite differences in buyer needs or preferences. Because preferences can be influenced to a certain degree by the available product offerings, an enterprise can mould demand to conform to products that have in fact been developed for other markets.

IKEA provides an excellent example. In 2000, the Swedish furniture seller opened its first retail outlet in China. Even though Chinese preferences with respect to furniture and interior design are totally different from those of clients in the West, the firm offers the same products in China as in Europe. IKEA takes into account quite consciously the fact that, because it is different, the furniture store will at first attract namely 'visitors', but relatively few buyers. The objective is to familiarize the young generation gradually with Western furniture and thus to influence the preferences of Chinese buyers (Blume, 2000, p. 32).

The IKEA example demonstrates that a supplier's actions can – to some extent – shape local demand and national consumer preferences. And IKEA is not the only company that tries to influence local market conditions to its advantage and is successful in that. Global brand leaders such as Coca-Cola or Kellogg have pursued similar strategies. Thus, product standardization can be viewed as not only being a function of local preferences – feasible if local preferences are similar – but also driving local or national consumer preferences towards higher conformity.

The degree of product-core standardization can be broken down into four basic types:

Differentiated products

For *differentiated products*, the product core reveals a high level of country-specific adaptation. For such products (such as food), there is little attempt to standardize the core, compared to the other product forms.

Modular design

If customers in different countries have essentially similar product requirements, a *modular design* may be used. That is, if only certain product components need to be varied country-by-country, because, for example, of differing technical standards or legal systems. In such a case, the product can be designed so that a core product that is already used in other markets, can be adapted for new markets through integrating special components (Jeannet and Hennessey, 1998, p. 380).

The automobile industry provides a good example. Using a standardized base product, country-specific adaptation is provided through the inclusion of special modules. Thus, for example, the bumper height is varied according to the country norm, or the position of the steering wheel is changed (to suit left- or right-hand drive).

Built-in flexibility

This is a more advanced form of standardization and entails integrating the necessary adaptation potential, with the greatest possible exploitation of standardization. The objective is to ensure that the product can be used within the technical environment of both (or all) countries. The task of adaptation is frequently transferred to buyers, so that they can carry out the process themselves.

Many electrical goods have this flexibility. The consumer can switch an appliance to the voltage that is used in a particular country (from 110V to 220V, for example). Other appliances are supplied with adapters which allow for different electricity networks.

Standardized products

This refers to products that do not need to be changed at all, and are sold in the identical formulation worldwide. Watches, cameras, pens and so on provide good examples.

Packaging

Packaging refers to any form of covering of one or more products. The increasing significance of product packaging in the past was caused by changes in demand for packaging, and by changes in the functions to be fulfilled (see Figure 5.16).

Particularly with respect to standardization potential, packaging

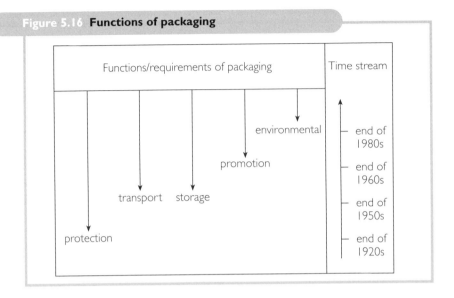

Figure 5.16 Functions of packaging

decisions are problematic. On the one hand, largely identical packaging raises the level of recognition considerably. For example, even without any lettering, the majority of smokers recognize their brand by the pack, irrespective of whether it is Camel, Marlboro, or any other. On the other hand, country-specific regulations set tight limitations on the standardization of packaging.

Australia and New Zealand have set very restrictive requirements on the import of wooden palettes. The fifth continent has imposed these due to its island location. Imported wood, even in the form of palettes, is subject to special requirements in terms of wood treatment, to avoid pests being released into the countries. In particular, Australia is keen to avoid the so-called *Sirex* wasp, which has, at the time of writing, so far been kept out of the country. The AQIS (Australian Quarantine and Inspection Service) therefore requires, from sellers using wooden palettes, treatment against the pest. Furthermore, the treatment must not have taken place more than 21 days before dispatch and a so-called Sirex Certificate, proving that the palettes have been treated, has to conform to certain requirements in terms of such factors as the use of gas or impregnation.

Labelling

Because it can generally be assumed that, in seeking products that satisfy their needs, customers can turn to many different sellers, the individual seller may be well advised to attempt to develop, beyond the basic utility, product identification and a worldwide image transfer.

Product identification is always necessary to ensure (as much as possible), that repurchases are not made from competitors. Labelling can ensure that a product can be differntiated effectively from those of rival sellers. Various product indicators, special designs and names, can be used to label a product. The objective is to enable the customer to identify a product by the label alone as that of a particular company. However, this makes sense only if the company can, in fact, provide consistant product quality in foreign markets as well. If this succeeds, the brand becomes part of the 'Esperanto of international trade' (Kapferer, 1997).

Product Name

With respect to labelling, the product name assumes particular significicance, because it exerts a major influence on the repurchase rate. If the same product name is to be used in several country markets, the following factors need to be taken into account (Kulhavy, 1993):

‣ The product name should be easy to pronounce in the language of the target country. Specifically, the use of sounds that are not internationally familiar, should be avoided. These include German umlauts, French accents and the linked consonants used in the Slavic countries.

> In several countries, it has to be to remembered, that the population is not able to pronounce certain syllables. Asians, for example, have some difficulties in the pronunciation of the letter 'r', and French people have problems with the pronunciation of the letter 'h'. That is one reason why Motorola used Chinese characters to name its products 'mou-tuo-luo-la', which – by the way – has no specific meaning in China (Zhang and Schmitt, 2001, p. 314)

> The Chevrolet company provides another good example. In the 1980s, the Chevy Nova was introduced to the Spanish-speaking market. The name seemed to be a good choice, because it could

easily be pronounced by Spanish-speaking people and 'nova' (new) has positive connotations. What was overlooked, however, is that together, the words Chevy Nova cannot be distinguished from 'Chevy no va' which means 'the Chevy does not go' (Ricks, 1983). Other firms have, in the past, clearly devoted too little attention to the potential problem of negative associations with respect to their name selection processes. The Italian automobile manufacturer's Lancia 'Dedra' sounds far too much like 'dead' and Volkswagen's Jetta means 'bad luck' in Italian. In Scotland, Volkswagen's 'Sharan' was greeted with amusement, because it resembles the dialect 'sharn' which means cow excrement. Nike products were forbidden in some Arabic states, because the name is the same as an Arabic swearword. Pepsi-Cola also had negative experiences with the introduction of 7UP in China. In Chinese, the name means 'death by drinking'. It is also important to avoid negative product-name connotations in foreign markets. Attention must be paid to the semantic meaning of the name in different cultures and countries.

▸ A brand name should also mean something to buyers in other countries, which raises the level of recall.

In Asia, for example, the Colgate-Palmolive company chose special Chinese characters to name its toothpaste 'highly clear and clean' instead of Colgate. Another example is Coca-Cola's rumoured failure to introduce the world's most famous soft drink in China, where the pronunciation of the original name meant 'bite the wax tadpole'. Coca-Cola changed the Chinese characters and nowadays, the brand name means 'tastes good and makes you happy'. Consequently, the Chinese consumers are able to realize that Coca-Cola is something to drink (or to eat). Nissan, for example, used to name its cars differently in various parts of the world. One reason to do this was the fact that the consumers should be able to realize what the car was made for. Figure 5.17 gives an overview of the Nissan brands. The model D 21, for example, is called 'Pickup' in Europe, since 'Nissan Truck' (USA) could be considered as a big US trailer-truck.

▸ Finally, the selection of a brand name must take into account the potential for protection by patent and other means in the target market.

Figure 5.17 Differing product names in various country markets

Model	Europe	North America	Japan	Latin America
A32	Maxima QX	Infiniti I30	Cefiro	Maxima
D21	Pickup	Nissan Truck	Datsun	Nissan Pickup
H41	Cabstar	–	Atlas	Cabstar Atlas
S14	200 SX	240 SX	Silvia	200 SX
B14	Sunny	Sentra Sedan	Sunny	Sentra

Source: Keegan and Schlegelmilch, 2001, p. 376.

In the early 1990's, the firm Kraft Foods, marketed a chocolate product in Italy under the name Lila Star, which was already used in Germany. Immediately after the market launch, which had involved an extremely expensive communications policy, the firm discovered that the product name 'Star', is legally protected in Italy by a food manufacturer active country wide. Consequently, Kraft Jacobs Suchard was forced to rename and relaunch the product almost immediately after the original launch, this time under with the name Lila Dream.

Product Logos

While the product name is one element of the brand that can be transmitted verbally, the logo is one that can be recognized visually, but only expressed with great difficulty verbally. A product logo can be in the form of a symbol, a graphic, typical colour or a combination of these (see examples in Figure 5.18).

Furthermore, the logo can be linked with the brand name by developing the brand name into itself a logo. Coca-Cola is a typical example, where the nature of the lettering is the equivalent of a logo. However, Figure 5.19 makes it quite clear that this link between brand name and logo almost inevitably limits the potential for standardization, if markets are to be served in which different types are script are used. Even Coca-Cola, which is generally considered to be a typical global company, has, through this linkage of brand name and logo, to use different logos in different countries.

Figure 5.18 Examples of international product logos

Figure 5.19 Coca-Cola product logos

Source: Bovée and Arens, 1986, p. 605.

Product Design

The non-verbal 'symbolization' of products may also be a component of product design. Also with respect to the design of products, brand protection assumes a particular significance in order to prevent 'brand piracy'.

The negative consequences of imitating established product designs can again be illustrated through the example of Coca-Cola. In 1994, the American soft-drink manufacturer controlled 44 per cent of the market in Great Britain, and was market leader in the lemonade segment. In the summer of 1994, the retailer Sainsbury copied the product design of Coca-Cola (labelled Virgin) and even used a red can in the British market. Because this almost identical copying could barely be distinguished from the real Coca-Cola right next to it on the shop shelves, Sainsbury gained huge market shares initially. In some stores, the share of Coca-Cola dropped to 9 per cent (Tödtmann, 1995).

For their entry into new countries, international enterprises must decide if their products are to be marketed under the same product name, logo and design as those used in current markets. This decision does not necessarily have to apply to all elements of branding. For example, it may be highly advisable to use country-specific brand names in new country markets, but the same logos as in established markets.

The black and yellow design for Henkel's Pattex adhesive has been copied by a number of competitors (see Figure 5.20). Such copies of Lacoste shirts, Rolex watches, Cartier jewellery or Boss men's clothing,

Figure 5.20 Imitations of the 'Pattex' product design

Original   Imitation

have also appeared on the market. While in the past, product piracy occurred mainly in the Asiatic countries, in recent years, 'fake factories' have also been springing up in the EU states.

Langnese-Iglo GmbH sells its ice-cream under the same logo in all country markets (see Figure 5.21), but using eighteen different names. Interestingly, the expensive communication mix used to change the logo in 1998 was not used to standardize the brand names internationally.

Figure 5.21 **Standardized logos and different brand names of Langnese-Iglo GmbH**

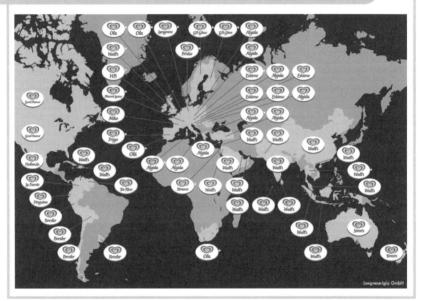

Services

Because of the transition from a sellers' to a buyers' market, many industry sectors are becoming increasingly competitive, and additional services are becoming a more prominent part of the marketing mix. The question now is, if and to what extent services can be standardized internationally. The standardization potential cannot be determined on an overall basis, and it depends primarily on the following three dimensions of the service:

▶ the point in time of performance;
▶ the proximity of service location to buyer; and
▶ the nature of the goods for which the services are provided (see Figure 5.22).

In particular, the service category 'after sales' has the potential to be standardized to a high degree, because most customers, irrespective of country of origin, have similar preferences relating to client service, spare parts delivery, training and so on.

On the other hand, those services that were provided with the purchase reveal a relatively lower potential for standardization. In the consumer goods area, instruction manuals with a product provide a good example. Sometimes such manuals contain a complete set of instructions in the language of the target country only, so that this service is not standardized. If, on the other hand, the instruction manual contains various different sets of translated instructions for some, or even all, target countries, the manual is standardized to a greater or lesser degree. Figure 5.23 gives an example from the company 3M of instructions for making overhead transparencies. They are given in English, French, German and Italian.

A standardization of services provided with industrial goods is also frequently problematical. For example, if complex machinery is offered to industrial, emerging and developing nations, the need for services often differs quite considerably (Backhaus, 1999). In particular, buyers from developing and emerging nations seldom have sufficient know-how to operate complex equipment efficiently, and therefore need more training than do customers in industrialized countries.

With respect to the question of whether it is advisable to standardize services together with, or after, a purchase, the specific situation of the seller company must be considered, if an appropriate decision is to be made. The so-called teleservice provides a good example. This is characterized by 'communicative support for installation, fixing breakdowns, maintenance and repair of machines and equipment (Burger *et al.*, 1998, p. 37). Because of its standardized services, teleservice is able to offer medium-sized companies, in particular, the opportunity of implementing internationalization strategies (Handge, 1997). The reason is that an after-sales service offered through a communications network, for the most part, eradicates the restrictions of a traditional

Figure 5.22 Service classification

Product proximity

	High		Low	
	Consumer goods	Industrial goods	Consumer goods	Industrial goods
Prior to purchase	• advice • catalogues	• portrayal of offer • demonstration	• children's area • parking area	• presentations • problem analysis • consultancy
With purchase	• trial period • instruction manual • trial installation	• assembly • training	• extra gifts • packaging service • delivery service • financing/leasing	• financing/leasing • barter or countertrade services
After purchase	• repair service • spare parts service	• repair service • spare parts service	• customer clubs • customer magazine	• employee training

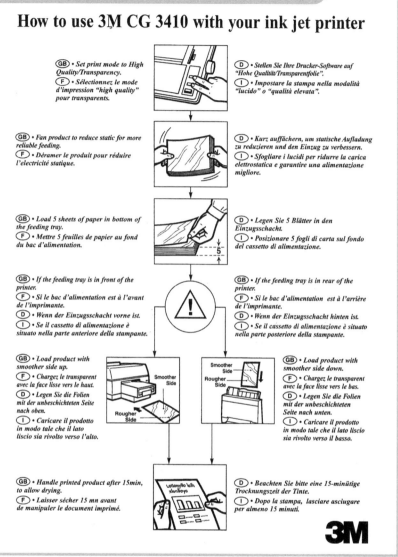

Figure 5.23 Instructions from 3M for making overhead transparencies

location-bound system. This alters the cost situation decisively for the seller, which can now offer a predominantly standardized service with constant quality to any part of the world without having to be there on the spot with the service organization. How great these savings are, varies from case to case, and depends on the extent of the services offered. The processes also offer clients considerable advantages: reaction times are shorter, because teleservice operates around the clock, with no time lags. In this manner, geographic distances play a subordinate role, so that even very distant sellers become part of the potential delivery network.

Giuliani, for example, is an Italian producer of machine tools for the global security industry. Alongside its traditional services, the company now offers a teleservice for its machines currently in production and existing machine installations. The teleservice function will allow the machines to be connected by remote access to a Giuliani computer using a modem and direct wiring, regardless of the machine's location. The function enables Giuliani to check processes such as machine troubleshooting and instant machine software modifications as required. Examples of other companies in a comparable business have shown that travelling costs (for example, for engineers) can be reduced by about 30 per cent and labour costs by 16 per cent.

CyberRep is another example of a teleservice provider. As well as several direct-marketing activities, the company offers an order-fulfilment system. This Internet system supports logistics managers in various areas, such as inventory level control, delivery schedules and back order status. In addition, CyberRep established partnerships with US Postal, FedEx and UPS to manage pick, pack and shipping systems for inventory warehouses. CyberRep interfaces primarily with its clients via a TCP-IP (Transmission Control Protocol – Internet Protocol) using standard technologies and languages such as Visual Basic and HTML.

The 'Optimal' Degree of Standardization During Market Entry

Degree of Standardization and supplier-based interdependencies

The introduction of differentiated products to new country markets generates additional costs dependent on the degree of differentiation, which in turn results from the necessary production processes and development costs. These costs of differentiation are acceptable only if they are accompanied by an accordingly greater willingness to pay on the part of buyers in the target country, and/or there is additional demand (quantity), in comparison to the situation for standardized products. A product variant that has been developed for a particular (country) target group, and where additional costs have thus been incurred, must then generate sufficient additional revenues.

A standardization of product policy can, in turn, create considerable cost-reduction potential. It thus becomes possible, on the basis of standardized products, to produce large quantities at a low unit cost, thus achieving economies of scale. Furthermore, production can be centralized, which increases scale effects still further.

If buyers' preferences in the target market reveal a certain level of heterogeneity in comparison to established markets, some degree of revenue loss can be expected as a result of the high level of standardization. This can occur because of a declining willingness to pay on the part of buyers, who want products that are better adapted to their preferences or needs. Indeed, this may in fact be provided by competitors. With an increasing standardization of product policy with a heterogeneous demand structure, it is necessary to identify the optimal degree of differentiation. This occurs in a balance or trade-off between the savings and losses, both of which are incurred through standardization or differentiation. The costs and revenues can be compared and contrasted with one another to determine the optimal level of standardization/differentiation.

This calculation is based on the assumption that buyer preferences in the individual country markets reveal a certain level of heterogeneity at a given point in time. This is a condition for assuming an additional willingness to pay for product differentiation, or for a better adaptation to specific preferences. If this is not the case, and buyer preferences are completely homogeneous, product differentiation is not economically advantageous because of the additional costs involved.

In the following section, these issues are used to formulate a specific model for optimization. The following simplifying assumptions are made:

▸ As the independent variable to be optimized, the degree of product differentiation influences the revenue earned, as shown in Figure 5.24.
▸ In the interests of simplicity, the demand in units in the relevant spectrum of potential degrees of product differentiation remains constant. This assumption facilitates an isolated observation of the

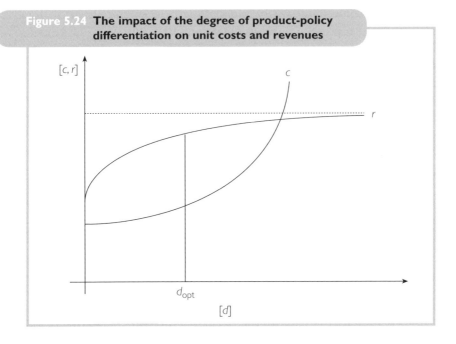

Figure 5.24 **The impact of the degree of product-policy differentiation on unit costs and revenues**

impact of standardization on overall results. The observation can then proceed for the level of unit costs and revenues.

▸ We assume, further, that the unit costs of developing, manufacturing and distribution (c) increase more than proportionately with the degree of product differentiation (d), while the average revenues per unit (r) approach, with a rising level of product differentiation, a certain value asymptotically. At this value, the heterogeneity of the market has been 'exhausted' from an economic perspective.

The overproportional increase in unit costs with a rising degree of product differentiation reflects the increasing complexity of production and its impact on cost. On the other hand, a rising degree of product differentiation has a positive impact on average unit revenues. This can be attributed to a buyer's willingness to pay more for product adaptation to their preferences. This increasing willingness to pay is reflected in positive marginal utility achieved through product differentiation. However, it must be assumed that the buyer's willingness to pay more decreases with more adaptation. Thus, the marginal utility gained from a comprehensive adaptation to buyer preferences, although positive, declines. The additional willingness to pay that can be achieved through additional product differentiation, becomes ever smaller, because buyers do not yield an infinitely high level of preference heterogeneity. Furthermore, each buyer has a maximum willingness to pay, even for a product that is modified optimally in terms of the buyer's preferences. In other words, the willingness to pay for a rising degree of differentiation will increase, but at a decreasing rate for increasing adaptation.

According to these assumptions, the optimal degree of product differentiation, lies with monotonous cost and revenue functions where the marginal cost of differentiation ($c'[d]$), equals the marginal revenue ($r'[d]$) (see Figure 5.24). At this optimum, the difference between the costs of, and returns from, differentiation are at a maximum.

If we now alter the model, so that a rise in the degree of product differentiation exerts an additional (positive) effect on demand, this effect must also be considered as an additional differentiation-related variable. A positive effect can be expected, because, through a higher number of variants, there will be a more effective adaptation to a heterogeneous buyer preference structure. The market rewards this better adaptation to preferences, through increased demand with respect to a particular seller. This additional demand can be achieved through new customers who previously purchased from competitors, or from increased purchasing by existing customers. The extent of increased turnover derived from a given increase in product differentiation depends on the resulting extent of additional adaptation to buyer preferences in absolute terms, and their perception of alternative offers from the competition. In general, we can assume that the probability of purchasing will rise with increasing product differentiation. The positive marginal purchasing probability, however, declines. This effect is due to the declining marginal utility of consumption: the more we consume of a certain product or product attribute, the less we value additional consumption of it. As a result, purchasing probability increases with increasing product differentiation (we get more of something we value), but at a declining rate. The larger this quantitative effect, the higher the optimal degree of product differentiation will be.

In principle, this approach can be used to determine the degree of standardization of both a complete product and individual product elements. The necessary pre-condition is that it is possible to operationalize the level of standardization monotonically (neither entirely non-increasing nor non-decreasing). This will *not* always be possible. If the degree of standardization can only be measured discretely (through, for example, the number of possible product variants), the same issues apply in principle, even if the optimum cannot be derived through marginal analysis, but only through comparing all possible situations with respect to the impact on cost and revenue. Furthermore, it is fundamental to be able to determine cost and revenue with sufficient precision, with respect to the various levels of differentiation.

The Degree of Standardization and Demand-Related Interdependence

Our discussion so far ignores the impact of demand-related feedback. This occurs when there are price or quality differences in the various country markets which enable arbitrage profits to be earned. It is debatable as to what impact differentiation-related quality differences will have on the exchange of goods. Two basic cases are conceivable:

▸ the extent of arbitrage *depends* on differentiation; and
▸ the extent of arbitrage is *independent* of differentiation.

Differentiation-dependent Arbitrage

Where arbitrage is dependent on differentiation, the *lower* the degree of differentiation of a product in the various county markets, the *more* extensive arbitrage will be. For arbitrageurs and their clients, the country-market-specific products become more readily comparable, and the prices more transparent, because quality differences, which would otherwise distort, for example, nominal prices, are no longer prevalent. The familiar (from experience) willingness to pay for a standardized product in various country markets – based, for example, on a comparison of price lists – reduces the uncertainty surrounding arbitrage profits. To the extent to which maintenance or service supplies are necessary to maintain product performance, the work of arbitrageurs is made easier by substantial standardization, because they otherwise must have differentiated services and spare parts on offer. Conversely, with increasing differentiation, price differentiation would become less transparent and arbitrage profits smaller and/or less certain.

From these considerations, it is evident that, with increasing standardization, the extent of arbitrage, and thus demand-related feedback for given price differences, will increase to the extent that there are arbitrage-relevant price differences between country markets (price differences > transactions cost of arbitrage). This situation is assumed with respect to the following discussion, because a consideration of demand-related interdependency would otherwise be irrelevant. Increasing demand-related feedback results in arbitrage and a decline in the average price level, because arbitrageurs are able to buy the same product made by the same manufacturers, but through cheaper sources. The greater the share of arbitrage in total turnover, the greater the negative revenue effect. As shown in Figure 5.25, the unit revenue function from our model in the previous section is affected.

The impact of demand-related feedback on buyers' willingness-to-pay function alters the optimal degree of differentiation. The *optimal degree of differentiation for co-ordination* becomes *greater* the further the unit-revenue curve is rotated downwards by arbitrage. An increase in the optimal degree of differentiation for co-ordination is

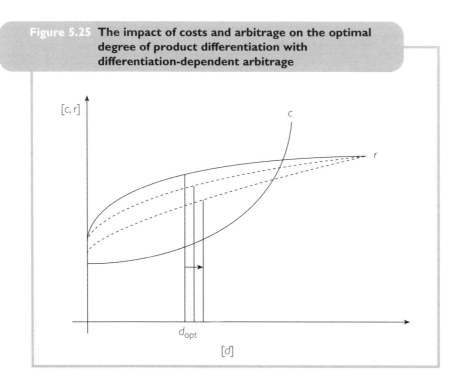

Figure 5.25 **The impact of costs and arbitrage on the optimal degree of product differentiation with differentiation-dependent arbitrage**

thus a reaction to the arbitrage that takes place, and will be exactly at a level that compensates for the cost impact of the additional differentiation.

If, in dependence on the degree of differentiation, the cost function is very steep over a particular segment, the increase in optimal differentiation for co-ordination will be relatively low, and vice versa.

Differentiation-independent Arbitrage

In the case of *differentiation-independent arbitrage*, these effects do not occur. The reason is that differentiation-dependent quality differences would have to be directly convertible or 'translatable' by buyers into arbitrage-relevant price differences. Even where there are substantial quality differences, the resultant arbitrage profits will be more transparent, or more certain.

As a result, the unit revenue function will not rotate dependently of differentiation, but will shift in parallel (Figure 5.26). Arbitrage would then have no impact on the optimal degree of differentiation.

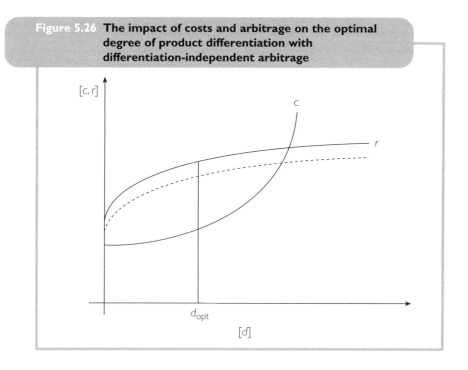

Figure 5.26 **The impact of costs and arbitrage on the optimal degree of product differentiation with differentiation-independent arbitrage**

The Degree of Standardization and Technical Norms

Typically, an enterprise cannot influence the formation of the level of standardization if this is already prescribed by a technical norm. Such a norm refers to a specification, for example, AEEE–802.6, which is defined and accepted by the various market participants.

It is important to note that norms are not legally binding. Instead, they constitute the results of a process of agreement involving all participating market partners. Through communication and the transfer of information, subject to a co-ordinative function generally on the part of governmental standardization institutions, agreements of this kind come into operation. It is possible, in terms of jurisdiction or the nature of content, to distinguish between institutions which set standards or norms. While in Germany, all relevant standards are set by the Deutsche Institut für Normung (DIN), at the European level, general issues are handled by the European Committee for Standardization (CEN). This organization must be distinguished in turn from the European Committee for Electrotechnical Standardization (CENLEC), responsible for the electronic aspects and the Telecommunications Standards Institute (ETSI), responsible for this particular sector. Furthermore, there are numerous other industry-related standardization bodies such as the European Computer Manufacturers Association (ECMA), which is responsible for the data processing area. Various institutions co-operate with one another at the international level. Apart from the International Organization for Standardization (ISO), there are also the International Electrotechnical Commission (IEC) and the International Telecommunications Union (ITU).

These standardization institutions, which are closely linked functionally and organizationally, claim to pursue the goal of identifying the 'best' possible available solution as the norm. Because the area of validity of a standard (region, country, global), also constitutes geographical applicability, a presence in these markets requires adaptation to the standards. For this reason, enterprises try to influence standardization decisions in advance. Through their involvement in working groups and technical committees, firms attempt to ensure that the standard is as similar as possible to what they prefer. Particularly when it seems likely that the suggestions of competitors will become the standard, it may be advisable for a firm to delay the standardization process actively. The behaviour of Microsoft in the context of the planned standardization process of the programming language, Java, provides a recent example of such a 'delaying tactic'.

The programming language, Java, developed in the mid-1990s by the firm Sun Microsystems, enables applications programmed with it to be used (partly) irrespective of the (overall) operating system. This has major implications for software markets. Previously, the selection of operating systems determined the software that could and could not be used. If, for example, Unix was selected, only applications developed for this system were usable. If, on the other hand, the user had selected a Microsoft product, such as Windows NT, this would restrict the user to Microsoft-compatible software. Indeed, Microsoft, in particular, benefited from this technical linking of software applications to operating systems. Because Microsofts operating systems, Windows and Windows NT, had already achieved high market penetration, the company dominated the market for standard software with its 'Office family' almost unchallenged.

Against this background, it is obvious that Microsoft would regard Java as a serious threat. Particularly between 1996 and 1999, Microsoft railed vehemently against the attempts of Sun Microsystems to make Java technology into an international standard. The attempt at standardization described in Figure 5.27 suggests that Microsoft used all possible means to prevent Java becoming an international standard.

Technical norms, whether achieved through official standardization or customary *de facto* standards (Backhaus, 1999), are of considerable importance in international marketing. This is mainly because standards eliminate a substantial degree of the latitude that firms would otherwise have for differentiation from competitors. Thus, for example, it is quite irrelevant where in Europe a mobile telephone is purchased, because it will function in all GSM markets. This creates an important basis for demand-related feedback. If the price differences are sufficiently large, this results in arbitrage. Standardization, therefore, reduces the available latitude with which differences in national preferences in international marketing can be exploited. On the other hand, standardization can, apart from

Figure 5.27 Microsoft's attempts to prevent the standardization process for Java

Date	Action
07/1995	Sun Microsystems introduces the programming language Java.
10/1995	The *Economist* magazine regards Java as the most important software development in 15 years.
08/1996	At the request of many buyer groups, Sun Microsystems submits Java to the ECMA for standardization.
12/1996	The ISO announces its interest in a standard for Java. A spokesperson stresses that the standard could be formalized within two years.
03/1997	Sun Microsystems submits Java to the ISO for standardization.
05/1997	Microsoft officially declines the standardization of Java.
07/1997	Sun Microsystems wants to gain the status of a 'Publicly Available Submitter' (PAS) for Java from the ISO. This would give the company the right to be responsible for the entire further development of Java. At the same time, Sun Microsystems wants to retain the rights to the name Java.
09/1997	Microsoft suggests standardizing Java, provided Sun Microsystems allows free use of the name.
11/1997	In the face of bitter resistance from Microsoft the ISO awards Java the PAS status.
07/1998	The responsible Joint Technical Committee requires Sun Microsystems to submit the specificactions for the planned Java standard by February 1999.
10/1998	Sun Microsystems allows Java licensees to influence the future development of Java.
01/1999	Under pressure from Microsoft, the Joint Technical Committee changes the PAS rights.
02/1999	Sun Microsystems breaks off the ISO standardization process.
04/1999	Sun Microsystems resubmits Java to the ECMA for standardization.
06/1999	The ECMA forms a working group to prepare the standard. In this context, Microsoft pushes for an open source procedure.
12/1999	Sun Microsystems breaks off the EMCA standardization process.

leading to substantial economies of scale in production and development, also expand the operational market. It was only with the introduction of the GSM standard that the international use of mobile telephones (roaming) was possible, and thus provided customers with additional benefits. None the less, standards constrain product policy, thus pushing pricing policy into the forefront of international marketing decisions.

Pricing

Factors Influencing the Extent of International Price Differentiation

In the area of pricing policy, an international enterprise must make a decision as to the relationship of price in the new country markets in relation to prices in current markets. Ultimately, this relates once again to the question of whether a policy of price standardization or differentiation is to be followed.

Price differentiation results from the individuality of country markets, and attempts to handle them effectively through a country-specific adaptation of prices, thus exploiting the differing willingness to pay (Hollensen, 2001, p. 458–61). The basis for determining optimal prices is an approximate determination of the national price–response function for each product. Expert appraisals, customer surveys using conjoint analysis and an analysis of historical data can be used for this purpose. Taking into account the often substantial international differences in buying power, this form of price setting leads to possibly large price differences between country markets and can therefore only be used if there are *weak market interdependencies*.

The opposite pole from price differentiation is *price standardization*. In the extreme, such a policy would entail a complete harmonization of products, prices, distribution structures and so on (Porter, 1986, p. 17). Market homogeneity and grey markets in particular, work in favour of a standardization policy. Harmonized prices mean sacrificing the potential exploitation of a differential willingness to pay. Consequently, this form of pricing policy should only be used where there is *a very high level of integration* of the various country markets, and where both physical and virtual arbitrage activities occur even with small price differences.

The extent of economically viable price standardization or differentiation is determined by a number of factors (see Figure 5.28). These include not only buyer- and seller-specific factors, but also environmental conditions such as inflationary and currency variables (Hollensen, 2001, p. 458; Forman *et al.*, 2000, p. 33).

Image

If a firm offers the same products and/or services in different country markets at significantly varying prices and is unable to conceal from or

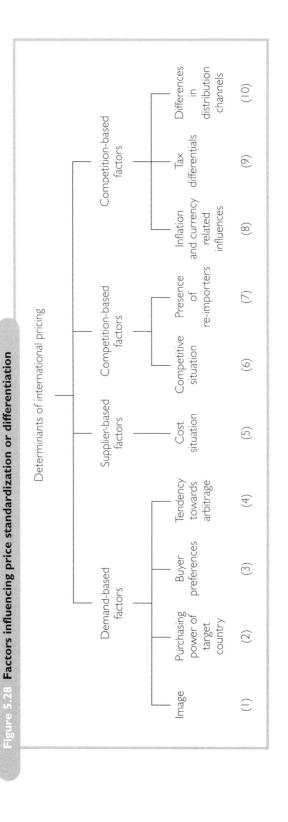

Figure 5.28 Factors influencing price standardization or differentiation

Determinants of international pricing

Demand-based factors
- Image (1)
- Purchasing power of target country (2)
- Buyer preferences (3)
- Tendency towards arbitrage (4)

Supplier-based factors
- Cost situation (5)

Competition-based factors
- Competitive situation (6)
- Presence of re-importers (7)

Competition-based factors
- Inflation and currency related influences (8)
- Tax differentials (9)
- Differences in distribution channels (10)

justify these differences to buyers, this can create dissatisfaction and loss of image (Channon and Jalland, 1979, p. 282). Although this problem can be observed with respect to both consumer and industrial goods, it seems particularly important for the latter. This is attributable at least partly to the greater transparency that prevails in industrial-goods markets. The result can be a shift in demand to other sellers, or a failure to purchase at all. Lutz (1994, p. 154), for example, demonstrated that, even without arbitrage, buyer negotiation power caused by price differences in various countries can be a decisive reason for price harmonization.

Purchasing Power of Target Countries

In order to answer the question as to whether a standardized pricing policy is appropriate, the level of purchasing power in the target country must always be taken in account. If, for example, it is highly divergent, unitary prices may be problematic if a firm wants to serve all similar customer segments in all countries.

Figure 5.29 gives an example of the purchasing power parity 'Big Mac' index, published regularly in *The Economist* magazine. This index reveals some very substantial differences between country markets. For example, the 'Big Mac' index for the Philippines reveals a purchasing power that is more than 70 per cent below that of Israel. It is generally more feasible to use standardized prices in countries that have a similar purchasing power, than for countries where the buying power diverges substantially.

The so-called 'big' pharmaceutical companies recently had to learn this simple lesson rather painfully (Grill, 2001). For years, these companies had been selling medication for AIDS patients at a similarly high price in both industrialized and developing countries. Because the purchasing power in developing countries is considerably lower, few HIV patients or public health care institutions could afford to buy the necessary medication. In order to improve the situation with respect to AIDS medication, the South African government decided to allow the production of cheap generic substitutes and thus defy international patent law. In order to prevent the enactment of the South African government's Medical Control Amendment Act No. 90, the pharmaceutical firms took the government to the South African high court. But in the wake of massive international protest, the companies felt compelled to accept an out-of-court settlement.

Figure 5.29 **The 'Big Mac' price index 2001, using McDonald's price data**

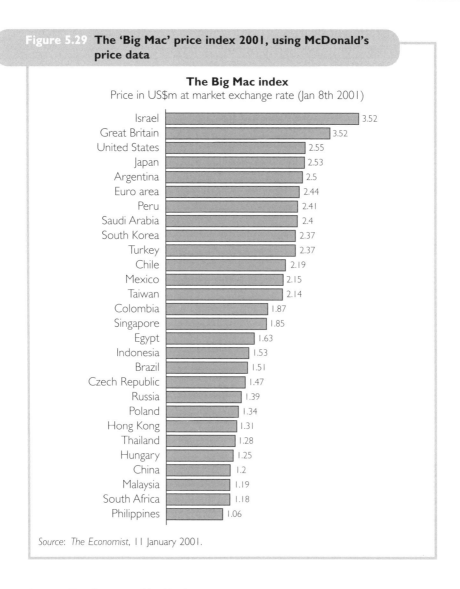

The Big Mac index
Price in US$m at market exchange rate (Jan 8th 2001)

Israel	3.52
Great Britain	3.52
United States	2.55
Japan	2.53
Argentina	2.5
Euro area	2.44
Peru	2.41
Saudi Arabia	2.4
South Korea	2.37
Turkey	2.37
Chile	2.19
Mexico	2.15
Taiwan	2.14
Colombia	1.87
Singapore	1.85
Egypt	1.63
Indonesia	1.53
Brazil	1.51
Czech Republic	1.47
Russia	1.39
Poland	1.34
Hong Kong	1.31
Thailand	1.28
Hungary	1.25
China	1.2
Malaysia	1.19
South Africa	1.18
Philippines	1.06

Source: The Economist, 11 January 2001.

Buyer Preference Similarity

Furthermore, the viability of similar pricing in different country markets also depends on the extent to which buyers have similar *preferences*. While purchasing power comparisons place willingness to pay in the forefront, the analysis of buyer preferences stresses the impact of preferences on this willingness to pay. For example, a cross-country comparison of the level of purchasing power may reveal similarities that indicate the viability of consistent prices. However, if buyers in fact have different degrees of willingness to pay, standardized pricing will fail, despite the similarity in buying power.

In the 1990s, a pharmaceutical manufacturer was able to position a so-called 'dietary supplement' successfully in the high-price segment of the German market, although the product was significantly more expensive that those of competitors. The company could justify this high price because, in contrast to most other products in this market, their product contained no chemicals and thus suggested risk-free weight loss. When the company subsequently attempted to enter the American market, it placed the product similarly in the high-price segment, not least because of the similar level of purchasing power in the USA. However, the product launch threatened to fail. Market research revealed that American clients simply were not interested in the risk aspect of dietary preparations. Therefore, in contrast to German customers, they were not prepared to pay a higher price than those of competing products that contained chemical ingredients. The company had to reduce its prices substantially in America, despite the country having a similar purchasing power to Germany.

Tendency towards Arbitrage

The tendency towards arbitrage is an additional demand-related factor influencing the selection of the level of standardization within international pricing policy. If the arbitrage tendency is taken to refer to the tendency of buyers, with a certain profit level (arbitrage profit = price difference – transactions costs), to have a preference for acquiring a particular product though the 'grey market' beyond the regular distribution channels, then the latitude for a price-policy differentiation declines with an increasing tendency towards arbitrage.

The arbitrage tendency of buyers depends not only on their general price sensitivity, but also on such factors as product complexity, or credence attributes. For example, the arbitrage tendency for pharmaceutical products is generally lower than for automobiles, because it is significantly more problematic to verify the quality of pharmaceutical products.

It can be assumed that the share of those buyers in the high-price country, who will, as a result of anticipated arbitrage profits, prefer reimported products from the original manufacturer, will rise with increasing arbitrage profits. Backhaus and Voeth (1999) differentiate between the functional interrelationships depicted in Figure 5.30 and the resulting share of buyers who are willing to undertake arbitrage (arbitrage tendency functions).

Function (a) in Figure 5.30 is a case of 'complete arbitrage', where it is assumed that with non-negative arbitrage profits, all buyers in the high-price country will satisfy their demand through reimports. On the other hand, functions (b), (c), (d) and (e) are examples of 'incomplete arbitrage'. In these cases, the share of buyers willing to undertake arbitrage rises monotonously with increasing profits. As we will see in the following example, function (e) is often a good approximation of reality. From function (a) to (e), the profit-maximizing level of price differentiation increases. This is due to the declining influence of arbitrage on total profits.

The question as to which of the arbitrage-tendency functions in Figure 5.30 applies to a specific situation in reality, and which parameters characterize the relevant function, can only be determined case by case. As an analogue to determining the price-response function (Simon, 1992, p. 109), the arbitrage tendency can be determined through historical market data and surveys of experts and buyers.

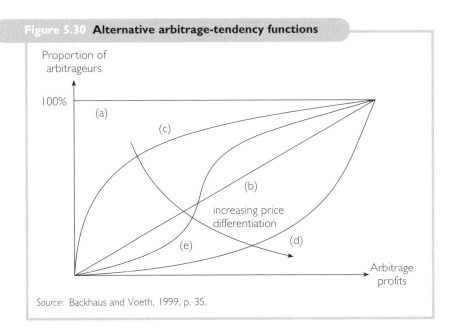

Figure 5.30 **Alternative arbitrage-tendency functions**

Source: Backhaus and Voeth, 1999, p. 35.

However, because historical market data and expert evaluations are not always available, or cannot be generated with reasonable ease or at reasonable cost, firms may be forced to determine arbitrage functions through customer surveys. The direct form of surveying ('at what price advantage would you be willing purchase a reimported product?'), has the disadvantage that the reimport decision is not regarded as a whole, but rather as the 'price advantage' criterion in isolation. Consequently, as in the case of estimating the price-response function, the estimation of the arbitrage-tendency function may have limited validity (Simon *et al.*, 1998, p. 790).

The errors can be avoided by using conjoint analysis (Hair *et al.*, 1998, p. 387). Because with conjoint analysis, the criterion of prices is not considered in isolation but in terms of a trade-off, the process can be regarded as particularly powerful for determining information that is relevant for pricing policy (Simon and Kucher, 1993, p. 222).

In the context of an empirical investigation of the automobile market, Lampert (2000) demonstrates how an arbitrage function can be determined empirically with the aid of conjoint analysis.

In Lampert's investigation, an automobile manufacturer was confronted with the problem that an increasing number of buyers in Germany were no longer prepared to buy the high-priced automobiles intended for the German market, but preferred lower-priced re-imports from other European countries. The task at hand was therefore to determine buyer tendency towards arbitrage in Germany, and on the basis of that information, to optimize the pricing in both high-price German and other low-price, European countries.

For this purpose, a conjoint analysis was conducted with current and potential customers, in which the following criteria and criteria categories were used:

▸ type of mid-range automobile (categories: *re-import; non-reimport*);
▸ distributor (categories: *franchised dealer; independent dealer*); and
▸ price (categories: €10 950; €12 200, €13 450)

The breakdown of the re-import phenomenon into the two criteria *type of mid-range automobile* and *distributor*, seems appropriate in terms of the investigation, because it is assumed that the utility advantages were derived not only through purchasing from an independent dealer, but also because the buyer would purchase an automobile that may be clearly recognizable as a re-import. Furthermore, the *price-category* criterion would be selected in such a manner that, apart from the

Figure 5.31 Part-worth utilities for one respondent as determined by conjoint analysis

Constant	Reimport		Distributor		Price		
	Yes	No	Franchised dealer	Independent dealer	€10,950	€12,200	€13,450
6.500	−0.6667	0.6667	0.8333	−0.8333	4.0000	0,0000	−4.0000

price asked by a manufacturer in Germany, those for re-imports could also be covered on the basis of the pricing policy of the manufacturer elsewhere in Europe, through the margin that is set (the maximum internal European price differentiation between any two country markets was about €2000.

The complete conjoint design that emerges from the above criteria and criteria categories, comprises 12 ($2 \times 2 \times 3$) full profiles. These were presented to the 53 participants in the survey, who were requested to rank the full profiles. On the basis of these empirical data, the utility components were then determined for the criteria groups by means of a least squares estimate. Figure 5.31 gives an example of the results for one respondent.

If, for this respondent, a price advantage is now to be determined for a re-import from an independent dealer, which would equal or outweigh the benefits of the offer for an original automobile from a franchised dealer, it must be borne in mind that the associated transition from the criteria 're-import' to 'distributor', will lead to a lower utility for this respondent. For the criteria 're-import', the reduction in utility is 1.3333 – transition from 'non-re-import' (0.66667) to 're-import' (−0.6667) – and for the criterion 'distributor' 1.6667. The utility reduction for the criteria 'type' and 'distributor' therefore adds up to 3. The re-import must compensate for this utility disadvantage with an appropriately more attractive price. If it is assumed that the part-worth utility for the criterion 'price' develops linearly between the categories, a minimum price advantage will emerge, which the re-importer will offer according to the following principle: a price reduction from, for example, €13 450 to €12 200, would create a utility advantage of 4 (difference between the utility components of the categories '12 200' and '13 450'), and thus yield a higher utility than is necessary. Because the intention is to create a utility advantage of 3 for the criterion 'price', this value is precisely the disadvantage suffered by the re-importer for the remaining criteria. Thus, (Equation 5.1) applies for the necessary price advantage (p) for the respondents under consideration:

$$\Delta p = \frac{€13\ 450 - €12\ 200}{4} \cdot 3 = €937.5 \qquad (5.1)$$

Only beyond this price advantage would this respondent prefer to purchase a re-imported automobile from an independent dealer rather than a non-reimport. In this manner, the price beyond which each individual respondent will prefer to buy a re-import from an independent dealer can be determined. On that basis, the share of respondents who will prefer to buy a re-import for a given arbitrage price advantage can be found. (With respondents, for whom the utility components for the categories of the 'price' criterion do not distribute symmetrically around the mean '€12 200', a linear interpolation between the outside categories '€10 950' and '€13 450', was undertaken for reasons of simplification). Figure 5.32 shows the arbitrage-tendency function obtained from the conjoint data in this example. Data suggest an optimal price differential of €800–900.

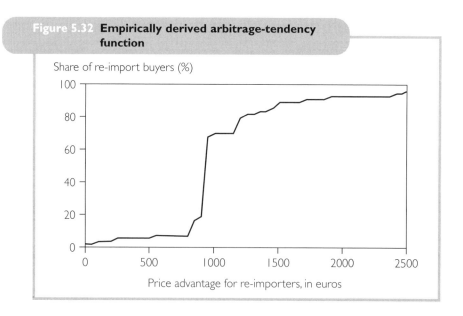

Figure 5.32 **Empirically derived arbitrage-tendency function**

Cost Situation

An argument frequently put forward against a standardization of pricing policy is that transport costs alone constitute a relatively large proportion of total costs and should be reflected by corresponding price differences. This is only partially true, for two reasons:

(i) This argument does not apply if enterprises in the target country have organized their production locally, so that transport costs outside the home market are not higher than in the domestic market. Particularly in industry sectors in which transport costs comprise a large proportion of total cost, as in some sectors of the food industry, for example, sellers make serious efforts to reduce costs. The establishment of production facilities in foreign markets is then a logical necessity. This requires clear self-awareness as an internationally operational company. That is, not as a German or French company, but as a 'global enterprise', and therefore with decentralized production locations.

(ii) Entering additional country markets will also create additional demand, particularly important for manufacturers with high fixed costs. Even where there are high transport costs, unit-cost savings may still enable a profitable unitary price to be charged.

None the less, the cost situation of a company may in fact be responsible for international price differences, if the company in question incurs country-specific distribution and marketing costs. The varying availability of distribution channels or differences in profit margins may, at least in part, be responsible for diverging prices internationally.

Competitive Situation

The extent of economically viable price differentiation in international markets is also influenced by the competitive situation in the target markets. In general, if the competitive situation between the various countries differs substantially, so too can prices.

Presence of Re-importers

The environmental factor 'presence of re-importers' is associated closely with the criterion 'arbitrage tendency of buyers', which was discussed above in the context of the standardization decision. The larger the price differences implemented by the manufacturer and the higher the estimated arbitrage tendency of buyers, the more attractive it will be for a firm to operate as a re-importer. In this context, the re-importer purchases goods from a manufacturer in a low-price country, and re-imports at his own risk in the high-price country with the intention of selling below the manufacturer's price to buyers there. Apart from the criteria 'extent of price differentiation' and 'arbitrage tendency of buyers' mentioned above, the presence of re-importers will also be influenced by the cost of re-importing and of arbitrage.

In recent years, re-importers have established themselves in various industry sectors. This is illustrated by the following examples.

Global Vehicles is a British car dealer located close to Tenterden, Kent. The company imports (for example, Fiat Punto) and re-imports (for example, Rover Discovery) cars from several regions of Europe, where they buy the vehicles at for a cheaper price. Global Vehicles transmits this cost advantage to its customers by offering the cars in Great Britain for a price that is lower than the UK list price. At the time of writing the company imports/re-imports cars worth over £12m per year.

However, re-importers exploit not only the prevailing price differences in Europe. For example, SamTrex Trading GmbH in Cologne, specializes in exploiting the price differences that exist between Germany and South Africa. For example, office materials, such as photocopier barrels or printer toner, are purchased in large quantities in South Africa, re-imported at the company's own risk back to Germany and redistributed by trading companies at prices below those asked by manufacturers in Germany.

Pharmaceutical companies are also confronted with problems resulting from re-imports. This is very obvious in the European Union, which has a long history of pharmaceutical re-imports (Mutimear, 2000, p. 15–18). In 1974, for example, the Dutch company Winthrop, sued Centrafarm for re-importing a drug called Negran. Centrafarm bought the genuine Negran in the UK and imported it into the Netherlands. In another case, Centrafarm bought Valium, a drug produced by the Swiss-based company Hoffman-LaRoche, in the UK and repackaged it for sale on the Continent, marking the new packs with the trade marks Valium and Roche.

Inflation and Currency-Related Influences

Apart from the factors that have already been discussed, inflation and currency fluctuations further influence pricing decisions and should not be underestimated. They are relevant partly because of the direct impact on revenue in the home currency. Furthermore, it is also important to safeguard business transactions from currency-related risk, which occurs during the time-lag between taking the order and receiving payment. For example, the long-term upward trend of the euro in the first half of 2002 reduced sales opportunities for European exporters, by making the goods more expensive in terms of foreign currencies.

> For example, the pharmaceutical manufacturer SmithKline Beecham, found that products introduced into various European markets around 1990 were subject to substantial exchange-rate fluctuations. Figure 5.33 shows that exchange rate changes alone imposed price differences of up to 40 per cent on this firm.

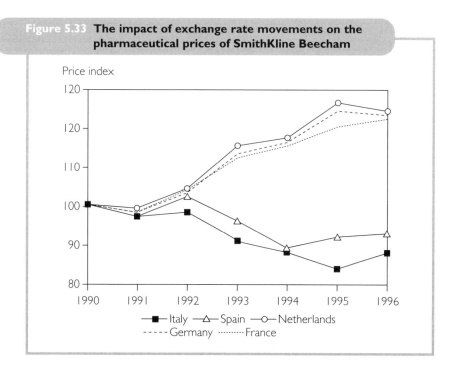

Figure 5.33 The impact of exchange rate movements on the pharmaceutical prices of SmithKline Beecham

Changes in exchange rates also have an immediate impact on price differences, which arbitrageurs are able to exploit in a particular currency.

The decline of the lira in the first half of the 1990s, for example, resulted in a considerable increase in the re-importing of vehicles from Italy. Within a relatively short period of time, the purchase prices for German arbitrageurs declined considerably, *independently* of any price reductions introduced by German manufacturers. Therefore, DM–lira exchange rate developments were a key factor in price formation.

Taxation Differentials

Price differences in international markets can also be attributed to the fact that taxation systems vary between countries – in some cases, substantially. Various taxation rates and supplements or surcharges, such as special luxury taxes, may force an enterprise to use differentiated net prices. This is particularly necessary in those countries where supplementary taxes are substantial, so that lower net prices are necessary in order to ensure that the gross price does not become excessively high.

However, arbitrageurs can exploit precisely these net price differences. The arbitrageur generally pays only the net price in the country of origin, if the purchase is destined for export, and only on import into the target country do the local (sales) taxes fall due.

The example given in Figure 5.34, demonstrates that international taxation differences create opportunities for arbitrage. In this example, it is assumed that buyers in Countries A and B together constitute 100 per cent of the willingness to pay for a particular product. Because the taxation rate is 25 per cent in Country A, the international enterprise in question sets a net price of 80 in Country A. In contrast, Country B has a taxation rate of 33 per cent. In order to avoid exceeding the maximum (gross) buyer willingness to pay, the firm can only charge a net price of 75 in Country B.

Now, if an arbitrageur buys in Country B and exports to Country A, he pays only the net price of 75. If this net price in Country A is subject to the taxation rate of 25 per cent in Country A, there will be a gross price of 93.75 (75×1.25) for the re-imported product. Provided the re-importing can be achieved at a lower cost than 6.25, the arbitrageur is able to undercut the manufacturer's price in Country A.

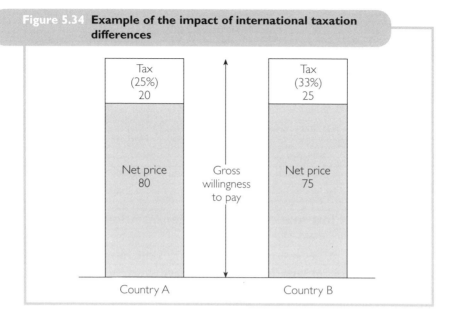

Figure 5.34 Example of the impact of international taxation differences

Country A	Gross willingness to pay	Country B
Tax (25%) 20		Tax (33%) 25
Net price 80		Net price 75

That taxation differences are directly responsible for the emergence of re-imports, is demonstrated by the international automobile market. Denmark in particular has developed into a popular country of origin for re-imports. Because the taxation imposed on automobiles, including the luxury-goods tax, can comprise as much as half the gross price, and manufacturers have thus been compelled to reduce the net price, the arbitrage process described above prevails in an extreme form.

Differences in Distribution Channels

Finally, it is necessary to bear in mind that the price ultimately paid by the final consumer is the result of a process determined not only by the manufacturer, but also generally by various distribution channels. Because manufacturers seldom have complete power over retail margins in a particular market, especially when they first enter that market, this has to be taken into account when developing a pricing policy. As the following example from the pharmaceutical industry demonstrates, differences in margins can lead to very substantial price differences.

The distribution of pharmaceutical products is traditionally organized in several phases. Manufacturers deliver to wholesalers, who in turn distribute the goods further. Table 5.2 shows the differing profit margins that accrue to wholesalers and pharmacies in various European countries.

If we now consider a medicine for which the European manu-facturing price is €100, Table 5.2 shows that, purely though differing profit margins within the distribution process, major price differences arise. In Austria, for example the price of this particular medicine is approximately 35 per cent higher than in Sweden.

The Extent of International Price Differentiation

On the one hand, several factors that tend to discourage firms from using price differentiation, including image loss, arbitrage or re-importing, have, with respect to many industry sectors, played a rela-tively small role in the past. But on the other hand, differentiated prices allow the comprehensive exploitation of country-specific differ-ences in willingness to pay, and thus raise the overall (international) profitability of the enterprise. Consequently, substantial prices differ-ences can indeed be found in many industry sectors.

In the past, this applied particularly to high-priced luxury consumer goods, because here, in comparison to many industrial goods markets, there is limited international informational trans-parency, and price differentiation seldom causes image problems. At the same time, there are huge differences in consumer willingness to pay, so that the instrument of price differentiation is particularly prof-itable (Czinkota and Ronkainen, 1998, p. 603). Table 5.3 shows that, in practice, some very large price differences prevail for selected consumer goods.

The last column in Table 5.3 demonstrates the difference between the highest and lowest price for the product in question in the coun-tries investigated. For example, the price for an IKEA 'Porfylit' table lamp in the USA is 162 per cent greater than the price for the same product in France.

However, international enterprises that differentiate to this extent are coming increasingly under pressure. The reason is the increasing informational transparency in many markets, and the increasing activ-ity of re-importers, which creates a parallel increase in demand-related feedback.

Table 5.2 The impact of differing distribution-channel profit margins in the pharmaceutical sector in Europe

Country	Austria	Belgium	Germany	Denmark	Spain	France	Finland	Greece	Italy	Ireland	Luxembourg	Netherlands	Portugal	Sweden	Great Britain
Wholesale premium on manufacturer's price (%)	16.7	15.1	14.0	7.0	13.6	10.7	8.3	8.4	10.5	15.0	14.9	22.0	12.4	4.2	14.3
Pharmacy premium on wholesaler's price (%)	52.4	44.9	47.2	34.0	42.7	36.0	55.8	35.0	33.1	33.3	47.1	28.9	25.0	26.6	20.9
Pharmacy price (manufacturer's price = €100)	177.9	166.8	167.8	143.4	162.1	150.6	168.7	146.3	147.1	153.3	169.0	157.3	140.5	131.9	138.2

Table 5.3 International price differences for selected consumer goods

	Germany	France	Sweden	Great Britain	USA	Difference between highest and lowest price (%)
IKEA 'Porfylit' table lamp	19.96	12.04	17.30	16.53	31.51	162
Bosch PSR 9.6 drill	51.60	77.45	99.00	98.68	–	92
Kodak 'Advantix APS' 200 ASA,	4.06	5.86	6.73	8.00	7.11	97
GAP 'Big Oxford' man's shirt	35.29	38.13	69.52	49.27	39.48	97
Clinique 'Dramatically Different', 50 ml moisturising lotion	22.23	21.28	27.27	23.23	13.11	101
Energizer AA 1.5 v batteries (4 pack)	4.66	3.56	4.91	5.68	5.74	61
Calvin Klein 'Eternity' aftershave, 100 ml	39.51	36.29	55.13	48.98	56.06	54
Pokemon cards, starter set	13.56	12.32	13.56	11.47	7.56	79
Timberland cargo pants, model 387	97.96	72.71	81.13	89.06	52.94	85
Dockers trousers, K1	77.15	78.86	90.31	96.87	53.81	80
Panasonic SL-SX 270 CD Player	91.93	135.90	130.68	124.75	78.57	73
Levi's 501 jeans	76.92	70.32	79.54	77.09	45.26	76
Nintendo Gameboy Color	73.89	75.80	85.89	111.27	89.06	51
CD – No. 1 in the current charts	15.20	17.57	20.09	22.29	17.60	47
Barbie 'Cool Clips' doll	24.58	21.13	31.73	22.90	21.06	51
Chanel No. 5 Eau de Toilette, 50 ml	48.33	47.67	54.64	59.90	59.54	26
'Virtual Tennis' Game for Sega Dreamcast	48.95	56.03	64.78	66.78	50.18	36

Source: The Economist Intelligence Unit, November 2000.

In view of this growing risk for enterprises that price according to country-specific willingness to pay, international price optimization is becoming increasingly necessary.

Optimization Approaches for International Pricing Policy

If there are demand-related interdependencies between the new target markets or between the new and 'old' ones, pricing co-ordination problems arise. These may be attributed to the fact that price differences can lead to arbitrage profits, thus constraining price differentiation. There is always a need for pricing co-ordination, if internationally co-ordinated prices would lead to higher overall corporate profits. A negative impact, because of demand-related feedback, can thus be expected if the negative impact of arbitrage overcompensates for these other positive effects.

Because prices in interdependent markets depend on one another, a process of *simultaneous* planning is necessary in order to consider adequately the feedback between the various country markets. The results of an appropriate optimization approach depend, most of all, on assumptions about the arbitrage-related behaviour of buyers. In this respect, it is important to distinguish between the extent of arbitrage that occurs for various given price differences. In the following model, the extent of arbitrage always depends on the price difference in the currency that is relevant to the arbitrageur. Initially, the currency is irrelevant; what matters are only the price differences that can be achieved at a particular point in time. However, these differences can be attributable to changes in exchange rates between the country markets in question. In terms of the consequences for pricing policy and co-ordination, on the other hand, the cause of the price differences is inconsequential.

Price co-ordination for a market entry poses a static problem, because an initial price must be found in the new market. The first step is a simple, microeconomic optimization model. The second step is to refer to some considerably more complex optimization approaches that can be found in the literature.

Price Optimization in Dependence on the Tendency towards Arbitrage

The extent of viable price differences is limited by many variables, in particular arbitrage costs and buyer arbitrage tendency. In the following section, a simple optimization model is presented with special emphasis to these demand-side factors. For simplicity, a distinction is made between:

▸ *complete* arbitrage; and
▸ *incomplete* arbitrage.

In the interest of simplification, in the case of incomplete arbitrage, the arbitrage tendency function is assumed to be linear (see Case (b) in Figure 5.3 on page 186).

Price Co-ordination with Complete Arbitrage

Although the assumptions underlying complete arbitrage are not fulfilled in every respect in reality, the principle of price co-ordination can be illustrated well by means of the following example.

It is assumed that an enterprise is operating in two markets, Country A and Country B, where the prices need to be co-ordinated. The isolated price-response function comprises $X_A(p_A)$ and $X_B(p_B)$ for a given, standardized product in both country markets (see Equation (5.2) and (5.3)). Price co-ordination in the context of market entry does not necessarily mean that the price in the new markets must be adjusted to the price level in current markets. Rather, the prices in all (old and new) markets need to be re-evaluated in a common planning process, and co-ordinated in this sense. Therefore such a planning process may well lead to changed prices in the established markets.

$$x_A(p_A) = 30{,}000 - 4\,p_A \qquad (5.2)$$

$$x_B(p_B) = 30{,}000 - 6\,p_B \qquad (5.3)$$

with

p_j = price in country j,
x_j = sales quantity in country j.

The enterprise finds itself in a monopolistic supply situation, because the prices of competing products have no impact. This is a substantial simplification of the model. Independently of the level of turnover, the enterprise incurs units costs in both countries of 2,000 MU (monetary units) for production and distribution. Furthermore, no additional costs are incurred – in particular, no fixed costs. Consequently, we consider only the impact of demand-related feedback in this model, because no change in units costs is incurred with the rising quantity sold. The enterprise knows that buyers in both Country A and Country B are characterized by a strong arbitrage tendency. Costs of 500 MU are incurred in the process of arbitrage and it is assumed, for reasons of simplicity, that when the price difference exceeds 500 MU, *all* buyers in the high price country will cover their demand in the low-price country. The impact of co-ordination emerges from a comparison of price co-ordination with an 'uncoordinated' country-specific optimization.

Profit situation for isolated (country-specific) pricing:

If price-setting in Countries A and B proceeds in isolation, this means that potential demand feedback not taken into account. Thus prices are planned in isolation from one another in Country markets A and B. For Country A, the revenue function is $R_A(p_A)$ and the cost function $C_A(p_A)$ (see Equations (5.4) and (5.5)).

$$R_A(p_A) = x_A(p_A) \cdot p_A = (30{,}000 - 4\,p_A) \cdot p_A$$
$$= 30{,}000\,p_A - 4\,p_A{}^2 \qquad (5.4)$$

$$C_A(p_A) = x_A(p_A) \cdot 2{,}000 = (30{,}000 - 4\,p_A) \cdot 2{,}000$$
$$= 60\,\text{m} - 8{,}000\,p_A \qquad (5.5)$$

as well as the country-specific profit function $\pi_A(p_A)$ (Equation 5.6)):

$$\pi_A(x_A) = 38{,}000\,p_A - 4\,p_A{}^2 - 60\,\text{m} \qquad (5.6)$$

Through maximization of equation (5.6) an optimum price of 4,750 MU is calculated for Country A and an optimal price of 3,500 MU for Country B. Figure 5.35 now shows that the planned sales volume for Country A of 11,000 units and for Country B of 9,000 units, will not be achieved because of arbitrage. Instead, in line with the assumptions, all buyers from the high-price Country A will buy in Country B, where, despite arbitrage costs of 500 MU per unit for re-importing, a profit of 750 MU is yielded. With respect to determining the amount of arbitrage, it should be borne in mind that not only buyers from Country A, who wanted goods at a price of 4,750 MU will become arbitrageurs, but also those buyers who were willing to pay only a lower price. Every potential buyer from Country

Figure 5.35 **Determining the amount (quantity) of arbitrage**

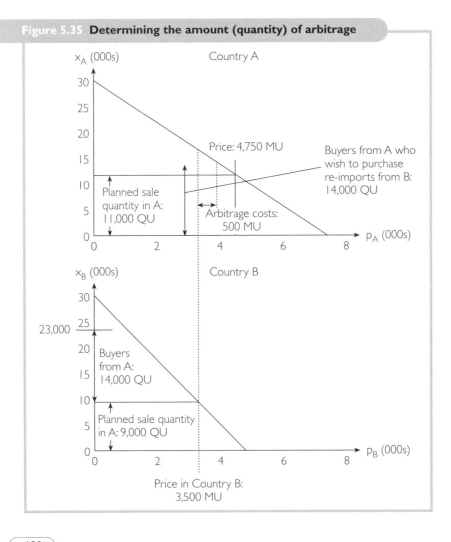

A, who is willing to pay at least 4,000 MU for the product (= the price in Country B including arbitrage costs), will become an arbitrageur.

In this extreme case, in Country A there will be no remaining demand, and in Country B, instead of the expected 9,000 units, 23,000 units are sold. The following profit is yielded in this situation:

Country A: $\pi_A(p_A) = 0$
Country B: $\pi_B(p_B) = R(p_B) - C(p_B) = 23,000 \cdot 3,500 - 23,000$
$\quad\quad\quad\quad \cdot 2,000 = 34.5 \text{ m}$
Total profit: $\pi(p_A, p_B) = \pi_A(p_A) + \pi_B(p_B) = 34.5 \text{ m}$

Profit situation with co-ordinated (international) planning

A co-ordinated reaction to the demand feedback proceeds on the basis that the price difference between the country markets has a maximum of 500 MU, because otherwise all customers will migrate to the low-price market. Consequently, the profit function $\pi(p_A, p_B)$ for the enterprise as a whole is:

$$\pi(p_A, p_B) = \pi_A(p_A) + \pi_B(p_B) = 38,000 \, p_A - 4 \, p_A{}^2 + 42,000 \, p_B$$
$$- 6 \, p_B{}^2 - 120 \text{ m} \qquad (5.7)$$

subject to the supplementary condition: $|p_A - p_B| \leq 500$ (5.8)

in order to achieve a maximum. If one replaces the maximum price difference with the variable d and solves the maximization problem with the aid of the Lagrangian method, this yields as optimal prices:

$$p_A = 4,000 + 0.6 \cdot d \qquad\qquad (5.9)$$

$$p_B = 4,000 - 0.4 \cdot d \qquad\qquad (5.10)$$

$$\lambda = 4.8 \cdot d - 6,000 \qquad\qquad (5.11)$$

Through applying optimal prices in the total profit function in Equation (5.7), one obtains Equation 5.12:

$$\pi(c) = 40 \text{ m} + 6,000 \, d - 2.4 \, d^2 \qquad (5.12)$$

This function, which is depicted in Figure 5.36, achieves its maximum at a price difference of 1,250 MU, which is exactly the difference obtained with isolated price-setting without arbitrage.

Because Function (5.12) rises monotonously for price differences

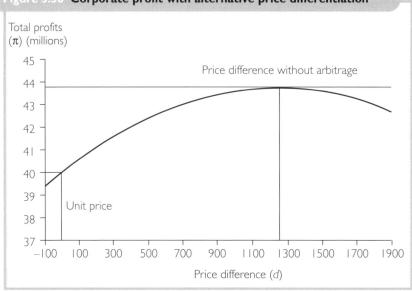

Figure 5.36 Corporate profit with alternative price differentiation

smaller than 1,250 MU, a price difference of exactly 500 MU dominates any *smaller* price difference. Consequently, for this strategy of hindering arbitrage processes, it is advantageous to maximize the price difference – that is, to set it at 500 MU.

If one now applies Equations (5.9) and (5.10), gaining for *d* a value of 500 MU, one obtains the optimal prices:

$p_A = 4,300$
$p_B = 3,800$

Individually, for this strategy, the following overall profits can be achieved:

Country A: $\pi_A(p_A) = R(p_A) - C(p_A) = 29{,}44$ m
Country B: $\pi_B(p_B) = R(p_B) - C(p_B) = 12{,}96$ m
Total Profit: $\pi\,(p_A, p_B) = \pi_A(p_A) + \pi_B(p_B) = 42{,}4$ m

Figure 5.37 shows a comparison of the profit situation for non-coordination and optimal price co-ordination. The *returns from co-ordination* will be determined by the additional profits earned through co-ordinated pricing in Country A. While in the case of an isolated price setting in Country A, no revenues are achieved, the country profit runs at 29.44 million MU for an optimised co-ordinated activity. However, this additional profit can only be achieved

Figure 5.37 Derivation of co-ordination profit

	Country-specific planning and arbitrage	Profit with co-ordinated planning and arbitrage	Results of co-ordination
Country A	$p_A = 4,750, x_A = 0$ $\pi_A = 0$	$p_A = 4,300, x_A = 12.800$ $\pi_A = 29.44$ m	$\Delta\pi_A = 29.44$ m
Country B	$p_B = 3,500, x_B = 23,000$ $\pi_B = 34.5$ m	$p_B = 3,800, x_B = 7.200$ $\pi_B = 12.96$ m	$\Delta\pi_B = 21.54$ m
Total	$\pi = 34.5$ m	$\pi = 42.4$ m	$\Delta\pi = 7.9$ m

through a profit reduction in Country B. Here, the profit drops by 21.54 million MU through co-ordination. This loss comprises the *costs of co-ordination*. Overall, the situation improves through co-ordinated pricing.

Complete arbitrage, which is in some cases quite unrealistic, creates a tendency towards a standardized pricing policy in the (old and new) country markets that are affected by demand feedback. The maximum price difference corresponds to the transaction costs incurred by buyers in the process of conducting arbitrage. The lower these are, the smaller the difference between the country-specific prices.

A decision as to standardized or differentiated prices in new and established markets, can, as a result, only be made in the context of (depending on) transport costs (as a primarily external condition) *and* on country-specific buyer willingness to pay in those markets. This is demonstrated by the considerations below.

In principle, it is conceivable that, by setting price differences above 500 MU, arbitrage is facilitated consciously. Because, in the example discussed here, it is assumed that all buyers will cover their demand in the low-price country, the planning problem reduces to that of price setting in the low-price country. Because the larger degree of price sensitivity in Country B automatically makes this country low-price, the question arises as to what (total) price-response function arises. In order to determine this, two transformation steps are necessary.

The first step lies in determining the demand from Country A, which depends on the price in Country B. Because the arbitrage costs must be taken into account, the price-response function of demand from Country A emerges geometrically through a parallel shift of the original price-response function. Thus:

$$p_B\,(x_A) = (7{,}500 - 0.25\ x_A) - 500 = 7{,}000 - 0.25\ x_A \qquad (5.13)$$

where the term in brackets corresponds to the original price-response function.

The second step includes the demand from Country B, which is dependent on the price level in Country B, which is, in turn, dependent on the demand in Country A. This yields the (total) price-response function seen in Equation (5.14):

$$x(p_B) = 58{,}000 - 10\,p_B \qquad\qquad (5.14)$$

Through maximization of the (total) profit function in Equation (5.15), an optimal price of 3,900 MU is obtained for Country B, with a maximum profit of 36.1 million.

$$\pi(p_B) = 78{,}000\,p_B - 10\,p_B^{\,2} - 116\ m \qquad\qquad (5.15)$$

In the example under discussion, a strategy of allowing (complete) arbitrage leads to a lower profit than with an avoidance of arbitrage processes through setting a maximum price difference at the level of the transaction costs incurred by arbitrageurs (Bucklin, 1990). Under these conditions, the optimal co-ordination approach lies in preventing arbitrage through a standardized pricing policy that allows the maximum price differences between the new targeted markets and established markets at the level of the arbitrage costs.

Price Co-ordination with Incomplete Arbitrage

It is more realistic to assume that the tendency towards arbitrage increases with increasing arbitrage profits and thus remains 'incomplete' for a certain range of price differences. In this 'zone', not all buyers take advantage of the opportunity to purchase in foreign markets, so that a certain proportion of national demand remains in the home market even in the presence of arbitrage profits. In comparison to complete arbitrage, this means that, under these conditions, a seller can set price differences in terms of the incomplete arbitrage tendency of buyers *and* the transaction costs. The objective would be to use the differing willingness to pay in the individual country markets in order to maximize profits.

In the following example, only Case (b) from Figure 5.30 (see page 175) will be considered. For simplicity, it is assumed that the arbitrage tendency b of buyers has a linear dependence on potential arbitrage profits (see Figure 5.38). According to this assumption, arbitrage will occur when the price difference $(p_A - p_B)$ lies above the arbitrage costs. Only beyond a certain level of arbitrage profit $(p_A - p_B)^*$, will complete arbitrage ($\beta = 1$) be achieved. The assumption of a linear function simplifies the analytical solution of the problem and facilitates a relatively straightforward solution. The following applies:

$$ß = b\,(p_A - p_B - d) \tag{5.16}$$

where:

ß = share of arbitrage demand in the high-price market
b = arbitrage tendency
d = arbitrage costs

In this case, the total profit function looks as follows:

$$\pi(p_A, p_B) = [(p_A - 2{,}000)\,((1-\beta)\cdot(30{,}000 - 4\,p_A)] + [(p_B$$
$$- 2{,}000)\cdot ß \cdot (30{,}000 - 4\,(p_B + d)] + [(p_B$$
$$- 2{,}000)\cdot(30{,}000 - 6\,p_B)] \tag{5.17}$$

where:

$[(p_A - 2{,}000)\cdot(1-\beta)\cdot(30{,}000 - 4\,p_A)]$ is the demand from Country A in Country A,
$[(p_B - 2{,}000)\cdot ß \cdot (30{,}000 - 4\,(p_B + c))]$ is the demand from Country A in Country B (arbitrage),
$[(p_B - 2{,}000)\cdot(30{,}000 - 6\,p_B)]$ is demand from Country B in Country B.

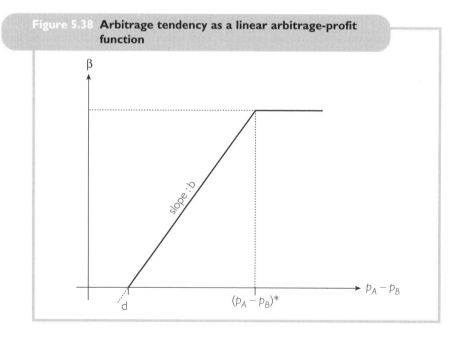

Figure 5.38 Arbitrage tendency as a linear arbitrage-profit function

Despite the simplicity of the assumptions, the marginal-analysis approach to maximizing this function remains complex. The derivation of Equation 5.17 according to p_A or p_B leads, with an assumed low arbitrage tendency ($b = 0.000001$) and arbitrage costs ($d = 500$), to an optimal co-ordination solution ($p_A = 4,738.48$; $p_B = 3,512.41$), which is almost identical to the solution for isolated country markets. If, on the other hand, a higher arbitrage tendency is assumed ($b = 0.0004$), the country prices are already, with $p_A = 3,384.83$ and $p_B = 3,756.41$, almost at the level of an optimal solution with complete arbitrage.

As with the case of incomplete arbitrage discussed here, it is advantageous *not* to adapt prices on entry to those in the established market, but to determine new prices and to implement them. What is remarkable about a co-ordinated pricing policy in integrated markets is that price standardization in the realistic case of incomplete arbitrage does not under any circumstances maximize profits (Bucklin, 1990).

Additional Optimization Approaches in the Literature

The literature offers a variety of further approaches on price optimization in international markets. To some extent, these overlap with the concept already presented here, but they do move in other directions as well or involve a considerably higher level of complexity. This is particularly the case, because, for example, in these approaches, the focus is not only on buyer arbitrage tendency, but also partly includes such related issues as the problems associated with exchange-rates. Berndt *et al.* (1997, p. 173) provide a good overview of the optimization approaches discussed in the literature. The essence of the various approaches are presented in Figure 5.39.

The *cost-orientated* approaches attempt, using certain modes of calculation, to set international prices in such a way that a particular profit margin is achieved over and above country-specific costs. Differences between prices in international business with respect to these approaches arise in the first instance through diverging production and distribution costs.

By contrast, the *competitor-orientated* approaches link price determination with the pricing and supply-related behaviour of competitors,

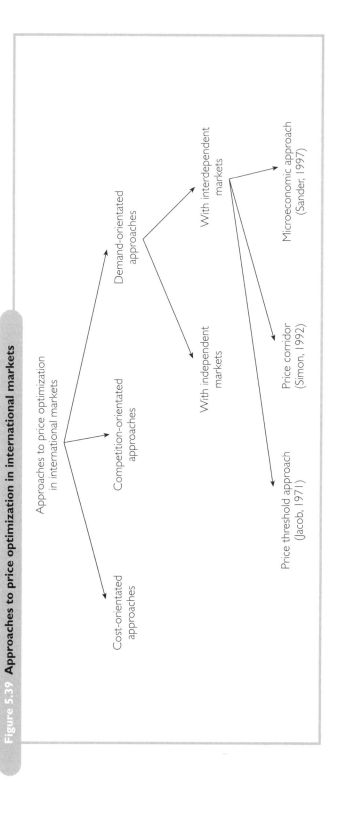

Figure 5.39 Approaches to price optimization in international markets

so prices can be orientated towards those of competition, or a conscious counter-strategy can be pursued. In each case, however, pricing will proceed less in terms of cost aspects or a demand perspective, and more in terms of the country-specific competitive situation.

In the context of price policy, supplier and competitor-based (sometimes), and, inevitably demand-related feedback, must be taken into account. Thus, the use of cost- and competition-orientated approaches to solving price co-ordination problems do not seem particularly useful, since demand-related feedback is not considered. Such a consideration of demand-related feedback is only possible in demand-orientated approaches, which make explicit the quantities that can be sold at different prices, and thus have the price-response function as the basis of the international pricing decision.

However, with demand-oriented approaches, the price co-ordination problem described above can only be solved if the approach is based upon feedback between country markets, and not by performing isolated price optimization. Among the demand-oriented price optimization approaches for interrelated markets, the models developed by Jacob, Simon and Sander are particularly interesting.

In his *price-threshold* approach, Jacob (1971) assumes that buyers who are resident in a country market, or a segment of such a market, will buy in another country market or segment if the prices offered by sellers in these other potential areas exceed a certain threshold. This means, in essence, that Jacob is assuming that the total profit function (in a two-country case) is formed from the single (linear) price-response functions and can be maximized subject to the following supplementary condition:

$$|p_A - p_B| \leq c_{A,B} \tag{5.18}$$

In order to solve this problem, Jacob suggests a rather complicated, indirect mode of solution. He first determines the isolated Cournot country–price optimum and only later the deviation from these profit-maximizing prices, which is necessary in order to fulfil the supplementary conditions that emerge from the required threshold values. He succeeds, in that he minimizes appropriately the sum for all country markets of profit losses created by the deviation from the Cournot prices (Jacob, 1971, p. 90).

$$\sum_{i=1}^{n} [(p_{c,i} - k_i) \cdot X_{c,i} - (p_i - k_i) \cdot x_i] \rightarrow \min!$$

where:

$P_{c,i}$ = Cournot price in Country i
p_i = price to be set in Country i
k_i = variable unit costs in Country i i,
$X_{c,i}$ = Cournot quantity in Country i
X_i = quantity sold in Country I

If the threshold value is equated with the transactions and arbitrage costs, Jacob's approach corresponds exactly with the procedure described above in the context of price co-ordination with complete arbitrage. However, Jacob's indirect method of finding a solution creates a level of mathematical complexity that arguably is not necessary.

Simon's (1992) price-corridor approach can be regarded as a further demand-orientated methodology for interdependent markets. In this approach, it is assumed that in international markets, country-specific optima frequently cannot be achieved, because of the potential danger of arbitrage processes. As, on the other hand, a unitary price is associated with a substantial reduction in profits (because of a possible incomplete exploitation of country-specific willingness to pay), Simon suggests implementing a price corridor, which should be set just high enough to prevent arbitrage.

If one denotes the width of the corridor as 'r' and regards this variable as the percentage reduction in the high price in the high-price country, Equation (5.20) below must apply to the prices to be set in country markets A and B:

$$p_B = (1 - r) \cdot p_A \tag{5.20}$$

In Simon's approach, on the other hand, the total profit function derived from the (linear) price-response function, which is based on the supplementary condition specified in Equation 5.20, is maximized with the aid of Lagrange's method. The following applies to the two-country case:

$$p_B^* = \frac{1}{2} \cdot \frac{(1-r) \cdot (b_A \cdot c_A + a_A) + b_B \cdot c_B + a_B}{b_A \cdot (1 - r)^2 + b_B} \tag{5.21}$$

where:

a_A = absolute term in the price-response function of Country A
a_B = absolute term in the price-response function of Country B
b_A = contribution of the gradient factor in the price-response function
  of Country A
b_B = contribution of the rate of increase in the price-response function
  of Country B
c_A = variable costs in Country A
c_B = variable costs in Country B

Equations (5.20) and (5.21) make it clear that the only difference with respect to Jacob's approach and that discussed earlier with respect to price co-ordination with complete arbitrage, is that the price difference allowed is not given in absolute terms, but determined as a percentage.

For the example given earlier, the application of Simon's approach, the optimal prices given in Table 5.4 apply with the variation caused by the price corridor at the basis of the approach.

Sander (1997) presents a third demand-orientated approach for interdependent markets which considers explicitly the behaviour of individual economic subjects (see also Berndt *et al.*, 1997, p. 194). In essence, Sander does not consider arbitrage tendency in the sense of 'complete arbitrage' but in terms of individual demand. For Sander, the arbitrage tendency of individual buyers does not depend only on the price differences set by sellers, but also on the geographic or spatial distance of buyers from the domestic and foreign points or sale (sales locations). Figure 5.40 clarifies the linkage of arbitrage costs and spatial distance selected by Sander.

If one takes the spatial difference of the individual buyer to the domestic or foreign sales location as the standard (magnitude) for determining individual arbitrage costs (difference between costs for purchasing domestically and overseas), then the individual buyer will only purchase in a foreign market if the arbitrage costs referred to above are lower than the price differences set by the seller. On this basis, Sander determines the profit-maximizing price for the enterprise in question, by using not only individualized transaction or arbitrage costs but also, simultaneously, the individual price-response function.

Sander's approach, in which he was the first to attempt to consider the arbitrage tendency not only as being dependent on price differences, and thus to arbitrage revenues, as in the case of price co-ordination with incomplete arbitrage described above, but

Table 5.4 Optimal prices and profits in the context of the price corridor

Price corridor [r]	Prices		Turnover quantity		Profit		Total profits	Profits sacrificed (%)
	p_A	p_B	x_A	x_B	G_A	G_B		
0.00	4,000.00	4,000.00	14,000.00	6,000.00	28 M	12 M	40 M	8.57
0.05	4,137.02	3,930.16	13,451.94	6,419.01	28.75 M	12.39 M	41.14 M	5.97
0.10	4,277.65	3,849.89	12,889.39	6,900.68	29.36 M	12.77 M	42.13 M	3.72
0.15	4,421.12	3,757.95	12,315.54	7,452.31	29.82 M	13.10 M	42.92 M	1.90
0.20	4,566.33	3,653.06	11,734.69	8,081.63	30.12 M	13.36 M	43.48 M	0.63
0.25	4,711.86	3,533.90	11,152.54	8,796.61	30.24 M	13.49 M	43.73 M	0.03
0.263158	4,750.00	3,500.00	11,000.00	9,000.00	30.25 M	13.50 M	43.75 M	0

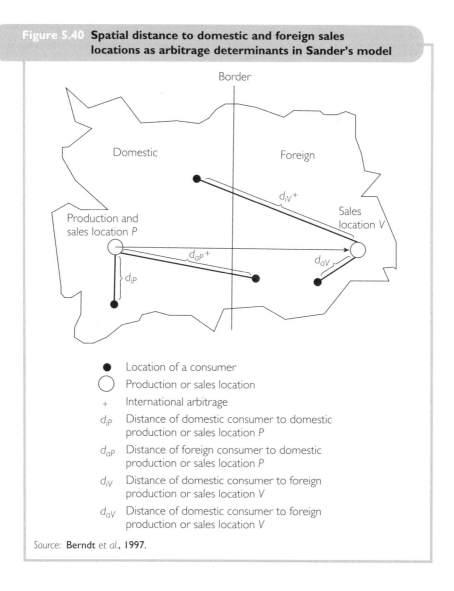

Figure 5.40 Spatial distance to domestic and foreign sales locations as arbitrage determinants in Sander's model

Border

Domestic   Foreign

d_{iV}^+

Production and
sales location P

Sales
location V

d_{aP}^+ d_{aV}

d_{iP}

●   Location of a consumer
○   Production or sales location
+   International arbitrage
d_{iP} Distance of domestic consumer to domestic
      production or sales location P
d_{aP} Distance of foreign consumer to domestic
      production or sales location P
d_{iV} Distance of domestic consumer to foreign
      production or sales location V
d_{aV} Distance of domestic consumer to foreign
      production or sales location V

Source: **Berndt** et al., 1997.

also simultaneously to integrate the arbitrage tendency with other factors (distance to domestic and foreign sales location). However, in practice, this approach is marred by some central weaknesses:

▸ The application of the model assumes comprehensive individual customer data input. Individual buyer price-response functions or data on domestic and foreign sales locations can generally not be collected in sufficient detail in mass markets.

- ▶ Sander's emphasis on the distance between seller and buyer in domestic and foreign locations necessarily places considerable emphasis on transport costs, because it can be assumed that this factor rises in significance in proportion to distance. None the less, arbitrage costs are influenced not only by transport, but also by factors quite independent of distance, such as exchange rates, information costs, duty and so on.
- ▶ Furthermore, grey markets arise in most sectors, not as a result of individual foreign demand, but through foreign demand that is organized, for example, by re-importers. Because, in this case, domestic buyers can acquire the products of original manufacturers and re-imports domestically, Sander's variable 'distance' plays no role.

In particular, the magnitude of (individual demand) data input necessary for Sander's approach, renders it questionable as to whether this model can really be used to solve price-setting problems in international marketing. Instead, because of the non-availability of individual data, one would frequently be compelled to estimate (total) arbitrage exclusively in dependence on possible arbitrage revenues, and thus ultimately on the price differences on the seller's side. In this case, adequate results can be obtained from the concept of price coordination with incomplete arbitrage that has been introduced, in which the arbitrage tendency depends on the price differences that have been captured.

Methods of Price Co-ordination

Historically, many enterprises make decentralized pricing decisions (Govindarajan and Gupta, 1991, p. 21). This results in part from better market knowledge on the part of local managers, and also because of the greater flexibility with which they can react to changes in buyer behaviour or competitive conditions. However, if homogeneity and thus the integration of country markets, increases, we can, as has already been shown, no longer use isolated pricing decisions in order to achieve international profit maximization.

The Process of 'Going Against the Stream'

The 'against the stream' process (Sander, 1997, p. 287; Berekoven, 1985, p. 172) offers a solution through organizing pricing decisions. Here, the subsidiary initially sets the optimum price for its own country, although this can be modified in agreement with the central office in the light of prevailing interdependency.

Lead-country Concept

The lead-country concept is a further means of organizing pricing (Raffee and Kreutzer, 1989, pp. 43–57). For this concept, some countries are designated as 'lead countries', according to certain factors such as turnover, profits or market share, and there, profit maximizing prices are determined.

For the lead-country concept, one country is frequently allocated the overall leadership role within pricing policy. Such a country would generally be a market of particular importance for the company, in terms of turnover, for example. In consequence, the 'non-lead countries' must orientate their prices around those set by the lead country. To the extent that at least the arbitrage costs are (approximately) known to the international enterprise, in order to avoid arbitrage, prices in the remaining country markets can move within a price corridor, the middle of which is defined by the price in the lead country, and the entire breadth comprises double the arbitrage costs (Figure 5.41).

Often the domestic market, is designated as the *lead country*. If the arbitrage costs are known, then the prices in the new foreign target

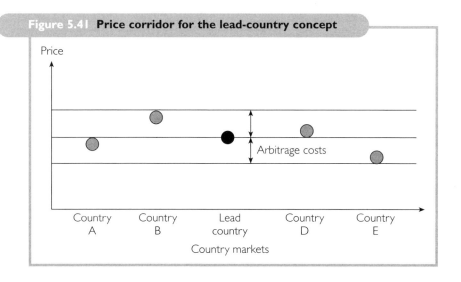

Figure 5.41 Price corridor for the lead-country concept

markets, in comparison to the price in the home market, have a maximum (positive or negative) difference amounting to the level of the arbitrage costs.

Even if the application of the lead-country concept fails to yield optimal co-ordination, an extension of the example given earlier shows that firms perform better with it than if they do not consider demand feedback at all.

For the extended example of complete arbitrage tendency discussed originally in the section entitled 'Optimization Approaches for International Pricing Policy, on pages 187–204, it will be assumed below that:

▸ so far, the enterprise has been active only in market A and now wishes to enter country market B as well;
▸ the enterprise knows only the price-response function of the domestic market (derived from historical data, for example);
▸ it is known only that the willingness to pay in market B is considerably lower than in market A;
▸ in reality (without the enterprise knowing this), the price-response function given earlier for Country B in fact applies; and
▸ it is known that the arbitrage costs amount to 500 MU.

In this situation, the application of the lead-country concept means that the enterprise demands an optimal price of 4,750 MU, thereby achieving a turnover of 10,000 MU and a profit of 30.25 million MU.

Because the firm knows that buyer willingness to pay in Country B is low, and that the arbitrage costs amount to 500 MU, it sets a price corridor, specifying that the price in Country B may not be more than 500 MU lower than that in A. If, therefore, a price of 4, 250 MU(4,750 MU − 500 MU) is demanded:

$$x_B(p_B) = 30,000 - 6\, p_B \tag{5.3}$$

$$\Rightarrow x_B(4,250) = 30,000 - 6 \cdot 4,250 = 4,500 \text{ QU} \tag{5.22}$$

Furthermore, with variable costs of 2,000 MU, this price setting leads to the following profit in Country B:

$$\pi_B(x_B) = (4,250 - 2,000) \cdot 4,500 = 10,125 \text{ m} \tag{5.23}$$

In total, therefore, with the aid of the lead-country concept, the enterprise can earn a profit of 40,375 million MU. Although this lies below the profit that would be achieved with optimal coordination (42.4 million), it is none the less clearly greater than the 34.4 million MU that is yielded if arbitrage is ignored.

Apart from the co-ordination methods discussed here, national sales organizations and subsidiaries of parent companies should, in principle, be provided with stronger incentives to coordinate their activities with each other. Once these incentive systems have been implemented, they have the effect that a subsidiary no longer sets a price that is optimal for it alone, but creates an incentive for arbitrage. In other words, interdependencies are taken into account. An international enterprise should therefore reward its managers, for example, not only according to turnover or profits, but also according to their willingness and ability to co-operate with other subsidiaries and the home office (Assmus and Wiese, 1995, p. 37).

Proactive Co-ordination: Separating Markets instead of Standardizing Prices

In contrast to the classical methods of price co-ordination, proactive strategies attempt to prevent the development of interdependent markets by ensuring that prices are *not* transparent. The objective is to make it increasingly difficult for customers to compare national prices with one another. Compared to a situation of differentiated prices in separated markets, price equalization is always associated with a negative impact on profit.

For internationally active enterprises, this may mean that they no longer differentiate prices by country, but rather by customer. This suggests that long-term co-ordination of manufacturer and retailing activities through *key account management* may be advisable. The international *key account customer* negotiates worldwide with only one contact person in the enterprise. The customer-related price for the key account customer is thus independent of the country and determined in price negotiations between manufacturer and customer. The exploitation of country-specific price differences will thus be countered, and at the same time, a closer relationship will be established with the customer. The potential for customer-related price differentiation is, however, of the highest priority for such enterprises, which have a manageable (but not excessive) number of major international customers. Enterprises which, because of their customer structure, are unable to practise a customer-related price differentiation may use *product differentiation* in order to reduce price transparency. With the aid of price differentiation, prevailing regional price differences become less transparent and make arbitrage profits smaller or less certain. In the context of product policy, a decision must thus be made, as to which components of a product programme in the target country markets are to be standardized or differentiated.

Communication

With respect to market entry into new target markets, international enterprises are confronted with the question as to whether, and to what extent, independent communication objectives, strategies and measures can be developed in these markets. An alternative to a country-specific formulation of communication policy is the transfer of policies that are already used in other country markets. It is also possible to unify communications policy over both old and new markets. Thus, within the communications policy, a differentiation-standardization decision must be made.

Determinants of the Co-ordination Decision

The decision as to the extent of standardization or differentiation of communication policy strategies and measures constitutes a *trade-off between cost* and *impact*.

The *cost* aspect refers to a standardization of communications policy instruments, which is advantageous if multiple (duplicated) investments for international marketing communications can be avoided. That is, the danger of seller-related feedback can be reduced through a unitary communications policy in both old and new markets. Although the literature suggests that a standardization of communication is often based upon an overestimation of its cost-reducing potential, a common communications policy developed for many different countries leads to 'once-only' cost savings with respect to conception, production and control. Similarly, it is sometimes the case that a consistent concept only needs be conducted in one country, in a one-off test phase.

The extent to which a consistent, unitary communications policy reduces costs depends to a large degree on the share of (communications) development costs. In this context, Merkle (1984) established that, for many international enterprises, the share of development costs comprises less than 10 per cent of the communications expenses. Consequently, the cost-reducing possibilities yielded by a standardized communications policy are limited.

While a standardized communications policy varies in terms of the cost savings it can achieve, other impacts can be more significant. The impact can be increased, among other measures, through an increase in communication effectiveness, a bundling of financial resources, the use of international media, and exploitation of spillover effects.

Higher effectiveness

With a standardized communications policy, an international application of creative resources facilitates a greater impact on performance. Such a 'quality push' emerges when the prevailing marketing know-how of the individual subsidiaries is pooled and, for example, international working groups improve the effectiveness of international communications.

Bundling of financial resources

If an independent communications policy is pursued in every operational country market, only a fraction of the total available communications budget is available for each. In such a case, more elaborate conceptions may not be possible, as they would exceed the budget allocated to an individual country.

> The integration of the tennis star Boris Becker into the world-wide marketing of Philips Hi Fi equipment, was only possible though combining the communications budgets of several subsidiaries. An individual subsidiary would not have been able to secure the contract with Becker, given that it cost US$2.5 million for the three-year contract (Becker, 1986).

The use of international media

A unitary communications policy opens the 'gateway' to international media, which will certainly increase in significance and usage over time, particularly global data networks (the Internet) or satellite television.

The importance of international media will grow for a number of reasons, not least of which being the fact that these media have recognized that (foreign) languages still constitute a central barrier to media acceptance. Consequently, many international media have for some time, been offering their services in the language of the relevant target country. Figure 5.42 gives the example of the news broadcaster CNN, which currently offers information in more than ten languages.

Spillover effects

Programmes broadcast by satellite can be received in a number of regions neighbouring the intended target zones. For example, the German TV station, ARD, which can be received through the Astra satellite on Transponder 19, is in fact broadcast over a large area, as shown in Figure 5.43. It is evident that the programme can be received in all western and central European countries.

Increases in impact can be achieved through the exploitation of so-called spillover effects. While such spillover effects for a standardized communications policy instrument leads, through a deliberate multiple communications policy, to an anchoring of the brand and the advertising message in the minds of buyers, a differentiated communications policy may irritate buyers.

On the other hand, communications policy standardization can be associated with a *reduction in impact*. A unitary approach to country markets makes it difficult to consider country-specifics in the way that would be possible with a differentiated communications policy. Consequently, a policy developed jointly for several countries, and a unitary application of communication instruments, can lead to a decline in turnover, because buyers do not relate to the unspecific communications message and turn to local suppliers (Buzzell, 1968). If enterprises use the same picture in new target markets as they do in the domestic market, it may turn out that these images produce quite different associations in the different countries. Empirical studies confirm that buyers in various countries perceive the same visual images differently and have different associations with them. Dmoch (1996), for example, reports the results of such a study that investigated the images German and French sample groups associated with

Figure 5.42 Country-specific CNN Internet Services (as at 5 February 2001)

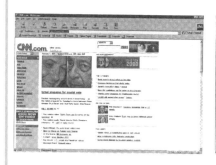

CNN (USA)

CNN (Europe)

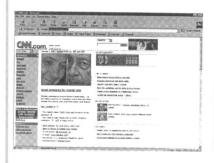

CNN (Portugal)

CNN (Spain)

CNN (Sweden)

CNN (Italy)

Figure 5.43 **Regional broadcasting zones for the TV station ARD through the Astra satellite**

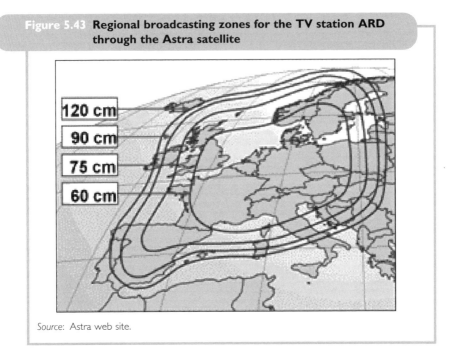

120 cm
90 cm
75 cm
60 cm

Source: Astra web site.

'the Caribbean'. As shown in Table 5.5, the results for the two national groups are quite distinct.

Furthermore, Tostmann (1985) draws attention to the danger that the impact of a message may also decline because a standardized approach to communications policy instruments is inevitably associated with a reduction in communicative power. The danger of

Table 5.5 **Primary image associations for 104 German and 112 French respondents to the concept of 'the Caribbean'**

German respondents (%)		French respondents (%)	
palms	30.8	sea	30.8
sea	16.4	island	17.3
sun	10.6	palms	15.4
island	8.6	sun	13.5
beach	7.7	beach	6.7

Note: German n = 104; French n = 112.

'message cannibalization' is always present, if the core message is reduced to the lowest common denominator with respect to preferences in the various country markets. This often leads to unsatisfactory results, when common motifs and slogans are used for distinct groups and cultures.

Studies show that these cost and impact considerations really do affect the extent of to which communications policy elements are standardized. Went (2000), for example, questioned sellers and advertising agencies in the shampoo market as to their views of the core advantages and disadvantages associated with a standardization of international communications policy. Table 5.6 indicates that many of the influence factors are indeed regarded as relevant by the responding companies.

Table 5.6 Advantages and disadvantages of standardizing advertising campaigns for shampoo brands

Advantages	%	Disadvantages	%
Unitary visual brand images	77	Insufficient consideration of country-specific aspects	71
Cost reduction, particularly of production costs	71	'Foreign' appearance of advertising resulting from inappropriate use of puns (linguistic jokes), irony etc.	18
Use of synergy effects	24	Level of costs for country adaptation	6
Brand internationalization	18	High risk	6
Use of advertising spillover	12	Low level of reaction to changing market conditions	6
Expensive production potential through high budget	12	Time and cost intensity of concepts for international market	6
Time savings in *rolling out* advertising concept	6	'Not-invented-here' syndrome in country subsidiaries	6
High process certainty through lead function of agency and corporate head office	6	Search for lowest common denominator	6
Concentration on product-specific core competencies	6	Insufficient attainment of country-specific communication and marketing objectives	6
Recovery of brand and corporate relevance	6		
Increasing competitiveness	6		
Improved negotiating position with retailers	6		

Source: Went, 2000, p. 263.

Determining the Optimal Degree of Standardization

The objective of determining the level of standardization/differentiation within communications policy is to achieve a level of optimization for which the marginal cost savings for a successively increasing level of standardization are equal to the marginal impact or revenue loss that occurs simultaneously (see Figure 5.44).

The determination of the degree of differentiation/standardization in target and currently operational markets within communications policy assumes that alternative communications policy strategies are possible that are characterized by a differing level of standardization. This is necessary, because, in contrast to pricing policy and analogously to product policy, in the context of the degree of differentiation/standardization, we are dealing not with a continuous, but rather a *categorical* variable. The impact on revenue shown in Figure 5.44 would, in reality, constitute a series of points and not a consistent function.

For the area of international advertising, Berndt *et al.*, (1997) developed a method of categorizing the level of differentiation/standardization. Figure 5.45 shows five phases associated with a particular level.

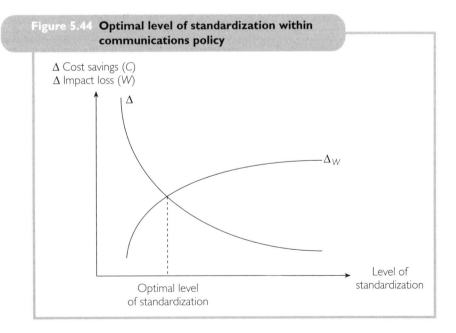

Figure 5.44 Optimal level of standardization within communications policy

Δ Cost savings (C)
Δ Impact loss (W)

Δ

Δ$_W$

Level of standardization

Optimal level of standardization

Figure 5.45 Levels of standardization in international advertising

	Complete differentiation	Large degree of differentiation	Partly different partly standard	Large degree of standardization	Complete standardization
		Supranational media co-operation		Supranational media	
Media strategies	National independent media	Several publishers	One publisher	With regional participation	Without regional participation
Advertising Formulation strategies	Differing national advertising images	Differing advertising media, but some global elements, e.g. photos slogans	Differing advertising media, but many identical elements	The same advertising image, but text in different languages	One supranatural advertising image
Combined media and advertising formulation strategies	National media, differing images	National media, differing images, but some global elements	National media, differing images, but many identical elements	Media co-operation, the same image	Supranational media, the same image

Source: Berndt et al., 1997, p. 271.

In order to choose the optimal level of communications standardization, the cost and impact effects for the various levels must subsequently be quantified. While the costs can be determined relatively easily, measuring the impact effects is not so straightforward.

Determining the communication impact effects and associated impact on revenue is problematic in two respects. For one thing, the level of standardization of communications policy instruments is often difficult to measure.

The development of scoring models such as that of a comparison of similarity in international advertising, is an attempt at measuring the degree of standardization in the context of international communications policy and thus for solving the above problem. In this context, at the end of the 1980s, Whitelock and Chung (1989) developed a model that measures the level of standardization of international advertising on the basis of various criteria. These are visual image (picture), size of advertisement, colour, general layout, headline and explanatory text.

Mueller (1991) suggests a more differentiated catalogue of criteria with eleven criteria and a different aggregation rule, with all basic criteria having the same weighting.

Even if the scoring models of Mueller, and Whitelock and Chung, provide a first approach for 'measuring' the standardization of international advertising, Schlöder (1998) and Backhaus et al. (2001) indicate that the weighting of criteria in the above-mentioned models is relatively arbitrary and not based on consumer response. Therefore, Backhaus et al. (1999) suggest developing a criterion weighting in terms of significance within the similarity evaluation. In order to determine the influence of individual criteria on the similarity of international advertisements from the buyer perspective, they use conjoint analysis.

Consumers were asked to compare international advertisements from a particular company with respect to their perceptions of similarity. The similarity of the advertisements is related to a base advertisement (see Figure 5.46). The advertisements to be evaluated are selected in such a manner that they contain a systematic variation from one another with regard to formulation. This variation facilitates measurement of the relative significance of the individual descriptive criteria such as colour and image, which can then be evaluated empirically.

Figure 5.46 Conjoint analysis determination of the significance of various formulation elements of international advertisements with respect to evaluating similarity

Basic advertisement

Please sort the following advertisements with respect to similarity to the advertisement above. Please give the first place to the advertisement with the greatest similarity to the basic advertisement.

card 1
SPURTREUE UND TRAKTION IN SERIE

card 2
BMW TRACTION CONTROL.

card 3
DARE TO COMPARE

card 4

This consumer perspective using conjoint analysis to determine the relative weighting of criteria, can then be used as weighting factors in the scoring models of Whitelock & Chung, and Mueller. In this manner, the models can be improved, because the criteria weighting is no longer arbitrary.

In addition, in the context of market entry, it is not generally possible to use historical data, so that the revenue impact of varying degrees of standardization in advertising concepts can only be estimated. Therefore the objective of determining the 'optimal' level of standardization of communications policy measures in new and established markets can often only be determined by means of what seems plausible. The impact of the influences discussed above will be estimated approximately, and then contrasted with one another.

Distribution

In the context of distribution decisions, enterprises must determine distribution channels for the new country markets. Furthermore, it is important to ensure, through appropriate measures, that the services to be offered in foreign markets are available in the required quantities and quality at all times.

With respect to the question of whether similar distribution channels can be used for entry into the new markets, the following considerations are important:

▸ The choice of organizational form (see Figure 5.7, p. 122) narrows down the possibilities open to the firm in terms of distribution policy. If the decision has been taken to operate in foreign markets through representative offices or branches, no additional channel decision is imminent. In turn, similar distribution channels in both new and old markets assume compatible organizational forms.

▸ Only those distribution channels can be used, which are available in the countries in question and/or if these channels are of significance in these markets. This latter condition may not always be fulfilled outside the home market.

In Japan, for example, large supermarkets are less significant than in Europe or North America. This is partly because many households in densely populated areas, such as those surrounding Tokyo, do not have cars, because parking is restricted and costs prohibitive. Furthermore, real estate costs have led to a situation in which most families, as well as single households, live in relatively small homes. Thus, many people do not have cellars or deep freezers necessary for medium-term storage. Consequently, the shopping trip that households in America and Europe undertake once a week, is rare, and shopping is done several times a week. The large supermarkets such

Figure 5.47 Main entrance to the 17,000 squ. m. Carrefour self-service warehouse in Tokyo

as that opened recently in Tokyo by Carrefour (Figure 5.47) are not practical with the long distances that buyers have to travel to reach them.

Apart from these limitations, seller-related feedback needs to be taken into account in the selection of distribution channels:

▸ If the above-mentioned limitations do not apply, it may be appropriate to establish a similar distribution channel to those used in current markets. In this respect, past experience in established markets may be of use to management with regard to handling channels in the new markets.

▸ However, seller-related feedback can provide a case against using the same intermediaries in various country markets, if this would lead to a power shift to the detriment of the international enterprise. For example, the intermediary could attempt to use its increased significance to demand higher margins.

▸ The case study of Corical discussed in Chapter 2 (see pages 17–19), showed, furthermore, that it is equally possible that the intermediary will develop feedback quite deliberately on the manufacturer's side, so that it can exploit its market position in order to influence the manufacturer's channel decision in other country markets. In the case of Corical, the enterprise had to assume that the wholesalers in the targeted Austrian market would only represent them if they distributed through this retailer in Germany as well.

Against this background, the international enterprise needs to consider the opportunities (for example, market situation in the target country, transfer of experience in channel management) and risks (control of intermediaries) associated with the establishment of a similar distribution system in each market. On the basis of these considerations, a decision must also be made as whether to use the same distribution-instruments, and whether to work with the same intermediaries.

6 Decision-making Interdependencies in 'Going International'

In the context of decision-making about going international (market selection and entry decisions with respect to timing, choice of organizational form for foreign business, and the formulation of marketing instruments), an important variable to consider is the need for international co-ordination. It is clear that for all individual country-specific decisions in the targeted markets, the following subsequent impacts must be considered:

▸ other markets which are to be entered; and
▸ the markets which have already been entered.

International market interdependencies manifest themselves as linkages between individual decision-making areas (Zentes and Swoboda, 2001, p. 33). Thus far, we have considered these effects only peripherally. For reasons of completeness, however, these factors will be discussed in more detail in this chapter.

Figure 6.1 shows that 'going international' decisions must be integrated not only in terms of

(1) current markets, but also
(2) simultaneously for future target markets.
(3) The selection and timing of market entry are closely interrelated. With respect to the market selection decision, it is necessary to take into account whether the entry strategy fits with the selected timing strategy. A shower entry strategy brought about by short product life cycles and rapid technological obsolescence may require different target markets than a waterfall strategy. Smaller 'trial markets' favoured by stepwise risk-reducing entry can be incompatible with the demand for the fast build-up of large-scale production.

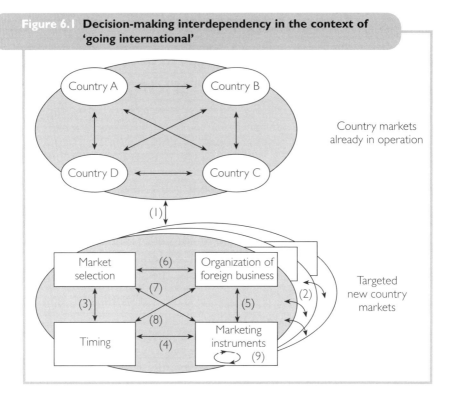

Figure 6.1 Decision-making interdependency in the context of 'going international'

(4) The linkage between timing strategy and the formulation of marketing instruments has already been demonstrated by the example on pages 111–118. Dynamic pricing (skimming in this case) interacts with timing of market entry as it may or may not facilitate a simultaneous entry. In order to determine the timing, it is necessary to know what price developments are planned in the country markets.

(5) The dependence of distribution policy decisions on the choice of organizational form for foreign business is discussed in the section entitled 'Distribution' at the end of Chapter 5. Similarly, for the selection of an appropriate organizational form, the distribution policy options in a particular country must be known. Direct export can be incompatible with the distribution in a country in which powerful 'mega-retailers' dominate the scene.

(6) The weighting of risk factors within the market selection decision depends to a large degree on which organizational form

will be used later in the foreign market. If the main source of value creation remains in the domestic market (for example, through exporting), risk aspects will play a lesser role. They will, however, assume a far greater significance if the value-creation focus is to be in the foreign market.

(7) There are also independencies between market selection and the formulation of marketing instruments. If, for example, an enterprise is searching for further sales areas for a standardized product, where a decision in favour of standardization has already been made in the context of product policy, then other markets which demand an adapted solution are inaccessible.

(8) If an enterprise fixes a timing strategy without advance consideration of the advantages and disadvantages of alternative organizational forms for foreign operations, there is a danger that the selected timing strategy will not be compatible with any available organizational form. For example, a shower strategy assumes that markets will be entered within the shortest possible time-frame. However, if a time-consuming establishment of subsidiaries is necessary, it is questionable as to whether a shower strategy can really be implemented in the new markets.

(9) Finally, the individual marketing instruments reveal their own interdependencies. In particular, the standardization/differentiation decisions that were discussed separately in Chapter 5, are in fact reciprocally independent. Irrespective of what marketing instrument (for standardization) is chosen, this decision will inevitably create pressure to standardize other marketing instruments. This principle is illustrated by the following examples:

▸ An enterprise that has decided in favour of product standardization puts pressure on its own price-setting. Because standardized products create the basic conditions for arbitrage, the enterprise will then have difficulty in implementing differentiated prices.

▸ If an internationally standardized communications policy is to be used, this will create pressure to standardize products and pricing policy. An identical product 'promise' in various country markets provides less leeway for differentiated product or pricing policies.

▸ A unification of distribution policy influences the optimal level of standardization of other marketing instruments. If, for example, the same intermediary is used in several country markets, he or she will then press the manufacturer for identical prices and (standardized) products.

▸ Finally, the decision as to whether to exploit the differing willingness to pay in the various country markets, to practise international price differentiation, influences the degree of freedom in the areas of product, communications and distribution policy. This has a bearing, for example, on potential arbitrage processes. Furthermore, differentiated prices limit the level of standardization in communications policy, because differing prices may require differing communication messages and statements, and also other communications instruments. For distribution policy also, differentiated prices have an impact on the optimal level of standardization. The larger the price differences required by the manufacturer, the greater the pressure also to serve varying distribution channels.

In view of the many dependencies that prevail between the various aspects of (country-specific) 'going international' decision-making, a simultaneous planning process is necessary in order to take into account both established and new target markets.

7 Case Study: Cotel

'If Brazil wants to upgrade its telephone network to twenty-first century standards – and indeed it *must* do so in order to achieve its objectives – this is our big opportunity,' concluded Mr Brown, the CEO of Communication and Telecommunication Inc. (Cotel) at the meeting of the company's Strategic Planning Commission on 25 March 1999. 'As you know, only once in fifteen to twenty years do we get a strategic window of opportunity like this, where an entire country wants to install a new telephone system. Not since the beginning of the 80s, have we had such an opportunity. If we aren't there right from the start of the network development and participating in decision-making for a particular system, we lose the market for the next few years. Certainly the Brazilians will decide in favour of two or three suppliers to avoid being dependent on just one. But these companies will then settle things among themselves for quite some time.'

For this reason, Mr Brown had asked his departmental heads to present, at the next planning-commission meeting, the documents needed to develop a strategy. He appointed Mr Smith and Mr Gerstner as the responsible co-ordinators.

Cotel has been part of telecommunications since the beginnings of the industry. In the past, it has been responsible for some major, trend-setting technological developments, which have earned it a reputation as a technologically outstanding enterprise. Cotel has always been particularly proud of its illustrious past and developmental role in the telecommunications industry.

The Historical Development of Telecommunication Networks

The age of electronic communication systems began in 1833 with the needle telegraphic machines of Friedrich Gauss and Wilhelm Weber. Commercial telegraphic systems began with Samuel Finley Breese's Morse alphabet and David Hughes' printed telegraphic messages. These forerunners of telex machines remained operational from 1860 until 1930. In the second half of the nineteenth century, continental telegraph networks were established across national borders in Europe and America. As early as 1858, an undersea cable was laid, although it remained operational for only a few weeks. In 1869, a transatlantic cable finally established a lasting link between Europe and America. In the same year, the telegraphic link between London and Calcutta truly ushered in the age of the global communications network.

Individual communication began in 1876, with the patenting of Alexander Graham Bell's telephone. An irony of fate: on 14 February 1876, only two hours after Bell, Elisha Gray patented a similar telephone. Both inventions were based on technology which enabled the conversion of sound waves into electronic impulses, which could then in turn be converted back into sound waves. Three scientists played particularly critical roles in the paving the way for telephonic communication – Page (1837), Bourseul (1854) and Reis (1861). In October 1877, information about the Bell telephone reached Europe through a publication. Experiences with the telephone were so positive that the invention soon became popular. In America, the first hand-operated long-distance telephone installation was opened in New Haven in 1877. In England, a similar installation emerged in 1879 and also developed rapidly. While in America and England, private telephone companies were responsible for establishing and operating long-distance installations, in Germany, the law that guaranteed a state monopoly for telegraphic communication was applied also to telephone communication.

Telephone users were linked to a switchboard in a star-like formation. Initially, every telephone had its own battery to feed the microphone and a handle to generate current for the call. By rotating the handle, the caller could contact the switchboard: the current would activate a magnetic 'calling key' which alerted the switchboard operators. The operator then connected the caller with the person being called, through linking a plug from the caller into a socket relating to the other party. A request for a link to a participant in the local network would take place through the switchboard operator, who placed the plug linked to the caller into the socket linked to the appropriate person being called. The operator then placed the calling key in the resting position to conclude the switchboard operation and the two participants were connected. Because the second participant was as yet unaware of being called, the caller would have to activate the inductor again, so that the recipient's appliance would ring. Neither the calling key of the caller nor that of the recipient would ring at the switchboard, because the relevant connection had been severed mechanically. It was not therefore possible to monitor if the call actually took place or when it ended. Because the costs and servicing of the local batteries proved too expensive, they were later replaced by a central battery at the switchboard. In large cities, exchanges with 10,000 participants and 50 operator places were installed. Approximately 150,000 calls were connected each day.

By 1879, the Americans Conolly and McTighe had already applied for a patent for an automatic exchange. However, it was only the invention of Almon B. Strowger that provided the necessary technological breakthrough. Further developments from Strowger and his son, as well as from the telephone technicians Keith and Ericsson culminated in the 'Strowger caller'. The first exchange went into operation in 1892 in La Porte, Indiana. The dial developed in 1896 by Ericsson enabled the caller to operate directly through a circuit breaker. This meant that participants were independent of operators in their local area. Telephones remained essentially unchanged until the introduction of push-button phones and electronic components between 1960 and 1970.

The electronic age began with the development of the transistor by John Bardeen, Walter H. Bratthain and William Shockley. In 1965, the first electronic switching system (ESS No.1) was introduced in the USA. The ESS No. 101 system was the first local exchange system with amplitude-modulated multiple switching through pulse amplitude modulation. The ESS No. 4 system was the first longdistance switching system with pulse-code modulated multiple switching.

Subsequently, the EWSA system (analogue electronic dialling system) was introduced, and in 1985, the system operating at the time of writing, the local and long-distance electronic dialling system (EWSD), as well as the System Alcatel 1000 S12 by the firm Alcatel. This entailed the installation of the digital 64 kbit/s network ISDN (Integrated Services Digital Network), which has become the standard system since 1989.

Cotel: Background to the Company

Cotel is an internationally-active telephone manufacturer which plans, develops and markets public exchanges and local networks. In terms of the international market, Cotel is a highly-rated company, which competes keenly with its major rivals such as:

▸ Western Electric, USA
▸ Alcatel, USA
▸ Ericsson, Sweden
▸ Nortel, United Kingdom
▸ NEC, Japan
▸ Philips, Netherlands
▸ Siemens, Germany
▸ Thompson, France

With EWSA and EWSD, Cotel has two quite different exchange systems on the market, and the older EWSA is still in common use:

▸ EWSA Technology (analogue electronic dialling system)

The EWSA is in fact a semi-electronic system which uses an ultra-rapid mini-relay as its main switching component. The major advantages of the EWSA are speed, reliability and low maintenance. Through its compact design, a minimum of building space is utilized.

EWSA technology has been installed in many countries, but has often been replaced by the newer, digital EWSD technology because of increasing communicational demands from both private households and industry. Cotel has an excellent market base and reputation, particularly in Europe, because of the wide use of its EWSA systems (see Table 7.1).

EWSD Technology

Cotel developed and introduced this technology in the 1980s and has improved it consistently since then. Because of the many innovations relating to this technology, Cotel regards it as being fully competitive well into the twenty-first century. In the context of the deregulation of telecommunications markets, Cotel has been able to expand its market shares considerably with digital technology. Although the German and British market were 'conquered' only a few months later than the USA

Table 7.1 Financial data for EWSD technology, 1999

Financial data, 1999 (adjusted for inflation)	USA	Great Britain	Germany
Sales (000s US$)	2,373,200	295,690	507,892
Fixed costs (000s US$)	1,220,146	65,012	98,041
Variable costs per unit	428	354	329
Number of units sold	3,400,000	597,354	1,067,000

Table 7.2 **Forecast statistics for EWS technology for 2008**

Forecasts for 2008 (adjusted for inflation)	USA	Great Britain	Germany
Sales (000s US$)	3,685,507	459,197	788,740
Fixed costs (000s US$)	730,546	38,925	58,701
Variable costs per unit	315	261	242
Number of units sold	8,818,724	1,549,382	2,767,523

market, because of the particularly high R&D costs (included in the fixed costs for the USA in 1999) and the high annual fixed costs, it was not possible to amortize the EWSD technology immediately. EWSA and EWSD technology are not compatible.

The Internet euphoria in the USA and in many European states has forced telecommunications equipment providers to cope with ever-increasing demands. Conservative estimates suggest that the consequent market growth for EWSD could develop as shown in Table 7.2 (estimates for 2008).

Independently of the technology, a telephone system (network) generally encompasses several installations that operate in unison (see Figure 7.1). At the lowest level of the system are the final communication points (FCPs), between which no *direct* communication occurs.

Figure 7.1 **The components of a telephone system**

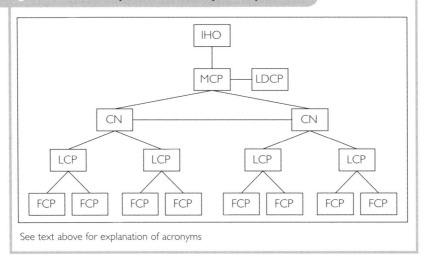

See text above for explanation of acronyms

This always occurs through the local communications points (LCPs), which in turn can be linked through communication nodes (CNs). Direct communication is possible between the CNs and between the main communication points (MCPs), and in some cases also through the long-distance communication points (LDCPs), at which there is a manual linkage of calls. The international head offices (IHOs) are the superordinate units of a national telephone system.

The Brazilian Market Segment

Brazil has always been an important market for Cotel, which even participated in setting up the first manual exchange there in 1889. In the 1980s Cotel participated with Alcatel, Ericsson, Siemens and Nortel in a major telephone system development plan with the objective of establishing national production sites. However, at the end of the run-up phase, in which direct deliveries were made from the USA, the national installation of EWSA technology was discontinued, because of the prevailing political situation, technical compatibility problems and various other factors. None the less, the Brazilian market continued to be regarded as interesting. National developments were observed keenly, and Cotel still received orders from rural areas.

In 1997, when Brazil conceived a new telephone development plan to co-ordinate the still strongly decentralised telephone system, and to monitor the 'catching up' process as well as the future development of local manufacturing, Cotel management was unanimously in favour of participating from the start. This opinion was confirmed retrospectively, after the Brazilian plans were formalized at the end of 1997 with the founding of Telebras, which, as a central holding, reduced the previous number of approximately 800 business units to one per province.

On the basis of this development, a large number of orders was expected, so there would be a good chance of entering the market alongside the firms already operating there. However, the potential market entry would be subject to two conditions:

▸ the Brazilians demand a high proportion of locally-manufactured components; and
▸ it is necessary to adapt to the prevailing price level in the country and to operate with Brazilian currency.

In view of the anticipated orders, the key question arose as to whether Cotel should indeed establish a local manufacturing facility.

However, even if they did so, it would take 2–3 years to become fully functional.

Some Cotel managers were determined to enter the Brazilian market in order to use it as a platform for further penetration of the South American region. However, other managers held diametrically opposing views. Thus, at the beginning of 1998, a market study was undertaken in order to predict the market volume in Brazil and determine the level of country risk. There were also concerns as to how to beat the competition, and to where competitive advantages could be achieved in the future.

Mr Smith presented the results of this analysis in a paper, reproduced below.

Analysis of the Brazilian Market – late 1997/ early 1998

Market Growth

There are currently about 2.3 million telephone units in Brazil. On average, the investment per unit is around US$325. The first draft of Telebras's telephone development plan envisages an increase to about 20 million units within nine years. This plan is based on gross national product (GNP) and population-growth statistics, according to which Brazil should achieve an international standard of telephone-network density by 2008. Not surprisingly, the country strives towards the calibre of system as utilized in the leading industrial nations.

These considerations were supported by an investigation in the *Telecommunication Journal,* which indicated that network density correlates strongly with GDP, *and* that strong GDP growth can be expected in Brazil (see Figure 7.2). In the past, Brazil has proved that such ambitious goals are achievable (for example, in energy provision, petrochemicals, street construction and transport technology).

Economic viability estimates for potential direct investment in Brazil are shown in Table 7.3. (The projections for the Brazilian development plan were based on an internal organizational estimate. Discrepancies between this calculation and calculations based on GDP or trend-extrapolations are thus unavoidable.)

The most recent Letter of Intent (LoI) contained the following numbers of telephone units provided during 1997 by the various competitors:

Ericsson	750,000
Alcatel	450,000
NEC	240,000
Cotel	180,000
Nortel	30,000

The statistics make it quite clear that, in 1997, Telebras favoured Ericsson and Alcatel with orders of 1,200,000 units in total. This is partly attributable to the fact that both suppliers are already operational in the country. The sales-planning department of Cotel believes that product quality was not the issue, because Cotel's products are in fact better than those of the competition. However, Telebras criticized Cotel for not remaining in the country, and thus not participating in the process of technical adaptation. This also applied to NEC, but this company had assured Telebras that these problems would be overcome by a new factory they had established in Brazil.

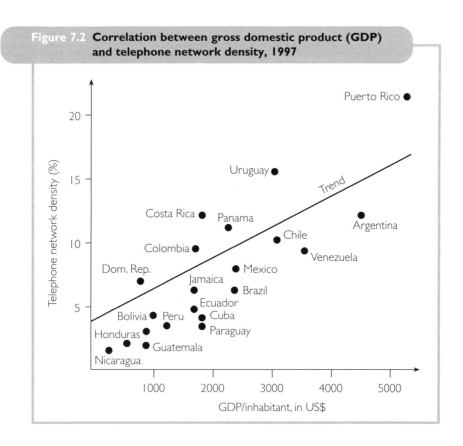

Figure 7.2 **Correlation between gross domestic product (GDP) and telephone network density, 1997**

Table 7.3 Local manufacturing project, Brazil

Financial data (000s US$) (adjusted for inflation)	2000	2001	2002	2003	2004	2005	2006	2007	2008
Revenues	65,000	81,536	91,320	102,279	114,552	128,298	143,694	351,762	428,350
Expenses for current assets	60,400	50,100	40,910	13,100	8,900	7,100	6,975	5,100	4,185
Fixed assets	37,400	35,400	30,435	15,120	16,200	17,400	18,200	19,400	23,715
Operational expenses	92,600	96,304	104,008	112,329	121,315	131,021	141,502	298,700	362,450

Was this perhaps the reason why NEC was to receive larger orders than Cotel? Or was it the lower prices from the Japanese that mattered? With the prevailing price level and volume of demand, Cotel could not afford to build its own 'organization on the spot'. Its own product development, sales, service and assembly organization would require a substantial commitment in terms of personnel and training. Furthermore, intensive support from Cotel USA with respect to the new EWSD technology would be necessary. While the Brazilian labour market offered an abundance of unskilled labour, skilled people were in short supply.

Cotel discovered that Telebras had made it a condition that Nortel was to provide a quality guarantee because of poor-quality deliveries in the past. Furthermore, it was known that the Brazilians had made it clear to the British Telebras was not satisfied with the service they were receiving. Spare-parts deliveries were often unsatisfactory and frequently had to be imported, putting foreign exchange reserves under stress.

The percentages of EWSA telephone units installed at the time of writing by the various firms are as follows:

Ericsson	45%
Alcatel	35%
Nortel	10%
Cotel	8%
NEC	1%
Philips	1%

The objective of Cotel's sales planning is to achieve a rising annual delivery quantity up to approximately 1,318,000 units by 2008.

Country Risk

The sales-planning department is of the opinion that political risk in Brazil is not substantial. In fact, they are convinced that Brazil is one of the most stable countries in South America. With respect to *economic* risk however, there *are* problems, particularly with respect to sub-contracting.

The Brazilian currency is highly unstable, so currency risk is substantial. Furthermore, the Brazilians tend to be heavy-handed with import tariffs. Changes of 30 per cent cannot be excluded, and at the time of writing, tariffs are running at 70 per cent of delivery value for imports from the USA. Also, bureaucratic delays caused by the

Brazilian authorities lead to stock accumulations in the USA. This causes assembly delays and may lead to punitive tariffs.

The Relevant Competitive Situation

Figure 7.3 shows the market shares of Cotel and its main competitors as of 1999, and the basic situation with respect to these is as follows.

Ericsson

Undaunted by any potential problems, the company plans to invest in factory capacity (local and long-distance) with the objective of achieving 1.1 million units annually, by the end of 1999. Ericsson holds back, however, on the latest technology which is in principle available in Sweden, and offers Brazil analogue EWSA technology. The results for the second half of 1998 were negative, with a –21 per cent return on investment. It is a joint stock company with a 26 per cent Brazilian holding. The pricing is favourable through minimal tariffs because of the high local manufacturing content. The company has an extensive and competent sales, service and assembly team on the spot.

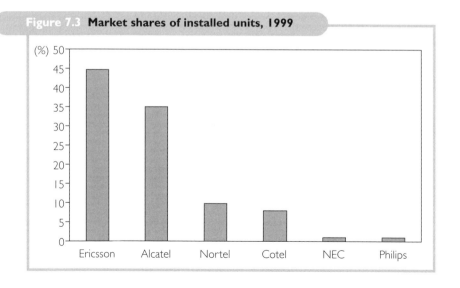

Figure 7.3 **Market shares of installed units, 1999**

Alcatel

Has similarly negative results. Negotiations over Brazilian capital participation are stagnating and nothing definite is known about the possible construction of a new factory. Alcatel has so far been very expensive. It also delivers EWSA technology and, as with Ericsson, the mother company does have newer technology available. Alcatel has its own manufacturing, sales, service and assembly capacity in the form of a wholly-owned subsidiary.

NEC

The new factory will be operational soon. The quantitative situation is similar to that of Cotel and the attainable price does not cover costs. It is difficult, therefore, to understand why NEC insists on being a 'cheap' supplier. NEC has an extensive sales and service organization in Brazil and offers high-quality goods. The company has both EWSA and EWSD technology, but will probably offer EWSD to Telebras.

Philips

According to the latest plans, Philips to be considered again as a supplier. Because the 'ancient technology' will no longer be allowed after the end of 1999, difficulties are likely to occur. Apparently manufactures in Recife, but whether the new technology can be manufactured there is questionable.

Nortel

Continually declining in significance and has no clear strategy or vision. The company experiences problems with quality, service, delivery and price.

Cotel

Cotel offers the new EWSD system with a more advanced technology than that of Ericsson and Alcatel, and is far ahead of Nortel. It is more expensive than NEC, partly because of the lack of local production. It is not present 'on the spot' and thus has no sales, service or assembly team in Brazil.

On the basis of this report, there were mixed views at Cotel as to the appropriate strategy. Mr Gerstner believed the best approach was to 'wait and see' if the planned and anticipated increases in demand really materialised. If this turned out to be the case, *then* they could 'go all the way' and set up a manufacturing facility with sales, service and assembly personnel. He summed it up as follows: 'If the market really grows, we'll certainly earn a decent rate of return on our direct investment. But if Telebras slows down the process, we'll be stuck with our investment.'

Mr Smith expressed a different view: 'Mr Gerstner, if we wait too long, our competitors will already have the orders, and once Telebras has decided on a particular system, we won't stand a chance. Furthermore, it would be some time before our "organization on the spot" was able to strike back quickly and powerfully. I believe, therefore, we need to make a decision as to whether to continue delivering from the USA, or to manufacture locally. If we consider that our new technology has so far only been installed in Germany and Great Britain, it's clear that we are a long way from amortizing our investments. Furthermore, I have heard from a reliable source, that not only Brazil, but also Argentina and Peru, want to update their telephone systems. Therefore, I have had market and economic feasibility studies prepared for these countries as well, with respect to potential direct investment in the new EWSD technology.'

Market Analysis for Argentina

Argentina has approximately 36 million inhabitants. It borders Bolivia and Paraguay in the north and, extending from the north-west to the east, Peru, Brazil and the Atlantic Ocean. Chile is the western neighbouring state. Argentina can be divided geographically into three large regions – mountain, highland and plains. With a telephone density of just over ten connections per hundred inhabitants, Argentina is an undeveloped market compared to the industrialized nations.

Market Analysis for Peru

Peru has a population of about 24 million, with a density of roughly eighteen inhabitants per square kilometre. Approximately half the population lives in the coastal lowlands (forty-five inhabitants/km^2); 40 per cent in the mountainous region; and about 10 per cent in the Amazon lowland (two inhabitants/km^2).

Up to the time of writing, Peru has a telephone density of fewer than three connections per hundred inhabitants, and is thus one of the least telephonically connected countries in South America. In the past, Cotel has not taken this market seriously and left it entirely to the competition.

Summary Evaluation of Argentina and Peru

In a similar manner to Telebras in Brazil, the state-controlled telephone companies of Argentina and Peru will be completely refurbishing their run-down and outdated networks. Because of their economic relationship with Brazil, both countries have behaved very opportunistically in recent years with respect to economic and political decisions (taxes, tariffs, transport technology, currency). Consequently, it can be assumed that they will proceed with their telephone-system modernization in a similar manner to Telebras. Experts reckon that Argentina's modernization will occur as early as 2002, Peru in 2004 and that no direct investment will be expected from the companies (see Table 7.4).

After Mr Smith had explained the reports, he emphasized once again that, for a possible Brazil entry, it was critical to bear in mind that the high research and development costs for the manufacture of a new telephone system such as EWSD demanded high turnover in order to be economically viable: 'System production is a high-risk business. We need incredibly high sales to cover the initial costs of developing a new system at the prevailing international price level. We have to think in quantitative terms, and all the more so because technological process is becoming ever more rapid.'

Mr Brown wanted to evaluate the studies as quickly as possible and therefore set up, for the following month, a meeting of Cotel's management at which a decision would be made.

Questions in the Case of Cotel

During the meeting of the Strategic Planning Commission, it became clear to Mr Brown that Mr Gerstner was against direct investment in Brazil. In contrast, Mr Smith would presumably attempt to bring about a decision in favour of direct investment.

Table 7.4 Estimated payments for Argentina and Peru until 2008, in 000s US$

	2002	2003	2004	2005	2006	2007	2008
Revenues							
Argentina	68,000	94,683	111,726	131,837	155,568	157,288	113,016
Peru	109,000	122,472	129,821	190,642	122,042		
Expenses							
Current assets for Argentina	3,283	3,783	4,183	4,476	4,789	5,124	5,347
Current assets for Peru	2,876	3,050	3,202	3,362	4,209		
Operational expenses Argentina	10,212	11,744	13,506	15,532	17,861	51,336	79,152
Operational expenses Peru	10,123	11,135	12,249	46,574	93,068		

With respect to making a decision, he did not want to rely exclusively on the scepticism of Mr Gerstner, or on the euphoria of Mr Smith. He wanted answers to the following questions:

1 Which interdependencies (supplier-based, demand-based and/or competition-based) must be taken into account with regard to the decisions about future activity in Brazil?
2 Prepare an economic feasibility study, on the basis of which Cotel could make a decision about possible business plans in Brazil.
3 From your calculations, make a specific recommendation.
4 Analyse *critically*, the premises (in 2) that form the basis for the recommendations.

Co-ordination Decisions in the Context of 'Being International'

8 Co-ordination Problems and the Dynamics of Country Markets

If an international enterprise has completed the internationalization process and is present in all target markets, it could be assumed that, initially, no further co-ordination decisions will be necessary. That is, there will be no further major tasks within the field of international marketing: it would seem that, in the context of 'going international', the firm would have its marketing strategies and measures so well in place in the foreign markets that these would correspond optimally to feedback between the markets.

In the context of ongoing market operations – that is, 'being international' – there are no co-ordination problems, if no changes in interdependencies occur between the markets over time. In this situation there will be no additional need for co-ordination between the country markets.

In practice, this case is a theoretical extreme and will rarely, if ever, occur. In fact, firms are generally confronted with constantly changing market conditions, which demand ongoing co-ordination of activities in the various country markets. *Country market dynamics* are thus decisive for the tasks of international marketing in the 'being international' phase, and these require constant attention (see Usunier, 2000, p. 56 on the meaning of dynamics in international marketing). Each time the nature and degree of interdependence between two target markets changes, a new co-ordination problem arises in international marketing. In this sense, the feedback-related dynamics of country markets are the decisive instigator of ongoing co-ordination problems. Four levels of market change that are relevant to co-ordination can be distinguished (see Figure 8.1).

Changes which have an impact on country market co-ordination may derive indirectly from institutional (environmental) conditions or directly from changes in market transaction partners and their relationships to one another. Both aspects will be considered below.

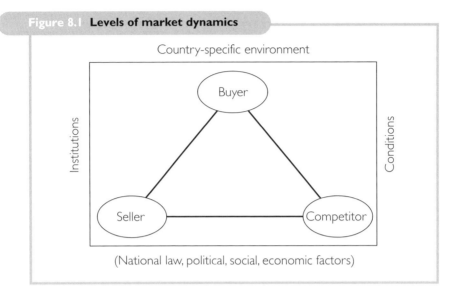

Figure 8.1 Levels of market dynamics

Country-specific environment

Institutions

Conditions

Buyer

Seller

Competitor

(National law, political, social, economic factors)

Changes in Institutional (Environmental) Conditions

The environmental framework in which market operations take place is frequently exposed to rapid and quite dramatic change. Changes in such elements as the law, politics, and social or economic factors are relevant to marketing and change the structure and nature of competition. With respect to interdependence between country markets, whether or not such changes are limited to individual country markets (country-specific change) or to several countries simultaneously (international changes), is of particular relevance.

It is always necessary to consider whether country-specific changes do in fact have ramifications for international co-ordination. In this respect, changes in individual country markets will create independencies in terms of other country markets. Both possibilities are conceivable, as the following examples show:

▶ In Country A, a cigarette manufacturer has so far only advertised by means of a country-specific communications strategy on TV and in print media. Country A now prohibits cigarette advertising in all media. The national marketing strategy needs to react to this (national marketing problem), but this environmental change does not *necessarily* have an impact on the market presence in other country markets.

▸ Country B has so far only allowed foreign firms market entry at all if they manufacture in the country and thus provide a certain share of value added. (The USA and UK have such regulations in the auto-mobile industry and Japanese manufacturers have to comply with specific value-added quotas. As a result, some of these manufactur-ers have established factories in these countries.) We now assume that the legal framework has been changed appropriately, so that direct export is also possible. This enables a seller to produce goods elsewhere for Country B. This is achieved through a centralization of production in order to achieve higher economies of scale. The resulting change in the cost situation affects all country markets supplied from this location, not only Country B (seller-related feed-back).

Country-specific changes in environmental conditions need not, therefore, lead to co-ordination challenges in every case. The situation is quite different for changes in *international environmental conditions*, however, which invariably cause integration problems. These constantly occurring co-ordination problems can be attributed to the fact that in this case, several countries are affected simultaneously.

Ohmae (1996) sees the causes of such international or country-specific changes in institutional environmental conditions in the fact that the borders of many national states do not coincide with natural economic or cultural regions. Against this background, Ohmae predicted the end of many nation states and the development of so-called regional states. These would encompass fundamental economic and cultural regions comprising either parts of individual national states or combinations of more than one country:

The glue holding traditional nation states together, at least in economic terms, has begun to dissolve. Buffeted by sudden changes in industry dynamics, available information, consumer preferences, and flows of capital; burdened by demands for the civil minimum and for open-ended subsidies in the name of the national interest; and hog-tied by political systems that prove ever-less responsive to new challenges, these political aggregations no longer make compelling sense as discrete, meaningful units on an up-to-date map of economic activity. They are still there, of course, still major players on the world stage. But they have, for the most part, lost the ability to put global logic first in the decisions they make . . . By contrast, the territorial dividing lines that do make sense belong to what I call 'region states' . . . In a borderless world, these are the natural economic zones. Though limited in geographical size, they are often huge in their economic influence . . . These region states may or may not fall within the borders of a particular nation. Whether they do is purely an accident of history. (Ohmae, 1996, pp. 79–81)

If one follows through Ohmae's predictions about the decline of national states and emergence of so-called 'regional states', two clear strands of change can be distinguished:

▶ regional states evolve through the joining of individual national states, if the traditional formation of states is located within a unitary 'natural' economic and cultural region; and
▶ regional states evolve through the division of individual national states, if the observed national state emerged through the 'artificial' fusion of various economic and cultural regions.

Heterogenization and *homogenization* are thus two manifest forms of change in institutional environmental conditions (see Figure 8.2). Homogenization includes all forms of international unification of legal bases for marketing or political, social and economic factors ('formation of regional states through the fusion of individual national states')

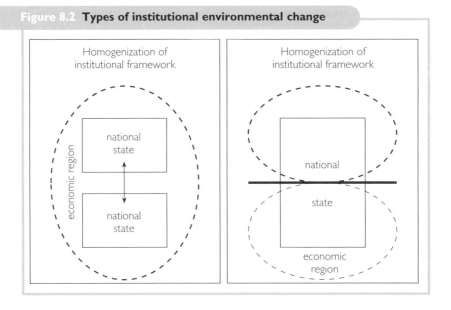

Figure 8.2 Types of institutional environmental change

and by heterogenization, all forms of breaking up of formerly unified regions ('formation of region states through splitting up former national states').

Homogenization of Institutional Environmental Conditions

Stages of Homogenization

In international markets, the homogenization of environmental conditions is a familiar and increasingly prevalent phenomenon (Hill, 1996, p. 7) which aims to eliminate hindrances to economic exchange processes either completely or at least in part. Depending on the targeted depth of integration and the level currently prevailing, various different levels of environmental homogenization can be distinguished. In this context El-Agraa (1989, p. 151) differentiates between the following levels of integration:

▶ Preferential trade zone
  Preferential trade zones refer to the lowest level of integration between country markets, when two or more countries have a bilateral or multilateral agreement so as to give preference to trade in particular goods (for example, low tariffs or higher import or export quotas than for other goods).
▶ Free trade area
  While the preferential conditions in a preference zone generally relate to specific goods only, a *free trade zone* generally includes the sum total of foreign trade. The member states commit to removing barriers to trade as much as possible and thus to guaranteeing free trade. However, member states often do not have a consistent trade policy with respect to non-member states, so that differing external tariffs still prevail. In order to prevent non-member states from exploiting these differing external tariffs by exporting goods to the member state with the lower external tariffs and transferring them tariff-free from there, free trade zones control the flow of goods, through, for example, certificates of origin.
▶ Customs union
  Apart form eradicating internal trade barriers, a customs union is characterized by a unitary external tariff among the member states. By so doing, controls on the flow of goods as are typical for free trade zones, become superfluous.

▸ Common market
In contrast to preferential trade zones, free trade areas and customs unions, where the elimination of barriers to trade is limited to trade in goods, a *common market* also ensures the unlimited mobility of factors of production (freedom to establish a business enterprise, uninhibited right to work and the free movement of capital).

▸ Economic and currency union
If, alongside free trade and the completely free movement of factors of production, economic union also harmonizes all other areas of economic policy. In this context El-Agraa (1989) discusses an intermediate phase of a common 'market order', in which economic policy focuses purely on specific markets. The complete harmonization effected in an economic union, extends simultaneously to competitive, social, fiscal, monetary, employment, growth, transport and industrial policy. As a rule, an economic union also entails a *currency union*, because a common economic policy is based on fixed parities between its currencies, as well as completely free convertibility of the currencies of its members. Because of the ease with which it can be implemented politically, in comparison to an economic union, El-Agraa (1989) believes that a currency union can be a prerequisite to economic union.

▸ Complete political integration
The highest level of integration is achieved when all economic-policy decision-making and administrative functions rest with a supranational authority, which ensures that diverging policies are impossible.

Homogenization Tendencies in Practice

Soon after the end of the Second World War, the first attempts at integrated international trade emerged in the context of GATT (General Agreement on Tariffs and Trade), now called the WTO (World Trade Organization) already showed signs of homogenization (see Figure 8.3). The UNO (United Nations Organization) and the OECD (Organization for Economic Co-operation and Development) played a significant role in this process. As early as 1951, the Federal Republic of Germany, Belgium, France, Italy, Luxembourg and the Netherlands formed the European Coal and Steel Union, which was to be extended through the 1957 Treaty of Rome in particular. The objective of the European nations was to overcome relatively small national markets.

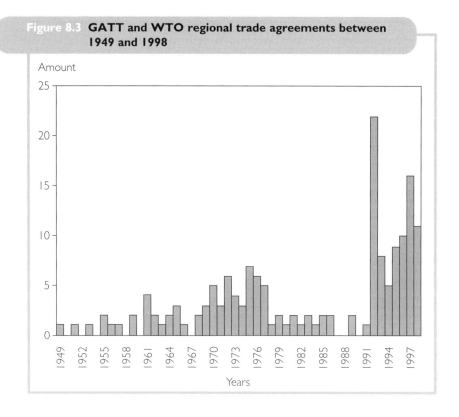

Figure 8.3 **GATT and WTO regional trade agreements between 1949 and 1998**

Although the European 'idea' was already imitated in other parts of the world even in the 1950s and 1960s, the alliances so created achieved little more than the status of loose arrangements, generally preferential trade zones. The basic problem is the fact the formation of trade agreements is generally plagued by difficulties in dismantling the following barriers:

▸ physical;
▸ administrative
▸ fiscal (tax); and
▸ technical.

Physical barriers arise through the differing infrastructures and level of development of the various member states as well as through other such constrictions on trade as border controls. In the first instance, *administrative barriers* refer to all attempts made by countries to protect their local markets though quotas or other methods of promoting local industry. Administrative barriers may or may not be legalized and thus can form part of actual administrative regulations or exist merely in the informal way in which a country behaves towards others. *Fiscal barriers* derive from differing taxation systems in the individual member states, while *technical barriers* include various product-related requirements with which products have to comply.

The removal of technical barriers is a difficult but most important problem, because they provide a very strong hindrance to cross-border trade. To categorize technical barriers and the differing rules and regulations on which they are based, de Zoeten (1993) developed a typology of the basic alternatives (see Figure 8.4) which can initially be distinguished one from another in terms of whether common technical regulations apply or not. The first attempt can thus be made to unify such regulations. A distinction must be made here between 'dual-regulation approaches' and complete 'legal consistency'. The particular characteristic of the dual regulation approach is that national regulations can exist alongside the planned common technical regulations. Accordingly, there will be a further differentiation as to whether some of the common regulations supersede and override the previous national regulations to

Figure 8.4 Basic options for eradicating technical barriers

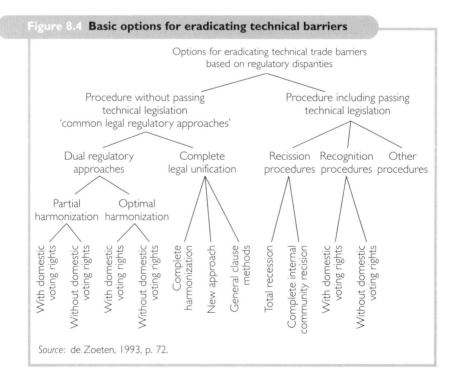

Source: de Zoeten, 1993, p. 72.

create a 'partial harmonization', or whether importers will have some degree of choice between the two sets of regulations, depending on the specific situation (case-by-case). For both partial or optional harmonization, enterprises can have a so-called 'domestic choice of laws'.

In contrast, 'complete legal unification' replaces national laws comprehensively, although even here, depending on the level of detail of common law, some case-by-case differentiation is still possible. With 'complete harmonization', technical requirements are formulated in detail, for the 'general clause method', with respect to private norms, and for the 'new approach', without reference to private norms. The latter two have a lower level of regulatory intensity.

Apart from these approaches, which assume the application of technical regulations for the community, there is also a second general possibility, namely dispensing altogether with the formulation of common technical regulations. With a cassation procedure, the desired dismantling of technical standards is achieved by removing all national regulations for the area in question and without any alternative regulation. If this applies only to enterprises from member states, de Zoeten (1993, p. 75) refers to this as 'complete internal cassation', whereas 'total cassation' refers to a situation which also applies to sellers from non-member states. In contrast to cassation processes, recognition processes do not entail a general relinquishing of regulations. National regulations remain valid, but their area of application changes. Because, for this process, each member state accepts the regulations of all other member states, it is sufficient for trade within the community if sellers satisfy the technical requirements of a member state, generally that of the country of origin.

Because, each of the basic options changes (in various ways), the competitive situation of firms in the planned common market, there are 'winners and losers'. Consequently, the necessary agreement constitutes a major political problem, which may conflict fundamentally with the formation of common markets.

Only since the end of the 1980s, can trends be observed to implement higher levels of integration. Interestingly, the motives of the participating states vary considerably, depending on the particular level of economic development. Since the 1980s, many industrial nations have faced saturated domestic markets. They therefore attempt to open up new markets for their products by initiating trade agreements. On the other hand, it is precisely this economic power that the developing countries fear. Therefore, many see the solution as joining

Figure 8.5 Integration tendencies outside Europe

Regional integration agreements

Name	Members	Date of entry into effect
North America		
NAFTA (North American Free Trade Agreement)	Canada, Mexico, United States	1 January 1994
FTAA (Free Trade Area of the Americas)	Canada, United States, all Latin American countries apart from Cuba	December 1994
APEC (Asia Pacific Economic Cooperation)	Australia, Brunei, Canada, Chile, China, Hong Kong, Indonesia, Japan, Korea, Malaysia, Mexico, New Zealand, Papua New Guinea, the Philippines, Singapore, Taiwan, Thailand, and the United States	January 1989
Latin America		
CACM (Central American Common Market)	Costa Rica, El Salvador, Guatemala, Honduras and Nicaragua. Panama is not formally a member, but has limited bilateral preferential agreements with individual members of CACM	1960
Andean Pact	Bolivia, Colombia, Ecuador, Peru and Venezuela	1969
LAFTA (Latin American Free Trade Area)	Argentina, Bolivia, Brazil, Chile, Colombia, Ecuador, Mexico, Paraguay, Peru, Uruguay and Venezuela	1960
CARICOM (Caribbean Community and Common Market)	Antigua and Barbuda, Bahamas, Barbados, Belize, Dominica, Grenada, Guyana, Jamaica, Monserrat, St. Kitts and Nevis, St. Lucia, St. Vincent and Grenadines, Trinidad and Tobago	July 1973
ACS (Association of Caribbean States)	37 Caribbean Basin and Central American states, including those belonging to CARICOM), Colombia, Mexico and Venezuela	July 1994
G3 (Group of Three)	Colombia, Mexico and Venezuela	June 1994
MERCOSUR (Common Market of the South)	Argentina, Brazil, Paraguay and Uruguay. Chile and Bolivia became associate members of MERCOSUR in October and December 1996, respectively	March 1991
Asia, Middle East and North Africa		
ASEAN (Association of South East Asian Nations)	Brunei (since 1984), Indonesia, Laos (since July 1997), Myanmar (since July 1997) Malaysia, the Philippines, Singapore, Thailand and Vietnam (since July 1995)	August 1967

Figure 8.5 *continued*

Regional integration agreements

Name	Members	Date of entry into effect
Asia, Middle East and North Africa (*continued*)		
SAPTA (South Asian Preferential Trade Agreement)	Bangladesh, Bhutan, India, Maldives, Nepal, Pakistan and Sri Lanka	April 1993
GCC (Gulf Cooperation Council)	Bahrain, Kuwait, Oman, Qatar, Saudi Arabia, and the United Arab Emirates (UAE)	May 1981
Sub-Saharan Africa		
ECOWAS (Economic Community of West African States)	Benin, Burkina Faso, Cape Verde, Côte d'Ivoire, Gambia, Ghana, Guinea, Guinea Bissau, Liberia, Mali, Mauritania, Niger, Nigeria, Senegal, Sierra Leon and Togo	1975
UEMOA (Union Économique et Monétaire Ouest-Africaine)	Benin, Burkina Faso, Cote d'Ivoire, Mali, Mauritania, Niger, Senegal.; Guinea Bissau joined the group in May 1997	1973; changed name to UEMOA in 1994
COMESA (Common Market for Eastern and Southern Africa)	Angola, Burundi, Comoro, Djibuti, Ethiopia, Kenya, Lesotho, Malawi, Mauritius, Mozambique, Namibia, Rwanda, Sudan, Swaziland, Uganda, Tanzania, Zambia and Zimbabwe	1981
CEMAC (Communauté Économique et Monétaire d'Afrique Centrale)	Cameroon, Central African Republic (CAR), Chad, Congo, Gabon, Equatorial Guinea (since 1985)	1966
SADC (Southern African Development Community)	Angola, Botswana, Lesotho, Malawi, Mauritius (since 1995), Mozambique, Namibia, South Africa (since 1994), Tanzania, Zambia, Zimbabwe and Swaziland	1992
SACU	Southern African Customs Union	1910

Source: World Bank website, 5 August 2002.

forces with other developing countries in order to increase their political power. Figure 8.5 provides an overview of regional trade agreements outside Europe (see Altmann and Kulessa, 1998; Keegan 1999, p. 140).

Given the large number of regional trade agreements that are already in force and are being planned, this factor can be regarded as being of some significance for the future. It should be borne in mind that individual states are not obliged to be members of only one agreement. For example, in the past, the USA was the driving force behind NAFTA. However, this did not prevent the USA from developing ties with the Asia-Pacific trade alliance APEC, and more recently, from negotiating a transatlantic trade agreement with the Europeans. Also, even if the so-called TAFTA (Transatlantic Free Trade Area) is not regarded as being particularly likely to materialize (on TAFTA, see Schott and Oegg (2001)), the development none the less reveals the dynamic nature of trade agreements. This phenomenon of dynamics is, from a marketing perspective, of particular significance. The tendencies towards change, the converging markets and associated preference zones create a need for enterprises operating in such regions to adapt their marketing to such challenges.

Heterogenization of Institutional Environmental Conditions

The reverse of converging markets is the phenomenon of the institutional fragmentation of markets. 'Fragmenting markets' refers to the division of a market into several, legally independent market components. This process of splitting is accompanied by a heterogenization of formerly unified environmental conditions.

In cross-sectional observation, the phenomenon of 'market splitting' reveals various market stages. Accordingly, Figure 8.6 is divided into:

▸ the global market;
▸ regional markets; and
▸ individual country markets.

Fragmentation of the Global Market

Fragmentation can occur on a global scale. The global or world market can be understood as all currently existing markets, of which most joined the GATT after the Second World War. The objective of this tariff and trade agreement was, from the beginning, to establish internationally accepted rules for, and to liberalize, world trade (Hill 1996, p. 7). Because the successor to the GATT, the World Trade Organization (WTO), established on 1 January 1995, continued to

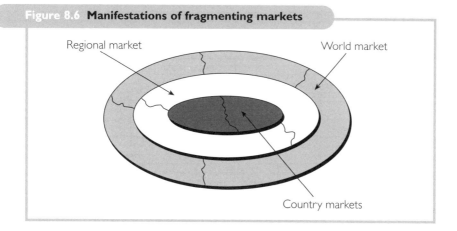

Figure 8.6 Manifestations of fragmenting markets

Regional market

World market

Country markets

pursue these goals, is organized in 120 countries and encompasses over 90 per cent of world trade, the GATT/WTO can be regarded as an attempt to create an integrated global market.

Although the declared goal of the WTO is to promote free trade, more recently some counter-tendencies have emerged (Jeannet and Hennessey, 1998, p. 42). Thus the USA, for example, an early protagonist of worldwide free trade, resorted increasingly towards protectionist tendencies in the 1990s because of chronic trade deficits. These tendencies included the pursuit of non-economic objectives.

The trade dispute between the USA and Japan has received particular attention in the past. Because of the rapidly-growing trade deficit with Japan in the second half of the 1990s, the US government has made serious attempts since 1993 to encourage Japan to open up its markets to American goods. Even though the Japanese government agreed to American demands in many respects, this did little to alter the practical difficulties that firms encountered in dealing with the Japanese market. The reasons lie in traditionally established structures of relationships between manufacturers and suppliers on the one side, and the intertwined distribution structures on the other hand. For this reason, the changes made at governmental level did little to reduce the sealed-off nature of the Japanese market, as expressed in the cartoon in Figure 8.7.

The objectives of the WTO have also been undermined by the regional integration tendencies discussed above. On the one hand, this has reduced the isolation or 'sealing off' of individual states and thus intensified international trade. On the other hand, however, such

Figure 8.7 **Caricature of the agreement made by the Japanese government in the trade dispute with the USA, 1994**

Source: Siems, 1994, p. 34.

regional integration tendencies have often impeded trade from non-member countries. For example, in the first half of the 1990s, the USA, in particular, constantly rebuked the European Union (EU) for becoming a 'Fortress Europe' that is protecting itself against external trade (Adam, 1993a and 1993b). Indeed, since its foundation, the EU *has* undertaken a variety of measures which place outsiders in a worse position than member states. This is demonstrated by the example below of the EU banana market regulations.

The Banana Market

Because of the necessary climatic conditions, the growing of bananas is limited to certain regions of the world. There are traditional banana farming regions in southern Europe (EU bananas), in Africa and the Caribbean, as well as in South America (dollar bananas).

Banana farming in various regions is, however, associated with various problems. EU banana farming is confronted mainly by geographic and climatic problems. In the agricultural regions of Portugal, Spain and the French overseas regions, the soil and climatic conditions are such that the bananas are both quantitatively and qualitatively poor. The African, Caribbean and Pacific states (ACP) have a similar fundamental problem. Added to this are geographic and climatic problems, which, from time to time, render agricultural production impossible. In contrast to the EU and ACP farming regions, the conditions in South America are generally far more favourable. Apart from the optimal climatic conditions, farming in Ecuador, Costa Rica, Colombia, Honduras and Panama is characterized most of all by large plantations which, because of lower wages and rationalized harvesting methods, have substantial production advantages over EU or ACP sellers. The European market share held by 'dollar' bananas was accordingly high in the past.

Total world production for 1991 amounted to 48 million tons, of which 20 per cent were for export. In view of the cost and quality advantages described above, it is not surprising that dollar bananas comprise 80 per cent of worldwide banana exports. In Europe as well, at the beginning of the 1990s, dollar bananas comprised a market share of approximately 66 per cent despite tariff protection (see Table 8.1). Furthermore, 35 per cent of the global demand for bananas

Table 8.1 EU banana imports, by region of origin, 1991 (per cent)

Member state imports	EU bananas	ACP bananas	Dollar bananas	Share Europe
Belgium/Luxembourg	–	0.6	99.4	5.6
Denmark	0.1	5.0	94.8	1.5
France	59.1	40.9	–	13.8
Germany	–	0.1	99.9	37.2
Greece	–	7.4	92.6	1.1
Netherlands	–	2.8	97.2	2.0
Republic of Ireland	–	3.6	96.1	1.2
Italy	–	11.1	88.9	14.3
Portugal	–	4.7	95.2	2.7
Spain	100.0	–	–	9.3
Great Britain	0.3	79.4	11.2	11.2
EU total	17.5	16.7	65.8	100.0

Source: Read, 1994.

comes from Europe, so it is the most important banana importer. As a result, the excessive weighting of dollar bananas constitutes a major problem for the banana-producing states of the EU.

The EU Banana Import Regime

For this reason, the Council of the European Union passed its Decree 404/93, the so-called 'Banana Import Regime'. It established a common market organization for bananas and banana-based products in terms of a consistent EU agricultural policy. Apart from quality and marketing norms, in which minimum standards were set for non-European bananas, with respect to length, diameter, curvature, consistency and susceptibility to damage, the Banana Import Regime served most of all to regulate (read: hamper) imports from non EU and non-ACP states through import tariffs and quotas. Depending on the prescribed quotas, the degree specified varying tariffs for dollar and (through a guaranteed import quantity, so-called non-traditional) ACP bananas. The tariff rates given in Table 8.2, led to a price rise of 20 per cent for dollar bananas to the extent that the quota was not exceeded (1995: a total of 2.2 million tons), and to an increase of 170 per cent where the quota was exceeded.

The Consequences of the Banana Market Ordinance

The banana market ordinance had various impacts in the EU member states. In countries such as France or Spain, in which dollar bananas were previously not allowed to be distributed, the introduction of contingents led to a reduction in the price level. Conversely, in countries such as Germany, the Netherlands or Denmark, where dollar bananas are common, the opposite effect could be observed. The tariff-induced price increase in dollar bananas, reduced the demand. All in all, the introduction of the EU banana ordinance led to a 30 per cent decline in demand.

Table 8.2 **Tariff rates for banana imports in the EU in 1995 (EU replaced by €)**

	Quantities imported within the quota	Quantities imported in excess of the quota
Dollar bananas	100 €/t	850 €/t
Non-traditional AKP bananas	0 €/t	750 €/t

The production and distribution of Latin-American bananas is dominated in the first instance by American (US) concerns. The price and quantity developments in Europe as a result of the EU banana market ordinance led to these concerns diverting freed up capacity to other markets. Apart from more intensive market operations in Eastern Europe, large quantities were diverted to the USA, the largest single market in the world, but the increased supply in the USA led inevitably to price declines there. Thus the sealing-off of the European market led to changed seller strategies in 'non-participating' country markets. Despite adaptation measures, producers and importers of dollar bananas could not avoid losses of several hundred million US dollars. For example, the American banana exporter, Chiquita Brands International, admitted to a profit decline in the 1990s of US$350 million as a result of the EU banana ordinance (Gersemann, 1999, p. 25).

Not least because of the massive political influence of the American concerns, in 1999, the US government threatened to place comprehensive punitive tariffs on exports from the EU. The goods potentially subject to these tariffs had a value of approximately US$520 billion (Hotze, 1999, p. 60; Dunkel and Gersemann, 1999, p. 30).

For one thing, the example of the EU banana market ordinance shows the protectionist tendencies that can emerge from regional alliances. In order to protect internal European enterprises, the EU accepted a trade war with America. The case also demonstrates the limited trade policy of the WTO. Despite being condemned four times by the WTO, the EU refused to withdraw the ordinance. Thus, it can be assumed that increasing regional integration in many parts of the world will fragment the global market.

The Fragmentation of Country Blocs

Just as individual countries can form joint economic units, such regional markets can also split up again. The most well-known example is the dissolution of COMECON in 1991.

Parallel to the integration efforts made by Western Europe in 1949 under pressure from the USSR, seven Eastern European States (USSR, Bulgaria, Hungary, Poland, Romania, Czechoslovakia and Albania) formed COMECON. Subsequently, the German Democratic Republic

(GDR) joined in 1950, the Mongolian People's Republic in 1962, Cuba in 1972 and Vietnam in 1978. From the start, the objective of the COMECON was to create a common market to ensure the supply of raw materials and a greater sales area for member states.

The dissolution of COMECON in June 1991, created major problems for the former members, also for those states which had been passive followers of the USSR. The comprehensive supply chain networks that had been developed proved to be particularly constraining. Through the dissolution of COMECON, this network collapsed, because previous suppliers withdrew from the market or required 'hard' currency, which was in short supply in all COMECON states. The breakdown in production was accelerated further by the fact that the remaining firms had to compete with the West and it was therefore extremely difficult to find buyers.

The Disintegration of Individual Country Markets

The disintegration of markets can also relate to individual country markets. Czechoslovakia, the USSR or Yugoslavia are good examples. Furthermore, this is not a phenomenon that occurs only in Central or Eastern Europe. The striving towards independence of the Canadian province of Quebec or of the Flemings in Belgium (Berschens, 1998), show quite clearly that disintegration tendencies also occur in other regions.

The main reason for the fragmenting of a national market lies in the 'artificial' grouping together of essentially autonomous economic regions or ethnically heterogeneous groups.

▸ Sometimes the tendency towards disintegration of different economic regions is caused by wealth gaps between them. For example, a major impetus for the efforts made by Flanders to achieve independence is the reluctance 'of the affluent Flemings to continue to support their poor Wallonian fellow citizens through taxation and welfare payments (Berschens, 1998, p. 51).

▸ There is an even greater disintegration potential if individual states have heterogeneous ethnic structures. The disintegration of the former Czechoslovakia was driven largely by the Slovakian population group, even though they profited quite considerably from the economically stronger entity of the former Czechoslovakian state.

Figure 8.8 Percentages of ethnic minorities in the states of south-eastern Europe

Percentage of ethnic minorities in the total population	Before the Division of Czechoslovakia and Yugoslavia	After the Division of Czechoslovakia and Yugoslavia
Less than 10 per cent	Albania, Hungary, Poland	Albania, Hungary, Poland, Slovenia and the Czech Republic
10–25 per cent	Bulgaria, Romania	Bulgaria, Romania, Croatia, Slovakia
25–40 per cent		Macedonia, Montenegro, Serbia
More than 40 per cent	Yugoslavia, Czech Republic	Bosnia, Herzegovina

Source: Based on Hatschikjan 1995, p. 15.

However, the background to these strivings was the fact that the Slovakians do not identify with the Czechoslovakian state, so wanted to break away from it despite economic disadvantages.

Figure 8.8 shows that, even after the breaking-up of Czechoslovakia and Yugoslavia, further disintegration in south-eastern Europe is possible, because a number of states still contain strongly ethnically heterogeneous groups.

▸ Finally, efforts at disintegration can also be caused or encouraged by language (and the associated cultural) differences. The separatist movement in the Canadian province of Quebec can be attributed to the fact that the population of this province is predominantly French-speaking, whereas English dominates elsewhere in the country.

The journal article shown in Figure 8.9, however, shows quite clearly that the separatist movement in the Quebec region had major difficulties after the referendum in 1995, which failed by a narrow margin.

Independently of whether the market dynamics in a country are characterized by a heterogenization of environmental conditions, a disintegration of country blocs or individual country markets, these processes are highly relevant for the marketing activities of internationally-operating enterprises. A distinction must also be made as to

> ### Figure 8.9 Part of a journal article on separatist efforts in the French–Canadian province of Quebec

WORLD IN REVIEW

Quebec's Lesson
A Path of Peaceful Separatism

*T*he recent tragedy in Kosovo of a minority's struggle for self-determination has unfortunately been representative of the violent ethnic conflict that prevails across continents. Groups with different religions, languages, or ancestry from their neighbors fight the perceived tyranny of existing borders to win recognition, liberty, and political autonomy. Too often, frustrated at the slowness and intransigence of the larger nation-state to

grant concessions, ethnic groups escalate their tactics to violent and destructive levels. However, one ethnic sub-region, Canada's *Province du Québec*, stands out as a place where leaders of an independence movement have relied on legal, codified avenues to win their ends. The case of Quebec may be seen, paradoxically, as a triumph for institutionalism.

Laying Claims

The French explorers Samuel de Champlain and Jacques Cartier, as well as the Briton Henry Hudson, first laid claim to the territory of Canada four centuries ago. Both France and England established colonies throughout the continent, but at the end of the French and Indian War in 1763, France was forced to abandon all of its North American colonies. Over the next century, Upper Canada, the region now known as Ontario, outpaced Lower Canada (now Quebec) in its industrialization, so that by 1867, the two Canadas were substantially different places: one was predominantly urban, Protestant, and anglophone, the other

agrarian, Roman Catholic, and francophone. The British crown issued an Act of Confederation in that year uniting the two regions as the Dominion of Canada. Gradually more provinces, all English-speaking, joined the Dominion, until the current nation took shape. Quebecois nationalist sentiment finally exploded when French President Charles de Gaulle visited Canada in 1969 on an official diplomatic mission. While addressing a feverish crowd from a Montreal balcony, de Gaulle cried out the now famous epigram, "*Vive le Québec libre!*" Ottawa immediately asked him to leave the country, but the forces his statement unleashed would not be contained.

Immediately thereafter, a group of young separatists calling themselves the Front de Libération du Québec (FLQ) began a campaign of angry activism throughout the province. Although the group postured as the "working people of Quebec who are committed to do everything they can for the people of Quebec to take their destiny in their hands," the activists' tactics included mailbox bombing, as well as the 1970

kidnapping and murder of a Quebec cabinet minister. Judgment from the people of Quebec was harsh; while many endorsed the FLQ's ultimate end, very few supported its means. The Quebec government asked the federal government for 10,000 troops to arrest and dissolve the FLQ. Quebecois society had long been stabilized by prominent social structures including the Catholic Church and the French civil code, both of which the FLQ explicitly railed against. Seeing the FLQ as a destabilizing, non-democratic presence, very few Quebecois could support the nascent group despite their sympathy for its cause. The FLQ's death outlined the future course of Quebecois separatism.

In 1982, the federal government won true independence from Britain, establishing or "repatriating," with the agreement of the British Parliament, its own constitution. Quebec refused to sign the new document. The long process of union and sovereignty had been carried out within an explicitly legal framework. Unlike many of Canada's fellow Western hemisphere nations, there was no war of Canadian indepen-

SAMEER DOSHI, Senior Editor, *Harvard International Review*

18 HARVARD INTERNATIONAL REVIEW • Summer 1999

whether these changes have an impact on so-called 'internal sellers', or relate rather to 'external sellers'. *Internal sellers* are those located within the fragmenting markets and *external sellers* are those in which there are no changes in market structure. None the less, even for the latter group, because of structural dynamics in their foreign markets, there are impacts on marketing activities.

Within the context of fragmenting markets, the speed of change creates a particular problem for both internal and external enterprises. It can be shown that, for converging markets, the restructuring process often takes decades and is thus relatively slow. In contrast, the 'erosion effects' in Eastern Europe are characterized by 'shock-inducing' speed (Losonez, 1990, p. 341). At the same time, fragmentation is accompanied by regional or country specific efforts to adapt economies to the free market model. This adds to the intensity of change and, possibly, fragmentation as the speed and direction of transformation among former block members differs.

One of the main problems for enterprises in fragmenting markets is the fact that the process destroys, partially or totally, the value chain of enterprises. Particularly in those industry sectors characterized by a high level of division of labour, disintegration can be highly disruptive.

Changes at the Level of Market Partners

Changes that have an impact on co-ordination do not only occur at the level of environmental conditions. Such changes may also occur at the level of market partners and be caused by changing demand, supply or competitive behaviour.

Demand-Related Change

Convergence Processes in Buyer Behaviour

One of the most important characteristics of demand-related change in international marketing is the assumed homogenization of buyer behaviour (Levitt, 1983; Ohmae, 1985). According to this opinion, target groups that can be identified across borders converge ever more in terms of similar buying (procurement) behaviour caused by converging preferences. This development is regarded as a decisive condition for geocentrically-orientated international marketing (Levitt, 1983). At the core of the convergence theory is a growing cross-border similarity in consumer habits, buying processes, and converging lifestyle.

It can be assumed that the convergence of buying behaviour in industrial goods markets is considerably more advanced than that for many consumer goods, for which regional or national preferences remain, at least to some extent, of considerable importance. In contrast, for some individual subsidiaries, many enterprises have to deal with the procurement guidelines of public institutions for certain purchasing problems (for example, machine tools, power-generation equipment, telecommunications equipment). Furthermore, ever more enterprises seek alternative suppliers internationally. The trend towards similar, or even absolutely identical, customer problems internationally increases this tendency. Thus, in an empirical study of the market for freight transport services, Backhaus *et al.* (1992), conducted a survey in France, the Netherlands and Germany, which failed to identify any national preferences or differences in the procurement of these services.

The convergence of buyer behaviour is particularly noticeable in the highly industrialized nations (HICs). Because the so-called 'emerging nations' imitate the industrialized nations, the convergence theory also applies to this former group to some extent. Kreutzer (1989, p. 41) provides the following explanation for the growing similarity of consumer preferences, as shown in Figure 8.10. That the causes of convergence are to be found not only in the level of demand, but also in new technologies. The figure shows that convergence is caused by many factors. It is difficult to separate clearly their influence.

Sociodemographic Developments

Over the last 20 years, the leading industrialized nations have been characterized by similar sociodemographic developments. Minimal, or even negative, population growth has led to a reversal of the age pyramid, indicating that the population in the industrialized nations is ageing increasingly. Furthermore, the trend away from large to small families that started towards the beginning of the twentieth century has continued, so that the number of single-person households has increased consistently. These parallel sociodemographic developments

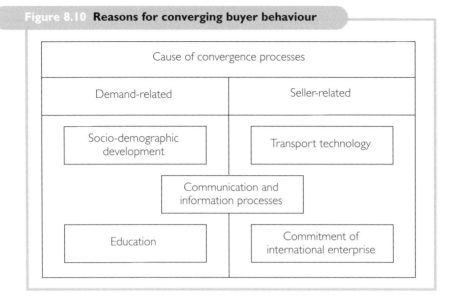

Figure 8.10 Reasons for converging buyer behaviour

have contributed substantially to a process of customer preferences and buyer behaviour convergence through lifestyle assimilation.

Education

The high level of education of the population, particularly in the industrialized nations, is a further demand-based reason for convergence tendencies. Strongly declining rates of illiteracy, improved education, and a strong interest in other cultures have undoubtedly led to a growing similarity in buyer behaviour. A high average level of education has encouraged people to deal with foreign cultures from an early age and to be open minded with respect to foreign sellers and their products.

Communication and Information Processes

The revolutionary development of communications technology cannot be allocated clearly to either the buyers' or sellers' side of the market, because this development has changed buyer behaviour through an explosive increase in the level of information, as well as opening up the potential for a parallel development of foreign markets to firms (Keegan, 1999, p. 19).

With respect to buyer behaviour, it is precisely the fact that consumers in different countries have access to the same information, and this information stimulates similar needs, that promotes the convergence of customer preferences and modes of behaviour.

In some new approaches, marketing integration processes are explained entirely in terms of information and communication processes. Hinzdorf (2001), whose work relates in the first instance to industrial goods analyses market convergence from an information process perspective.

An international seller (sender) provides a number of possible communications instruments. He informs through the application of communicative marketing instruments such as advertising, public relations or personal sales. The products themselves that are sold in the various country markets also carry information that is relevant to buying. Also transmitters of information, are those institutions that provide access to information, thus enabling third parties to conduct arbitrage. International companies and their subsidiaries, arbitrageurs, buying consortiums, trade journals and associations are examples of such senders.

The information exchange between country markets is a necessary process for establishing integrated markets. This includes the flow of arbitrage – relevant information within the firm, in which the receiver of arbitrage-relevant information and the decision-maker in purchasing may not be the same person. This is the case, for example, if purchasing decisions are made centrally by one organizational unit of a parent company, this unit then depends on the purchasing departments of subsidiaries for information.

None the less, particularly trade barriers between the procurement and home markets can hinder the transfer of an arbitrage good. Accordingly, *trade barriers* constitute a possible component of the marketing integration process. Market integration can also be purely information-induced if a large customer forces suppliers to abandon country-differentiated pricing due to his purchasing power. The following model can be derived (Figure 8.11).

Four factors influence market integration. The diffusion of arbitrage-relevant information in the market and within the company, transfer barriers and buying power (Figure 8.12) (Hinzdorf, 2001).

Information exchange with respect to price differences can lead to purely *information-induced*, and *transfer-induced*, market integration. The higher the speed of diffusion of pricing information for such a product between country markets, the higher the degree of

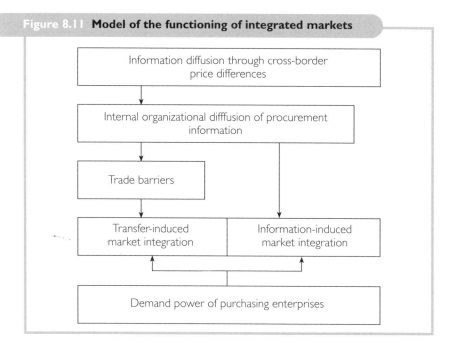

Figure 8.11 Model of the functioning of integrated markets

market integration between them. The extent of market integration also depends on *internal corporate diffusion of price difference information.* We assume that with an increasing speed of diffusion of price information in internationally sourcing enterprises, the degree of marketing integration between country markets increases.

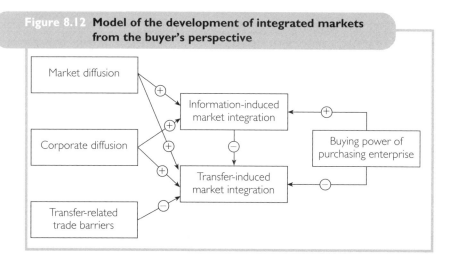

Figure 8.12 Model of the development of integrated markets from the buyer's perspective

Furthermore, the extent of market integration is determined by *trade barriers that hinder transfers*. In this respect, it can be supposed that the stronger these barriers between country markets, the lower the probability of transfer-induced market integration. With rising demand power, an internationally sourcing enterprise raises the probability of an information-induced market integration. With declining demand power on the other hand, the enterprise can only undertake classical arbitrage with the physical transfer of goods between country markets. In this case, we are dealing with transfer-induced market integration. This suggests that the stronger the internationally sourcing enterprise integrates markets via virtual information-based arbitrage processes, the weaker the transfer-induced market integration processes.

Hinzdorf (2001) tested this model empirically, and was able largely to confirm these hypotheses. He showed that the four determining factors explained 41 per cent of the variance in information-induced market integration and 51 per cent of the variance in transfer-induced market integration. The model as a whole revealed a high fit level. It can therefore be concluded that the diffusion of arbitrage-relevant information, is a key factor in market convergence. The emergence of classical, physical arbitrage is not necessary for the integration of markets.

Similarly, the increasing speed of information transfer and resulting high level of market transparency brought about by new information and communication technology, have an impact on buyer behaviour. If one considers, for example, that satellite television programmes can be received simultaneously by viewers in all parts of the world, it is evident that its impact on strategy can be substantial. Global news or entertainment TV networks with their broad reach and appeal can indeed be powerful sources.

Transport technology

Transport technology has undergone dramatic change similar to that of communication technology. Modern transport systems enable sellers to cover large geographic distances at relatively low cost (Keegan 1999, p. 19). The resulting potential for serving all desired markets independently of geographic location, has characterized the convergence process, because global product presence has contributed to stimulating similar customer needs and preferences.

The Commitment of International Enterprises

Internationally-active enterprises contribute both consciously and unconsciously to an increase in convergence tendencies. In this manner, through marketing aimed at overcoming national differences, such enterprises focus consciously on structural change in terms of the needs of the customers in question. If, for example, a firm that has introduced a new product successfully in Country A attempts to do the same in another country for which there are so far no preferences for this product this enterprise contributes potentially to the convergence of consumer preferences.

Similarly, such enterprises *un*consciously support convergence tendencies. They overcome national differences through the intensive international flow of communication, personnel transfer or management and/or technology know-how.

Regionalization of Buyer Behaviour

The regionalization of buyer behaviour refers to a process of growing dissimilarity of consumer behaviour and purchasing processes. The regionalization of buyer behaviour describes a procedure by which buyers break away from overall national consumer or purchasing characteristics and relate rather to those of a region. The subsequent evolution of 'buying regions' can override original national boundaries (Ohmae, 1996). The causes of the regionalization of buyer behaviour are manifold, and relate to the following aspects:

▸ internal country tensions;
▸ striving towards a differentiated satisfaction of needs; and
▸ cross-border, regional development programmes.

Internal country tensions caused by political, cultural, religious or ethnic conflicts between national groups, have been observed ever more frequently in recent times. Examples such as India, Sri Lanka, the Lebanon or the former Yugoslavia show that political processes can lead to a disintegration of former national markets. Because of their long-term and often strong impact, the influence of cultural and religious norms is substantial (Perlitz, 2000).

The development of regional particularities cannot be attributed only to extreme cases of national collapse. Similarly, regional cultural characteristics can create market regionalization. This may, for example, be caused by the urbanization of society (Hünerberg, 1994), coupled with an intensification of the disparity between rural and urban regions, the emphasis of regional identities ('we in the north . . .'), or strivings to maintain cultural identity ('back-to-the-roots syndrome'). Such developments lead to efforts to achieve a *differentiated needs satisfaction*, which manifests itself in the form of a regionalization, or even individualization, of buyer behaviour, the 'multiple option society' (Naisbitt, 1984).

Seller-Related Changes

If cross-border procurement processes become increasingly similar, it will become more attractive for sellers not to concentrate solely on the domestic market. Furthermore, competitors from other countries are in a similar initial situation and accordingly operate increasingly in foreign markets. This creates a substantial globalization pressure: sellers in homogeneous markets are forced increasingly to be 'global players'.

A failure to internationalize will then lead to a loss of market share to international competition. In many industry sectors, additional turnover in foreign markets can lead to cost advantages as a consequence of the scale sensitivity of modern production technology (Ghemawat and Spence, 1989). Experience-curve effects favour those sellers with the highest cumulative output. The positioning as a 'global player' often does not constitute an independent strategic choice, but rather strategic necessity.

Convergence processes operate mainly in the markets of the leading industrial nations. The focus in these markets is thus frequently geocentric. For this reason, the concept of global marketing is closely associated with that of the triad. This concept, developed by Ohmae, demands that sellers must be active in all of the USA, Western Europe and Japan. Only this puts firms in a position, to amortize, within a reasonable period of time, fixed costs, such as those relating to research and development. As a result of increasingly short product life cycles, this can only be achieved through a simultaneous presence in all parts of the markets that make up the triad. Of course this compelling rationale depends on a company's actual relationship between production volume and unit costs. This relationship can reveal diseconomies of scale or increasing unit costs as production increases beyond the unit cost minimum. This effect limits seller-related feedback and sometimes motivates companies to organize production into multiple, yet independent units.

Figure 8.13 Reasons for maketing globally

Causes of global marketing	
Seller-related	Buyer-related
▶ economies of scale	▶ homogeneity of customer needs and behavioural patterns
▶ improved access to resources	▶ convergence of technical standards
▶ rapid amortization of investment caused by rapidly shortening product life cycles	▶ favourable economic and political environmental conditions

It is not always Japan, Europe or the USA that are the focus of attention for global business. Instead, with the aid of a global strategy, those country markets should be targeted in which substantial portions of world trade are conducted, and where in addition there are similar, if not identical, customer preferences and buyer behaviour.

A focus on the triad and the associated attainment of *global marketing* cannot be regarded across the board as the appropriate strategy. Rather, it is important to weigh up the pros and cons of potential globalization quite carefully. Figure 8.13 outlines the advantages and disadvantages of globalization.

Apart from considering what relevance these factors have in specific industries and corporate situations, it is necessary also to consider the advantages of other internationalization strategies. Figure 8.14 shows a grouping of selected industry sectors positioned not only in terms of possible globalization advantages, but also in terms of possible advantages to be gained from a polycentric orientation.

Changes in Relative Competitive Position

Co-ordination problems can arise for international enterprises through a change in the relative competitive position. Such a change occurs if competing enterprises in one or more country markets deliberately undertake a strategic change. Despite constant buyer behaviour, stable environmental conditions and unchanged market operations by an international enterprise, co-ordination problems can still arise if the competition alters the rules of the game. A strategic change from a

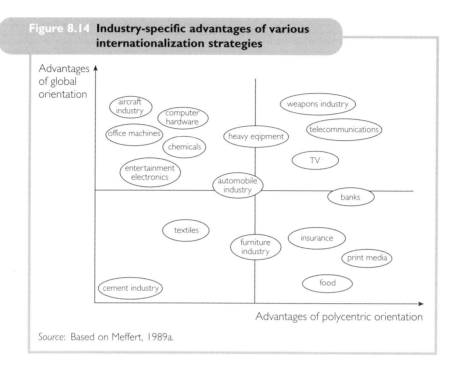

Figure 8.14 Industry-specific advantages of various internationalization strategies

Source: Based on Meffert, 1989a.

competitor in one or more country markets changes the competitive position, and not only in this or these markets. The effects can easily spill over into other markets, as shown in the following example from the automobile industry.

In the second half of the 1990's, Ford and General Motors were having to contend with a slow but steady decline in market shares (Figure 8.15).

The reasons for the continually worsening market position were manifold, but, for both companies, can be attributed mainly to the following errors of judgement (Linden, 1998; Appel, 1999; Schneider, 2001). As the world's largest automobile manufacturers, Ford and GM misjudged the international competitive network in the 1990s. The enterprises believed that their market position would, in future, be attacked mainly through Asian, and particularly Korean, concerns. For this reason, Ford and GM focused mainly on the strategies of these Asian competitors and attempted to emulate their 'world-car' strategy. Both companies subsequently

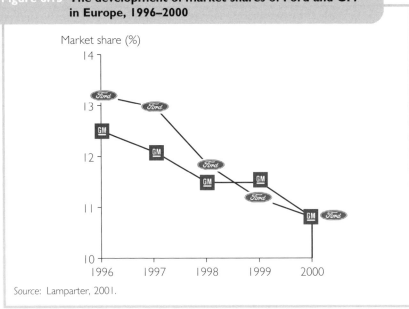

Figure 8.15 **The development of market shares of Ford and GM in Europe, 1996–2000**

Source: Lamparter, 2001.

pursued, without further product adaptation, global automobile concepts in the USA, Europe and Asia. Thus, model development was centralized in Detroit, and special models were no longer developed for the European or Asian markets. However, after 1995, the companies came under massive attack, not from Asian, but mainly from German manufacturers. These competed in Europe against the 'world cars' of Ford and GM with cars that were specially adapted to the needs of European customers. Because the attacks by the German automobile manufacturers in Europe increasingly jeopardized the market position of Ford and GM towards the end of the 1990's, they gave up the world-brand concept that they had been previously propagating enthusiastically. However, the responsibility for model development was not re-delegated back to the European subsidiaries. For example, GM is planning a new production facility in Thailand, in which a model is to be built especially for the Asian market. The changed competitive situation in Europe thus led both enterprises not only to develop a revised European strategy, but also to changes in all other markets.

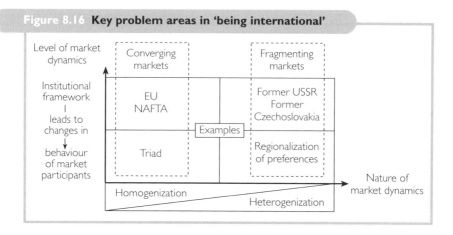

Figure 8.16 **Key problem areas in 'being international'**

'Being International': A Problem Map

The dynamics of country markets in the form of a change in environmental conditions or the behaviour of transactional partners, determines the situative context of international marketing. The specific problem areas can be delineated as shown in Figure 8.16.

The four quadrants of this matrix describe the various starting points for international marketing in the area of 'being international'. The direction of *market dynamic* (homogenization versus heterogenization) is of particular importance, because of its fundamental impact on international marketing.

The particular characteristic of the country market define the fundamental nature of the co-ordination problem. A variety of co-ordination problems arise for internationally active enterprises. In a market environment that is becoming *homogeneous*, the application of standardization strategies is easier, because an efficient, broad application of consistent marketing instruments is possible. The connection between homogenization and co-ordination requirements becomes clear if one considers the (theoretical) extreme of a complete homogenization of operational country markets. In this case, there is no demand-related co-ordination problem, because identical products can be offered through identical distribution channels in the various country markets. The basis for arbitrage is removed through the consistency of operations and related variables. The situation is quite different, however, if buyer preferences become *more heterogeneous*. Heterogeneity is the basis for a successful policy of differentiation, and thus also for a possible exchange of goods between country markets. This goods exchange creates demand-based feedback, which grows in parallel with increasing homogeneity. This applies provided that the preferences of buyers are not so divergent that the basis for arbitrage is removed though a lack of product acceptance.

It is clear that the dynamics of country markets, described here in terms of the nature of changes in buyer behaviour, relates to a spectrum of various country market similarities, in which co-ordination problems manifest themselves in a number of forms. It is characteristic of this spectrum that, at its extremes (complete homo/heterogeneity), there are no co-ordination problems.

For the various possible positions between the extremes, the question arises as to the manner in which the internationally active enterprise should react to co-ordination problems. In this respect, a differentiation can be made between:

▸ the *origin* of the co-ordination problem;
▸ the *extent* of the co-ordination challenge; and
▸ the *selection* of alternative co-ordination strategies.

These issues are to be discussed in the following chapters.

9 Co-ordination in Converging Markets

The Origin of Co-ordination Problems in Converging Markets

An increase in seller, buyer and competitor-based feedback caused by the convergence of the behaviour of market participants and/or the eradication of trade barriers which hinder the movement of products, people and capital, is characteristic of co-ordination problems in converging markets. The need for co-ordination, increases with a rising level of integration, especially if a seller in a converging market attempts to maintain a *degree of differentiation* in the product programme. As a result of possible arbitrage (demand-related interdependency), differentiation-related cost impact (seller-related interdependency) or limited competitive networks (competitive-based interdependency), the results in the market may be sub-optimal. This interconnection between seller marketing strategy, the degree of integration of country markets, and the resulting co-ordination problem, can be well illustrated by means of the European automobile market.

The emergence of re-importing and parallel imports in Europe is the result, of an increasing integration of country markets of member states of the European Union, through declining transaction costs. They alone, however, do not explain the existence of the grey car market. It is also an inevitable consequence of the attempt of automobile manufacturers to maintain a high level of price differentiation between country markets for virtually identical products. Figure 9.1 shows the average price differences (before tax) which prevail between high- and low-price European countries with respect to various manufacturers. Combined with more fluid exchange conditions, this behaviour on the part of sellers leads to arbitrage processes. A pan-European standardization of pricing strategy which reduces price differences to the level of arbitrage costs alone, would, however, remove the basis for arbitrage.

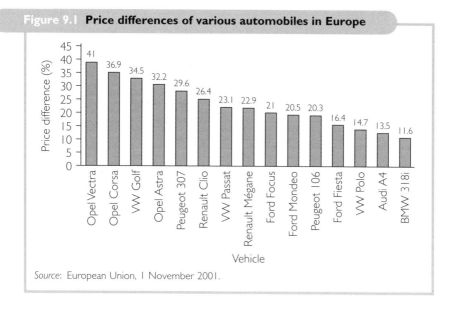

Figure 9.1 Price differences of various automobiles in Europe

Source: European Union, 1 November 2001.

From time to time, a co-ordination problem derives from distribution channel differences. For example, in converging markets, the price differences that lead to arbitrage processes need not necessarily be caused by a conscious process of price differentiation by the seller. Instead, differing requirements from distribution channels in the various country markets may be responsible for price differences, as is demonstrated by the case of prescription medication.

The sometimes substantial price differences for pharmaceuticals in Europe are the result in particular of varying gross margins in wholesaling and retailing (pharmacies). While, for example, the average margins for wholesalers is only about 4 per cent in Sweden, it is as high at 22 per cent in the Netherlands. The margins earned at pharmacies in Europe also vary considerably. They vary from 56 per cent in Finland to 21 per cent in Great Britain. If the diverging value-added taxation rates are also taken into account, it is clear that, despite identical prices from manufacturers, final users are confronted by very substantial price differences, as shown in Table 9.1. Note that, in this case, market transfer at the retailing level does not affect the manufacturers' profits.

The impact of this spread of margins is decisive. It may lead to sub-optimal results if there are no attempts at co-ordination. A

Table 9.1 Emergence of price differences for pharmaceuticals in Europe

Country	Manufacturer's price	Wholesaler's margin (%)	Retail pharmacy price (%)*	Value added tax in (%)**	Final price
Austria	100	16.7	52.4	20.0	213.42
Belgium	100	14.1	44.9	6.0	175.25
Germany	100	14.0	47.2	16.0	194.66
Denmark	100	7.0	34.0	25.0	179.23
Spain	100	13.6	42.7	4.0	168.59
France	100	10.7	36.0	2.1	153.71
Finland	100	8.3	55.8	12.0	188.98
Greece	100	8.4	35.0	8.0	158.05
Italy	100	10.5	33.1	9.0	160.31
Ireland	100	15.0	33.3	21.0***	185.49
Luxembourg	100	14.9	47.1	3.0	174.09
Netherlands	100	22.0	28.9	6.0	166.69
Portugal	100	12.4	25.0	5.4	148.09
Sweden	100	4.2	26.6	0.0	131.92
Great Britain	100	14.3	20.9	0.0	138.19

Notes:
* Premium on wholesale price; ** Rate for prescription medicines; *** 0% for oral, 21% for non-oral medicines.

possibly negative result of demand-related feedback is the emergence of parallel imports or re-importing. However, the demand-related feedback can positively impact profit – as we will see later. In order to determine whether or not this is the case, the phenomena which surround the development of a grey market must be analysed in greater detail. The alternative possible reactions of buyers to re-imports and parallel imports form the initial starting point for this analysis. What needs to be done is a closer analysis of the magnitude of the following options along with their impact on the profit of the company:

(1) The purchase of reimported goods from the same seller
   In this case, the grey market reduces the average price and entire revenue earned. The average price declines, because the purchase of reimported products lowers the price in the market. The impact on total revenues earned is thus *negative*.

   German car manufacturer, Audi, had a significant re-import problem in the late 1980s and 1990s. At the time, about one third of all sales of new Audi 80s in Italy actually went to German owners. Since the price for a new Audi 80 was much lower in Italy, this led to a decrease in the average price for an Audi 80 in Europe.

(2) Winning new customers who previously preferred other brands
   The typically lower price level in the grey market entices customers previously served by other sellers. Because new customers are attracted, the effect on revenue is *positive*.

   It is clear that the availability of a cheaper 'Italian' version of the Audi 80 sold by re-importers attracted new buyers. Ford or Opel owners who previously could not afford a new Audi, now could. This enlarged Audi's market in Europe. The reason is price differentiation, which always increases a vendor's market reach.

(3) Customers migrate to other sellers
   In principle, it is possible that customers migrate to other manufacturers as a result of differing prices for products offered in regular and grey markets. Such market activities are associated with *declines* in revenue.

(4) No change in buyer behaviour
   The offers of a re-importer or parallel importer do not necessarily lead to changes in buyer behaviour. This is particularly the case if the price difference for a product is regarded by buyers as being too

low. This phenomenon is observable in consumer goods markets with small margins. Small margins lead to small transnational price differentials. Even if these are substantial enough to attract some arbitrage, the majority of consumers might be unimpressed by it. They will prefer service from established and 'brand-certified' distribution channels.

Assuming that geographical shifts in the sales have no impact on the cost situation, an impact on the results of demand-related interdependency, and thus a co-ordination problem, will prevail, if the total revenue losses [(1) + (3)] would be greater than the revenue gained through the emergence of grey markets in (2). If, in addition, cost changes also enter the picture, these must be contrasted with revenue changes. The cost impact for (1) can be excluded, if the country of origin has no impact on the cost position, so that it has no cost impact in terms of the alternative country markets in which a unit of the product in question can be sold. A positive cost impact (cost reduction) will be exerted by (2) if additional quantities sold lead to economies of scale. Accordingly, for (3), the cost situation will worsen through diseconomies of scale.

In the extreme, with completely integrated markets and completely homogenous buyer behaviour (identical product preferences and willingness to pay), and an identical legal framework, the demand-related co-ordination challenge disappears if sellers standardize marketing instruments fully. Of course, this extreme case is hardly observable in practice. It applies, if at all, to certain industrial or high-tech markets (commercial airplanes, IT hardware, enterprise software) in which buyers try to solve very similar or even identical problems.

Only as long as the operational country markets are not fully integrated from the buyer perspective, will there be differing product evaluations and a difference in the willingness to pay. Under these conditions, it is profitable to exploit these differences through a differentiated marketing programme, provided that the revenue impacts so obtained (marketing effectiveness), exceed the additional costs associated with differentiation (marketing efficiency). An increasing similarity of buyers' preferences and buying behaviour puts pressure on that practice. We have described that process as increasing market interdependency.

The co-ordination problem in converging markets can thus be attributed to two causes:

▸ the extent of market integration and the associated potential for a profitable differentiation of marketing strategies; and

▸ the extent of virtual and physical arbitrage in country markets resulting from differentiation.

Through a standardization of the legal framework, converging markets lead to declining transactions costs. Therefore, market integration leads, *ceteris paribus*, to increasing arbitrage profits. The level of arbitrage profits depends on the extent of differentiation of the product programme. The greater this is, the larger the arbitrage profits (with constant transactions costs).

If, with a complete standardization of market operations, the potential cost savings are so large as to more than compensate for the potential revenue loss due to lack of differentiation, there is no potential for profitable differentiation. In this case, the question of whether a seller is active in interdependent markets is unimportant, because the basis for arbitrage disappears as a result of the absence of product and price differentiation. A co-ordination problem in the sense described here no longer exists. Only when there is potential for profitable differentiation can the issue of whether operational markets are interdependent be significant. Both causes must prevail *together*, for reciprocal market co-ordination to emerge as an international marketing problem. Co-ordination problems in interdependent and converging country markets only exist *if market operations are not completely standardized*.

The Extent of Co-ordination Problems in Converging Markets

The extent of the co-ordination problem can be attributed to the increase in seller, demand and competition-related feedback between country markets with a simultaneous differentiation of market operations. This increase in interdependency can be observed on two levels:

▸ aggregated market; and
▸ individual company.

The *corporate level* is most decisive for the internationally active seller, and reveals the need for immediate co-ordination. The *market level* is an aggregate of the single-company perspective at the dimension of the overall co-ordination problem, is also significant. It is an indicator of the sum of individual co-ordination problems.

The Extent of Co-ordination at the Market Level

The extent of co-ordination problems in converging markets depends on the extent of feedback between them. Institutional integration is an important factor, providing additional feedback and dynamics to the process of convergence. It facilitates market feedback from the demand and the suppliers' side. The EU provides a good example of branch-specific variation in market feedback caused by integration.

Figure 9.2 shows that the impact of institutional integration is at its largest, where the legal barriers were greatest in the past. Here, the removal of legal hindrances has, accordingly, the greatest impact. In this area, on the other hand, the strongest impact of the institutional standardization of the European markets can be found where the previous linkages of market partners were low and the relatively strongest homogenization tendencies prevail. This applies to sectors such as

Figure 9.2 Industry-specific impact of linkages within the EU

		Degree of market integration within EU	
		Low	High
Significance of legal barriers	Low	• metal-working • tools and metal products low impact of EU	• agricultural machinery • machine tools • textile machinery • machines for food and chemical industry low impact of EU
	High	• naval construction • railroad materials • medicinal, surgical and orthopaedic devices strongest impact of EU	• office equipment and electronic data-processing • long-distance communications, computers • electro-medicinal tools high impact of EU

shipbuilding, the procurement of medical equipment, or of materials for railways. These examples are typical of industries in which the public sector is the customer, and where the applicable regulations favour national sellers.

However, the removal of trade barriers leads to noticeable impacts in those sectors in which the economic linkages were already substantial before the establishment of a common market. This applies particularly to the data processing sector, in which market feedback has been fostered by the introduction of international standards. The impact of the EU is low where trade barriers were already of minimal significance.

Despite the industry-specific differences in the impact of removing legal trade barriers, the economic effects of the convergence of markets can be captured in a model (see the so-called 'Cecchini Report' – Cecchini, 1988) based on the following assumptions (Cecchini, 1988; Emerson 1989; Hermann *et al.*, 1990; de Zoeten, 1993):

▸ the removal of legal trade barriers leads to a reduction in transaction costs (direct reduction of initial costs);
▸ the removal of legal trade barriers intensifies competition (greater competitive pressure), which leads to attempts at rationalization to compensate for declining prices (indirect cost reduction); and
▸ the declining price level leads to rising demand, which creates growth effects and renewed cost reduction through the exploitation of economies of scale.

The model basically describes the impact of market alliances. The interrelations assumed in the model do not relate specifically to the European market. The model uses general observations, which are independent of individual cases. It is an attempt to differentiate the various effects of market integration based on cost reduction and increasing competition. However, the relationships assumed in the model should be viewed critically. As every model, it simplifies the complex structure of cause and effect in economics. Against this background, de Zoeten (1993) concluded:

▸ The interrelations assumed by the model with respect to converging markets may, but need not necessarily, occur. There is no automatism.
▸ The impacts emerging from the convergence process can only be determined case-by-case in terms of the particular market circumstances.

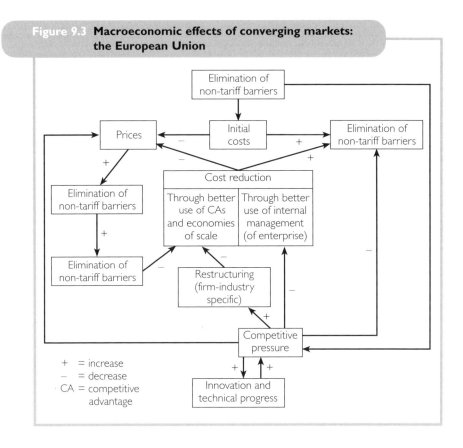

Figure 9.3 **Macroeconomic effects of converging markets: the European Union**

None the less, the model offers an insightful approach for determining the main impacts of country market integration (Jeannet and Hennessey, 1998, p. 172). Attempts have therefore been made to quantify the qualitative impacts of converging markets for the EU, as described in the Cecchini model.

The central impacts of market integration are regarded as the reduction of costs by removing barriers to trade, and in the potential for utilizing economies of scale in production following price reduction and demand expansion. It is estimated that, based on the assumptions, the economies of scale would comprise 70–90 per cent of the welfare effect in the EU. This would amount to 216 billion ECU. The variation can be attributed to the differing methods of forecasting and data used. This estimate seems rather conservative as it is based on cost reduction primarily. Increasing competition motivates companies to innovate and develop new markets. The estimated increase in welfare depends on the number of integrated country markets in the EU, because this number determines the total market size achieved, and resulting cost-reduction effects through volume of sales. We can expect this effect to be greatly enhanced by the enlargement of the EU to EU–25/27.

The effects of the integrated European market anticipated by the EU Commision in 1993 relate particularly to *seller-related*, but in part also to *competition-related* interdependency in European market operations. They constitute, in particular, an aggregation of the cost impact derived from eradicated barriers to trade on the seller side. The quantitative estimates show that this seller-related feedback is regarded as being the dominant effect of market integration. For a single seller, this is a rough indicator of the effects that can be achieved (on average) through European integration. The Cecchini model suggests that these effects can only be achieved if the individual European country markets are integrated simultaneously.

Interestingly, the integration model of the EU Commission, and the resultant estimates of welfare effects, assume that *demand-based feedback* will have no immediate impact on market convergence. In the case of integration this may be justified by the following reasons:

- The removal of trade barriers is a major challenge for sellers, because it affects access to individual markets. The result is not necessarily a change in buyer behaviour.
- However, over the long term, the pursuit of standardized, cost-optimized marketing concepts may initiate a trend towards higher similarity of buying behaviour, for example standardized advertising and product policy may accelerate the emergence of homogeneous transnational consumer segments. As a short-term consequence of market integration, changes in buyer behaviour could be negligible.
- In many industry sectors the markets of the EU, independently of the eradication of legal barriers to trade, already reveal a high level of demand-based integration.

However the absence of demand-related feedback is not a necessary consequence of market integration. In sectors with minimal interweaving linkages, the eradication of trade barriers will have an impact on buyer behaviour. In the medium to long term, the impacts are difficult to quantify. They can be attributed, among other factors, to the breaking down of perceived distance between countries and cultures as a result of the eradication of trade barriers (Kreutzer, 1989).

The Need for Co-ordination at the Corporate Level

The effects estimated by the Cecchini model are differentiated neither in terms of industry sectors nor companies. In view of the need for information by decision-makers in the political and macroeconomic spheres, this is not surprising. Figure 9.2 (see page 282) has already shown that the effects assumed in the model with respect to various industries and companies can be quite varied. Thus, for example, the starting point for a single seller, and thus the extent of individual feedback caused by market integration, depends, among other factors, on whether the relevant legal regulations for the entire market correspond with the previous national laws or not, because the adaptation to new regulations entails additional costs.

In principle, the extent of seller, buyer and competition-related feedback determines the extent of interdependence of country markets, and thus the extent of co-ordination problems. Because this extent depends also very strongly on the individual situation of a firm, the company needs indicators in order to operationalize the degree of interdependence of the relevant markets.

Indicators of Seller-Related Interdependency

The effects derived from the Cecchini model are based mainly on the cost impact of market integration, and thus on seller-related feedback as a result of market convergence. At the centre of these cost and competition effects lies the experience curve as the basis for quantifying the impacts of increased production volume (Figure 9.4).

This experience-curve concept is based on empirical investigations, which suggest a relationship between unit costs and the cumulative production volume of a product (Henderson, 1980, p 19; Bartlett and Goshal, 2000, p. 701). The concept assumes that, with each doubling of the cumulative production volume, unit costs (adjusted for inflation) decline by 20–30 per cent. Originally proposed by Bruce Henderson from the Boston Consulting Group, this relationship between accumulated volume and costs has been observed in many industries. Fixed-cost degression and the learning-curve effect contribute to cost reduction as well as the option to switch to more

Figure 9.4 The experience curve

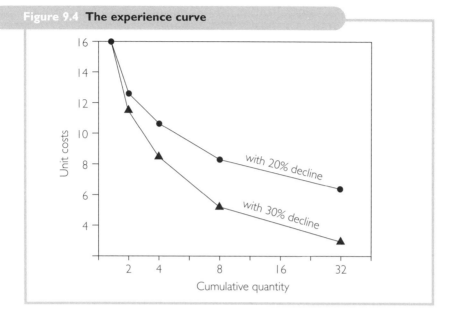

cost-effective production technology with growing production volume. NASA has estimated experience curve effects in practice range from 10–15 per cent in repetitive electronics manufacturing, 15 per cent in aerospace and 25 per cent in the machine tool industry. The rationalization potential may extend beyond the productive process (such as to efficient distribution) and encompass the entire value chain of an enterprise (Henderson, 1980, p. 26).

The direct and indirect cost impacts of market integration depend strongly on the cost changes caused by situational conditions relating to a particular company. Incumbents in a certain industry may deliberately choose different production technology to account for different production volume and risk preference. The following are the main influences on enterprise-specific cost changes, and thus constitute indicators of seller-related interdependency:

▸ cumulative production quantities;
▸ the enterprise-specific potential for achieving greater sales as a result of market integration;
▸ the phase in the life cycle of the product in question;
▸ the timing of market entry;
▸ the degree of product standardization; and

▸ the degree of centralization (international configuration) of production within the internal value chain.

Accumulated production volume and the additional potential unit sales that lie in the future are fundamental for the cost-reduction potential based on the experience curve of an enterprise. Because of its relation to accumulated volume, this cost-reduction diminishes over time. In order to achieve a doubling of the total production quantity starting with low cumulative volume, a considerably smaller production quantity is needed than with a high volume. Accordingly, only exponentially increasing production volume delivers a constant cost reduction each year. Conversely, with a high total production quantity, accordingly high additional quantities of output will be necessary to double that output. In this manner, the point in time at which the cumulative production quantity is observed exerts a strong influence on the remaining potential experience-curve effects. At the end of the product life cycle, the impact of the experience curve on a change of cost position relative to competitors is small.

The additional output actually achieved determines the real, enterprise-specific cost reduction facilitated by market integration. These cost reductions, however, are not dependent purely on sinking prices as a result of higher competitive pressure, as assumed in the EU model. Thus, apart from the price, the quantity of a product sold also depends on other factors which interact reciprocally with one another.

If products have a *reciprocal relationship*, a product will, for example, be used as a system component. The demand for this product will be determined by demand in the related system markets. The demand may therefore have a market and enterprise-specific price elasticity. The *current phase of the product life cycle* has a fundamental impact on the quantity of goods that can additionally be sold. Products in late phases of their life cycle tend to have a lower remaining potential than those in earlier phases. The potential (total) turnover is also dependent on the number of operational country markets, and thus on the *timing strategy* of an enterprise. With the number of simultaneous market operations, turnover potential within a particular time frame increases. The selection of a shower strategy leads to greater sales potential, and thus to a higher potential cost impact of market integration.

The concept of an experience curve assumes that a standardized product will be manufactured. The offerings in the various country markets will then be similar or even identical. With a *declining level of standardization*, the potential for cost reduction also declines, if specific production facilities would be needed to manufacture differentiated products. Because the experience-curve effects refer to particular product technologies and equipment, these 'split up' with increasing differentiation, so that synergistic cost reduction effects are smaller. In the extreme they only apply to R&D costs, which are also fixed, but independent from the configuration of production. There are more production facilities with corresponding fixed costs, and these have to be spread over relatively low production quantities. This problem increases with increasing fixed costs intensity. As a result, the international *product strategy* has an impact on the cost effects of market integration and thus on the extent of cost-related (seller-related) interdependency.

In summary, it is clear that, for an integrated (total) market, the anticipated cost impact is only a rough indicator of the seller-related feedback that arises from market integration. The integration effects reveal a high level of industry specificity. A number of company-specific factors influence the extent of individual cost effects. This means that, at the same time, substantial factors driving supply-related feedback can be influenced by management, and must be regarded as instruments of international marketing. An analysis of the extent of supply-related feedback caused by converging markets cannot therefore be generalized, but applied in terms of the specific circumstances of an enterprise. Accordingly, for example, the seller-related cost-feedback created by integration, will, *ceteris paribus*, be all the greater:

▸ the smaller the product-related cumulative production volume;
▸ the larger the remaining enterprise-specific potential of additional sales as a result of market integration;
▸ the larger the number of country markets in the converging market in which the enterprise in question operates;
▸ the longer the anticipated market presence of the product in question;
▸ the greater the degree of possible standardization of the products offered in the country markets; and
▸ the greater the degree of centralization of production.

The connection between the cost situation of an internationally active enterprise and the degree of centralization shows that the configuration of international activities, in this case production, is a core influence on seller-related feedback. Bartlett and Ghoshal (1990) make this quite clear in recommending the development of well-defined roles and responsibilities in order to achieve the greatest possible global efficiency and national effectiveness in the context of transnational enterprises. In this respect, they suggest a high centralization of production to minimize manufacturing and transport costs for a product which can be standardized.

Indicators of Competition-Related Interdependency

The experience curve affecting seller-related feedback in converging markets (which form the centre of focus), can be affected not only by the seller in question, but also by its competitors. Thus, for competitors as well, market integration also leads, under certain circumstances, to a rise in cost-induced feedback between the enterprises in which they operate. Decause of these basic considerations, the Cecchini model proceeds on the assumption of generally rising competitive pressure, which in turn is responsible for price declines and thus for a rise in demand.

For a seller, an increase in cost-induced interdependency on competitors is equivalent to a rise in competitive-based feedback. The more the operations of competitors in these markets depend on one another, because of, for example, internal corporate cost effects, the more likely it is that measures undertaken by the seller in question in selected markets to adapt to competitors' actions in other markets will compel the seller to undertake appropriate counter-measures.

Figure 9.5 illustrates this relationship of cost-induced interdependency between competitors, and the competition-related interdependency of the seller in question. In this respect, it can be assumed initially that market integration on the part of a competitor leads to a rise in cost-induced feedback (1). If a seller changes the nature of its operations in the country markets in which the competition is present, in this case in Country B (2), then, on the basis of growing interdependencies, the competitor will be forced to change its marketing activities not only in this, but in all other country markets (3). This now leads to necessary adaptation by the seller in markets A, C and D (4). However, if the marketing approach is changed in these markets, the seller may be compelled once again, to make adaptations in Country B (4).

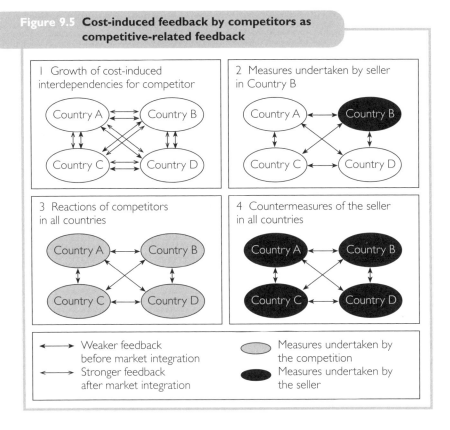

Figure 9.5 Cost-induced feedback by competitors as competitive-related feedback

Because the increase in cost-induced feedback with respect to competitors can lead to growth in competition-related feedback for the seller in question, the indicators described in the previous section should be determined not only for the company's own enterprise, but also for the relevant competitors. The stronger these indicators for competitors, the more closely the competition-related feedback must be monitored by (analysing) enterprises in converging markets.

Indicators of Demand-related Feedback

A step-wise removal of trade barriers between country markets and a (partial) resulting standardization of buyer behaviour is characteristic of converging markets. This homogenization leads to improved opportunities for buyers, and better information about the supply situation in other country markets. In order to answer the question as to the extent to which foreign procurement is an economically viable option, a series of indicators is available.

Information Exchange

Purchasing in converging foreign markets, and the necessary comparison of advantages between domestic and external purchasing options, depends initially on the availability of alternative suppliers, and the relevant prices and qualities. For the buyer, it is decisive if, and at what cost, this information is available. The convergence of a market is thus beneficial to the basic information-creation process and reduces the associated costs.

If they are relevant to purchasing and available in a specific purchasing situation, information about country-market specific alternatives can therefore trigger off arbitrage processes. It is thus necessary to have an appropriate supply of information, and to use it appropriately.

The Supply of Information

The evolution of integrated markets promotes the development of cross-border media which are relevant to purchasing processes and provide purchasing-related information. These media are provided not only on the seller side by enterprises, but also by public institutions, which hope to accelerate the integration of country markets through instigating adaptation processes on both buyer and seller sides.

An institutionalized price comparison of the automobile market provides an example of an international and relevant (to purchasing) medium of information. At regular intervals, the EU Commission publishes a 'price mirror' which shows the price differences (adjusted for country-specific taxation differences) between the approximately 70 models of automobile offered in the European market. The price differences are determined by the EU Commission, partly in order to determine the extent of market integration in the industry. However, this information can also provide buyers with cheap information on price comparisons between country markets, to achieve what they would regard as an optimal choice of purchasing market.

Apart from public providers of information to buyers, there are also private enterprises which provide such services in the course of their business. Of note are those consumer goods companies that market their products directly across Europe through mass media or the Internet. Products may be purchased by telephone or online.

Parallel to the pool of information on the European automobile market provided by the EU, the increasing number of reimporters has also increased the supply of information considerably. These sellers place advertisements in local and national newspapers, as well as in car magazines and other trade publications (see Figure 9.6). They use mainly the Internet to offer precisely specified models at favourable prices.

Figure 9.6 Example of an import offer in the automotive sector

Apart from a seller-inducted exchange of information, this can also be encouraged by buyers. This applies particularly in the sector of public demand, for which the EU has drawn up explicit regulations.

The objective is to eradicate the national character of procurement by government agencies.

The purchasing guidelines from the EU Council of 17 September 1990 made a substantial contribution to the removal of administrative barriers. In these guidelines, which relate to the tendering of contracts in the areas of water, energy, transport and telecommunications (90/531/EEC), the Member States were, for the first time, obliged to tender public contracts Europe-wide if they exceed the value specified in guidelines. With the aid of these guidelines, the Commission and Council of the EU took the first step to counter the tendency that had prevailed, for public bodies to award contracts only domestically. Independently of the previous, questionable success of these EU measures, the obligation to offer contracts Europe-wide has led necessarily to an improved level of information and thus to an intensification of information exchange.

The same applies to the trend on the part of private enterprises towards international, even worldwide searches for alternative sources of supplies. This development termed *'global sourcing'*, refers primarily to the delivery of interchangeable components whose high degree of standardization and relatively low complexity facilitate a high number of alternative sellers. Homburg (1995) and Backhaus (1999), confirm this not only theoretically, but also empirically. Based on 165 companies that purchase manufactured items, the investigation showed that the number of suppliers for a particular component increases with the increasing economic significance of this component. At the same time, the investigation comes to the conclusion that the number of suppliers declines with the increasing complexity of the procurement situation. For this procurement situation, it can be assumed that buyers seek, with increasing intensity, information about other suppliers. Because we are dealing here with less complex goods, the price will be the decisive decision-making criterion in selecting a supplier (Backhaus, 1999). Sellers with cost advantages on the basis of a low wage level, and resulting attractive prices, can thus improve their market position. Because they are located primarily in low-wage countries, interchangeable components lead to a trend towards globalization in the area of procurement, because of a cross-border search for alternative suppliers. This trend is reinforced further by the increasing internationalization of organizational buyers, who are able to simplify access to arbitrage-relevant information through their subsidiaries in foreign markets, through, for example, price comparison.

The result of this globalization of procurement processes is a cross-border search for information that is relevant to purchasing and has a positive impact on the supply of information. This process is *buyer-induced*, because internal organizational cost considerations trigger off this search for information. This applies, first and foremost, to the area of less complex, but economically significant, goods, as described above. For more complex goods with a lower level of interchangeability and a higher interaction intensity between buyer and seller, a trend towards *'single sourcing'* is evident (Backhaus, 1999).

The connection between the degree of complexity of the goods to be purchased and the sourcing strategy can be demonstrated effectively, again using the automobile industry as an example. The European manufacturers (OEMs) in particular, have, in recent years, developed the expectation that their suppliers would provide integrative services that they themselves had largely provided in the past (Adolphs, 1997). Figure 9.7 demonstrates that the share of (normal) components purchased by OEMs has declined significantly over time,

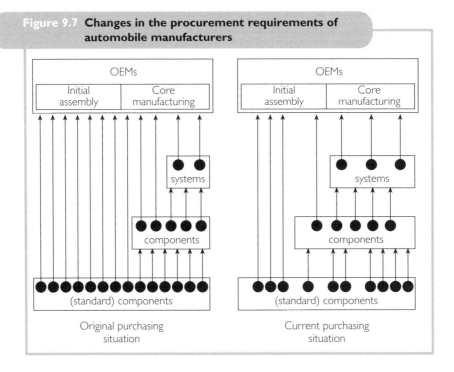

Figure 9.7 Changes in the procurement requirements of automobile manufacturers

Table 9.2 Trend towards reducing the number of direct suppliers in the automobile industry

		Number of direct suppliers	
Company	1996	Short term	Long term
Audi	900	400	90
BMW	900	450	100–200
Ford	900	600	100
Mercedes	1,200	600	40
Opel	1,400	1,100	300
Porsche	650	300	100
VW	1,500	950	100

in comparison to more complex components or modules. In other words, the OEMs have outsourced the integration aspect and thus increased systemically the complexity of the goods they purchase.

Parallel to this, the OEMs have, however, also reduced the number of their (direct) suppliers. Table 9.2 shows that, for example, all German automobile manufacturers have reduced the number of suppliers substantially, or will do so in the future.

In summary, it is clear that the extent of relevant buying information in a specific procurement situation changes as the following magnitudes alter:

▸ costs of information;
▸ internationalization of sellers;
▸ securing information that is relevant to arbitrage;
▸ purchase complexity; and
▸ economic significance of the procured object.

The Use of Information

The exchange of information about alternative sellers and their offers in various different country markets leads to changes in buyer behaviour, if this information is used by buyers. However, this information does not necessarily lead to arbitrage (procurement in foreign markets), as the following listing of possible reactions shows:

▸ (ultimate) backing out of purchasing decision;
▸ evading alternative offers with significantly lower price differences;
▸ (provisional) delay of purchasing decisions;
▸ procurement and use in the foreign market;

▸ procurement in foreign markets, re-importing and use in the domestic market;

▸ the impact of pricing concessions from original suppliers;

▸ no impact on the originally planned purchasing decision (no re-importing, no brand or supplier switching, and no refusals to make a decision).

Buyers have a variety of options open to them in terms of acting on price and quality differences that they have recognized. Thus purchasing decisions can be delayed temporarily, if, in future, a levelling-out of country-related price and quality differences can be expected. This is most likely to be the case if purchasing decisions do not have to be made under time pressure, and the perceived risk of such a pressured decision is high. A further convergence of price and quality differences can be expected if the first price-convergence movements in the market can be observed, no barriers (or only small ones) hinder exchange, or the existence of a large number of potential buyers is known and alters buyer behaviour. The reaction to a recognition of price and quality differences can therefore go so far that purchasing decisions are abandoned out of anger or frustration, or buyers switch to alternative products with lower price and quality differences that have a bearing on arbitrage. The background of both reactions can, for example, lead to perceptions that product and pricing policy by manufacturers are 'unfair'. If, on the other hand, arbitrage-related information becomes available for purchasing processes in foreign markets, there may be an immediate exchange of goods.

The Exchange of Goods

Demand-related feedback only occurs if information about price and quality differences, which can lead to arbitrage, lead to a change in buyer behaviour. The exchange of goods is a central indicator of changes in buyer behaviour. In order to measure the extent of goods exchange, and thus of its growth in converging markets, the concepts of (the extent of) *grey markets* and *price differences*, is important. It measures the demand-related degree of integration of country markets in question (Ravallion, 1986; Silvapulle and Jayasuriya, 1992).

The concept of price differences as an indicator of horizontal or geographical market integration is used particularly in the economic policy of developing countries to identify regions that are subject to food shortages and thus susceptible to hunger and starvation, with a simultaneous provision of aid. For example, the proposition that relates the topic to famine is that poorly-integrated markets constitute one factor (among many others) that make a region more vulnerable to famine. If a peripheral market is poorly integrated with a central market that constitutes an important source of supply, then big price movements over a long time period may be necessary to bring supplies to the peripheral market (Wyeth, 1992: 3). Hunger crises in a region with a varied degree of welfare among the population occur when the region is weakly integrated with other, well-provided regions. The low level of integration means that high price differences for the product in question between the regions do not disappear. This is due to bottlenecks in supply in the regions threatened by starvation. Chronic price differences in the context of development policy are a motivation to combat price differences through governmental trading organizations which facilitate the exchange of goods between weakly integrated regions.

The development of price differences thus becomes an indicator of the level of integration of the relevant regions. In the case of high integration, arbitrage leads to a levelling-out of price differences to the level of transaction costs, without governmental intervention being necessary (Wyeth, 1992). Weakly integrated markets, on the other hand, reveal stagnant or constant price differences (Figure 9.8).

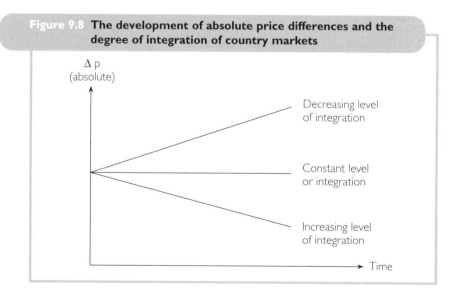

Figure 9.8 The development of absolute price differences and the degree of integration of country markets

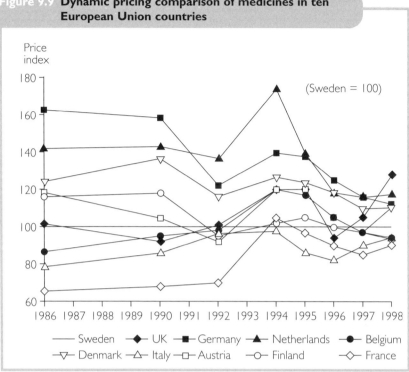

Figure 9.9 **Dynamic pricing comparison of medicines in ten European Union countries**

Price index

(Sweden = 100)

Legend: —— Sweden —◆— UK —■— Germany —▲— Netherlands —●— Belgium
—▽— Denmark —△— Italy —□— Austria —○— Finland —◇— France

If, for example, the pharmaceutical market is used as an example, in Figure 9.9 the dynamic pricing comparison of medicines in ten European Union countries shows, on the basis of pharmacy prices, that price differences have declined considerably since the late 1980s.

The concept of price differences can only be applied under certain conditions. The basic condition for this approach is that the product, with an appropriate level of integration, is offered, preferably in the identical form. The observed price differences and their changes over time can only be effective if they relate to a comparable basis. With an increasing degree of product standardization, there is an increase in significance of the indicator for the measurement of the degree of integration. Accordingly, in practice, integration is measured with the aid of price-difference application examples, mainly for commodities such as rice (Timmer, 1974; Ali, 1984; Ravallion, 1985; Tabor, 1989; Ellis *et al.*, 1991); for wheat

(Cummings, 1968); or money (Hakio and Rush, 1989; Karfakis and Moschos; 1990).

What is also decisive is that the degree of standardization – that is, the level of comparability of products in the country markets – does not change over time. On the other hand, it is unclear to what extent price convergence can be attributed to arbitrage or fluctuating quality differences. For the purposes of measurement, furthermore, sufficiently large price variations in the reference market are necessary, in order to observe, at all, the impact in other markets. Therefore, the concept can only be applied where prices are not completely constant over time.

An additional influence on the measurement of integration, and one that should not be neglected, is the prevalence of differing inflation rates. These must be considered in processing price series over time.

Co-ordination Strategies in Converging Markets

An increasing interdependence of country markets creates a continuous need for co-ordination within these markets. An enterprise can react to this need for co-ordination by adapting market operations continually to changes in environmental conditions (increasing buyer, seller and competitive interdependence) or through attempting to influence the degree of feedback itself. While reactions to interdependence constitute a pure *adaptation strategy*, influencing the degree of interdependence itself is a *countering strategy*.

For an adaptation to changing environmental conditions, an enterprise regards market changes as unalterable. Adaptation measures are aimed accordingly at fulfilling the need for co-ordination. Covering the external need for co-ordination entails optimizing country-specific market operations with respect to the new market conditions, either through an adaptation of marketing instruments or adaptation through the timing of market exit. In any event, adaptation to the growing degree of market interdependence assumes a *reaction* to changing buyer- and seller-related feedback. The extent or development of feedback between the operational country markets is thus regarded by the buyer as given and unchangeable.

On the other hand, a counter-strategy is based on the assumption that the degree of interdependence of country markets can indeed be influenced (by the firm itself). On the basis of this assumption,

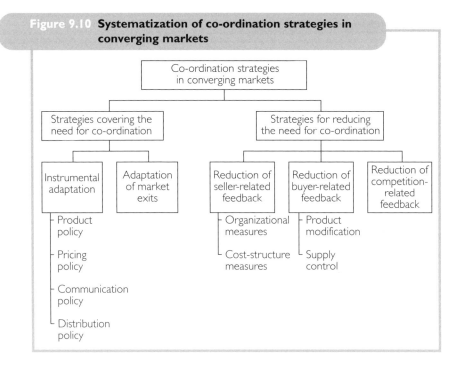

Figure 9.10 Systematization of co-ordination strategies in converging markets

approaches are followed that aim at changing the degree of interdependence in a targeted manner (measures to reduce the need for co-ordination). This strategic approach can thus be characterized as an active intervention with respect to changes in buyer, seller and competitive feedback.

Figure 9.10 shows a systematization of co-ordination strategies, and makes it clear that, within the specified strategy types, there are partial strategies (strategy components) that international enterprises can use for the purposes of co-ordination.

The following observations on individual strategies for overcoming co-ordination problems in international marketing are not intended to imply that they can, or should, be applied in isolation. On the contrary, one must assume that enterprises will use them in *combination*. This applies particularly to strategies aimed at fulfilling or reducing the need for co-ordination. In general, it can be assumed that a firm is not in a position to undertake measures that completely eradicate interdependencies between country markets (to the degree that this would be economically advisable). Consequently, a parallel application of co-ordination measures may be necessary.

Co-ordination Strategies

Instrumental Adaptation

Through a change in marketing operations (instrumental adaptation), a reaction to increasing interdependency, subject to changed environmental conditions, may optimize the total profit of the enterprise. With respect to the instrumental adaptation by internationally active enterprises to converging markets, *product, price, communication and distribution policy* are the central decision parameters. With respect to converging markets, and therefore often in the context of a market entry decision, international enterprises have established to what extent these instruments should be standardized or differentiated. Through changed interdependency between country markets in the context of convergence, the initial decision must now be re-made in terms of the level of standardization of instruments. Because convergence frequently is associated with an increase in feedback, there is a need in all decision-making areas, at least to some extent, to implement a high level of standardization of marketing instruments.

However, it is less clear as to what level of standardization is optimal at a specific point in time, depending on the level of integration and, of course, also on the cost situation. In principle, this co-ordination problem can be resolved so as to achieve, with a given level of market integration, the profit-maximizing level of standardization or differentiation relating to the extent of buyer, seller and competition-related feedback. The co-ordination problem in dynamic, converging country markets is therefore reflected in the identification of an optimal *standardization path*, which, with increasing market integration, relates to the temporal sequence of the profit-maximizing level of standardization of market operations, subject to cost (learning effects, spreading of fixed costs, economies of scale) and revenue aspects (willingness to pay, arbitrage). In this context, Figure 9.11 demonstrates that determining the optimal level of standardization is a static problem, whereas, through the (dynamic) permanent determination of the particular extent of market integration attained through the *level* of standardization, the optimal standardization *path* may be obtained.

The individual marketing instruments can function as alternative or complementary reactions to increasing buyer, seller and competitive interdependency. They will be discussed separately in the following section, in order to clarify the isolated impact on the

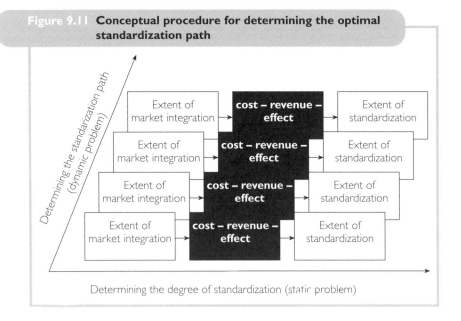

Figure 9.11 Conceptual procedure for determining the optimal standardization path

optimization approaches of determining the appropriate degree of differentiation and standardization within the context of going international.

Product Standardization

Formal Derivation of the Adaptation Path in Product Policy

In the context of *going international*, an analytical model for a static determination of the optimal level of standardization is discussed. The effects described apply to static market conditions, primarily because a constant degree of feedback is assumed. In converging markets with increasing feedback, dynamic effects should be included in the analysis. It is necessary to identify an optimal dynamic *standardization path for production policy*, which is dependent on environmental developments.

As a result of differentiation, in which buyer preference converge, market convergence has a particular impact on revenue.

The influence on costs can be ignored at first, because market integration influences only some elements of sales cost (for example, tariffs). In the broader context of all costs (including production and development, remaining sales costs), these seem negligable.

The convergence of buyer preferences leads initially to a decline in the marginal revenue of differentiation. With an increasing

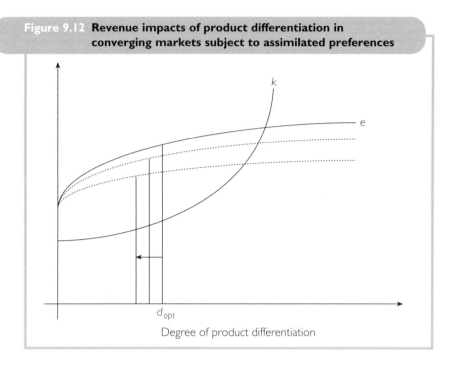

Figure 9.12 **Revenue impacts of product differentiation in converging markets subject to assimilated preferences**

homogeneity of preferences, the attainable advantage in willingness to pay, and in quantities sold as a result of product differentiation, will become progressively smaller. The greater the impact of buyer-preference convergence on the revenue function, the flatter the curve representing differentiation-related revenue (see Figure 9.12).

In the extreme of a completely homogenous preference structure, the revenue curve runs parallel to the x-axis and is independent on product differentiation (see Figure 9.12). A differentiation of products and services no longer leads to an additional willingness to pay and consequently not to additional revenues. As a result of this development, the optimal level of differentiation declines with an increasing standardization of buyer preferences, and vice versa. With completely identical preferences for all buyers, complete product standardization (zero differentiation) will be optimal.

Implementation of the Adaptation Path through Product-Policy Measures

In terms of implementing the formally-derived standardization path (shown above), two questions that build on one another arise for the enterprise that is active in converging markets:

▸ The enterprise must first determine if standardization measures should be implemented simultaneously with respect to all elements of product policy. Alternatively, the enterprise can focus its initial standardization efforts on certain elements only, and standardize others when the process of convergence in country markets is more advanced.

▸ Building on the above question, there is the further issue as to what specific measures will be used to implement the previously established standardization sequence (timing) of product policy elements.

Standardization Sequence of Product Policy Elements

The strategic process of increasing the level of standardization within product policy, will, of necessity, take place 'from inside out'. In a first step, enterprises focus their efforts on the product core. Furthermore, possible cost advantages arising from the experience-curve effects (as discussed earlier), can be given as a reason for efforts at standardizing the product core, first and foremost. Such cost reductions become more likely because there is no need for the product core to be affected by variations and adaptation. Standardized labelling, identical packaging, or similar or identical services, are less important. It thus seems appropriate that efforts at standardizing the core constitute the main objective of product policy.

Only if there is a complete standardization of the product core is it possible, through a standardization of labelling and packaging, to raise the overall level of standardization (see Figure 9.13). If it is also possible to standardize the additional services, the case of complete standardization will have been achieved.

Figure 9.13 demonstrates, in summary form, that the main objective of product-core standardization is product-policy adaptation in converging markets. On the other hand, standardization of the other elements are only supplementary goals, because, with their *help*, homogenization is possible, but they cannot solve the key interdependency problems. However, it is quite clear that the ideal situation can only be reached when a simultaneously high level of labelling, packaging and service standardization is attained. Consequently, all elements of product policy are taken into account in terms of converging markets.

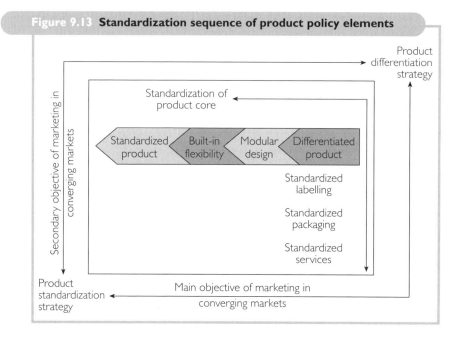

Figure 9.13 Standardization sequence of product policy elements

Dynamic Brand Management as an Example of the Operational Implementation of a Selected Standardization Sequencing

By way of example, the operational formation of an increased standardization of product policy elements is demonstrated against the background of brand management in converging markets. With respect to standardization in the previous country-specific markets, the potential goals of brand management should be observed. In principle, the brand is in the foreground with respect to creating additional utility which goes beyond the basic utility provided by the product. This additional utility or benefit can be justified, in that the buyer has clear quality expectations from future purchases.

In view of the fact that one of the main tasks of brand management is the development of *customer loyalty*, and that it should be the goal of internationally operating companies in converging markets to create such customer commitment to the brand beyond country borders, the establishment of an international brand is particularly important to avoid customer migration. Therefore brand standardization can contribute considerably towards product standardization, particularly from the point of view of buyers.

In terms of the dynamic aspects of converging markets, due attention needs to be given to the question of shaping the transition from a national to an international brand. A number of examples demonstrates this well (KKB → Citibank; Texaco → DEA; Raider → Twix or InterRent → Europcar). Kapferer (1989) differentiates among three different methods of transition between country-specific brands and an internationally standardized brand (see also Liedtke 1992):

▸ progressive 'blending';
▸ information-aided transition
▸ the 'clean break' method.

Progressive Blending

Progressive blending occurs if the brands that are to be newly positioned emerge from a linkage of earlier country-specific brands (brand components). The objective of this method of progressive blending is to standardize the brand internationally, without incurring recognition losses in the various country markets.

The French brand 'LU' provides a good example of internationalization. From the Pimm's brand which is used in France, the Pimm's De Beukelaer brand sold in Belgium, and the biscuit De Beukalaer sold in Germany, Pimm's LU was developed in three steps as shown in Figure 9.14.

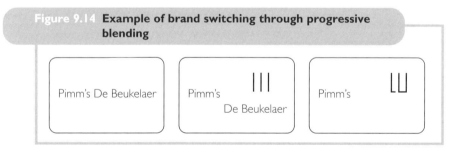

Figure 9.14 Example of brand switching through progressive blending

Progressive blending is often used by enterprises in the context of mergers for determining the company name. 'Thyssen-Krupp' or 'DaimlerChrysler' are examples of this kind of naming. Enterprises frequently use such methods if they believe they can exploit at least certain aspects of the value of both merger partners. The procedure also has the advantage of avoiding a long, involved process of name-setting. None the less, problems inevitably occur when it is unclear which partner, in an essentially equal alliance, should appear first in the combined name (Gutzmer, 2001).

Information-aided Transition

With an information-aided transition, the customer is explicitly and repeatedly prepared for the name change (Meissner, 1994), through, for example, using the two logos parallel to one another for the transition period. This is intended to facilitate a 'soft' movement from the old country-specific brand to the new, internationally standardized brand. Buyers are thus eased in to the new brand gently and gradually. This helps to achieve the objective of retaining the value of the 'old' brand.

This form of dynamic brand management is applied in practice by many enterprises. Typical examples are the transfer from Effem as well as Mars to Masterfoods (Figure 9.15), from InterRent to Europcar, Raider to Twix, Texaco to DEA (Bierwisch, 1994) or Melitta to Toppits (see Figure 9.16).

Figure 9.15 Information-aided transition form Mars to Masterfoods

Good-bye...

...hello!

Masterfoods

The firm Melitta is a medium-sized enterprise in Eastern Westphalia (Germany), which, as well as coffee and coffee filters, manufactures and markets a variety of household products. In 2001, the enterprise achieved a turnover of €1.1 billion, with 40 per cent outside Germany. The enterprise had gained market shares in various sub-sectors of the industry, including rubbish bags and food wrappings.

They were selling more than 210 products in more than 100 countries, and doing so under the single brand name 'Melitta'. Because the earlier individual Melitta brand had, over time, become a brand assortment, the enterprise feared a dilution of the brand profile. Consequently, the enterprise decided to revitalize its brand portfolio. To this end, in the second half of the 1980s, strategic marketing fields were established, in which similar products from the enterprise were marketed under one brand name. For example, all food wrappings for maintaining freshness, or for freezing or baking, were repositioned under the brand name 'Toppits' (Bieling, 1999).

Because the products were familiar to customers of the enterprise under the name 'Melitta' rather than 'Toppits', and it was desirable to transfer the high level of familiarly and brand value to the new brand, the enterprise decided to implement a twelve-year information-aided transition from Melitta to Toppits. Figure 9.16 shows the various phases of the process, and how the optical significance of the brand name Melitta declined in importance. It was removed altogether as a logo anchor in 2000.

Figure 9.16 Information-aided transition from Melitta to Toppits

 Before 1988

 1988–1993

 1993–1999

 As of 2000

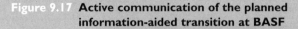

Figure 9.17 **Active communication of the planned information-aided transition at BASF**

In some instances, for this method of information-aided transition, there is even a clear statement of such planned step-wise change within the communication policy. Figure 9.17 is an example of an advertisement showing the information-aided transition from BASF to EMTEC.

The 'Clean Break' Method

With the 'clean break' method, one brand is replaced by another without any advanced warning. In this strategy, the brand value of the replaced brand is destroyed, so this method is use only if the value of the old brand was far lower than that of the new one and/or the new brand has a far greater brand value or growth potential (Liedtke, 1992). The attempt in 1986 by the firm Mars to replace the 'Treets' brand with

'M&M' without warning, is an example of the unintended use of the 'clean break'. Despite efforts at linkages though the message 'from the manufacturer of Treets' in the communication policy, which was intended to minimize damage to the brand policy, the level of familiarity of the brand declined radically, leading to major losses in market share in Germany and France (Kapferer, 1989).

However, clean breaks can sometimes be used with great success, as in the case of Albal/Handy Bag in France.

In the context of a joint venture, the Melitta enterprise group and Dow brands, a situation arose in the French market in which both enterprises had comparable brand strength in the market for aluminum foil for food wrapping. The Melitta enterprise group had acquired its French brand 'Handy Bag' in 1992 through a corporate takeover, and then decided not to replace it with 'Toppits-Melitta', because the Toppits name was quite unfamiliar in France. Because the brand of the joint venture was to be positioned in Southern and Western Europe under the name of 'Albal', and Dow brands had already placed this brand successfully in France, in March 1997, it was decided to withdraw the 'Handy Bag' brand from the French market. Through accompanying communication-policy measures (such as the advertising slogan 'Albal and Handy Bag are getting together to make you even more satisfied'), the joint venture managed to transfer the entire market share from Handy Bag to Albal (see Figure 9.18).

Price Standardization

Impact of Market Convergence on the Factors Determining International Price Differentiation

The consequences for pricing policy of market convergence have, in the past, been discussed with considerable controversy (see Gaul and Lutz (1993) for an example of an empirical investigation on the subject). Here, the discussion varies from the extreme position of 'maintaining price differentiation' and 'complete price harmonization'.

For example, Meissner regards the application of price differences after the removal of trade barriers in a common market as being almost impossible, because of potential trade diversion (Meissner, 1990). In a similar manner, Bridgewater and Egan (2002, p. 167) advise a standardized price in converging markets, which should be

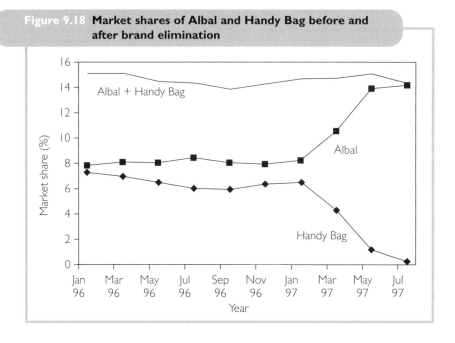

Figure 9.18 **Market shares of Albal and Handy Bag before and after brand elimination**

determined in consideration of the average distribution and logistical costs, just as the previous country-specific costs. Daser and Hylton (1991, p. 45) plead for a unitary European price and suggest a pricing policy which 'at least to some degree is adapted to the prevailing economic and cultural differences in the various markets'. In contrast, Meffert (1990) regards regional price differentiation as being necessary in order to be able to take advantage of existing buying power differentials and situational influences, such as differing value-added taxes.

In view of the lack of unanimity in the literature as to whether market convergence necessarily leads to a large degree of price standardization, the question arises of how the factors influencing decisions about the optimal extent of international price differentiation/standardization that can be observed will develop in converging markets.

In this context, Figure 9.19 demonstrates that, through the integration of markets, the influence factors that had earlier had an adverse impact on price standardization and work in favour of price differentiation, become weaker. For example, it can be assumed that, for converging markets, there will be a (slow) convergence of purchasing power; also buyer preference convergence cannot be ruled out.

Figure 9.19 Changes in factors influencing price standardization decisions in converging markets

Influence factors	In non-integrated markets	In converging markets
Image (problems) with differentiation	Largely unproblematic due to low informational transparency	Problematic due to increasing information exchange
Level of purchasing power in target countries	Varies to some extent	Possible convergence
Buyer preferences	Varies to some extent	Possible convergence
Tendency towards arbitrage	Generally low	Increasing tendency
Cost situation	Varied	Often not affected
Prevalence of reimporting	Minimal	Increasing
Inflation and exchange rate risks	At times substantial	Lower, and with currency union, zero

To what degree the prevailing inflation and exchange-rate swings are responsible for the emergence of price differences depends decisively on the adaptive behaviour of firms as a result of the development of exchange-rate swings. In this respect, empirical studies prove that, for example, exporters tend to keep either the price in the foreign market constant, or at least the original unit revenues in the domestic currency.

Simon (1992) analyses these two 'practitioner strategies', using the example of a German enterprise that exports to the USA. He assumes that the exporter is confronted with the following price-response and cost functions in the American market:

$$x = a - b \cdot p_{USA} \tag{9.1}$$

$$K = K_{fixed} + k_v \cdot x \tag{9.2}$$

Because we are dealing with an exporter, the price is assumed to be set in US\$, but the costs are in € (that is, originally in DM in 1992). If the exporter aims at maximizing profits, there will be an attempt to maximize the following function (9.3):

$$
\begin{aligned}
G€ = U - K &= x \cdot p_{USA} \cdot w - (K_{fixed} + k_v \cdot x) \\
&= (a - b \cdot p_{USA}) \cdot p_\$ \cdot w - K_{fixed} - k_v \cdot (a - b \cdot p_{USA}) \tag{9.3}
\end{aligned}
$$

$$\Rightarrow \frac{\partial G \euro}{\partial p_{USA}} = a \cdot w - 2 \cdot b \cdot w \cdot p_{USA} + k_v \cdot b \overset{!}{=} 0 \tag{9.4}$$

$$\Rightarrow p_{USA;opt} = \frac{1}{2} \cdot \left(\frac{a}{b} + \frac{k_v}{w} \right) \tag{9.5}$$

where w corresponds to the €/\$ exchange rate.

If the price in the USA is now adapted to exchange-rate swings (9.5), the enterprise achieves consistently higher profits in the US market than the above-stated practitioner strategies. Figure 9.20 demonstrates that this applies to rising and falling exchange rates.

Against this background, Simon (1992, p. 473) evaluates the practitioners' strategies accordingly: 'practices such as maintaining constant prices in the target market currency or the unit revenue in the currency of origin, lead to suboptimal results in the face of exchange rate fluctuations. Maintaining constant unit revenue in the home-country currency proves particularly disadvantageous.'

In developing further these considerations from Simon (1992), it is clear, at the same time, that exchange-rate fluctuations lead, in effect, automatically to changing price differences. If one assumes that, in the German home market, the original situation (w_0) is that the seller asks the same price as in the USA (merely converted into

Figure 9.20 **Profit developments of alternative adaptation strategies subject to exchange rate**

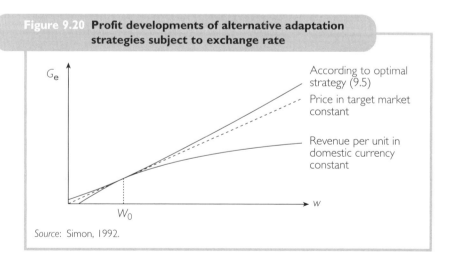

According to optimal strategy (9.5)

Price in target market constant

Revenue per unit in domestic currency constant

Source: Simon, 1992.

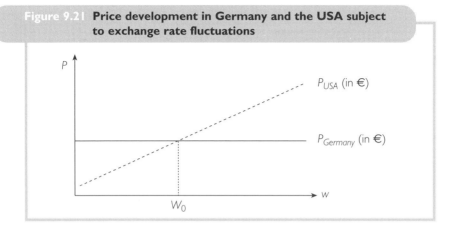

Figure 9.21 **Price development in Germany and the USA subject to exchange rate fluctuations**

€), in the USA, there will be a price that depends on the exchange rate (in Figure 9.21, the prevailing price in the USA would be converted into € for reasons of comparison), because it is not the conversion here, but the level of the optimal price according to Equation (9.5), that counts.

With respect to the above considerations, it should not be neglected that clear disadvantages of practitioner strategies can be attributed mainly to the fact that a comparatively simple model situation is assumed. This refers to the fact that typically a monopolistic situation is assumed in terms of an exporter in the foreign market. Löbler (2000) considers this to be an unrealistic assumption for many markets, and comes to different conclusions about advantages when considering a duopoly. The strategy, which depends on the exchange rate and attempts to achieve an optimal Nash equilibrium, does not always provide profit maximization, in comparison to the practitioner strategies.

Figure 9.22, which shows the profits of the practitioner strategies, less the corresponding profits from the use of the Nash equilibrium, and demonstrates that it is appropriate with a rising exchange rate to maintain a constant price in the currency of the target country – that is, constant in US dollars. Only with a very strong increase in the exchange rate ($w > w_1$), will a new Nash equilibrium contribute towards profit maximization. If, on the other hand, the exchange rate sinks ultimately from W_0, not striving towards a new Nash equilibrium will contribute towards profit maximization. Instead, the unit revenue in the domestic currency (€) should be kept

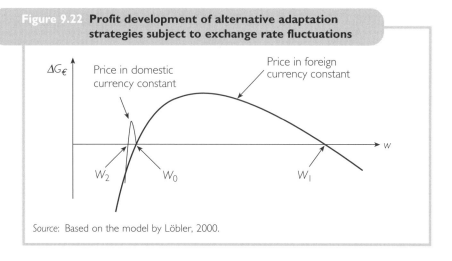

Figure 9.22 **Profit development of alternative adaptation strategies subject to exchange rate fluctuations**

Source: Based on the model by Löbler, 2000.

constant. Only when $w < w_2$ is it optimal in terms of profits to achieve a new Nash equilibrium.

With regard to the key question here, as to whether exchange rate fluctuations lead consistently to changed price differences, a small decline in exchange rates in Löbler's model does not make any difference to prevailing prices. In other words, if it is optimal in this situation to keep unit revenue constant in the domestic currency, this means that, subject to identical costs, there will be no price differences between the domestic and foreign markets at that time.

Furthermore, through the convergence, the impacts which the ten stated factors were already exerting on price standardization will increase further. The elimination of trade barriers makes it easier for exporters to transport goods at low cost across national borders. Similarly, it is clear that in integrated markets, buyer tendency towards arbitrage rises, and enterprises that insist on maintaining price differences will have to contend with image losses. Because of an improved flow of information, the price differences will be far more evident to buyers.

Above all, if there is a currency union in the converging markets, price differences will be revealed. In such a situation, there are no conversion problems for consumers, and price differences are obvious and transparent to buyers. This is also one of the reasons why the introduction of a common currency, euro (€), within the EU is regarded as having a major impact on the pricing policy of international enterprises, and is accorded due attention in the literature (Bridgewater and Egan, 2002, p. 66). However, it should not be overlooked that many of the problems cited in the literature that are associated with a common currency, are not *inter*national, but rather national marketing problems. These include the group of problems associated with price thresholds in the context of currency unification (Bridgewater and Egan, 2002).

There are various possible reasons why enterprises in converging markets should increase the extent of price standardization. However, it cannot be assumed that there will be no differences in purchasing power or consumer preferences between converging markets. Furthermore, complete informational transparency is hardly possible in real markets, and arbitrage costs cannot be eradicated completely. None the less, this does not mean that complete price unification should be implemented. Instead, the issue here is the optimal formulation of a pricing policy adaptation path. This applies all the more because convergence generally occurs in the form of a gradual process, which requires a successive increase in the extent of price standardization.

Derivation of the Optimum Pricing Standardization Path

Because, in contrast to fragmenting markets, the convergence of country markets generally occurs in a step-wise process, the problem of price co-ordination does not arise as *static problem* (at a single point in time), but rather as a *dynamic problem* relating to a broader time frame. In other words, this means that, depending on the degree of convergence that has been achieved in the operational, and now converging, markets, prices must constantly be coordinated optimally with one another (Backhaus and Voeth, 1999).

For this reason, Simon and Kucher (1993), for example, recommend a step-wise, converging price-setting process within the (internal) European market process (see the upper chart in Figure 9.23), which would cope effectively with the step-wise creation of the European market. Most of all, the aim is to avoid the 'nightmare' scenario that would occur if, because of arbitrage and competitive pressure, the prices set by international enterprises approach, step-wise, the lowest level that prevails in the country markets (see the lower chart in Figure 9.23).

These considerations can now be formulated specifically with the aid of the co-ordination approaches. In this context, the nature of pricing-policy adaptation is determined largely by the factors that influence

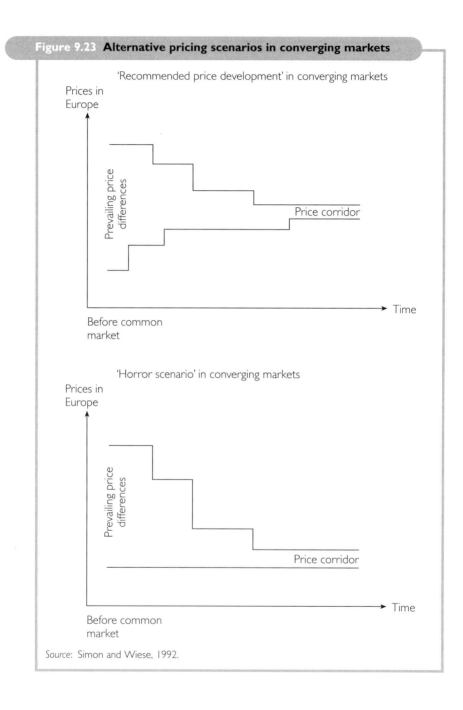

Figure 9.23 Alternative pricing scenarios in converging markets

'Recommended price development' in converging markets

Prices in Europe

Prevailing price differences

Price corridor

Time

Before common market

'Horror scenario' in converging markets

Prices in Europe

Prevailing price differences

Price corridor

Time

Before common market

Source: Simon and Wiese, 1992.

pricing decisions through the convergence process. Among others, the progress of country integration can find expression in:

▸ declining arbitrage costs over time; and/or
▸ an increasing tendency towards buyer arbitrage.

Declining Arbitrage Costs with a Complete Arbitrage Tendency

If the impacts of declining arbitrage costs in converging markets are analysed in isolation, it is necessary to make an assumption about the extent of the tendency towards buyer arbitrage. For reasons of simplicity, we shall assume at first that the tendency towards arbitrage is complete. In comparison to 'incomplete arbitrage', this is a simpler case to describe. As explained earlier, there is complete arbitrage when all buyers in a country market become arbitrageurs, if they can gain arbitrage profits for a particular product. This is the case if the price differences set by a company exceed the arbitrage costs incurred by the reimporter. In order to clarify the effects associated with declining arbitrage costs, we refer to the case of static price co-ordination with complete arbitrage.

In this example, it was evident that co-ordinated, cross-border planning in the country markets A and B, led to a maximization of total corporate profits. In order to achieve optimal prices, the following is yielded in dependence on the transaction or arbitrage costs d (see page 191):

$$p_A = 4{,}000 + 0.6 \cdot d \tag{5.9}$$

$$p_B = 4{,}000 - 0.4 \cdot d \tag{5.10}$$

Because the enterprise assumed arbitrage costs of $c = 500$, in Country A, a price of $p_A = 4300$ was set, and in Country B, $p_B = 3{,}800$.

If one now assumes that the country markets converge, and that this means the arbitrage costs are reduced step-wise, partly through the progressive dismantling of barriers to trade which still prevail. Consequently, it is optimal in terms of profits for the enterprise to adapt prices constantly. If, for example, the enterprise suspects that the dismantling of the previously prevailing tariff barriers will mean that the transactions or arbitrage costs will be reduced annually by 50 MU within the first six years of market integration, and that they will finally settle down to a level of 200 MU, then the enterprise should adapt the function presented in Figure 9.24 annually to the changing conditions.

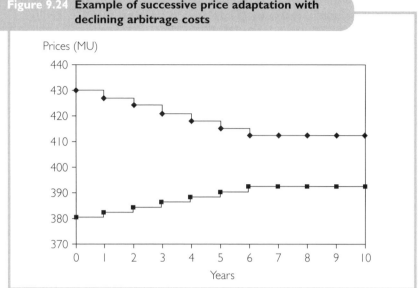

Figure 9.24 Example of successive price adaptation with declining arbitrage costs

The step-model developed by Simon and Wiese (1992) uses a similar process of adaptation. The breadth of the price corridor corresponds to the termination of transaction costs of re-importing (200 MU) which no longer arise after the end of the market integration process.

Increasing Arbitrage Tendency in a Model of 'Incomplete Arbitrage'

The impacts of an increasing arbitrage tendency in converging markets can only be analysed within a model of incomplete arbitrage, because in a model of complete arbitrage, the arbitrage tendency is already at a maximum and thus cannot be increased further. In order to clarify the impacts on price co-ordination here too, the static price co-ordination model discussed in Chapter 5 will be used.

In the case of incomplete arbitrage, it can be assumed that, with a rising price advantage accruing to re-importers, the percentage of buyers willing to purchase re-imported goods will rise. This leads to market convergence, initially with constant arbitrage costs of $d = 500$, so that the arbitrage tendency b rises with a constant price

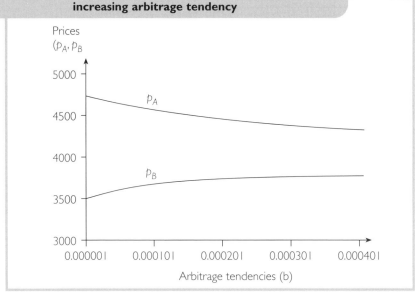

Figure 9.25 Example of successive price adaptation with increasing arbitrage tendency

advantage for re-importers of $(p_A - p_B - d)$, which covers a large part of the demand in the high-price country through re-importing. This will, through differentiation from the static situation, lead to the known profit function (5.17), with the optimal price adaptation shown in Figure 9.25.

$$
\begin{aligned}
G\,(p_A, p_B) = &\; [(p_A - 2,000) \cdot (1 - \beta) \cdot (30,000 - 4\,p_A)] \\
&+ [(p_B - 2,000) \cdot \beta \cdot (30,000 - 4\,(p_B + d)] \\
&+ [(p_B - 2,000) \cdot (30,000 - 6\,p_B)]
\end{aligned} \tag{5.17}
$$

where:

$[(p_A - 2,000) \cdot (1 - \beta) \cdot (30,000 - 4\,p_A)]$ is the demand from Country A in Country A,

$[(p_B - 2,000) \cdot \beta \cdot (30,000 - 4\,(p_B + d)]$ is the demand from Country A in Country B (arbitrage),

$[(p_B - 2,000) \cdot (30,000 - 6\,p_B)]$ is the demand from Country B in Country B.

Also, where there is an increasing tendency towards arbitrage, it is in the interests of profit optimization to equalize prices progressively. However, in this context, the enterprise tolerates a certain amount of re-imports, because these will optimize profits for the enterprise. If, for example, the arbitrage tendency rises to $b = 0.0004$, it will then be appropriate for the enterprise to set a price of $p_A = 4,384.83$ MU, and of $p_B = 3,756.41$ MU. For such a price difference of 628.42 MU, it will pay reimporters to acquire the products of a manufacturer in the low-price country and to transfer these to the high-price country, because, in view of the transactions costs or arbitrage costs of $d = 500$ MU, they can still offer their customers a price advantage of a maximum of 128.42 MU.

$$\beta = b\ (p_A - p_B - c) \tag{5.16}$$

With this price advantage, Equation (5.16) emerges, which, for a constant arbitrage tendency and given level of arbitrage costs, determines the share of re-importing customers from the high-price country, a β-value of 0.051. In other words, in this situation, 5.1 per cent of customers from the high-price country cover their demand through re-importing. However, this is advantageous for the company, because the additional profits gained through price differentiation with respect to customers with a low arbitrage tendency more than compensate for the 'losses' incurred with customers who have a higher arbitrage tendency.

If, in the model of incomplete arbitrage, not only the effects of an increasing arbitrage tendency are taken into account, but also declining arbitrage costs, then the effects described above will apply to a greater extent. In this situation, enterprises must converge their prices more strongly, because the proportion of re-importing customers increases strongly. This is caused by the rise of b and simultaneous decline in d in Equation (5.16), so that the β-values rise with a constant price difference. The pressure to raise the prices in the low-price country and to reduce those in the high-price country, and thus pressure towards standardization, is particularly strong when the arbitrage tendency rises and arbitrage costs decline simultaneously.

Price Co-ordination in Converging Markets in Practice

The above, formal considerations on price co-ordination in converging markets have shown, in essence, that market integration generally leads, or at least should lead, to a stronger price standardization by sellers. The question arises as to *if, how, and with what impact,* international enterprises really do co-ordinate their prices in converging markets.

The Meaning of Price Co-ordination (If?)

Particularly in the context of the founding of the European Union, a number of empirical investigations have been conducted which provide instrumental decision bases to aid firms in their adaptation processes. The majority of the studies came to the conclusion that the need for corporate change lies mainly in price and sales conditions, as demonstrated by the following example from the Gaul and Lutz study.

In the early part of the 1990s, Gaul and Lutz (1993; 1994) conducted a survey of 306 German, British and French enterprises in which they asked for an estimate as to which corporate decisions were affected in particular by Western European integration. The respondents regarded pricing and sales-condition policy as the most significant, ahead of distribution structures, market research, communication policy and product range and formulation.

Simon *et al.*, (1998) developed this work further in terms of the introduction of the euro, and considered what pricing-policy measures were particularly important for business enterprises.

The results shown in Figure 9.26, demonstrate that the respondents accorded price-strategy elements (criteria 1, 2, 4, 5 and 6) a relatively homogeneous weight, compared to operative measures. Interestingly, only 24 per cent of the respondents found the price-threshold problem to be significant, despite the prominence it has received in the literature.

In view of the results of the outlined empirical investigations on price management in converging markets shown here through the example of European market integration, the conclusion could logically be drawn that enterprises active in converging markets see their main challenge in the co-ordination of national prices.

Implementing Price Co-ordination (How?)

The actual implementation of co-ordinated pricing policy measures depends substantially on the corporate and industry-related situational contexts of internationally operating enterprises. For this reason alone, the question of 'how' will not be described in general terms, but by means of an example.

Figure 9.26 The Need for pricing-policy action as a result of the currency union

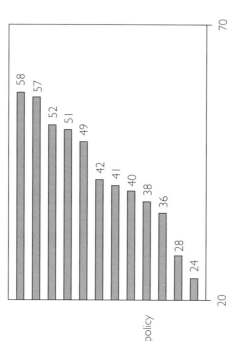

1. Adaptation of national prices in Europe
2. Introduction of a European pricing strategy
3. Employee training on euro strategy
4. Substantial standardization of price formation
5. European price formation for new products
6. Europe-wide price control
7. Introduction of dual price labelling
8. Price formation in various distribution channels
9. Integration of national taxation differences in pricing policy
10. Fixing the price-setting authority of sales personnel
11. Organization of price-setting authorities
12. Europe-wide consideration of price thresholds

Percentage of respondents. Scale values: 1 = less important; 5 = very important.

Source: Simon *et al.*, 1998, p. 787.

Case Study: **Continental AG**

The automobile tyre business in Europe is traditionally character-ized by large regional price differences. The so-called 'big six' enter-prises shared over 85 per cent of the European market until well into the 1990s (Michelin 32 per cent, Continental, 14 per cent, Goodyear, 13 per cent, Bridgestone, Sumitomo and Pirelli, 9 per cent each). These various companies charged varied prices in the European market. This was possible before the founding of the European common market, because:

▸ in the past, many customers were keen to buy local products (country-of-origin effect);
▸ the extent of motorization, size of vehicle fleets and thus the associated distribution of tyre dimensions and tyre speed cate-gories was very different across the European countries;
▸ there were market differences in buying power and purchasing preferences;
▸ there were exchange rate fluctuations and diverging inflation rates; and
▸ differing payment and delivery conditions prevailed in the country markets.

In the 1990s, the automobile tyre business in Europe changed considerably. Given a generally stagnating demand with a simulta-neous over-capacity on the part of established manufacturers, the competitive situation increased. This was exacerbated further by the Asian and Eastern European manufacturers who flooded the European market with cheap products. Furthermore, the EU jeop-ardized the pricing system of the European manufacturers, which was orientated towards price differentiation. The international tyre dealers, in particular, used the dismantling of trade barriers within the EU to improve their procurement conditions, so that they covered their need for tyres in the country market of a manufac-turer who offered the appropriate selection at the lowest price. Because the international tyre dealers were present Europe-wide, they could approach manufacturers' subsidiaries in various coun-tries, to find the cheapest country market. Also, re-importing was made easier for many tyre dealers through the willingness of manu-facturers to absorb transport costs themselves, if the dealer was prepared to organize the transportation. For example, an Italian dealer could buy tyres from a German manufacturer directly from the factory, at a price substantially lower than from a comparable German manufacturer who would have to include in the price the high costs of long-distance transport. None the less, many dealers exploited this situation, not in fact exporting the tyres at all, but selling them immediately in the country of origin, in this case, Germany.

For the tyre manufacturers, these increasing re-imports were associated not only with revenue losses. The purely nationally-operating tyre dealers were becoming increasingly unhappy. They had to observe increasingly active parallel-market re-imports, which were offering customers tyres sometimes below their own original cost.

In order to eradicate the consequences of uncontrolled re-imports, or at least to minimize them, Continental AG decided to establish a European price management system. This comprised essentially two modules, or measures:

▸ An initial lower (list) price limit was fixed for all country markets, which had to be observed by the regional management responsible for price setting. Furthermore, the companies dispensed with a fixed upper price limit, because they assumed that this would be determined, more or less, by the competition in each country market. Finally, maximum rebate conditions were set in each country market, which were to limit the latitude of regional management to allow discounts. These conditions were formulated in such a way that net prices in the European markets would differ from one another by less than 20 per cent.

▸ A second measure comprised the establishment of a pan-European price-control and information system. In this Continental Price Information System (COPIS), all regional subsidiaries had to capture all sales data, as well as dealer offers that were known to them, so it was possible for the head office to analyse these data and identify re-imports, locate their sources and undertake price-policy adaptation. This is demonstrated in the following example (Figure 9.27):

Figure 9.27 shows the prices allowed by the enterprise in countries A and B (Country A represents 100 per cent). However, the system also shows that, in Country A, one dealer offers its

Case Study *continued*

customers substantially different prices for larger tyres. The comparison with the price structure in Country B indicates that this dealer has acquired the tyres not in Country A, but in Country B.

Figure 9.27 International price comparison of Continental winter tyres with the COPIS price information system

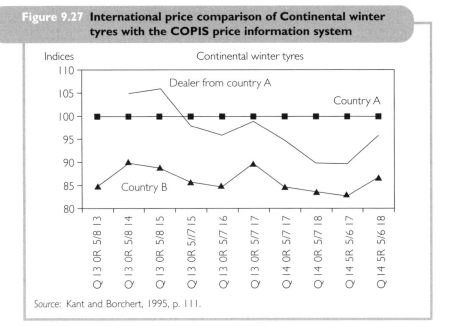

Source: Kant and Borchert, 1995, p. 111.

The case study shows that a central component, and frequently the first step in international price co-ordination, lies in capturing, and analysing systematically, information on the companies' own-price structures and possibly uncontrolled goods streams in operational country markets. If there is such a basic information system, it is possible to intervene and control the international pricing system of an enterprise.

Additional case studies on the implementation of international price management systems, such as for the adhesive 'Pritt' from Henkel (Bornfeld, 2000), for the heating appliances of Joh. Valliant (Backhaus, 2000) or for the 3M company (Huckemann and Dinges, 2000), show, furthermore, that in many enterprises international price management can be achieved with the aid of a price corridor.

The Consequences of International Price Co-ordination

Given that it has become clear that international enterprises in converging markets generally accord an increased weighting to their price co-ordination and, moreover, regard their pricing information and control systems as a first step towards a functioning means of price co-ordination, a final question arises as to whether the application of co-ordinated measures in converging markets are associated with the dismantling of previously prevailing price differences, as would be implied by the issues discussed earlier.

If such a question were to be investigated, not just for an individual enterprise such as the tyre manufacturer described above, but also for an entire industry, then the European automobile market provides a good case in point. This is a suitable example, because:

▸ there have been substantial price differences in the past;
▸ since the establishment of the European market, a number of re-imports have entered the market; several hundred German re-importers can be found on the Internet alone;
▸ the extensive public reporting of price differences and re-importing offers in the automobile market has led to an increase in the tendency for arbitrage among customers;
▸ The fact that car manufacturers lobby against EU law on car re-importing, shows that reimports have become a serious threat for automobile manufacturers; and
▸ a half-yearly report about price developments in this market will be presented to the EU Commission, which will analyse the changes or lack of them, in price differentiation practices of manufacturers.

The EU automobile market index has appeared bi-annually since 1993. To this end, fifteen European and eight Asian manufacturers are requested to state the net and gross list prices they charge in the EU Member States for their automobile models. Furthermore, the prices of add-ons must be formulated in such a manner that they adjust for differences in equipment or fittings between the base models. Once adjusted for equipment differences, the prices are then calculated in euros (formerly ECUs) and normalized, so that the lowest country price for a model constitutes 100 per cent. Since May 1993, these calculations have been available for approximately seventy models.

Figure 9.28 shows the results of an analysis of pricing developments for the models of eight different European automobile manufacturers. The graphs are based on the following considerations:

▸ Because re-imports, and thus the accompanying pressure on the previous price differentiation, can only occur between country

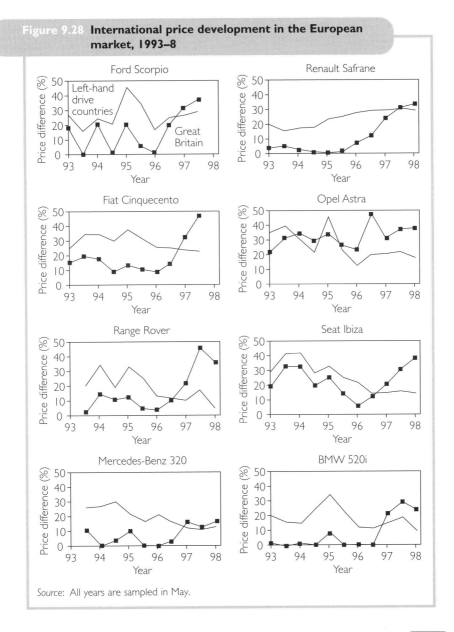

Figure 9.28 International price development in the European market, 1993–8

Source: All years are sampled in May.

markets in which similar products are offered, it is necessary to differentiate between left-hand-drive (LHD) and right-hand-drive (RHD) countries.

▸ Comparisons are made between the group of LHD countries, so as to establish the highest and lowest European prices. Because the EU Commission uses the lowest country price as 100, the data in Figure 9.28 represent the percentage deviations of the high-price country from the low-price country.

▸ In addition, the deviation of the price in Great Britain (RHD country) from LHD low-price countries is shown as a different function.

It is evident that price differences in the LHD countries have not developed in the same manner for all models. For some models, price differences between 1993 and 1998 have tended to remain constant (for example, Ford Scorpio), whereas in the case of the Renault Safrane, they have increased slightly. For the majority of models, there has in fact been a decline, as in the case of the Seat Ibiza.

Furthermore, it is conspicuous that for all the models shown in Figure 9.28, there is an increase in the price difference between the RHD country Great Britain and the low-price LHD country. The non-availability of re-import capabilities of the (cheaper) LHD automobile in the RHD market of Great Britain, seals this market off, protects it from re-imports from the Continent and enables automobile manufacturers to use price differentiation there.

The fact that not all the manufacturers presented in Figure 9.28, have implemented price standardization in the European market, should not be interpreted as meaning that sellers who have not reduced price differentiation set their European prices in an un-coordinated manner. Instead, it should rather be assumed that the models in Figure 9.28 do not all reveal the same arbitrage tendency. Particularly against this background, the maintenance of price differences and the accompanying tolerance of re-imports can optimize profits for the international enterprise. In summary, it is clear that price standardization certainly tends to be encouraged through market convergence, but it must be clarified case-by-case, if and to what extent, price differentiation can still be applied.

In the context of such an analysis of the European pricing system, the firm Porsche came to the conclusion in the summer of 1999 that fixing unified prices in all European countries (apart from Great Britain), would make economic sense.

Standardization of Communication Policy

The Impact of Country Market Convergence on the Optimal Level of Standardization

Market convergence also leads a change in the benefits to be derived from standardization, as opposed to differentiation measures within communication policy. With unchanged cost effects, those impacts that have so far facilitated a differentiated impact of communication policy strategies and measures, tend to lose significance. In particular, the homogenization of buyer preferences leads to a reduction of country-specific characteristics. In this context, the danger referred to by Buzzell (1968), of losing market shares to local sellers who cater more for the specifics of the market, will decline, because the extent of these specifics declines. Given that, at the same time, the potential for increasing the impact of standardizing communications policy in converging markets increases, through, for example the increased significance of international media, there is increasing pressure on international enterprises to adapt. This occurs because the decision made in the past as to the extent of standardization versus differentiation in communication, must be made again, because of the changed market conditions.

With respect to determining the optimal degree of standardization of communication policy measures in the context of the 'going international' model, Figure 9.29 shows the impacts of converging markets. The step-wise convergence of country markets means that, with an increasing degree of standardization, the declines in impact will be increasingly small. Because standardization is associated with a tendency towards constant cost-saving potential, the optimal level of standardization will grow in converging markets.

Formulation of a Standardization Path

The predominance of standardization versus differentiation options in converging markets leads inevitably to a situation in which co-ordination measures create an increasingly unified communications policy. In order to exploit the cost-reduction potential of standardization, without at the same time reducing the impact of communication and thus incurring declines in revenue, the standardization of communication policy occurs in dependence on a convergence of market conditions in the operational country markets.

The standardization path within communication policy depends substantially on the situational context of the international enterprise.

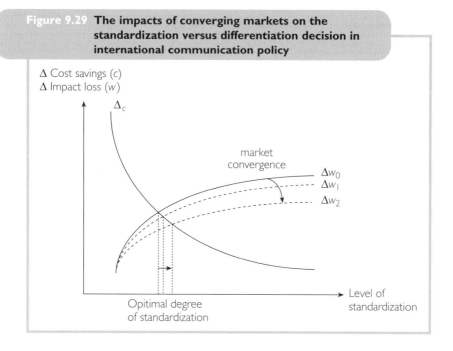

Figure 9.29 **The impacts of converging markets on the standardization versus differentiation decision in international communication policy**

In general terms, however, the standardization path can be described in the following terms:

▸ If the objective of communication standardization is to achieve cost savings without a parallel loss of impact, communication policy *processes* will be more standardized than the policy results. In the advertising of international enterprises, for example, standardized concepts of international agencies can initially be used (process components). Only subsequently will the results of communication policy be standardized.

▸ A standardization path orientated towards the specifics of communication policy measures means that the communication objectives are standardized rather than the communication strategies, and these earlier than the communication instruments (see Figure 9.30).

▸ At the end of the standardization route, there will not necessarily be a complete standardization of communication policy results. For example, in communication policy, in view of the differences in national languages that still tend to prevail, common linguistic or text elements can be found only in exceptional cases. Figures 9.31 and 9.32 provide an example from the consumer goods sector.

Figure 9.30 Formulation elements and phases of communication standardization

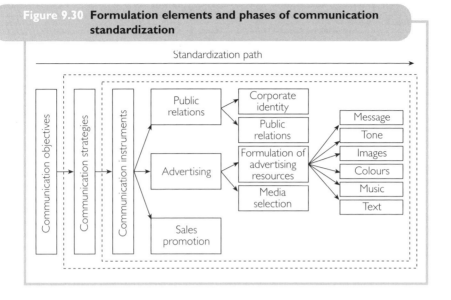

Advertisements from the company, Lancôme, for the German and Italian markets, differ very little.

What is clear, is that, in the context of communication policy in converging markets, the standardization path cannot be generalized. At any point within the dynamic process of converging market conditions, the extent of standardization of communication policy objectives, strategies and, in particular, instruments, must be set in such a manner that a maximum difference is achieved between cost reduction and impact increases on the one hand, and frequently non-avoidable impact reduction on the other. The wide-ranging discussion that can otherwise be found in the literature on potential for standardization of individual communication-policy decision elements (Killough, 1978), which has, become known as the 'standardization debate', helps only in so far as it enables the determinants of the standardization path to be specified (cost-reduction potential and impact reduction/increase).

Development of the Degree of Communication Policy Standardization of International Enterprises

With respect to the question as to whether, in corporate practice, there really is an increasing tendency towards standardization within

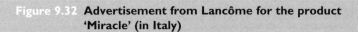

Figure 9.32 Advertisement from Lancôme for the product 'Miracle' (in Italy)

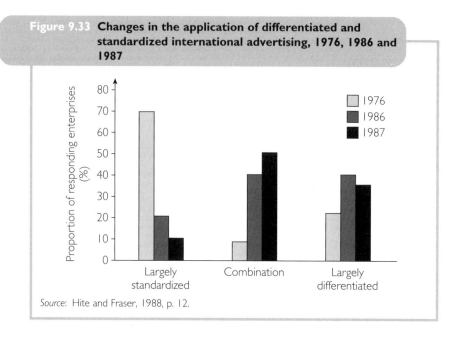

Figure 9.33 **Changes in the application of differentiated and standardized international advertising, 1976, 1986 and 1987**

Source: Hite and Fraser, 1988, p. 12.

communication policy, there are a large number of investigations in the literature (see the overview of Attour and Harris, 1999) which, to some degree, come to contradictory conclusions. While Kreutzer (1989), for example, presents an investigation with evidence of an increasing standardization of advertising of international enterprises, Hite and Fraser (1988) arrive at precisely the opposite conclusion. On the basis of a standardized questionnaire in which international enterprises were asked to specify the degree of standardization of their international advertising for 1976, 1986 and 1987, Hite and Fraser argue that they were able to prove that the standardization of advertising has declined in significance (see Figure 9.33).

However, the investigations such as that of Hite and Fraser must be used with extreme caution, especially if the results of questionnaires and written surveys are the basis of the results. It can be assumed that perceptions of what is really meant by 'largely standardized' or 'largely differentiated', will vary substantially on a subjective level. While one respondent considers the conceptual input perspective, and thus, for example, considers only the (various output based) advertisements as standardized, because these have been developed by an advertising agency, another respondent, looking rather at the output impact, will come to the opposite conclusion with respect to the same advertising campaign.

In order to evaluate the level of standardization applied by an enterprise within international advertising, it is first necessary to determine what exactly is meant by standardization versus differentiation. In most of the investigations in question, this has not been achieved sufficiently. In general, simple survey techniques, and barely adequate market research designs and methods have been used. Thus the investigations do not provide convincing results, so that the answers they provide on the question as to whether enterprises in converging markets implement increasing standardization of their communication policy, are largely unusable.

Since there is a lack of (methodologically) reliable empirical data on the development of differentiation/standardization behaviour in international enterprises within communication policy, the question can generally only be answered in terms of individual cases.

For example, an increase in the level of standardization of international advertising for the firm, Honda in Europe, is a good case in point. Print advertisements in Germany (see Figure 9.34) and Italy (see Figure 9.35) for the Honda Jazz differ substantially. The German advertisement provides significant more (written) information, whereas the Italian advertisement is largely devoid of it. The German advertisement alludes to the sporty character of the car, providing detailed information on engine size (1.4 litre) and power (83 HP). The Italian print provides the same information, but much less prominently. Instead, at the bottom it mentions the versatility of the interior of the car. Both however use the 'Power of Dreams' as the key slogan and place the car in the centre of the message.

Sabel and Weiser (1998) cite another example from the area of international advertising. They show the use of associated slogans by the Coca-Cola company in the USA and Germany (Figure 9.36), and specifically how they become more similar over time.

Changes in Distribution

In terms of distribution policy as well, market convergence changes the communication policy situation, in contrast to product and pricing policy (changes in demand, supply and competitor-based feedback). In the first instance, the supply-related feedback changes.

Figure 9.34 Advertising image for Honda Jazz in the German market, 2003

Figure 9.35 **Advertising Image for Honda Jazz in the Italian market, 2003**

Figure 9.36 Advertising slogans for Coca-Cola in Germany and the USA, 1970–93

USA	Year	Germany
It's the Real Thing	1970	Frischwärts
I'd Like to Buy the World a Coke	1971	
	1974	Trink Coca-Cola . . . das erfrischt richtig
Look Up America	1975	
Coke Adds Life	1976	Coke macht mehr daraus
Have a Coke and a Smile	1979	
	1981	Zeit für Coca-Cola
Coke Is It!	1982	
We've got a Taste For You	1985	Coca-Cola is it!
Red, White & You Catch the Wave	1986	
When Coca-Cola is Part of Your Life, You Can't Beat the Feeling	1987	
Can't Beat the Feeling	1988	
	1989	Can't Beat the Feeling
Can't Beat the Real Thing	1990	
Always Coca-Cola	1993	Always Coca-Cola

The increase in seller-related feedback, which exerts an impact on distribution policy, occurs in converging markets through a possible change in trade structures that can accompany market integration. The homogenization of the institutional framework give not only manufacturers, but also gives retailers, a more straightforward access to converging markets.

While, in the food industry, manufacturing enterprises such as Nestlé, Unilever or Coca-Cola have since the 1960s and 1970s, pursued a consistent strategy of internationalizing their business activities (for a discussion of the internationalization of Coca-Cola, see Oliver (1996), for example), food retailing was in the past generally national in orientation.

The improved possibilities for being active in additional European countries, which have arisen as a result of the creation of the European market, have, in the meantime, led to a situation in which many retailers in Europe have increased their foreign commitment substantially (see Kreke, 1991 on the impact of the European market on retailers). The Frankfurt-based research institute *M+M EUROdATA* even talks of a 'wave of internationalization' in food retailing (*M+M EUROdATA*, 1997).

The preferred market entry strategy of many retailers in the food industry is that of taking over competitors in the target markets. For example, in 1996, the Austrian retailer, Meinl, was taken over by the German Rewe group, which had previously taken over the Austrian market leader, Billa, in 1996. The French retailer, Intermarché, became the main shareholder of the German SPAR in 1997, which, in turn acquired a participation in the Austrian Adeg in 1998. In the past, the British market leader Tesco expanded its presence in Central and Eastern Europe through strategic take-overs (for example, Global in Hungary, K-Markt in the Czech Republic and Slovakia, and Savia in Poland.

Through this kind of market entry, some retailers have, in the meantime, increased their level of internationalization quite considerably. For example, the five largest European food retailing enterprises have been able to expand their European market share between 1990 and 2000 from about 14 per cent to 26 per cent (see Figure 9.37).

While some enterprises already achieve a significant share of their turnover in foreign markets, other retailers (for example, Edeka, Migros, Leclerc or Casino) still operate almost exclusively in their

Figure 9.37 Developments in the European market shares of selected food retailers (in per cent)

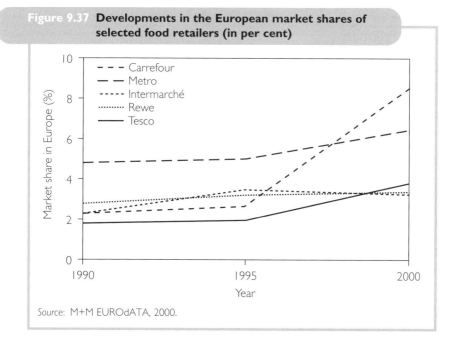

Source: M+M EUROdATA, 2000.

home markets. However, in future, these enterprises, will also need to increase their foreign operations if they want to avoid being taken over by the above-mentioned industry leaders (Hinrichs, 1989; Thiesing, 1989). The concentration process that characterizes European food retailing, will increase in future (see Schneider, 1999 for a discussion of further concentration).

The internationalization of retailing as a result of market integration (see for example, Schneider, 1999) is not without its impact on international distribution policy. These companies find themselves confronted increasingly by the same retailers in various country markets. This increases the level of interdependence of the operational country markets, because seller-related interdependencies increase: the distribution policy decisions can barely be made for specific countries any longer and must relate to all operational (converging) markets.

The outlined changes in retailing structures also have an impact on the formation of the remaining marketing instruments (product, price and communication). In pricing policy, for example, co-operation is possible with increasingly pan-European retailers, which makes price differentiation seem dubious, as shown by the following examples:

▶ In the mid-1990s, the retailing enterprise, Metro, requested the film manufacturer, Kodak, to replace its retailing prices, which had been negotiated nationally until then, with standardized conditions. These were also to remain at the low price level that Kodak had so far used only in the Southern European country markets. Kodak had to reduce its retail prices by, on average 20 per cent (Reischauer, 1997, p. 120).

▶ The increasing willingness of retailing enterprises, to use reimports to improve their sales conditions, is also shown in the following example:

The offer from the Belgian discounter was unbeatable. Such a favourable price for Henkel's washing powder Dixan, has not been available for a long time – so everyone bought enthusiastically. That the packaging looked a bit different and the instructions were in Spanish, did not seem to bother buyers particularly. The Belgian discounter had transported the powder in large trucks from Spain. The batch had originally been offered by an intermediary. This, on the other hand, had acquired the goods in an undisclosed manner in Spain. This convoluted path paid off: the washing powder was cheaper on the Iberian subcontinent than from the Belgian subsidiary of Henkel. What appealed to both the manager of the retail chain and the consumers, led to some concern in the Henkel head office in Düsseldorf. If such activities were to occur on large scale, the relatively high price level in many European countries would be jeopardized. (Jensen, 1998, p. 119).

The boxed examples show that the retailing structures in converging markets lead not only to adaptation within distribution policy. The optimal, and above all, viable levels of standardization and differentiation in the context of other instruments are also influenced. In this manner, once again, the proposition that has already been formulated is reinforced, namely that a decision about adaptation that is appropriate to co-ordination in the context of different instruments, cannot, strictly speaking, proceed in isolation, but must be simultaneous.

Choosing the Right Time for Market Exits

From the co-ordination perspective, the exit from country markets to converging markets can create an economically viable option for internationally active enterprises if individual country markets allow strong feedback to develop, which creates a mismatch between the revenue generated from these country markets and the co-ordination costs associated with maintaining a market presence there. The causes can be explained by means of a simple example.

An enterprise operates in the country markets A and B, and faces the following price-response functions:

$$x_A(p_A) = 225,000 - 2.5 \cdot p_A \tag{9.6}$$

$$x_B(p_B) = 100,000 - 2.5 \cdot p_B \tag{9.7}$$

Furthermore, it should be considered that assembly and delivery in both country markets is associated with different levels of variable costs. Thus, the variable unit costs in Country A amount to 40,000 MUs and in Country B to 30,000 MUs.

If one assumes that, before the convergence of the two country markets, there were insuperable trade barriers for imports, for example, then enterprises active in country markets A and B, could pursue an isolated price-setting process, which would yield the following country-specific optima:

Country A:

$$G_A(p_A) = (225{,}000 - 2.5 \cdot p_A) \cdot p_A - 40{,}000 \cdot (225{,}000 - 2.5 \cdot p_A)$$
$$= 325{,}000 \cdot p_A - 2.5 \cdot P_A^2 - 9 \text{ billion} \tag{9.8}$$

$$\frac{\partial G_A}{\partial p_A} = 325{,}000 - 5 \cdot p_A \overset{!}{=} 0 \Leftrightarrow p_{A,opt} = 65{,}000 \tag{9.9}$$

$$\Rightarrow G_A(65.000) = 1{,}562{,}500.000 \tag{9.10}$$

Country B:

$$G_B(p_B) = (100{,}000 - 2.5 \cdot p_B) \cdot p_B - 30{,}000 \cdot (100{,}000 - 2.5 \cdot p_B)$$
$$= 175{,}000 \cdot p_B - 2.5 \cdot P_B^2 - 3 \text{ billion} \tag{9.11}$$

$$\frac{\partial G_B}{\partial p_B} = 175{,}000 - 5 \cdot p_B \overset{!}{=} 0 \Leftrightarrow p_{B,opt} = 35{,}000 \tag{9.12}$$

$$\Rightarrow G_B(35.000) = 62{,}500{,}000 \tag{9.13}$$

In total, the enterprise could achieve a profit of 1,625 billion MUs.

In the event of convergence of the country markets A and B which are being considered by the enterprise in question, and thus the previously existing trade barriers are dismantled, the enterprise must, in view of the previous price differentiation, now consider possible re-imports. If one assumes that re-imports cause transaction costs of 20,000 MU, then remaining with the optimal prices derived above in the case of independent markets would lead to a substantial loss of profits (assumed for reasons of simplification, a complete arbitrage tendency of buyers). With non-coordination, all those buyers from Country A whose willingness to pay for the product lies above the price charged by the re-importer (price in the low-price Country B including the transaction costs incurred by re-importers), therefore above the level of 55,000 MU, cover their demand through re-importing, so that sellers in Country A will no longer achieve any sales. All in all, in Country B, the following sales quantity would be achieved (X_B) (sales in Country A are zero).

$$x_B{}^* = x_B(35,000) + x_A(55,000) = 12,500 + 87,500 = 100,000 \qquad (9.14)$$

In this manner, by dispensing with price co-ordination, the seller will achieve a profit of only 0.5 billion MU.

If, in view of the looming loss of profits of 1,125 billion MUs in the absence of a price corridor, the seller may decide to optimize his/her profits internationally. Thus, he/she must use the procedure explained earlier in Equation (9.15) in order to maximize his/her total profit function, subject to the condition of avoiding reimports.

$$G(p_A, p_B) = 325,000 \cdot p_A - 2.5 \cdot p_A{}^2 + 175,000 \cdot p_B$$
$$- 2.5 \cdot p_B{}^2 - 12 \text{ billion} \qquad (9.15)$$

$$|p_A - p_B| \leq 20,000 \qquad (9.16)$$

If this optimization problem is resolved with the aid of a Lagrangian solution approach, the following optimal values are obtained:

$$p_{A,opt} = 60,000 \Leftrightarrow x_A = 75,000 \qquad (9.17)$$

$$p_{B,opt} = 40,000 \Leftrightarrow x_B = 0 \qquad (9.18)$$

The result shows that it is obviously in the interests of profit optimization to exit Country B. However, if one leaves Country B, then it is no longer necessary to require a different price in Country A in comparison to an isolated price optimization. For this reason, it is optimal for the enterprise to require an (isolated) optimal price of 65,000 MU in Country A. By so doing, the firm can achieve a profit of 1,5625 million MU, which is 62.5 million MUs below the initial level of profit.

An evaluation of a selective market exit thus clearly poses the problem as to the relative economic significance of the operational country markets from the perspective of co-ordination. This arises not only with regard to the evaluation and selection of an appropriate country market, but also *after* entry in the case of converging markets and on a continuous basis. This relates particularly, in contrast to instrumental adaptation, not to an optimal reaction to the prevailing interdependency in the form of a comparison of the impact of isolated and co-ordinated market operation, but to a comparison of the total profit situation for a varied mix of country markets as the basis of corporate activity. Thus what hangs in the balance is less the 'how' of market operations, but rather the 'if' of market presence.

These considerations, as in the above example, show that the advantages of a selective market exit as an instrument of co-ordination, are determined by a number of factors:

- the number or size of the country markets, which lead to co-ordination problems;
- the extent of prevailing co-ordination problems;
- the co-ordination costs and revenues associated with market presence and the resultant profits of co-ordination, compared to an uncoordinated situation; and
- the profit situation on exiting the country markets that create the worst co-ordination problems.

Co-ordination problems between the operational country markets, can, as in the above example, be attributed to having few and/or small, country markets in the mix. As a consequence, the economic significance would be low in terms of the total context of a company. If it is to be expected that this will not change in the future, the exit option may be economically meaningful. This depends simultaneously on the extent of the co-ordination problems created by the country markets. The larger these are, the greater will be the losses suffered in the other country markets. This situation must be contrasted with the impact of the results of a market exit from the country markets that are causing the co-ordination problems.

The economic evaluation of exit options on the basis of quantitative criteria is, however, only achieved *partially* in many instances. Thus, individual quantitative aspects of a market exit cannot be evaluated immediately and accurately from an economic perspective. The (at least partly) negative signals conveyed to buyers in other countries should be borne in mind. The generally problematic evaluation of bundling effects between products, in the case of multiple-product enterprises whose markets can be affected in different ways by interdependencies, or quantification problems of these linkages, are significant issues. Although this problem is obvious, it is a central task in international marketing to make transparent the economic consequences of market presence and absence.

Strategies for Reducing the Need for Co-ordination

Instrumental adaptation and selective market exit are instruments which cover the need for co-ordination between country markets that arises as a result of interdependencies. A counter-strategy, on the other hand, has the objective of reducing the need for co-ordination between the various country markets. A reduction in the need for co-ordination leads to declining feedback between country markets. Consequently, differentiated marketing programmes can be used and maintained, in order to maximize profits.

Strategies aimed at reducing the need for co-ordination in converging international markets are an attempt to reduce the degree of interdependence between country markets. In essence (formulated in the extreme), we are dealing with an approach to limit the permeability of country borders (arbitrage) or adverse impacts of a cross-border market operation. This is appropriate if a reduction in the degree of independence between country markets creates new latitude in market operations (for example, the level of price differences). Our assumption is that this new latitude can be used profitably by the company. In this respect, the decisive question is, which factors determining buyer, seller and competitive feedback as a cause of co-ordination problems of the seller can be influenced in any way by the seller?

Reduction of Buyer-related Feedback

The reduction of demand-related feedback aims, most of all, at reducing the exchange of information and goods between country markets. Through a reduction in demand-related feedback, the seller attempts, ultimately, to reduce the negative impact of market convergence, or even to reverse it. In other words, various corporate measures aimed at reducing demand-related feedback can be categorized as an attempt to re-separate converging markets (see Figure 9.38). While strategies aimed at catering for the need for co-ordination are an adaptation to convergences, the following are just the opposite.

Because the flow of information in markets with a democratic-liberal societal and economic structure can rarely be limited by individual sellers, arbitrage is the central means of reducing demand-related feedback. Because the extent of arbitrage is *determined by the profits* that can be earned, a reduction of demand-related feedback can be applied using *price differences* as the factor determining arbitrage revenues and the *transaction costs* as the essential cost factor. An increase in the transaction costs incurred by arbitrageurs thus has an immediate impact on the extent of arbitrage. The change in price perceptions, on the other hand, aims at the *perceptions of* arbitrage profits and the resulting behaviour of arbitrageurs with given transaction costs and price differences.

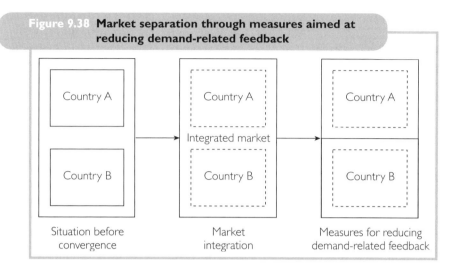

Figure 9.38 **Market separation through measures aimed at reducing demand-related feedback**

| Situation before convergence | Market integration | Measures for reducing demand-related feedback |

On the other hand, the simplest case of limiting demand-related feedback entails, independently of potential arbitrage profits, *controlling supply* in low-price markets. If, for example, it can be ensured that only national or regional buyers can be served excluding the additional demand from arbitrageurs, the basis for arbitrage will have been removed (independently of quality and price differences). However, this assumes that appropriate influence can be exerted on distributors. This applies most of all to contractually-based distribution systems.

Product Modification

With constant transaction costs incurred through arbitrage, the extent of grey markets rises with increasing arbitrage profits. A reduction in demand-related feedback can therefore be linked to the subjectively perceived arbitrage revenues. Thus the perceived arbitrage revenue will be determined not only by the nominal price differences between the products in two countries. For a country-specific product modification, and thus a country-specific product specification, the perceived *exchangeability* of *product variants* by buyers, is a further condition for a sufficiently precise prediction of arbitrage revenues.

Only if there is a complete exchangeability of country-specific product variants from the buyer's perspective, does the product variation exert no influence on perceived arbitrage revenues. But, this does not seem particularly realistic. The question should thus be posed as to the extent of modification of what product elements is necessary in order to change the perception of arbitrage revenues in such a manner that the exchange of goods will be reduced to the preferred quantity on the seller's side. In this context, informational product elements (for example, communicational positioning, labelling), as well as product elements themselves (for example, product characteristics), can be brought to bear on goal-orientated modification. Similarly, it is possible to differentiate according to the degree of potential for reversing modifications (reversible versus irreversible):

▸ Product variation leads to irreversible modifications, if these cannot be reversed by the arbitrageur.

> Such a case prevails if the enterprise consciously varies the packaging size of its products. The spirits manufacturer, Campari, used to sell its products in 1-litre bottles in Italy, but in 0.7-litre bottles in Germany. In such cases, the arbitrageur is not able to reverse the modifications.

▸ Product variation leads to reversible modifications if the arbitrageur can change them, with a corresponding increase in transaction costs, in this case – the costs of changing the product.

> Automobile manufacturers attempt to prevent possible arbitrage processes (re-imports) through product modification, by offering factory guarantees only in a specific country market. Arbitrageurs bypass this form of modification by offering their own guarantees for reimported products.

Elements of Modification Strategy

Actual Product Modification

In the national context, an extension of the marketing programme through a modification of the basic design is considered to be a product differentiation. Product differentiation refers to planned changes of components of a product or service, with the objective of creating a new product from the (own or external) original product, without this replacing the original product or moving totally away from the original intended use. In contrast to national product differentiation, modification in the international context does not serve to extend the product offer spectrum within a country market. The aim is much

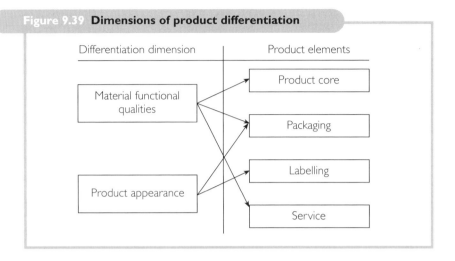

Figure 9.39 Dimensions of product differentiation

more, through variation between country-market-specific products, to reduce the value of price differentiation for arbitrageurs.

The product modifications themselves can be supplemented by additional services, or by means of the packaging. In contrast, the labelling is more suitable for an informational modification. Against the background of converging markets, a *product-core modification* plays a lesser role, because it is precisely through homogenization, such as through the legal framework, that the advantages of standardization are to be achieved. While a differentiation in packaging and services refers to functional qualities of the product, a communication-policy differentiation in general, and labelling in particular, are informational modifications (see Figure 9.39).

Packaging and Packaging Size

As in the case of brand modification, also in terms of packaging and parcelling policy, a country-specific adaptation of size, colour, form or materials is possible. However, differentiation, such as acquiring material for packaging, is also often a matter of necessity rather than choice for a firm. Climatic differences, a varied environmental awareness, or distance between production facilities and markets, forces enterprises to adapt the packaging of their products to the particular needs of specific countries. Cultural aspects, as well as legal aspects, also have an impact on packaging formulation. In the cultural context, the enterprise must be sure to conform to the linguistic peculiarities of a country.

An American manufacturer of golf balls sold its products in Japan in packs of four. However, the Japanese translation of the number four sounds like the word for 'death', so the product was doomed to failure (Hill and Still, 1984, p. 95).

The legal environment influences the formulation of packaging in various ways. For example, in Japan, cigarette packs carry only weak warnings ('Don't smoke too much'), whereas in Oman, a far stronger warning is obligatory ('Smoking is a major cause of cancer, lung disease and diseases of the heart and arteries'). Although, with the harmonization of institutional conditions, such a differentiation loses relevance, it cannot completely override packaging modification as an instrument of co-ordination.

Informational modification through instruction brochures or packaging constitutes a proven instrument for eliminating arbitrage. A product description purely in the country language and not, as can be observed mainly for technical products, in various languages, counteracts an international exchange process and facilitates the implementation of a differentiated pricing policy. The omission of certification is also appropriate as a further reinforcement. For buyers, there is considerable potential uncertainty as to whether the products are exportable if they do not conform to the measures relating to harmonization efforts. In principle, this problem can be solved. None the less, providing the necessary proof required by import regulations raises arbitrage costs, so that the exchange of goods may no longer be efficient.

The simplest form of product modification through differing packaging is a variation in quantity within a particular package. Examples are the 250-gram packets of pastry and the 500-gram containers of margarine or soap in-side various sizes of folding packaging. The example given earlier of Campari packaging shows how, through regional modification, international transparency can be influenced substantially. According to the form of packaging differentiation, this can be either reversible or irreversible.

Figure 9.40 shows three types of blister packaging for pharmaceutical products. If Type 1 is used, the reimporter can reverse the process easily by simply cutting open the blisters. For Type 2, this is considerably more difficult, and for Type 3, almost impossible.

Figure 9.40 **Reversible and irreversible blisters for pharmaceutical products**

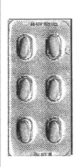

Type 1:
reversible
modification

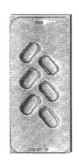

Type 2:
difficult reversible
modification

Type 3:
irreversible
modification

Offering Supplementary Services

A further means of preventing arbitrage processes lies in offering products with additional components that apply only to a particular market. The most significant are services such as free assembly or repair, advice, training, maintenance or guarantees. The totality of these services, which can be offered after the original purchase as well, also contribute towards ensuring that the product remains functional. Figure 9.41 shows product-related services which can be applied specifically at certain phases of the purchasing cycle.

As a consequence of supplementary services, price differences between country markets become distorted by the value of the services. Because, irrespective of the intended use, products can only be purchased together with services, this modification is irreversible. The arbitrage profit declines with the price difference, compared to an otherwise identical product without these services, because the sale proceeds without country-market-specific services.

With the aid of these product modifications, the results of the business operations can, on the one hand, be improved qualitatively (for example, shorter delivery times). On the other hand, a different formulation of the productive process (for example, remote diagnosis of defects though data transfer instead of personal customer service) is possible. Furthermore, product modification can be achieved through

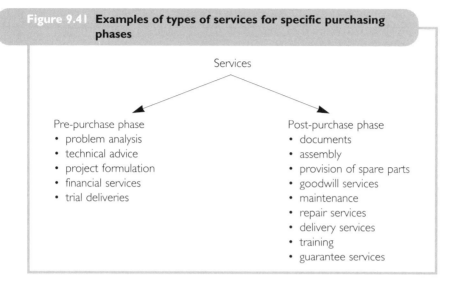

Figure 9.41 **Examples of types of services for specific purchasing phases**

Services

Pre-purchase phase
- problem analysis
- technical advice
- project formulation
- financial services
- trial deliveries

Post-purchase phase
- documents
- assembly
- provision of spare parts
- goodwill services
- maintenance
- repair services
- delivery services
- training
- guarantee services

an additive palette in the form of training and technical advice. If, either voluntarily or through obligation, buyers are to be induced to purchase products, country-specific customer loyalty is to be established or customers enabled to use products optimally, these service functions must be conducted in accordance with the specifics of the individual country markets, or in dependence on the needs structures of the target segments.

A country-specific formulation of the service offerings opens up the possibility of focusing on the specifics of a country without the risk of having to build an international brand.

Varying guarantees are the simplest form of product modification, While, for example, in Country A, the product is offered with a 48-month guarantee, the same manufacturer may only offer a 12-month guarantee in Country B for the full functioning of an identical product. Apart from the differentiation according to the length of guarantee, the content of the guarantee itself can be varied country by country. However, the harmonization of legal conditions often requires an internationally standardized guarantee, so the danger of parallel imports cannot be eliminated.

In summary, it is clear that product modification through additional services, especially for products with a high need for accompanying explanation and maintenance (for example, software), is well suited to avoiding the arbitrage arising from homogenization. Only if the additional services to buyers are perceived as being core elements of a product can the enterprise achieve a comparative advantage.

Informational Product Modification

A product modification relates to physical product elements or to supplementary services, and changes perceptions of price differences which have an impact on arbitrage. Informational product modification is based on a limited comparability of products threatened by arbitrage. Their basis is not physical, but informational and emotional. This includes contributions to the quality of life as a result of consumption of the product. They are a great help in raising the willingness to pay among buyers, particularly of consumer goods.

In the context of informational product modification, it is not the product itself ('the hardware'), but the informational–emotional exchangeability that changes from the perspective of the potential arbitrageur. Labelling policy in particular, is well suited to this purpose, because labels have a strong emotional appeal (for example, denoting prestige or status and so on), or convey important purchasing decision information (the brand as a quality criterion). The brand can therefore be used as an instrument for reducing feedback. In order to reduce the exchangeability of goods, or the feedback between country markets, it is possible to differentiate some or all of the elements of labelling. Apart from the advantage of preventing the customer from identifying the internationally diverging brands, and therefore from comparing prices, it is also advantageous that, in each country, the product name can be selected in such a manner as to promote positive associations with the relevant buyers.

> The Wybert GmbH, for example, offers their cough lozenges in Germany under the brand name 'Wybert' and in Switzerland, under the name 'Gaba'.

Brand differentiation that is undertaken as a modification is potentially more successful, the more important the informational–emotional product components are seen to be from the buyers' perspective. The consumer experience of informational value of the brand is lower with a differentiated brand in different country markets. It is decisive, whether or not the product itself is identical in the various markets. From the buyer perspective, the essential criteria are missing from the purchasing decision. The subjectively perceived exchange-ability declines with increasing brand differentiation.

The advantages that can be achieved through brand differentiation in the context of reduced exchangeability must be contrasted with the disadvantages from the seller's perspective. These disadvantages occur partly because of confusion of international target groups, or because of the higher costs of differentiated branding. A communication policy that places its focus on the brand can, similarly, be differentiated through labelling. Cost effective international media are thus not available, as it is necessary to stick to national media. The relevant additional costs are, consequently, similarly important for the issue of international labelling.

The Optimal Extent of Product Modification

Through an appropriate product modification, price differences for comparable products can be distorted deliberately, and perceived arbitrage profits changed in the minds of potential arbitrageurs. The optimal degree of product modification from the manufacturer's perspective is debatable – that is, what product elements are suitable for product modification aimed at reducing the need for co-ordination? Product modifications have consequences for manufacturers as well, because product modifications are generally associated with additional costs (for example, production costs). Potential arbitrageurs are also affected, because their potential revenues are reduced as a result either of a lower willingness to pay for modified products in the target country and/or the additional costs of measures to restore the original product qualities.

On the part of arbitrageurs, product modification leads to the following effects (see Figure 9.42):

▸ Reduction in arbitrage revenues caused by irreversible modifications; and
▸ an increase in the transaction costs of arbitrage for reversing (reversible) modifications, which depends on the extent of reversal that in fact occurs.

With an increasing degree of reversible modification, the costs of eradicating these effects rise initially ('change costs'), to the extent to which reversible modifications can in fact be reversed. This assumption seems meaningful only if the costs of reversal, independently of

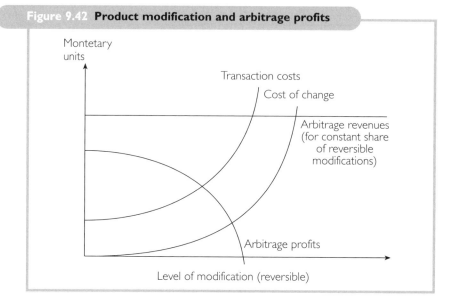

Figure 9.42 Product modification and arbitrage profits

the degree of modification, are lower than the price advantage that can be achieved. As a result, total transaction costs rise for the arbitrageurs.

The differences between change and transaction costs relate to the transaction costs that are independent of the modifications (contract initiation, control, transport and so on). Arbitrage revenues are independent of the degree of reversible modification, or are constant, because they cannot be entirely eradicated. However, they are affected by the degree of irreversible modification. The larger these are, the more substantially do arbitrage revenue decline, and the more the degree of arbitrage revenues will be shifted downwards (Figure 9.42). As a result, arbitrage profits decline with the increasing intensity of reversible (and irreversible) modifications.

From the *manufacturer's perspective*, it is now worth considering what extent of product modification is economically appropriate. In this respect, the cost impact of product modification should be contrasted with the effects resulting from the limitation of arbitrage.

Assume a manufacturer of film for small-format cameras provides a differentiated offer. An identical product is offered in low-price Country A, with a 'bonus', such as a development coupon, which can only be redeemed in Country A and not in Country B. The manufacturer would then be able to charge nominally identical prices, although there would be an effective price modification to the value of the coupon. In Country B, this coupon has zero value, because neither an arbitrageur nor his customers can use it. At best, the arbitrageur can replace it with his own coupon. However, this would only make sense if he were to incur costs for the coupon that are lower than the price difference. A change in packaging size, to 'triple packs', for example, in Country A, would be a reversible modification, because an arbitrageur could separate the packs for sale in Country B.

Declining arbitrage profits lead to a reduction in demand-related interdependency. As a result, a seller is able, for example, with an increasing (reversible and/or irreversible) degree of modification, to implement higher price differences in the operational country markets. The increases in revenue that arise from these higher price differences, can then be contrasted with the modification costs in order to determine the optimal degree of modification. For a given modification-induced reduction in demand-related feedback, and the resulting increases in revenue, modifications can be implemented that lead to the lowest costs on the part of the seller. For variable, modification-induced revenue increases, the optimum will be located where the marginal costs of modification correspond with the marginal revenue of modification.

These theoretical considerations of the behaviour of arbitrageurs clarify which decisions, from the manufacturer's perspective, are advisable for product modification in order to reduce the need for co-ordination. In order to optimize the degree of modification to reduce demand-related feedback, apart from the associated costs, the relative preferences of buyers for modified product components, and the resulting relative willingness to pay, are decisive. It is assumed that different product elements are available for modification, which will lead to varying modification costs for the manufacturer, and various costs for reversing modifications (by arbitrageurs) as well as differing willingness-to-pay effects on users of re-imports/parallel imports. Subject to these assumptions, it makes sense to modify those product elements that will cause the manufacturer the lowest possible additional modification costs, and which simultaneously will entail the highest possible reversal costs for arbitrageurs. By so doing, the economic viability of the reversal becomes questionable. If the modification is not reversible, at least not in an economically viable manner, the loss in willingness to pay on the part of arbitrageurs, or their clients should be at its highest. With respect to the willingness to pay, it is fundamental to the strategy of modification that these are made with respect to those product elements where the willingness to pay is not only varied, but is also higher in the *low*-price country than in the *high*-price country. Only these conditions lead to a relatively lower acceptance of re-imports or parallel imports in the high-price market, and thus to declining arbitrage profits.

In the context of measures aimed at satisfying the need for co-ordination, the identification of such product elements has thus become an important market-research task. Relatively low-cost modifications exert strong downward pressure on arbitrage profits.

These differences in relative willingness to pay can have various causes. Thus, for example, in the early 1990s, Audi offered its '100' model and the successor model 'A6' in Italy with a 2.0L 16V engine, which, in contrast to an only marginally stronger 2.6L engine, is considerably more tax-effective in that country. In Germany, the 2.0L model would be exposed to strong competition, because of the substantially lower difference in purchasing and running costs (including taxation) with respect to comparable models from other automobile manufacturers. The relative willingness to pay would therefore be lower than in Italy. For the current model (also called A6), Audi no longer offers the 2.0L engine. Now, as in Germany, a 1.8 20V engine with 125 kw or 150 kw (supercharged version) is offered. This product modification thus disappears. Conditions for arbitrage have therefore become more favourable.

Controlling Supply

Controlling supply refers to the controlling of *goods streams* between country markets. This encompasses all measures that serve to prevent or limit the sale of an industrial company's products to arbitrageurs. The potential for such control implies that a seller can influence the behaviour of product distributors in the sense of limiting demand-related interdependencies. This influence can be attributed to two causes:

▸ limiting national supply; and
▸ influencing the behaviour of distributors.

Limiting National Supply

The influence of demand-related feedback by controlling the quantity sold is based on the assumption that arbitrage can thus be prevented or reduced, and that the quantities sold by a seller to national distributors can be limited. Ideally, there will be no arbitrage if a seller in a national market can provide precisely the quantity required in that market, and no more. Only when national supply exceeds national demand, or arbitrageurs have a greater willingness to pay than national buyers, can arbitrage take place.

A central problem of supply control lies in the degree of precision with which *national* demand (quantities) can be estimated. Complete prevention of arbitrage through quantitative control is only possible if such estimates can be conducted with sufficient precision. However, because the demand for the products of a particular manufacturer are influenced by a number of factors, such predictions are difficult to achieve in practice. In this context, the level of experience of local management plays an important role.

Volkswagen AG and DaimlerChrysler have, in the past, attempted to stem the increasing number of re-imports of automobiles from Italy to Germany, by controlling and influencing the quantities sold by contract dealers. Estimates of 'normal' demand in a particular area from local customers form the basis of control. If the quantities delivered to dealers greatly exceed these estimated quantities, it is possible that the dealer in question is selling to reimporters. If, on closer analysis, these suspicions are confirmed, the quantities sold to dealers are limited even more strictly in terms of expected 'legitimate' sales. A further measure lies in paying the contractually agreed-upon commission on the sale of a new car only three months after the initial licensing in Italy, to ensure that the automobile has in fact been sold to an Italian customer. However, this latter measure merely increases the sales of so-called '3-month cars' in the grey market.

On the other hand, the comparison of quantities sold by *individual distributors*, particularly those operating under similar environmental conditions, is simpler. If the sales quantities from such dealers vary considerably from one another, this may be an indication that arbitrageurs are at work. A comparison between predicted and actual quantities gives some indication of the extent of the control problem. Depending on this extent, there may be a need for adaptation. This adaptation may be implemented dealer-by-dealer through individual control of quantities sold.

Influencing arbitrage by controlling the quantities sold, is only appropriate if dealers do not react to a limitation of their purchasing with measures that are counter-productive for the seller. These include:

▸ poor service with respect to goods or shelf space;
▸ aggressive sales of competitors' products; and
▸ a complete switch to the products of competitors.

Re-imports can be limited the most when the manufacturer is able to serve the final user directly in the target country. In essence, a 'purging' of a distribution channel is possible, with the following features (Schneider, 1995, p. 259):

▸ transition from indirect to direct export;
▸ increased tendency towards direct distribution; and
▸ reduction in the number (levels) of intermediaries.

With the *transition from indirect to direct exports*, the efforts of the manufacturer lie in marketing the company's products internationally. This does not necessarily mean that the company will sell its products directly to final users. Instead, distribution can proceed through importers or wholesalers (Dwyer and Tanner, 1999, p. 10). The market proximity as well as the control and monitoring functions are essentially forgone.

An even more comprehensive purging of arbitrageurs from the market can be achieved through the use of *direct distribution*. The manufacturer then assumes not only the cross-border marketing itself, but is also responsible for the majority of the functions that relate to the end user. With the implementation of direct export and associated distribution, there will be the simultaneous reduction of a multi-phase process to a single-phase distribution channel. Figure 9.43 shows how the number of phases can be reduced.

With the *reduction of the number of intermediate phases* in the distribution channel, the price difference between the low-price and high-price countries is available to the arbitrageur, because he or she is no longer able to benefit from low purchasing prices from dealers.

Control through Influence on Distributors

Counter-productive measures of the kind discussed above should be avoided most of all where there are contractual relationships between manufacturers and dealers which provide behavioural rules

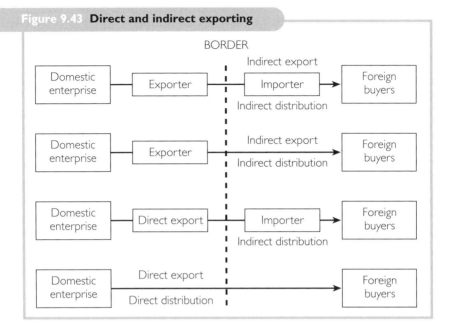

Figure 9.43 Direct and indirect exporting

for both parties. Because these behavioural rules relate to both parties, the legal latitude of the seller to control quantities plays a major role in the formulation of contracts. These measures aim less at avoiding price comparisons or informational transparency, and far more at purging the distribution channel of potential reimporters.

In the context of distribution policy, *contractual distribution systems* can be used to prevent parallel exports. They work through limiting distribution to certain dealers. Contractual distribution systems define contractual rights and obligations in the form of limitations on individual freedom of action in a business context. These are characterized by three criteria (Ahlert, 1996):

▸ co-ordination of market-orientated activities of manufacturer and intermediary,
▸ planned, lasting and individual contractually regulated use of selected dealers, which function as legally and economically autonomous enterprises in the sales network of the manufacturer; and
▸ co-operation with dealers who are not bound in any way and have no specific interests to protect.

As a form of contractual distribution system, *distribution restraint systems*, which can regulate and 'purge' distribution systems according to qualitative selection criteria, can refer to certain sales areas and specific buyer groups. While a *spatial channel restraint*, related to the external market, such as export bans for domestic operators, re-import bans for domestic exporters or re-export bans and forward export bans for foreign buyers, oblige intermediaries, through distribution channel limitations of a personal nature, to transfer goods to specific customer circles only (Ahlert, 1996). The exclusion of certain buyers has its limitations, however, especially in converging markets. Thus the contract on the founding of the European Economic Community in Article 19, para. 1, line 3, as well as in Article 85, para. 1, regulates the limitation of trade partners with respect to non-delivery to certain buyers. For example, the European Court prevented the enterprise called the United Brands Corporation from using an extremely differentiated pricing policy that would oblige its buyers to re-sell green Chiquita bananas to other countries only with the agreement of the supplier (ECJ 27/1976).

The *implementation of selective distribution* is an additional means of avoiding parallel imports to a large degree. This sales strategy applies when the manufacturer selects the number of intermediaries on the basis of qualitative demands. Examples of such criteria are: shopping centre image, type of business, creditworthiness, flexibility, supplier loyalty, average order size, the potential for effective and reliable customer service, ongoing personnel training and so on (Ahlert, 1996). With the aid of an exclusive distribution network, it is possible, for example, to exclude all intermediaries who do not conform to the necessary criteria. Furthermore, parallel imports can be prevented by obliging the members of this distribution form only to deliver from the manufacturer to approved dealers. Distribution through foreign dealers or domestic parallel importers is no longer possible.

For the choice of a selective distribution system, the relevant legal framework must, however, be taken into account. It is particularly important to bear in mind that the selection of intermediaries proceed according to objective criteria. Against this background, the European Court and the EU Commission have guaranteed selective distribution only for those enterprises that produce qualitatively high-value products that also require a high degree of accompanying information and explanation (Krämer, 1985, p. 93). The more the qualitative selection criteria relate directly to the functioning of the products, the more sympathy the authorities will have with selective distribution. For example, buyers of a technically complex product need ongoing qualified support from the dealer, so that distribution through exclusively qualified distribution channels does not constitute discrimination against less-qualified dealers. In terms of the problem of international co-ordination, which arises for the enterprise because of the homogenization of institutional conditions or converging buyer behaviour if distribution is achieved through dealers selected exclusively by qualitative factors, this is of lesser importance. Certainly, the exclusion of parallel importing dealers minimizes the potential for arbitrage processes. However, it cannot be assumed that, on the side of the final user, cross-border exchange processes will not occur. Consequently, manufacturers must have the objective of obliging selected dealers, through a limited distribution strategy, to sell their products only to final users in certain target countries. Even if the founding contract of the European Union sets quite strict limits on such practices, it can be observed repeatedly that dealers are careful to adhere to the preferences of manufacturers, in order not to lose their dealerships. In particular, the threat of manufacturers reducing discounts or setting delivery quotas has, in the past, led to a high level of 'dealer discipline', and thus to an accompanying reduction of parallel imports in many branches (Krämer, 1985, p. 93).

The Limits of Supply Control: The Example of the EU

If forms of supply control are applied by international enterprises, in order to reduce demand-based feedback in converging markets, there are often tight legal constraints. Because, with market integration, enterprises pursue the objective of combining previously separated markets into unified market areas to gain the advantages of freer flows of goods, personnel and capital, individual corporate measures for reducing demand-related feedback – particularly in the case of a homogenization of institutional conditions – are often limited by the state or treated as violations. This occurs in particular because the corporate measures described above counteract the original objectives of market integration.

At the end of the 1990s, the attempts of the EU Commission to discourage automobile concerns from using supply controls to limit re-imports, provides an excellent example of the above issues.

The price differences for automobiles discussed earlier are, in the first instance, the result of the contract dealer system in the automobile market. Thus automobile manufacturers have been able to retain their contract dealer systems in the European market. Because the contracted dealers are not allowed to sell the vehicles of several different manufacturers, and are further obliged to acquire automobiles through the country-specific channels laid down by manufacturers (for example, through a particular general importer), the automobile manufacturers are able to set country-specific price levels almost totally at will. In view of this comprehensive dealer control, it is possible for manufacturers to maintain a high level of price differentiation (Münster, 1999).

Because, despite rigid dealer commitments, the number of re-imported automobiles increased substantially in the 1990s, with automobile manufacturers suffering from substantial revenue losses as a result, manufacturers have, in the opinion of the EU Commission, attempted to force their contract dealers not to handle re-imports. For example, the general importers of Audi and VW in Italy, have, at the request of VW, refused to sell vehicles to customers from other EU states.

The Commission regarded this as discrimination against customers on the basis of their nationality, and threatened the manufacturers in question with draconian fines, amounting to up to 10 per cent of turnover in the relevant country markets. In January 1998, the EU Commission imposed a fine of approximately 200 million DM on VW, because, despite repeated warnings, the concern continued the practices described above. Furthermore, VW was obliged to terminate its illegal activities in Italy within two months.

Similarly, DaimlerChrysler, Opel and Renault were cautioned by the EU Commission for practices constraining competition (Anonymous, 1999b). In early 1999, DaimlerChrysler was rebuked by the Commission for ordering its subsidiaries in Spain, Belgium and the Netherlands not to sell any automobiles to foreign customers (Büschemann, 1999, p. 2; Fälschle, 1999, p. 100).

Finally, the newspaper clipping in Figure 9.44 shows that the EU Commission attempts to constrain such seller strategies of controlling parallel imports, not only in the automobile market, but also in the pharmaceutical market. In the past, sellers tried to control

Figure 9.44 **The battle between Glaxo and the European Commission**

Glaxo Wellcome battles with Brussels

By Emma Tucker in Brussels and David Pilling in London

Glaxo Wellcome, the British pharmaceutical company, is deliberately seeking to deprive British consumers of cheaper medicines and drugs, the European Commission alleged yesterday.

Opening the first stage of a legal battle with the company, the Commissioners said Glaxo was operating a system of double pricing in Spain that sought to stop wholesalers exporting competitively priced drugs to the UK. Brussels says the company's system of charging one set of prices for drugs produced and sold in Spain, but higher prices for the same drugs when they are sold abroad, was a restriction of competition and a breach of EU competition rules.

Brussels could ultimately fine Glaxo if the company, which suspended the scheme in January, reinstates the scheme. Brussels issued preliminary objections to the scheme last year.

"At this stage in the proceedings, the Commission envisages banning the double price clauses in Glaxo Wellcome's Spanish general conditions of sale," said a Commission statement.

Glaxo said it had sought to implement the scheme as a "test of principle (against) the current system, which basically exports Spanish prices into northern European countries". It said there was no question of being fined as it had gone through the legal channels and would not implement a scheme found to be in breach of EU regulations.

Glaxo, in common with nearly all pharmaceutical companies, has sought ways of preventing parallel imports across Europe. Because of what drug companies see as the anomaly of fixed (government set) prices in each country and the free movement of goods, an estimated 10 per cent of European drugs are "parallel exported" from low-priced southern countries to higher priced northern ones.

Brussels says that UK wholesalers should be able to import from other EU countries. Glaxo sales conditions notified to the Commission last year make it difficult, "if not impossible", to export from Spain to the UK.

"The Commission has observed that the export price levels set by Glaxo Wellcome are based largely on the British Glaxo Wellcome price levels," said the Commission. The Commission, supported by the European Court of Justice, believes that the existence of national price regulation does not justify impeding competition rules and, in particular, restrictions on parallel trade within the EU.

Glaxo said that it was disappointed by the Commission's finding and would appeal within the stipulated four months. It reserved the right to call an oral hearing of the case. The Commission had received four complaints against Glaxo's new conditions of sale in Spain, which was suspended temporarily by the Spanish competition authorities last October.

Source: *Financial Times*, 17 July 1999, p. 50.

country-specific distribution phases quite consciously (see the behaviour of GlaxoSmithKline in Spain described in Figure 9.44). That the EU Commission has also made moves against such practices is all the more remarkable as these strategies have not infrequently been regarded as economically desirable. This orientation is justified in that the various Member States of the EU have differing approval processes for pharmaceuticals. That the EU Commission is using counter-measures to supply control by sellers in just such a market demonstrates unmistakably the strong desire to bring about a convergence of grey markets.

Reducing Seller-related Feedback

At the heart of the discussion of co-ordination problems in internationally active enterprises *at the management level* is the question of the distribution of tasks between the corporate head office and the national organizational units (Hollensen, 2001, p. 590; Porter, 1986). In this respect, the objective is an optimal distribution of all international tasks accruing to the individual organizational units and their co-ordination, to achieve the overall objectives of the company. The need for co-ordination arises through the organizational interfaces, which in turn have their origins in the division of labour. The allocation of interrelated tasks to organizationally distinct areas (such as allocating the delivery of a certain product to a particular client at a certain point in time to the sections dealing with procurement, production, distribution and service) leads to a need for agreement and co-ordination between the various areas, because each can affect the overall results in a different way. In this respect, the task of management co-ordination is to secure goal harmony *within* areas of business and an exchange of information *between* them, so that an overall optimum is attained.

With respect to market operation, such organizational interfaces typically are caused by *country-based spheres of responsibility*. In particular, multinationally-organized international enterprises with 'strong' and well-equipped country management provided with far reaching decision-making authority, have broad organizational interfaces, when the individual national subsidiaries operate in country markets with strong interdependencies (Bartlett and Ghoshal, 1990). In view of the informational dependence of marketing decisions, an essentially decentralized approach towards decision-making for market operations will create additional (organizational) problems. However, this will not be the case if, with respect to market-related feedback, the markets are largely independent of one another, or if, because of a global orientation of the enterprise, decision-making for market operations is largely centralized.

These considerations show that the organization of an international enterprise exerts a considerable influence on the extent of possible co-ordination problems (not only) for international marketing. The root of the co-ordination problem is the organization of the division of labour for interdependent decision components. In this respect, there are various possible forms of division of labour:

▶ *Horizontal division of labour* – employing several people or institutions for the same work processes so as to raise capacity leads to the need for co-ordination with respect to the total volume of the results of this process. To allocate this capacity efficiently and to control product quality are key tasks.

▶ *Vertical division of labour* (specialization) – the division of the entire process into component parts, and the allocation of these to different individuals. This leads to the need for various sequential or parallel processes (e.g. purchasing, operations, sales and services) to be co-ordinated with one another. The search for the greatest possible specialization advantages creates such functional organizational structures.

The organization of international corporate activity is, according to Perlitz (2000), a function of the 'degree of specialization'. With an increasing internationalization of business activity, the following phases of organizational development can be identified (Perlitz, 2000, p. 617):

▸ export department;
▸ distinctly differentiated structures for domestic and international business; and
▸ integrated structures where domestic and international business are organized according to a common principle.

Subject to the assumption of operating interdependent markets, the co-ordination of marketing activities first becomes relevant when the internationalization of an enterprise takes on systematic characteristics and is comprehensive. The establishment of *differentiated structures*, such as the development of an export department into an international division (see the example given in Figure 9.45), shows an early form of organization which accords a relatively low level of significance to foreign activities.

According to Perlitz (2000), advanced international enterprises have *integrated structures*, for which there is a clear formulation for foreign and domestic business through:

▸ an integrated functional structure;
▸ an integrated product structure; or
▸ an integrated regional structure.

Figure 9.46, which shows the alternative forms of an integrated structure, demonstrates that, for an *integrated functional structure* and an *integrated product structure*, a differentiation is made between domestic

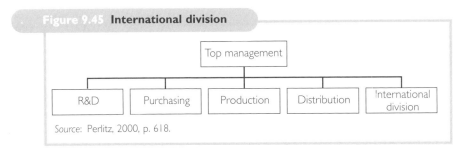

Figure 9.45 International division

Source: Perlitz, 2000, p. 618.

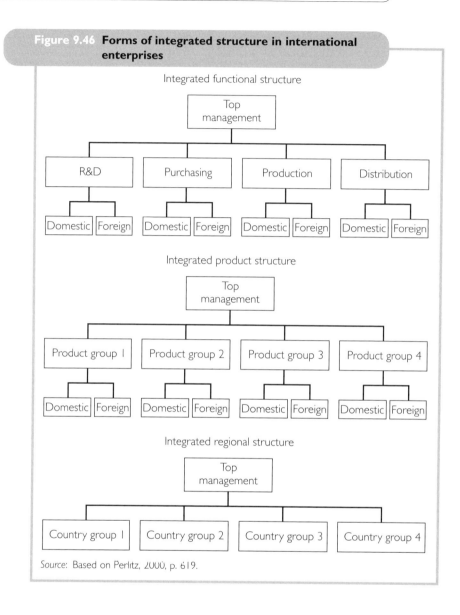

Figure 9.46 Forms of integrated structure in international enterprises

Integrated functional structure

Top management

R&D | Purchasing | Production | Distribution

Domestic | Foreign | Domestic | Foreign | Domestic | Foreign | Domestic | Foreign

Integrated product structure

Top management

Product group 1 | Product group 2 | Product group 3 | Product group 4

Domestic | Foreign | Domestic | Foreign | Domestic | Foreign | Domestic | Foreign

Integrated regional structure

Top management

Country group 1 | Country group 2 | Country group 3 | Country group 4

Source: Based on Perlitz, 2000, p. 619.

and foreign level only at the second level of the system. By contrast, the country markets for an *integrated regional structure* have related structural criteria at a higher level.

However, because the organizational forms shown in Figure 9.46 reveal specific weaknesses that derive from their one-dimensional structure, in practice a matrix organization is used in many enterprises

Figure 9.47 **Matrix structure**

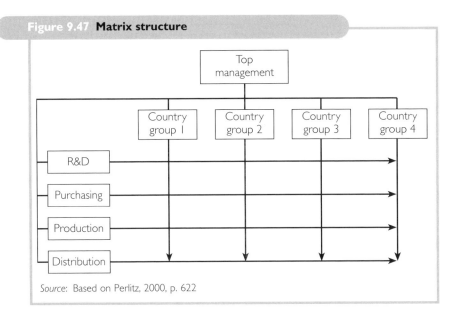

Source: Based on Perlitz, 2000, p. 622

(see Figure 9.47). Matrix structures are characterized by a combination of functional and objective-related organization. The objects are business areas in the form of product groups, customer groups or (global market) regions. A separation of matrix leadership, matrix units and interfaces (see Figure 9.47), is typical of the matrix structure. Matrix management has the task of ensuring overall goal attainment. Each matrix element is allocated either a functional or an object-related task. The interface fulfils a functional or object-related task. It reports to superiors in functions (e.g. R&D) and objects (country group managers). The objective of the matrix structure is, as in the example, the simultaneous co-ordination of specific tasks in both functional and country-market related aspects.

Differing organizational structures in international enterprises fulfil differing coordination functions. The organizational structure itself is the *result* of managerial decisions (Frese, 1992). Consequently, the prevailing need for co-ordination can be controlled through organizational measures. This includes measures for *centralized decision making*, as well as *formal co-ordination* in the context of existing organizational structures. In association with this, the organizational structure itself is a possible instrument for co-ordinating marketing in international enterprises. The decision between 'early' and 'advanced' organizational structures for international enterprises made by Perlitz (2000), already reflects their adaptation to various environmental conditions of corporate activity.

Centralization of Marketing Decisions

The shifting of decision-making authority with respect to the market operations of a decentralized corporate unit (for example, country representation), is a measure that contributes towards overcoming the (market) decision-making problems that occur between organizational interfaces. This will be the case when the respective decision-making authority for all countries affected by interdependencies is centralized in *one* location.

Thus, a manufacturer of pharmaceuticals, wishing to improve the overall profit situation of its enterprise through a country-specific pricing policy, would remove price-making authority from the country markets and place it in the hands of an international pricing manager. If this person is able to identify and implement optimally co-ordinating prices for the individual country markets, the interface problem will largely be solved.

In practice, there are various levels of centralization with respect to marketing decisions. A series of empirical investigations shows clearly that product-policy decision areas, such as product core formulation and labelling, tend to be highly centralized, while communication policy measures, in particular, tend to be decentralized (Wiechmann, 1974; Hedlund, 1981). Pricing policy measures, on the other hand, reveal a substantially varying degree of centralization. In this respect, the empirical results are not unanimous. This derives from a situation-specific allocation of tasks between central and national units, taking into account, for example, regional and industry-sector conditions. Welge (1989) established that decision-making should be centralized when:

▸ the problem itself is structured simply;
▸ the circumstances in the foreign country are clear;
▸ a quick decision is necessary;
▸ there are short communication paths between the participating organizational units;
▸ management in the foreign markets is not well qualified; and/or
▸ foreign management does not reveal a strong national or local character.

The effectiveness of a centralization of marketing decisions in the form of more effective on efficient actions lies in the potential for influencing centralized authorities as opposed to the country offices. Because the significance of representatives 'on the spot' decreases with centralized decision-making, resistance is to be expected. This resistance will be all the larger, the more important is the decentralized authority in the perception of national management in order to justify its own existence, and the larger the profit losses that can be expected at the national level resulting from a co-ordinated policy.

A reduction in the market-related need for co-ordination through the centralization of decision-making refers primarily to the problem of *organizational agreement* between the various corporate units affected by interdependencies. This problem is simplified through the centralization of decision-making, subject, for example, to the following conditions:

▸ Centralized decision-making authority ensures agreement regarding objectives (goal harmony) between the country-market-specific marketing decisions, by achieving profit maximization subject to consideration of feedback between country markets. This is synonymous with a strong focus of country-market-specific measures with respect to their impacts on other markets.
▸ Centralization ensures a rapid flow of information between organizational units, and thus for a *rapid* determination of the optimal decision for achieving co-ordination. However, this can only be significant if the speed of decision-making leads to some clear benefit for the enterprise.

The centralization of responsibility for interdependent country-market marketing decisions, on the other hand, does not constitute a reduction in the *informational* interfaces between marketing decisions. The task of identifying an optimal co-ordination policy is not affected by the organizational structure in which the decision is made. This occurs in essentially the same way in both centralized and decentralized organizations. The contribution of organizational measures in reducing the need for co-ordination provides, at best, better conditions for solving co-ordination problems.

Formal Co-ordination through Process Standardization

In contrast to the centralization of independent marketing decisions, formal co-ordination can cause a reduction in the informational interfaces between country markets. Formal co-ordination with respect to certain decision-making problems refers to a system of rules for categorizing and solving problems. Formal co-ordination mechanisms include all approaches to standardizing information, planning, control and monitoring processes for developing and implementing marketing measures. Company-wide process standardization of decision making is categorized in international marketing as *process standardization* (Meffert and Bolz, 1993, p. 55). An approach towards formal co-ordination could attempt to determine the interdependence of national marketing decisions through a mandatory inclusion of the impact of national decisions and their adaptation to an overall optimum of the enterprise.

National subsidiaries with their own research and development (R&D) and production capacity, can, for example, through rules and regulations, be ordered to consider the impact of a high level of product differentiation, not only with respect to its own cost situation, but also to that of other subsidiaries. A high level of standardization could facilitate product standardization in two country markets and thus led to a 'pooling' of productive capacity with synergistic cost impacts (economies of scale). This change of decisional basis can lead to better co-ordination.

In international marketing, a standardization of decision-making processes is generally considered from the efficiency perspective. This becomes clear from the associated objectives (Landwehr, 1998):

▸ reducing planning and decision-making authority through a standardization-orientated reduction of uncertainty and complexity as a result of establishing clearly the decision-making determinants that are to be used;
▸ achieving organizational cost reduction potential;
▸ simplification of co-ordination by making the decision process transparent;
▸ making international control easier; and
▸ ensuring a co-ordination of country-specific measures.

Kreutzer (1989) differentiates between process standardization of a problem, leading to the formulation of a measure for its resolution, and activities which derive from a particular problem. The problem defines the basis of the measures aimed at optimization. As such, these are, for example:

▸ the entry of new competitors into a country market;
▸ changes in transaction costs incurred by arbitrageurs;

▸ a change in the extent of integration of the operational country markets; and

▸ the increasing internationalization of the enterprise and the resulting interdependencies (for example, changes in costs).

Co-ordination and the Extent of Process Standardization

The above-mentioned incentives for taking appropriate actions or counter-measures are modified through the prescription of reactions, whereby their structure and content can be prescribed in various degrees of detail. Accordingly, a differentiation can also be made between different intensities of standardization with varying intensities of regulation (comprehensive process standardization, standardization of conditions (guidelines), and basic process standardization (Hill *et al.*, 1981). The optimal degree of process standardization is debatable, because, with an increasing intensity of regulation, efficiency advantages increase, but at the same time, the problem solutions tend to lose innovativeness and effectiveness. A decision as to the extent of process standardization is thus determined by a number of influences (Kreutzer, 1989).

Predictability of future planning situations
In an enterprise, planning processes can only be established for those situations that are reasonably clear and predictable at the time of planning. For exceptional business situations, standardized planning processes cannot be prescribed; a flexible plan designed for a specific situation is necessary. Media planning is an example of predictable planning situations, whereas new product development is particularly difficult in terms of predictability.

Repeatability of planning steps
The issue here is whether planning situations are unique, or whether they repeat themselves over time, which would then facilitate repeatable planning processes. Only in the latter case is standardization to be considered, because only here can formalization be of use.

Classification of problem
There can only be a standardization of planning processes if the incentive or reason to plan is not hampered by any difficulties regarding what class of planning scenarios apply to the particular situation and the necessary procedures within the planning process.

Stability of planning steps

Planning steps can only be established for those planning situations that are characterized by an operational goal formulation as well as existing problem-resolution mechanisms. On the other hand, situations that demand individual solutions do not lend themselves to standardization.

Apart from the factors discussed above, the environmental conditions must be fulfilled, or at the least, non-fulfilment must be excluded, if standardization is to be possible. Environmental *stability* and *homogeneity* are the necessary conditions.

Environmental stability

As usable dimensions of environmental stability, the number of changes in the environmental situation, the extent of change and its regularity, are frequently cited in the literature (Duncan, 1972; Kieser and Kubicek, 1992). The problem is that internationally operating enterprises are often confronted with a unique environment in each country market. Plus, environmental stability cannot generally be evaluated objectively. Decision-makers are therefore reliant on their subjective perceptions and evaluations.

For process standardization, the application of standardized processes is always problematic when the environments, specifically those in which the enterprise operates, are essentially unstable. In such cases, a large degree of standardization of internal corporate marketing processes prevents an immediate reaction to environmental changes.

Environmental homogeneity

With respect to the optimal degree of process standardization, the relationship between the relevant environmental factors is important. In contrast, process standardization becomes more limited, the more heterogeneous the relationship between the environmental factors that have an impact on decision-making. Limits arise not only through the heterogeneity of various environmental factors, but also because the similar environmental factors, such as between interest groups in the different markets, manifest themselves in varying forms.

Co-ordination in Independent Markets through Process Standardization

The ability to capture the relevant factors that create interdependencies with respect to international marketing decisions is decisive for successful process standardization. The definition itself, of situations that compel certain people or organizational units to react in a particular way, constitutes an important effect of formal co-ordination through process standardization. This creates the potential to use situations that are relevant to co-ordination, as instigators of action and a motive to undertake serious consideration of what steps are appropriate. This possibility should not be underestimated, because it leads automatically to a *prioritization of situations that require co-ordination,* through forcing some form of reaction (analysis of the situation, taking the appropriate steps). From the perspective of individual country managers, the significance, for example, of a change in the transaction costs of arbitrage or the meaning of a change in the extent of integration of the operational country markets, can vary substantially.

Process standardization is an instrument for determining reactions to co-ordination situations and measures (see Kreutzer (1989) on determining reaction patterns). Thus, national managers can be obliged to consider the impact of their actions on other country markets and on the overall situation of the country. A clearly-defined system of rules, such as in the form of control manuals, can prescribe the appropriate measures for reacting to specific situations in terms of objectives. By doing so, the interfaces between organizational units will be overcome from the start. Furthermore, such decision-making rules provide sound approaches for handling informational interfaces for international marketing co-ordination.

> Italian VW dealers, whose turnover rises through purchasing re-imports, will not automatically assume that this development needs to be changed. Their goal function will differ from that of VW AG. The same could apply to the German subsidiaries of VW in Italy, because the need for a reaction is perceived differently by the parent company in Germany.

Kreutzer (1989) determined, quite correctly, that the use of reaction models is a complex task which has to be considered in terms of the real objective of complexity reduction through process standardization. What is problematic is the attempt to find optimal coordination procedures that can also be used in a variety of different situations. Their application areas, and thus their impact on co-ordination, are otherwise severely limited. Less detailed processes (guidelines) facilitate more leeway and adaptation. Finally, this means that co-ordination through process standardization is a trade-off between rule flexibility and the process-related (standard) quality of co-ordination.

Coordination through Adaptation of the Formal Organizational Structure

Organizations are social networks which have a formal structure, by means of which the activities of its members are expected to pursue a specific goal (Kieser and Kubicek, 1992). This co-ordinated function of formal organizations is also described as *integration*. In this sense, the organization is an *instrument* for achieving objectives and, as such, *an object of formation.* An adaptation of the organizational structure with respect to operations in independent country markets is an option if (considered in a simplified manner and ignoring additional possible influences) the returns from specialization, for example, are lower than the co-ordination costs. Such an organizational structure, as well as any other structure, would be inferior because the difference between the returns from specialization and co-ordination costs are not maximized.

Organizational structure creates interfaces between distinct working units. Overcoming the co-ordination problems associated with these interfaces can be made easier through an appropriate adaptation of the formal and informal organizational structure. Informational interfaces between country-related marketing decisions, are, however, not necessarily affected. Thus, for example, optimal overall profit-maximizing country market prices are determined quite independently of the organizational structure. This is essentially an autonomous problem. In this respect, the informational interface problems must be overcome by making mutually dependent marketing decisions simultaneously. In this sense, the organization does not replace the approaches to decision-making in international marketing.

The discussion of differing organizational principles in international enterprises has clarified that it is possible to distinguish between relatively simple, one-dimensional organizational structures (such as a business section that is responsible for all foreign markets, or a global product structure) and complex, multidimensional matrix structures. With respect to the economic factors that influence organizational structures, the domains of the simple structures can be determined if:

▸ high returns from specialization can be achieved from a corporate business unit responsible for foreign business, but there is simultaneously only a low need for co-ordination with the 'national' activities in the domestic market; and

▸ with respect to a global product structure, the individual product divisions do not develop feedback with the achievement of high returns from specialization.

There would be a low need for co-ordination between national and 'foreign' marketing activities if the domestic market were not interdependent in any way with the foreign markets. This does not seem particularly realistic, where, for an ethnocentrically-orientated strategy, similar foreign target markets are sought out, or where attempts are made to achieve great synergy advantages. In general, simple international structures seem quite appropriate, if the need for co-ordination between country markets and productive organizational units is low. In this case, organizationally-related decisions are relatively simple.

This becomes more problematic if the activities of the individual organizational units cannot be conducted free of interdependencies, that is, if, in the sense of Hax (1965), the system cannot be 'broken down' completely. This is quite common in practice, and plays a central role in the formation of the breadth of corporate activities and the synergies obtained from economies of scale and scope. If these are significant, however, the individual activities cannot ever be separated from one another completely.

Substantial interdependencies between country markets should encourage enterprises in the form of centralized policies to integrate all marketing activities for strongly interdependent country markets. This could lead, for example, to the founding of a product division with global marketing responsibilities. This may break the existing dependencies between product divisions (for example, common production and R&D capacities). It could then become appropriate to use complex, multidimensional matrix structures to cope more effectively with non-'decomposable' systems.

An advantage of matrix organizations is the simultaneous co-ordination of activities according to various demands (Hollensen, 2001, p. 595). A matrix structured according to (global) product brands *and* functions leads, ideally, to the fulfilment of organizational tasks across both dimensions. In fact, this will only be achieved when goal conflicts between the product division and the functions can be resolved co-operatively and in the interest of the enterprise. A simultaneous monitoring of both definitions is necessary, not only for such goal conflicts: the allocation of authority between matrix dimensions plays a critical role. Only if each interface of both dimensions of a two-dimensional matrix is ranked equally, can this be achieved.

With its equal-parity dimensions, a mature matrix places high demands on those in charge, because the multiple and often conflicting objectives have to be reconciled in the best interests of the enterprise. This requires an accordingly high capacity for information utilization by the affected employees. Even if this situation prevails, a matrix organization inevitably means a relatively high number of employees who have co-ordinative responsibilities, which in turn means that the enterprise has high co-ordination costs. These can only be justified if very high returns from specialization can be achieved. In reality, this does not always seem to be possible. For this reason, multidimensional matrixes have been criticized severely, and their use has been recommended by Davis and Lawrence (1977) only as a last resort. The reason for this is the realization that the dependence on two equally-ranked superiors with quite different interests and objectives often fails to lead to optimal coordination, but results in inappropriate compromises, failure to make decisions at all, or a focus on internal organizational problems rather than on customers and competitors.

Despite their theoretical elegance as solutions to real-world problems, multidimensional organizational structures must be regarded with some scepticism. It is also questionable as to how an organization should react to increasing interdependencies between country markets. It would make more sense as a *first step*, to regard dependencies between county markets as a central managerial problem, to develop the right perceptions and, where necessary, acceptance, subject to the appropriate managers and their subordinates. This seems important, because it is the first step to a really desirable co ordination that is also implemented. Recognition of the problem is the beginning of the search for an appropriate solution. In this respect, no more changes are needed in the formal organizational structure. Such changes on the basis of country market interdependencies will only be accepted by employees if they have the necessary understanding.

Co-ordination is based on communication and overcoming information interface problems between organizational units. A sound *second step* is thus the establishment of communication channels between interdependent individuals. If country markets are mutually dependent, the responsible managers should exchange their information and set prices together. This can occur in a self-organized form, provided it leads to goal attainment. In this context, interventions in the formal structure may not be necessary. Only if an ongoing and significant need for co-ordination between organizational units emerges, does a *third step* seem appropriate. This step will be accepted if the first two have already been implemented.

Behavioural Co-ordination

The objective of co-ordinating various measures is to influence the decision-making (and implementation) behaviour of the individual organizational members, to the advantage of the entire enterprise. This objective can also be served by behavioural control. This includes the following instruments:

- corporate culture;
- selection and continuing education and training of decision makers;
- incentive systems; and
- goal systems.

Corporate Culture

The formal organizational structure comprises only one part of the co-ordinative authority of the enterprise. Every organization also develops informal organizational structures which have a co-ordinating effect. As such, corporate culture plays a central role as the sum of the values and norms that mould the behaviour of members of the enterprise (Kieser and Kubicek, 1992; Deal and Kennedy, 1982). Such 'dos and don'ts' with respect to the socialization processes of new members of the enterprise, for which corporate 'heroes' and rituals are significant, have a behaviour-controlling character. These behavioural effects may exert a positive or negative overall impact in terms of achieving the desired behaviour in the company.

The significance of corporate culture for co-ordination is based on the behaviour-controlling impact of a 'normative management through values and norms' (Ulrich, 1983). In order to achieve this objective, management has the task of developing such a system of normative rules (Beyer, 1993). This system is intended to lead the behaviour of the institution in the direction of values and objectives. In contrast to such guidance, the formative process does not consist of establishing norms and behaviour in individual situations, but in an appropriate ordering of abstract norms which will prevent undesirable behaviour, and thus establish acceptable behaviour (Ulrich, 1983).

With increasing interdependencies between country markets, the values and norms that prevail in an enterprise are of great significance, because they bring the pursuit of overall enterprise objectives into the foreground and prevent the pursuit of 'empire building' and egoistic self-interest. A behavioural influence in this direction must, therefore, be regarded as a major instrument of organizational co-ordination.

Selection and Continuing Education of Decision-makers

If current and potential corporate managers are willing, to varying degrees, to operate in the interest of the entire enterprise, their selection for higher management tasks can have an impact on the criterion of co-ordination. The objective behind the selection of managers is to choose what is best for the enterprise, and not for one particular section. These top managers will then promote co-ordination throughout the company. Such managers are particularly important in those enterprises where the tendency to pursue partial goals, such as those of a department, is at its highest. This managerial 'model' function should, over the medium to longer term, contribute towards changing corporate culture.

The co-ordination challenge of selecting the managers themselves lies in rendering measurable the motivation of individuals for pursuing enterprise-related goals and maintaining this motivation over time. It is necessary to measure the motivation for providing an efficient selection. This must be maintained in order to secure the right longer-term impact through sustainable interdependencies.

Co-ordination through the selection of managers can only succeed if there is a sufficient pool of suitable candidates available to the enterprise, both internal and external (Hax, 1965). Initial and ongoing training in the sense of *management development*, may be necessary in order to ensure that this potential is available. To this end, the appropriate programmes must be developed. Conveying the need for incentives and goal-setting processes for international marketing co-ordination, are the central focus.

Incentive Systems

The behaviour of managers and employees can be influenced quite substantially by appropriate incentive systems. Incentive systems contain income-based and non-income-based components. The latter refer, for example, to potential for personal development and recognition or to status in the enterprise. A goal-orientated formulation of incentive systems requires a differentiation between 'good' decisions (optimal for co-ordination) from individual employees, compared to 'bad' decisions which pursue individual or departmental objectives at the expense of those of the enterprise. Second, it can be observed that the impact of incentive systems depends on the cultural context (de Pay, 1989). The identification of 'good' decisions enables the appropriate reward and fostering of positive impacts. 'Bad' decisions can, similarly, be coupled with negative sanctions. Incentive systems will exert a co-ordinating impact if the incentives lead to the right kind of interlinked employee behaviour. A culturally differentiated employee background means that different types of incentive systems will be needed, which ensures that all follow the same overall goals.

Goal Systems

Goal systems play a major role in co-ordinating the performance of employees. Goals (objectives) relate to the desired future situation of the enterprise. Apart from their co-ordination function, goals also serve control and motivation functions. The co-ordination function is intended, most of all, to ensure that 'decentralized, interdependent decisions at various informational and decision-making levels are orientated towards the goal systems of the entire organization' (Heinrichs, 1973, p. 262). The following functions of goals must be fulfilled if co-ordination is to be achieved (Hax, 1965):

▸ operationality; and
▸ overall complementarity.

Apart from the measurability of goal attainment with respect to content, comprehensiveness and time-frame, it is also critical to establish if sub-goals complement overall enterprise goals. Thus the overall goal must be divided effectively into smaller, complementary, sub-goals.

If this is not possible, and departmental goals conflict, there is a *defective goal system*. In such cases, the effective co-ordination of sub-goals is not possible, even subject to the assumption that the objectives of the relevant employees can be converted into goal-orientated behaviour. In this case, 'the problem is that of finding a synthesis of variables of evaluation' (Adam, 1996, p. 12). This constitutes an attempt to cope with contradictory objectives and evaluation dimensions, whereby the essential goal conflict remains intact. There is, then, no attempt to find an optimal solution.

As a result, it is clear that objectives can only provide a co-ordinative function subject to certain conditions. These conditions prevail in the case of complementary sub-goals. However, if goal conflicts cannot be overcome, co-ordination through goals can no longer lead to acceptable results.

Cost–Structure Measures

The impacts on the cost situation of the enterprise as a whole are major elements of seller-related feedback from marketing measures in the operational country markets. The main causes are cross-border changes in cost as a result of operations in additional markets, and an increase in the degree of product differentiation. In both cases, the *high shares of fixed cost* and the associated cost impacts on entering new markets are the chief causes of cost-related interdependency.

A reduction in cost-related feedback will only be necessary if it results in an improvement in the enterprise's overall situation. In essence, high fixed costs are harmless if there is no volatility in sales. This would be the case if sales and production fluctuations occur and, with declining production, fixed costs could not be reduced, or could only be achieved with considerable delays. This risk grows with the share of irretrievable *sunk costs* (Funke, 1995).

Entry into new country markets and an increase in the quantity sold will thus only exert a positive impact on the cost situation (by reducing unit costs), if there are no fluctuations in future quantities sold. However, enterprises cannot rely on such a situation prevailing. Fluctuating sales and price levels, and thus uncertain revenues, render the share of fixed costs dangerous in terms of ensuring the desired profit situation. With declining revenues and an inflexible cost situation, profit deteriorates, and, analogously to the effects of entering new markets, this impact is international. The extent of this deterioration grows with an escalating turnover decline and increasing production centralization.

A reduction in cost-related feedback is a measure that contributes towards increasing corporate flexibility. Fluctuations in turnover have less of an impact on enterprises with a high share of variable costs relative to fixed costs. The question as to what share of fixed costs is optimal cannot be answered in general terms. This depends on the extent of expected revenue fluctuations and managerial risk preferences, or those of the enterprise's owners. In general, with an increasing degree of anticipated revenue fluctuation, the share of fixed costs should decline. The same applies if management or the enterprise's owners are risk-averse.

A variety of instruments which manage *cost structure* are available for reducing the share of fixed costs (Funke, 1995). Cost structure refers – in its simplest form – to the share of fixed and variable costs at any production level. This contrasts with *cost-level* management, where the objective is to reduce total unit cost at any output level. Funke (1995) suggests the following measures in order to manage cost structure effectively:

Reducing the share of value added

This means reducing the share of value added in one's own enterprise and relying more on suppliers. This would shift fixed costs (for example, depreciation of productive equipment, personnel costs and so on) to a supplier, whose (identical) services can be procured on the basis of flexible contracts. By doing so, fixed costs are rendered variable. However, contracts which define fixed sales quantities and purchasing prices are equivalent to fixed costs for the duration of the contract (Backhaus and Funke, 1996).

Removing barriers to reducing fixed costs

The conversion of fixed to variable costs may begin by removing the barriers to the reduction of fixed costs. Such measures are based on the fact that all costs are fixed for only a limited period of time, after which they become variable. Thus personnel costs, for example, are fixed only for the duration of an employment contract. The objective of these measures is to shorten the time-frame in which costs are fixed. Thus time-limited work contracts would be an appropriate measure.

A shift to cost structures with different proportions of fixed and variables costs constitutes an additional possible instrument that cannot be separated from cost-level management. This is illustrated in the following example.

For the manufacture of a product, an enterprise has two alternative technologies at its disposal (A and B), each of which has differing shares of fixed and variable costs (see Figure 9.48). In a particular area (the shaded column in Figure 9.48), the achievable production quantities with both technologies causes the cost level to differ only minimally. For production quantities which exceed this level substantially, technology B is cheaper, whereas A would be cheaper

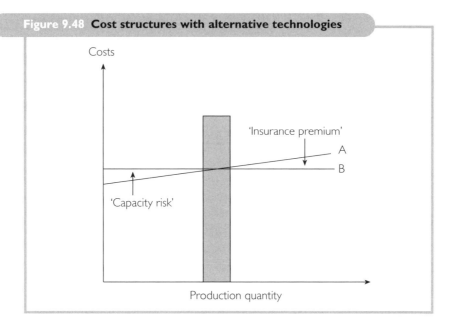

Figure 9.48 Cost structures with alternative technologies

in the reverse situation. If the enterprise now decides in favour of technology A, the strongly positive deviation in product quantities compared to technology B will lead to additional costs. That can be interpreted as *insurance premiums* for negative employment changes. Ultimately, which cost structure is in fact selected is a question of possible future fluctuations in production quantities and managerial risk preferences. The extent of reduced cost-related feedback with negative deviations from planned production quantities, and the resultant costs in the form of additional production cost with strongly deviating production quantities, need to be taken into account with respect to this decision.

Reducing Competition-related Interdependencies

A counter-strategy can ultimately succeed for enterprises in converging markets, by reducing the competition-related feedback between country markets. If such a form of feedback is understood to refer to the fact that corporate measures in one country will lead to competitive reactions in other markets, which in turn compel them to adapt again, then these reactions can only be reduced by the enterprise withdrawing at least partially from the pressure of international competition. In other words, the aim of the international enterprise is to break up the network of international competition, to increase its country-specific freedom of action.

Such measures include:

▸ co-operation with international competitors;
▸ the take-over of international competitors; and
▸ selective market exit.

If an enterprise succeeds in securing the co-operation of competitors, as in the form of strategic alliances (Backhaus, 1999), competitive feedback will then be reduced, as in the case of take-overs of foreign competitors. In both situations, the degree of dependence between operational country markets declines, because country-specific measures can be expected not to impose negative competitive reactions in other country markets.

Finally, the enterprise can exit certain country markets in order to reduce competitive feedback, and by doing so reduce international competitive pressure.

This issue can be demonstrated by means of the following example: Figure 9.49 outlines the network of international competition faced by a seller. This enterprise is active in countries A, B, D and E, while the competitor in question is present in countries D and E, but not in A and B. Instead, this enterprise is also present in markets F, G, H and I. The significance of these various markets for the enterprise is demonstrated in Figure 9.49 through the size of the various rectangles.

If the seller now finds that his/her measures in D, for example, lead to immediate retaliatory measures by the competitor in question in E, which in turn necessitates marketing adaptation in E, this market dependence can only be dismantled by the seller's exit from Country D – in this case, the market operated commonly with the competitors to Country E. As an alternative, the seller can enter Country C, for example, in which the competitor is not present.

The exit from D and simultaneous entry into C would, in the situation described, lead to a decline in competitive feedback, because the seller would now only be competing with international rivals in one market.

Figure 9.49 Reducing competitive feedback through market exit

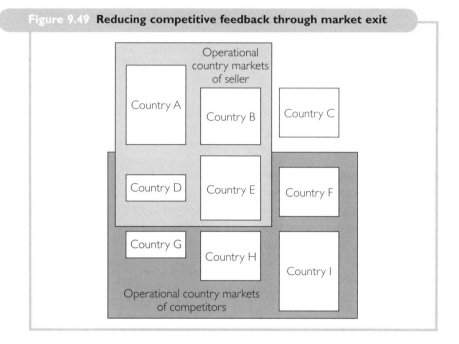

Case Study: PharmaCo

Background

The Pharma Corporation (PharmaCo) is a Dutch enterprise which evolved from a family business founded in Rotterdam, the Netherlands, in 1923. It is the subsidiary of a large French chemical conglomerate and represents the interests of the mother company in the pharmaceutical market When PharmaCo found itself in serious financial difficulties in 1982, the family shareholders sold out to the French concern. The major product of the enterprise is Multiprofen, a pain-reliever for various symptoms (rheumatic pain, accidental injuries and so on), which is marketed in the Netherlands and various other European countries. Because of its enormous popularity, the product accounted for over 95 per cent of the company's roughly US$40 million turnover in 2001. This popularity may be attributed to the exceptionally high physical tolerance to the product and the familiarity and trust it enjoys among patients. These qualities have secured it a near-monopoly position within its price range in the various country markets.

Through an injection of capital and know-how, the new owners established new markets in the entire Western European region as well as in some Middle and Eastern European countries, Canada and the USA. In these countries, Multiprofen is marketed, as in the home market, through wholesalers, pharmacies and hospitals, sometimes under different product names, but always with the identical chemical composition.

As an independent subsidiary of the French parent company, PharmaCo is managerially autonomous. Management decisions are not, in essence, influenced by the parent and control is applied only through financial indicators submitted monthly to France. The consistent profit-maximizing orientation of PharmaCo and its marketing organisation constitute an important change since the take-over. Previously, satisfactory profits ('satisficing'), were regarded as adequate.

PharmaCo's fourteen national marketing (trading) companies, including that in the Netherlands, are 100 per cent wholly-owned subsidiaries, whose activities are therefore focused entirely on the country market in which they operate. The marketing subsidiaries incur almost entirely fixed costs, because of the high contribution of personnel to costs. Variable costs are negligable, apart from delivery and related costs. The objective of the national marketing subsidiaries is profit maximization in that market. The marketing activities themselves focus on developing and maintaining relationships with intermediaries (wholesalers) and doctors; brand management; and, in particular, price formation. In this respect, the marketing subsidiaries have so far had complete autonomy and are controlled only through their national overall performance. No control is exercised over national management, through delivery quotas or limits, for example. This was not always the case. Only with the rising significance of foreign business (less than 40 per cent of turnover now occurs in the home market) was pricing policy transferred from the home office to the national marketing subsidiaries. This was done because it was evident that market knowledge 'on the spot' was extremely important for appropriate price setting.

Multiprofen is produced only at the Rotterdam factory. In this production process, constant marginal costs are US$300 per delivered unit. Product composition and branding are totally standardized. Until now, the product has been shipped at a unitary delivery price ex-works of US$400 per shipping unit to the marketing subsidiaries, which also have to carry country-specific transport costs. For example, in the Dutch market, transport costs of US$50 per unit are incurred in distributing from the factory to the Dutch retailer, and US$200 per unit for transport from the Rotterdam factory to the Swedish marketing company. However, no additional transport costs are incurred in Sweden, because, in contrast to the situation in Holland, the local wholesaler purchases 'free ex marketing company'.

Problem Formulation

The autonomy in price-formation enjoyed by the marketing subsidiaries has led to extremely mixed results. This is because of the high variability of customer willingness to pay for Multiprofen, because it is not a prescription drug in all countries, and thus may be sold 'over the counter' (so-called OTC medicine) in some markets and not in others. Because all marketing subsidiaries and their management are evaluated according to financial results, each strives towards a profit-maximizing price policy.

For the Netherlands, the least price-sensitive European country with respect to this product, the following per-unit price-response function (in US$) can be formulated on the basis of past experience:

$$p_D = 8,000 - \frac{1}{6} \cdot x_D \qquad (9.19)$$

In Sweden, where the European price sensitivity for Multiprofen is highest, the following price-response function applies (again in US$):

$$p_E = 4,500 - \frac{1}{4} \cdot x_E \qquad (9.20)$$

As expressed in this price-response function, the national marketing subsidiaries have thus far formulated an independent pricing policy. In the recent past, this practice has come increasingly under pressure in Europe, and not only consumer organizations and politicians have criticised the differential pharmaceutical pricing policy in this politically sensitive area. The increasing integration of the European market and the concomitantly simplified information and goods flows (quicker and cheaper), have given rise to trading enterprises which exploit price differences. These arbitrageurs (re-importers and parallel importers) purchase products in low-price markets and re-sell in higher-priced ones. This is profitable, provided the achievable (positive) difference between purchase and sales price is lower than the transaction cost (administration, transport and so on).

The grey pharmaceutical market created by arbitrageurs has grown continually in the last 8 years. As with many other firms in a similar position, PharmaCo has reacted by putting pressure on some wholesalers in the low-price countries that have grown suspiciously rapidly. Efforts have been made to prevent them from selling to arbitrageurs in an attempt to stop them re-importing. Furthermore, retailers in the high-price countries have been discouraged from stocking re-imported goods. However, because of the legal situation in the EU, this approach is not possible over the longer term. Furthermore, the EU authorities 'use' the re-importing, or parallel importing, consciously as a means of strengthening market integration. It thus opposes, both legally and through publicity, any efforts on the part of manufacturers to prevent the emergence of grey markets. The result of this development is a constantly increasing market share of grey products, precipitated largely through rising market transparency. In 2001, this exerted a significant downward pressure on profits in the high-price countries of the European market, such as the Netherlands.

The target markets of the re-importers and parallel importers are always those with the largest price differentials. In the case of Multiprofen, this has led mainly (but not exclusively) to goods flowing from Sweden into the Netherlands. Arbitrageurs purchase relatively cheaply in Sweden and, in terms of transaction cost, incur only transport costs of US$250 per sales unit for re-importing into the Netherlands and distributing to wholesalers there.

This development has become increasingly problematic for the home-office management of PharmaCo. The exploitation of national differences in price sensitivity, on which a substantial part of business success in the past years was based, is increasingly being jeopardized. The extent of the problem, and the likelihood that external circumstances (EU and national policy) would prevent a defusing of the situation, led PharmaCo to rethink its pricing policy. The key factor was the realization that the emergence of grey markets necessitates some form of co-ordination of national pricing policies. It is clear that, in future, national pricing decisions can no longer be separate from one another, at least not in the EU.

Questions Relating to the Case

1 What are the general co-ordination problems, and why did they arise? Ensure that your answer relates to the case.

2 What internal and external factors influence the degree of co-ordination difficulties encountered with respect to PharmaCo's pricing policy?

3 What is the impact of the deviation from the goal of profit maximization on marketing behaviour?

4 In order to gain an impression of the consequences of the emerging grey markets, the price-response functions stated earlier can be used to analyse a possible co-ordination of the pricing policy in the Netherlands and Sweden, as two 'extreme' markets.

It should be assumed that: the Swedish marketing subsidiary treats arbitrageurs as domestic clients with respect to pricing, arbitrage goods move physically between the countries; currency risks can be ignored; and the only transaction costs incurred by the arbitrageurs in the process of re-importing are transport costs.

(a) In the context of a 'worst-case' scenario, it should, for the moment, be assumed that in future, all Dutch wholesalers will be supplied by the Swedish marketing subsidiary of PharmaCo, provided the price difference between the two countries exceeds the transport costs. The aim is to compare the consequences of this scenario with the current situation (independent country markets) in order to determine the potential extent of co-ordination problems. In this context, the total profit earned by PharmaCo should be maximized; that is, including profit from the national marketing subsidiaries. Given the above assumptions, formulate an optimization function for optimal co-ordination between the Netherlands and Sweden.

(b) In the context of an alternative scenario, develop a function for a co-ordinated pricing policy between the Netherlands and Sweden, if the arbitrage quantity increases linearly with the (positive) difference between price differentials and transport costs. No information is available about the rate of increase of the function. Which changes will now occur with respect to the function formulated in the first step?

(c) What are the shortcomings of both functions? Refer to the assumptions in your answer. Do you still believe the model to be realistic?

(d) As a solution to the European pricing problem for Multiprofen, the management of PharmaCo is considering appointing a pricing manager who would be responsible for all markets affected by arbitrage. Alternatively, it would also be possible to diverge from the policy of a unitary price ex-works (adding full transport costs). What do you think of both ideas? What would be an optimal co-ordinating price ex-works for the Swedish marketing subsidiary with the given transport costs?

Co-ordination Problems in Diverging Markets

The Origin of Co-ordination Problems

After completing the internationalization process, enterprises face new international marketing tasks if the interdependencies, which applied at the time of market entry, subsequently change. In such cases (although not only in such cases), the enterprise is compelled to adapt its market presence.

Changed interdependencies in the context of *being international*, may be described and analysed not only through a homogenization of environmental conditions or a standardization of the behaviour of market parties, as in the previous chapter, where the emphasis was on the problems of converging markets. Furthermore, feedback changes and the accompanying need for change by international enterprises, also arise with the diametrically opposite processes, that is, a 'heterogenization' of institutional conditions and/or the behaviour of market parties. Buyer behaviour is the most important of these factors.

Current examples of such heterogenization tendencies can be seen in the fragmentation tendencies of world markets, the break-up of economic blocs and the disintegration of individual country markets. Not only the sectoral protection by the USA or Japan, which contravenes the worldwide rules of trade, but also the behaviour of economic communities such as the EU or NAFTA, render increasingly difficult exporting by enterprises into third countries. The disintegration of individual country markets constitutes a third form of heterogenization. Political motives are often responsible for the fact that country borders are redrawn, and that country markets disintegrate into smaller pieces. The dissolution of the former USSR, the fragmentation of Yugoslavia, the striving towards autonomy of the Flemings and Walloons in Belgium, or the attempts of the Canadian province Quebec to achieve autonomy, demonstrate the current significance of country-market disintegration.

The *heterogenization of the institutional environment* is characterized by the fact that enterprises operating in a variety of country markets face increasingly diverging legal, political, social and economic conditions. While, in the past, goods, capital and personnel flows operated in similar, or at least reasonably co-ordinated, frameworks, heterogenization means that such transfers are either impossible or expensive.

The *heterogenization of the behaviour of market partners* constitutes another type. Even if homogenization tendencies predominate in general, in many instances the opposite tendencies can be identified in specific industry sectors. Because of cultural, political or religious conditions, there are diverging buyer preferences between countries or within individual country markets *(heterogenization of buyer behaviour)*. Similarly, a heterogenization of the behaviour of market partners can take the form of international competitors exiting certain markets and thus causing a decline in the degree of competitor-based interdependence.

In summary, the heterogenization of environmental conditions, and of buying behaviour, can be described as *the problem of fragmenting markets*. With respect to coordination aspects, various forms of market fragmentation lead to similar problems in the context of being international:

1 With respect to the heterogenization of institutional conditions, such as in the form of protection of economic blocs, imports by enterprises from third countries are either not allowed or limited. The market area of the importing enterprise fragments, because an extensive market operation of the target markets from within the economic blocs is rendered difficult or even impossible. For example, feedback arises if the enterprise is unable to adapt its own productive capacity immediately to changing conditions. In such cases, the sealing-off of economic blocs leads to overcapacity which has an impact on marketing in other countries that are not immediately affected. For the importer, this may put downward pressure on prices in the non-affected markets, if the overcapacity demands quantity increases in the 'remaining' markets.

Precisely this phenomenon was demonstrated with the example of the EU banana market regulations given in Chapter 8 (see pages 256–9). Because the EU limited the imports of so-called 'dollar bananas', the American sellers were compelled to divert into the American market the formerly European sales capacity

> that had become free beyond their control. The results were a price decline and associated profit declines.

Similar feedback effects occur in fragmented markets. Instead of a unitary overall market, an enterprise is suddenly confronted by several country markets that are separated from one another. The effects associated with such fragmentation depend primarily on the question of whether the enterprise under consideration was already active internationally or not.

- For international enterprises, which, apart from fragmenting markets, also operate in other countries, there is a need to adapt to diverging institutional change. Apart from new country borders, which determine new tariff trade barriers, there may in particular be feedback to other countries, if, in the existing market components, the legal framework already implemented diverges from that in the past. In such a case, standardization decisions made in the past, for example, may require careful consideration and evaluation, because imports in the fragmented market require a differentiated formulation of individual marketing instruments. This creates adaptation pressure in other markets, because the data situation underlying the formulation of marketing instruments in other countries has changed.
- Two central problems arise for enterprises which have so far been active only in the fragmenting country market: first, the break-up of the domestic market may be accompanied by a need to internationalize. In view of the now-smaller domestic market, this enterprise is likely to have overcapacity. If this cannot be dispersed over the entire existing market, the enterprise will be compelled to secure new markets. This means *going international*. Second, this break-up leads to procurement gaps within the value chain of the enterprise. This applies in particular if the suppliers in the foreign country belong to the part of the total market that has now become foreign.

2 Finally, the heterogenization of buyer preferences renders more difficult, the application of standardized marketing, or enables an enterprise to increase the extent of differentiation of its market operations. If it can be assumed that a change in buyer preferences can be observed in only a part of the previous country markets, there will also be feedback in other markets that are characterized by

constant preferences, because international standardization decisions may now be sub-optimal.

Similarly, the degree of freedom enjoyed by the enterprise with
respect to market operations in the various country markets will
increase if the previously prevailing international competition fades
away or becomes simpler to handle, through, for example the
partial exit of competing enterprises. In this case, the enterprise can
implement country-specific measures without this leading to
competitive reactions in other country markets.

If, for example, the situation discussed earlier (Chapter 9)
applies with the competitor from Country D this is equivalent to
a break-up of the previously independent markets D and E.
The enterprise can, in this instance, enter Country E, without
there being any 'retaliatory' measures from this competitor in
Country D.

It becomes clear that an enterprise in fragmenting markets is
confronted by a change in the feedback situation, compared to the
circumstances that applied previously. Depending on the causes and
manifestations of this fragmentation, the possible interdependency
changes are shown in Figure 10.1.

Fragmenting markets lead predominantly to declining feedback,
because market separation reduces the level of interdependence.
Demand-related feedback is weakened, for example, by a fragmentation of the global market, the sealing-off of economic blocs, break-up
of individual country markets, or heterogenization of buyer behaviour,
because there is unlikely to be a decline in cross-border information
exchange, but it will always be more difficult, if not impossible, to
exchange goods. Apart from the fact that an 'untangling' of the international network of competition is accompanied by declining competitive-based feedback, seller-related feedback will also decline if

Figure 10.1 Changes in interdependency in different types of diverging markets

		Seller-related interdependencies	Buyer-related interdependencies	Competition-related interdependencies
Heterogenization of institutional conditions		Increasing	Decreasing	Constant
Heterogenization of behaviour of partners	Buyer behaviour	Decreasing	Decreasing	Constant
	Competitive situation	Constant	Constant	Decreasing

fragmentation is caused by a heterogenization of buyer behaviour. In such a situation, it may be essential (or at any rate possible) for the firm, to offer country-specific products using different prices; in other words, to decouple market operations in the fragmenting markets.

On the other hand, an increase in seller-related feedback will prevail if the enterprise is faced with a heterogenization of institutional conditions. In particular, if there are cost-related interdependencies between the country markets operated by sellers, the strategies used so far in countries not immediately affected by the fragmentation will come under pressure. This temporally-delayed impact of market fragmentation or heterogenization of buyer behaviour in other country markets, is referred to as the '*domino effect*' of fragmenting markets. The effect refers to the problem that arises in fragmenting markets when other markets operated by sellers are affected successively by the fragmentation. The way in which the domino effect functions, can be explained by means of an highly simplified example:

An enterprise succeeds in developing an innovative product, for which there is a high demand in the domestic market (Country A) as well as in Countries B and C. The manufacturing of the product, and thus the effective unit costs, are associated strongly with the experience curve, because, with growing cumulative sales quantities, rationalized production methods can be used. Furthermore, even before the introduction of the product, it is evident that the competition will bring a comparable product variant to the market in the medium term. Thus there will be a limited 'window of opportunity' for amortizing the R&D that has already been invested. Although there are significant differences between country markets with respect to the willingness to pay for the developed product, the enterprise decides to introduce it into all countries at the same price, because the extremely low transaction costs and high buyer arbitrage tendency is characterized by disadvantageous parallel imports. Against the background of a temporally limited product life cycle, the enterprise also decides for the quicker diffusion of the product with a constant price during the entire life cycle, which is not orientated to the actual development of effective unit costs (target pricing). In terms of price-setting, the enterprise orientates itself with respect to estimating the development of units costs, as well as for the total quantities that can be sold in Countries A, B and C, to the results of comprehensive market research activities (see Figure 10.2).

After the successful introduction of the product in Countries A, B and C, in t_1, Country C forms an economic bloc with Countries E and F, and simultaneously, bans imports from Countries A and B in order to protect the local economy.

The import ban by Country C has the effect that the originally anticipated path of the experience curve will no longer be achieved on the basis of the price-setting that has been implemented. For the enterprise, the reduced quantity of total sales leads to a slow decline in unit costs in Countries A and B. Consequently, the price originally planned for these countries cannot be maintained, and subsequent price rises will be necessary. This situation, is intensified further for the enterprise in question, when, as assumed in Figure 10.2, the price rise means it now exceeds the willingness to pay of buyers in Country B. Thus, in the subsequent period, the enterprise finds itself compelled t_2 to withdraw from Country B, because the new price eliminates demand completely.

The slowing decline in unit costs, on the other hand, necessitates a new price rise in Country A. Because here too the price exceeds what consumers are willing to pay (see Figure 10.2), a withdrawal from Country A will occur in t_3. The import ban in Country C has thus compelled the seller to withdraw successively from Countries A and Country B.

Figure 10.2 Pay-out effective unit costs and target pricing

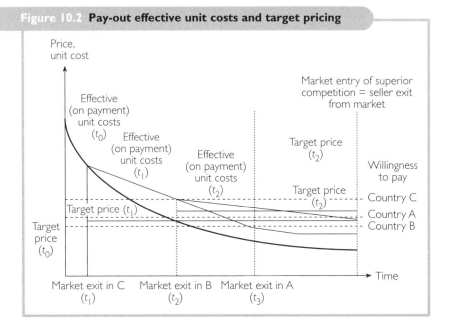

The Extent of Co-ordination Problems

Independently of whether feedback in diverging markets rises or declines, the international enterprise is always compelled to undertake adaptation measures. These depend to a large degree on the extent to which there is an increase or decrease in feedback, and thus on the market splitting process.

Such processes can be differentiated according to:

▸ market size and symmetry; as well as
▸ the degree of smoothness of market splitting (how sealed-off the market is in reality).

Market Size and Symmetry

With the fragmenting of markets, the extent of co-ordination for the various marketing activities of the international seller depends largely on the size of emerging market components for overall markets that are breaking up. In other words, the extent of co-ordination is influenced by the symmetry of the fragmentation.

Based on the example in Figure 10.2 above, if the market in country C, operated so far by the seller in question splits up, and this area cannot therefore be used in the same way by this seller (because, for example, the seller has no distribution channels in this region of the former Country C, because he/she used to serve the entire country from a distribution point in Country A), then the extent of co-ordination for this seller depends mainly on the significance, and thus the size, of the area that can no longer be reached.

International enterprises are confronted by similar issues if there is heterogenization of buyer behaviour, or if it comes to a break-up of the international competitive network. In the first case, the decline of buyer-related feedback, for example, will be particularly weak, if consumer preferences in a smaller market segment develop in their own individual way, so that the enterprise, because of the low significance of this segment, can dispense with a change in market presence where an independent operation in this market will no longer pay off. Analogously, the changes in feedback will be minimal if competitors withdraw from this unimportant market.

For the break-up of markets in the form of a heterogenization of institutional conditions, Ackermann (1997) describes the following types of market split in the context of the two differentiation criteria: *market size* and *symmetry*.

Because enterprises do not generally have the same level of access to all parts of a country or region, a differentiation must be made between 'active regions' and 'abstinence regions'.

Presence regions (P) refer to the part of the market in which the international enterprise, for example, concentrates its production and distribution facilities, and which, before the market split, served all remaining regions and the entire market. Accordingly, the regional market components, where the international enterprise does not have sufficient production or distribution facilities, are called *abstinence regions* (A).

Against this background, the various splitting scenarios can be constructed, which, for the enterprise in question, lead to a specific level of co-ordination. Figure 10.3 presents some particularly relevant scenarios.

For one thing, the degree of co-ordination depends largely on whether or not the market splitting process is symmetrical or asymmetrical. With a *symmetrical split*, the market volume in the former (total) market is halved, so it may be necessary to re-enter the part of the total market that is no longer operational, the abstinence market.

While, for a symmetrical market split, two (or more) economically equivalent market zones emerge through the fragmentation, an *asymmetrical split* is characterized by the fact that the market components are unequal in size. To the extent that the production and distribution capacities of the seller are located in the smaller market zone, the enterprise will be compelled to adapt. On the one hand, in this case it may again prove appropriate to secure the larger (split) market segment, or to reduce capacity significantly in the smaller remaining market area. Here, too, there will be a need for adaptation subject to coordination considerations, if the presence/abstinence areas of the sellers do not cover the newly-evolving country borders. A significantly lower need for co-ordination will ultimately prevail if precisely the opposite case emerges and the seller has capacity in the larger market component. To the extent that the segment that has split off reveals no particular significance for the seller in question, there will be no need for major adaptation, and the extent of co-ordination may be small. However, it remains possible that, even in this case, the extent of co-ordination will rise again if the new country borders do not correspond with the preference regions of the seller.

Figure 10.3 Alternative types of market split

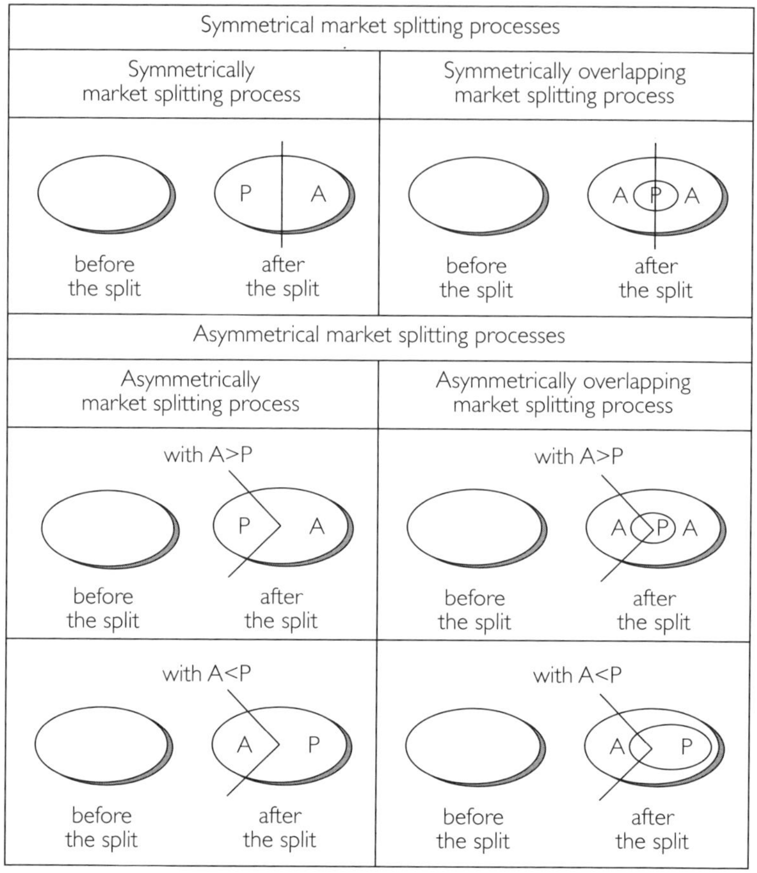

Extent of Market Split

The extent of market split (the degree to which it is clearly defined) will be determined by the prevailing, economically relevant relationships between the country markets or economic regions created by the split. We refer to a *soft market split* when:

▶ with a heterogenization of institutional conditions, the split is in the interests of all participants and thus, even after the economic separation, there is an intensive exchange relationship; and

▶ with the heterogenization of the behaviour of market participants (for example, in the form of a rationalization of consumer preferences), the deviations between the market components are small, so that no significant differences in preferences arise, or competitors accord a low level of strategic significance to a change in the network of international competition.

In contrast, fragmentation with a *hard market split* occurs abruptly and comprehensively. With a heterogenization of institutional conditions, the split often conflicts with the interests of one of the market sub-regions (market components) so that, after the split, economic exchange processes become considerably more difficult. Analogously to this, there is a hard market split with a heterogenization of the behaviour of market parties when, subsequent to the split, there are substantially differing market conditions between the market components.

As well as the stated extremes of hard and soft splits, intermediate forms are also possible, where the break-up reveals elements of both.

The degree of market split generally exerts an immediate impact on the extent of co-ordination within an international enterprise. The harder the market split process, the larger the changes in interdependency, and thus the need for co-ordination on the part of the firm. While, for a soft market split, with respect to the institutional conditions, the economic exchange conditions in the fragmenting market regions may barely be influenced, and thus a lower level of co-ordination is in fact needed for the enterprises active so far in the total market. Therefore the need for co-ordination may increase with an increasing degree of hardness. To the extent that the economic relationships between the splitting regions more or less settle down, it will become more difficult for the seller to serve the entire market.

On the basis of the typology criteria discussed above (market size, symmetry and extent), actual splitting processes can be classified. At the level of the entire market, Figure 10.4 shows a categorization of the Central and Eastern European markets in the 1990s with respect to market splits.

In terms of the market-split processes that have occurred during the 1990s and later, most of all in Central and Eastern Europe, virtually all the splitting processes described above can be found (see Figure 10.4). For example, the split of the country bloc COMECON can be categorized as an asymmetrical splitting process because the individually operating country markets after the split (such as Russia and Albania) reveal highly varying market sizes. Furthermore, the dissolution of COMECON was (primarily) a soft split, because it was generally in the

Figure 10.4 **Categorization of market splits in Central and Eastern Europe**

Region / Criterion	Economic block COMECON	Country markets		
		USSR	Yugoslavia	Czechoslovakia
Symmetrical form	Asymmetrical	Asymmetrical	Asymmetrical	Symmetrical
Level of business	Soft	Medium	Hard	Soft

interests of all former member states. And the destruction of the economic exchange relationships between the member states of COMECON was, furthermore, determined less by the dissolution of the country bloc and far more by the parallel transition from a socialist planned economy to a market economy.

In contrast to the asymmetrical and soft market splits with the dissolution of COMECON, the subsequent break-up processes of individual countries in Central and Eastern Europe belong elsewhere in the categorization. The break-up of the USSR, for example, is essentially an asymmetrical split, but a hard one. This is particularly the case because, for a long time, Russia railed against the splitting up of the USSR, as is evident from the problematic breaking-away of the Baltic states. As a consequence of the split of the Baltic states, which did not occur consensually, virtually all economic exchange between these states and Russia, or the remaining regions of the former USSR, have come to a standstill and been replaced by economic ties with the West.

In comparison to the above splits, the (asymmetrical) splitting process in Yugoslavia was even harder. The separation of Croatia from the Serbian-dominated remainder of the country met with massive disapproval in Serbia, causing a year-long, ethnically-based war.

The Czech Republic demonstrates that the splitting-up of country markets is not necessarily asymmetrical, and can also proceed 'softly'. Even after the market split, there are still intensive exchange relationships between the Czech Republic and Slovakia, so that the need for co-ordination on the part of firms that formerly operated in the total Czechoslovakian market, is relatively low.

However, such an overall market perspective can lead only to tentative conclusions about the need for co-ordination by individual international enterprises. The specific, enterprise-related need for co-ordination still depends on the particular situation and must be conducted case-by-case.

Co-ordination Strategies in Fragmenting Markets

Co-ordination strategies in fragmenting markets depend on whether the fragmentation leads only to a decreasing, or also partly to increasing (seller-related), feedback. The analysis of the origins of co-ordination have shown, in this context, that the former tends to be the case with a heterogenization of the behaviour of market participants, and the latter with the heterogenization of institutional conditions.

Co-ordination with Decreasing Feedback

In this case, fragmenting markets constitute the opposite of converging markets in the sense of dynamic market change. The resulting decision problem *principle* for international marketing is identical to that of converging markets and manifests itself in the question as to how one should react to market changes, or what need for co-ordination proceeds with respect to market operations.

Why the fundamental decision-making problem in international marketing depends initially on the orientation of market changes (homo/heterogenization), can be demonstrated with the aid of an example of price co-ordination from the area of instrumental adaptation to converging markets.

> The objective of price co-ordination is that of coordinating profit-maximizing, country-specific prices for the entire enterprise. This co-ordination is the result of changes in the market environment (with increasing market integration – for example, increased arbitrage) and identifies dynamic pricing paths which, in *converging markets*, reveal standardized prices (see Figure 10.5). Price co-ordination creates the task of determining optimal (co-ordinating) country prices at specific times.

Figure 10.5 Optimal co-ordinating pricing paths in dynamic markets

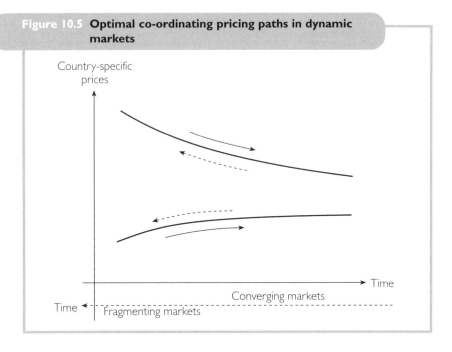

The lower the transaction costs of arbitrageurs, the stronger the tendency towards price standardization. In the case of *fragmenting markets*, with rising transaction costs, the opposite result will occur. Here, profit-maximizing prices have a tendency towards increasing differentiation, which becomes stronger if, for example, the transaction costs for arbitrageurs rise as a result of changes in institutional conditions (import quotas, tariffs and so on). The optimal price paths will, with precisely the opposite changes in the relevant environmental conditions and an otherwise identical initial situation, vary only with respect to the direction of change. The country-specific prices would then develop along the same pricing path for one country, but, in the diametrically *opposite direction*.

If, for example, a common market develops and, in this context, the arbitrage costs decline, as shown earlier, it may be appropriate for an enterprise that has so far pursued a differentiated pricing policy in the participating country markets, to even-out the prices in the sub-regions and position them in a pricing corridor, the breadth of which will be determined by country-specific willingness to pay and the level of prevailing arbitrage costs. If this common market breaks up once again, the enterprise can achieve a high level

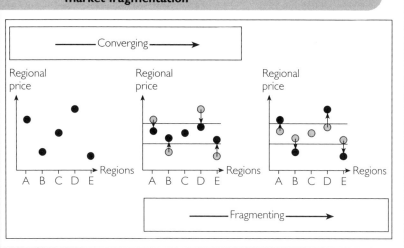

Figure 10.6 Reversal of pricing policy adaptation measures with market fragmentation

of price differentiation, because either the arbitrage costs will rise through the market break-up, or re-imports will become completely impossible. Figure 10.6 shows how this works through the creation and subsequent fragmenting of the common market caused by pricing-policy adaptation.

The similarity of the decision-making problem in the case of instrumental adaptation leads us to a similar category of solution approaches. For the pricing example, this means that the formal *optimization approach* for both fragmenting and converging markets is identical. All that changes is that the impact of time refers either to increasing or decreasing feedback. In both cases, the result would be an optimal adaptation process over time, which, in the case of *converging markets* would be an adaptation process with increasing standardization of country-specific prices (or generally of country-specific marketing instruments), and in the case of *fragmenting (converging) markets*, an adaptation with declining standardization. In this sense, the co-ordination approaches for instrumental adaptation discussed in the context of converging markets are also relevant and applicable here (as approaches dependent on the direction of change). However, they will lead from the results to the opposing direction over time. Thus the issue is that of decision-making problems for which solution approaches are developed, which are determined in the first instance through market dynamics, but not by their direction.

Co-ordination with Increasing (Supply-based) Interdependency

In this case, market fragmentation creates decision-making problems in international marketing, which are quite different from those in converging markets, but are familiar from the area of *going international*. Whenever a heterogenization of institutional conditions is responsible for parts of an operational market area splitting off from what was part of a single unified market, and the operation of this market is fraught with difficulties, or even becomes impossible, the enterprise is faced once again with the question of what countries are best suited for the location of the (productive) capacity that has been freed. However, this is not conceptionally different from the problems discussed in the context of going international.

In summary, Figure 10.7 shows that the co-ordination strategies in fragmenting markets do not reveal any conceptual uniqueness. If fragmentation leads only to reduced interdependency, as in the case of a heterogenization in the behaviour of market partners, a new differentiation/standardization decision will have to be made. This has already been discussed in connection with converging markets, albeit in the opposite direction. If, on the other hand, with a heterogenization of institutional conditions, there are increasing seller-related interdependencies, the enterprise must, once again, make market

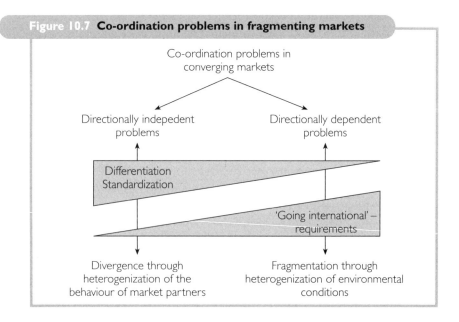

Figure 10.7 Co-ordination problems in fragmenting markets

entry decisions. This have been discussed in detail in the context of going international.

In view of the lack of conceptual completeness of co-ordination strategies in converging markets, it seems that a comprehensive treatment of such strategies is unnecessary. They can be inferred from the foregoing text.

Case Study: Petrolub plc

Petrolub is a Liverpool-based mineral-oil company which has been in operation since the 1960s. With an annual turnover of approximately £9 billion, it is a small firm compared to its international competitors. The company's shares are held mainly by British energy suppliers and banks, as well as by the giant American Oil (AMOIL). Its shares are not listed on the stock exchange, and only a small proportion are dispersed among other holders.

Over the last few years, the company's turnover has been constant. Management estimates that only in 1992 will turnover stagnate. 1992. Turnover trends since 1990 are shown in Figure 10.8. The figure also shows that the company is active mainly in the British market.

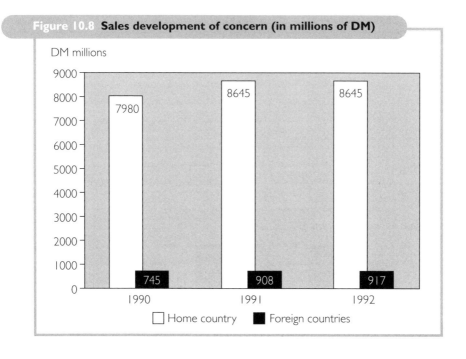

Figure 10.8 Sales development of concern (in millions of DM)

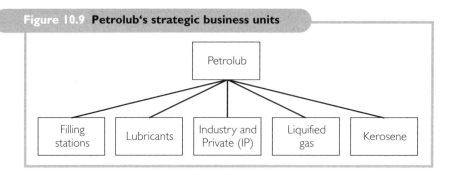

Figure 10.9 **Petrolub's strategic business units**

Petrolub concentrates exclusively on the 'downstream' area – that is, the marketing of mineral-oil products. It is not involved in the 'upstream' operations of oil extraction, but sources its oil products and liquid gas directly from refineries. In many cases, Petrolub sources from firms with whom it competes directly 'downstream'.

The company is divided into five Strategic Business Units (SBUs) as shown in Figure 10.9. Through its subsidiaries, the enterprise has a presence in Great Britain, Austria, Hungary and the former Czechoslovakia.

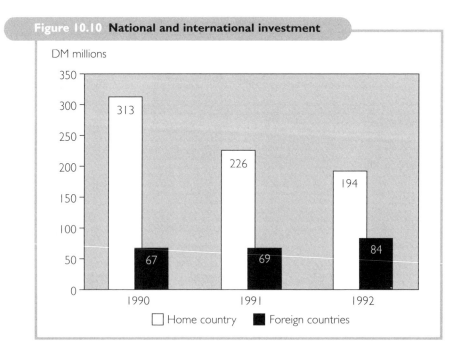

Figure 10.10 **National and international investment**

The firm's investments have been declining over the past few years, particularly in Great Britain. Only in selected areas was investment undertaken for the construction of new filling stations. However, most investment funds were used only for modernizing filling stations and for network maintenance.

Strategic Business Areas

The Core Activity – Filling Stations

The filling station business can be divided into the three areas of fuel provision, shop and services. Selling fuel through its retailer network has given Petrolub a high profile.

Apart from the size and location of the filling stations, the costs of establishing a station range from £0.5 to £1.5 million. The industry is thus relatively investment-intensive.

The fuels sold at filling stations are sourced from refineries, which in turn acquire unrefined oil on the open market. In the filling station business, prices are calculated according to replacement cost. The objective is to obtain sufficient revenue per litre to repurchase it from, for example, the Rotterdam market. Falling prices in Rotterdam are passed on directly to customers in order to maintain or expand market share.

Because world prices are quoted in US Dollars, the exchange rate against the German Mark exerts a major impact. Taxes, the price of unrefined oil and the US Dollar rate are thus the key determinants of the petrol price. The oil companies have little influence on these processes. The different levels of taxation create substantial price differentials within Europe, which even lead to 'tank tourism' in border areas (see Figure 10.11). Figure 10.12 provides an overview of European prices. The high market transparency intensifies both national and international competition. More than virtually any other product, filling-station petrol is characterized by 'visible' prices.

There are three types of contractual relationship between Petrolub and the filling stations.

▸ *Company-owned, company-operated (CoCo) service stations*: Petrolub both owns and operates the filling station. The complete control of the business is advantageous, but the additional need for personnel, and consequently high fixed costs, are disadvantageous.

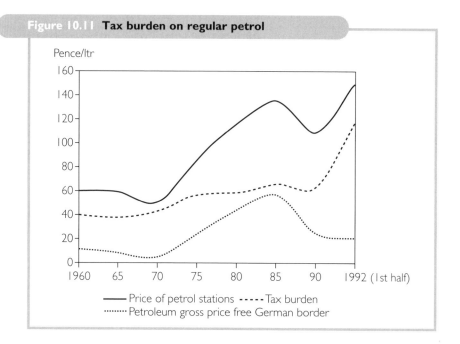

Figure 10.11 Tax burden on regular petrol

Pence/ltr

— Price of petrol stations ---- Tax burden
········ Petroleum gross price free German border

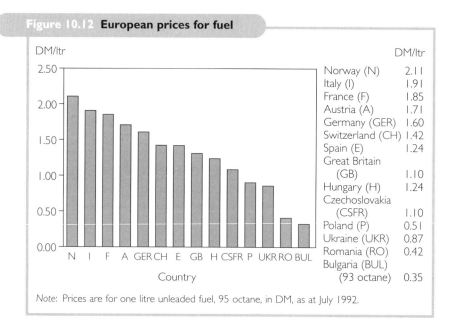

Figure 10.12 European prices for fuel

DM/ltr

	DM/ltr
Norway (N)	2.11
Italy (I)	1.91
France (F)	1.85
Austria (A)	1.71
Germany (GER)	1.60
Switzerland (CH)	1.42
Spain (E)	1.24
Great Britain (GB)	1.10
Hungary (H)	1.24
Czechoslovakia (CSFR)	1.10
Poland (P)	0.51
Ukraine (UKR)	0.87
Romania (RO)	0.42
Bulgaria (BUL) (93 octane)	0.35

Country

Note: Prices are for one litre unleaded fuel, 95 octane, in DM, as at July 1992.

- *Company-owned, dealer-operated (CoDo) service stations*: The operators of the filling station carry the operational responsibility. In this case, Petrolub receives rent from the filling-station operators, and in return, pays them a commission on turnover. Most of Petrolub's contracts work on this basis.
- *Dealer-owned, dealer-operated (DoDo) service stations*: The operator of the station is also the owner. Operational regulations constrain the autonomy of the operator only minimally. For the most part, the owner has only an acceptance or purchasing contract with Petrolub, does not use the company logo and is, therefore, a so-called 'independent filling station'.

In the filling-station business, the supplementary purchases (sales of food, souvenirs and so on in 'selection shops') as well as the service sector (car wash, repairs and so on) are becoming ever more important. The sale of fuel accounts for 60 per cent of filling-station turnover, but contributes only 29 per cent to income (see Figures 10.13 and 10.14).

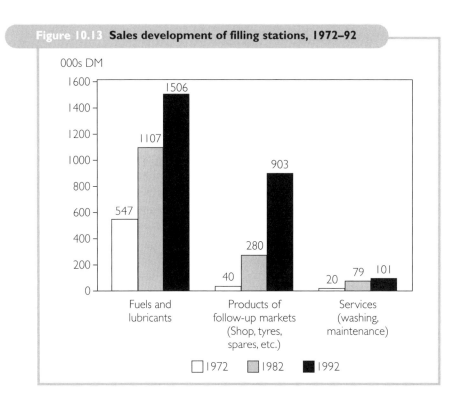

Figure 10.13 **Sales development of filling stations, 1972–92**

000s DM

	1972	1982	1992
Fuels and lubricants	547	1107	1506
Products of follow-up markets (Shop, tyres, spares, etc.)	40	280	903
Services (washing, maintenance)	20	79	101

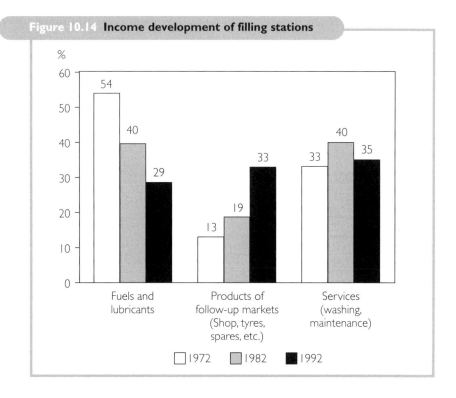

Figure 10.14 Income development of filling stations

The increasing importance of the shop-trade can be attributed to a distinct marketing concept. The so-called 'selection shops' are intended to emphasise their independent character, and thus signify a move away from the 'highway shop' image. Even 'non-petrol' customers should see the shop as more of a neighbourhood store. In this manner, filling-station shops increasingly assume the function of the ever-more-marginalized retailers, and satisfy consumer preferences for quick snacks and a high level of convenience. Customers are spared additional shopping visits with the inevitable waiting to pay; they quickly find what they want and have no parking problems. Under such conditions, customers are also particularly price insensitive.

In order to supply the filling-station shops, the Claris Sales and Service Company was founded, as a joint venture between Petrolub and Vergun Ltd, with each holding a 50 per cent interest.

Supplementary product lines

Lubricants

The company offers a range of about 400 lubricants, which are tailored specifically to the needs of customers in terms of general consumer preferences as well as those relating to specific countries or regions. Despite the large number of products, packaging and presentation are largely standardized for cost reasons.

Customers include large industrial firms, which use the lubricants in manufacturing processes – for example, machine, turbine and cylinder oils, regulator fluids, and lubrication fats. The entire automobile industry is a major customer for gear oil and various kinds of engine oils, brake fluids and so on, which are delivered directly to repair workshops.

Another marketing channel is though major retail chains, which sell a small proportion of the product range, primarily the popular engine oils, Herix (standard synthetic) and Herix Plus (highly synthetic), in 5-litre and 10-litre containers. The disadvantage of this form of branding is that the major chains also offer the products of competitors, so there is no clear or distinct profiling of the Petrolub range.

Liquid gas

The company's liquid gas sector is growing rapidly. A rising international environmental awareness on the part of consumers virtually guarantees massive increases in turnover over the medium term.

Liquid gasses are also known as propane and butane, which differ only in terms of their heating capabilities. Liquid gas is purchased from refineries, which generally have their own pipeline networks. Purchasers use their own containers and market under their own logos. Customers are mainly large manufacturing concerns, which use the gas as, for example, raw materials in petrochemical processes. Medium-sized firms and private households are also customers. The latter obtain the liquid gas in storage canisters delivered directly to them and used for such applications as domestic heating and running air-conditioners.

Aviation fuel

Petrolub sells kerosene at international airports to major airlines and private carriers. The kerosene is purchased from refineries and delivered directly to tank facilities at airports. Major international carriers such as British Airways are serviced directly from the Liverpool headquarters. A dedicated contact person within the company guarantees a sound customer relationship and a unitary pricing and invoicing policy. Less significant customers in terms of turnover (such as private and national airlines) are charged country-specific prices by the relevant country offices, and are also billed from there.

The ethnocentric internationalization strategy

Petrolub is an enterprise that is internationalizing and has a distinctly ethnocentric strategy. Its range of business extends to several countries, but the major markets are Great Britain and Austria. Furthermore, since the beginning of the 1990s, the firm has had a presence in Hungary and the Czech Republic, at first with lubricants and since the transformation progress started to show results, with a rapidly expanding filling-station network. Since 1991, there have been independent distributors for lubricants in Romania and Bulgaria, and since the beginning of 1992, also in the Ukraine. These distributors provide initial inroads to the market, and pave the way for the later introduction of other fields of business. These activities are co-ordinated from Vienna.

Austria is the largest foreign market and it is very similar in structure to that in the United Kingdom. It plays a significant role as a transit country for many Dutch, British and German holidaymakers on their way to Italy, Hungary or Croatia. Through a comprehensive network of filling stations, Petrolub has established a timely presence on the main transport routes.

However, 'tank tourism' still represents a problem for the Austrian management. Particularly in the border regions, consumers travel to Slovenia, Hungary or the Czech Republic, sometimes even Italy, because petrol and diesel prices in these regions are as much as 40 per cent below the Austrian level. The absence of mineral-oil taxes in these neighbouring countries is primarily responsible for the price differences. To date, the efforts of the entire mineral-oil industry and the Austrian government to get these countries to introduce mineral-oil taxes, have failed. In Italy, on the other hand, exchange-rate disparities are responsible for the price differentials. These problems are prejudicial not only to traditional business activities, but also with respect to the associated purchases – that is, the turnover of the shops. In other words, tank tourism has considerable knock-on effects.

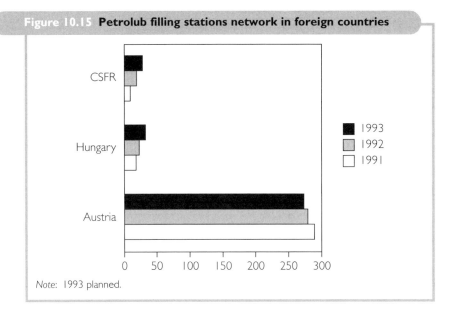

Figure 10.15 Petrolub filling stations network in foreign countries

Note: 1993 planned.

The development and planning dates of filling station networks, which will be established from Vienna for the Czech Republic and Hungary, are shown in Figure 10.15.

The foreign market in Czechoslovakia

The Czechoslovak market is regarded as particularly problematic. During the transformation process and in terms of potential EU entry, the government of Prime Minister Václav Klaus introduced a timely and comprehensive programme for Westernising the economy. How attractive the market and how effective production in Czechoslovakia are, is demonstrated by, for example, the substantial interest of international automobile manufacturers in SOD, which is now majority-owned by the Volkswagen group. The largest share of direct investment from German enterprises, apart from Hungary, flows into Czechoslovakia.

The geography of the country and the main national roads are demonstrated in Figure 10.16.

Mrs Smith, manager of Petrolub's International Activities Division comments: 'In the Czech Republic, we also commenced in about 1989 with lubricants only. Given our positive experiences in the market, we

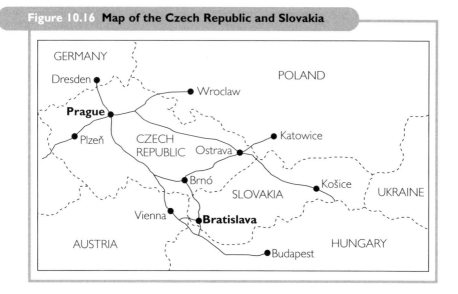

Figure 10.16 Map of the Czech Republic and Slovakia

then opened our first filling station in Prague . . . and plan to extend this network further.'

Filling stations

Petrolub owns nine stations in Prague and its environs, six additional stations on the highway to Prague, and is the only company represented in the Bratislava region, where it has three stations. Because of the general lack of motorized transport and low purchasing power, the network in the Slovakian region has not yet been developed significantly. Because of limited financial resources, filling stations were established in the strongly motorized Prague region. As in Hungary, at approximately 3 million litres per station, annual turnover in the Czech Republic is extremely high.

Apart from Czech goods, the shops also stock a small proportion of Western products, which have not yet developed into a viable segment, however, because of low purchasing power. Claris has its head office in Bratislava and supplies the entire Czech and Slovak networks as well as Vienna and Budapest. This Bratislava base was selected because of its proximity to the Vienna and Budapest regions as much as for the low wages in the Czech/Slovak area.

Figure 10.17 **Price–response function for regular fuel in Czech and Slovak markets**

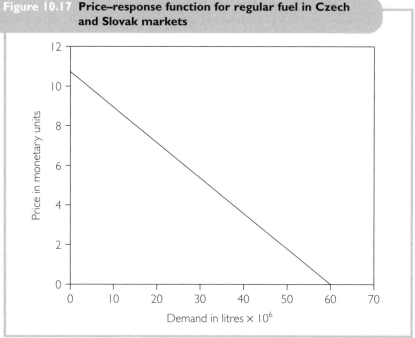

In order to measure demand in the Czech and Slovak markets most effectively, Petrolub engaged an Austrian market research agency. With the aid of state-of-the-arts research methods, particularly conjoint analysis, the agency established the following average price–sales function for the price of petrol in the Czech and Slovak markets:

$$p = 10.8 - 1.8 \cdot 10^{-7}x$$

(where p = price; x = demand in units)

The graphic application of the price–response function in Figure 10.17 shows that demand in these countries is relatively price-elastic.

Lubricants

Because of the heavy industry located in the Slovak region, the lubricant market segment is particularly important. This industry produces armaments (tanks and other equipment), machine tools, bicycles and so on, which are purchased mainly by Russian firms or the Russian and Hungarian governments. For historical reasons, there are strong ties to

Hungary. At the time of the Austro-Hungarian monarchy, Bratislava was the residence of the Hungarian king. Even today as in the early 1990s, there is a strong Hungarian minority of about 600,000 in Slovakia. The automobile industry is another important customer, particularly Skoda, but also automotive garages throughout the Republic.

Because of the proximity to most important local authorities and to the city's infrastructure, all activities are co-ordinated from Prague. A small office in Bratislava services customers in the south. Business is also conducted in the Czech and Slovak areas through regional distributors and wholesalers who offer a selection of the product range. The entire process, including the distributors, wholesalers and retailers, is handled by the Prague operation.

Aviation fuel

Because of the economic transformation processes, the Czech and Slovak markets are becoming increasingly significant. Representatives of foreign firms are also flying into Prague in ever greater numbers to establish initial business contacts or develop existing networks. This increasing interest has resulted in international airlines adapting to the new market conditions and offering more flights between Prague and smaller European or non-European airports. For the air-transport industry, this increasing air travel means a larger potential turnover for Prague airport, by extending the airport's capacity and envouraging interest from international customers.

Liquid gas

Management anticipates considerable growth, particularly in the liquid gas market. Thus, at the end of 1991, a liquid gas bottling plant was acquired in Plzeň for €20 m, the first Western enterprise in the Czech market. The plant will be written off over twenty years on a linear basis. In the meantime, Shell and Austrian OMVs (Österreichische Mineralölverwaltung – Austrian Mineral Oil Corporations) have entered the market.

However, because the plant is not yet at the technical level of Western Europe, there will still be investments in rationalization which, over the first four years, are estimated at £0.8 million. The plant is intended to serve the entire Czech and Slovak markets. At present, the plant is only operating at 70 per cent capacity. However, attempts will be made, particularly in Slovakia, to win new industrial clients for liquid gas. On the basis of the transformation process, 80 per cent capacity utilization (5 million litres) is expected for 1994, and 100 per cent by the millenium.

This is strategically necessary, because in the future years, new competitors will enter the market and put further pressure on the already narrow profit margins in this sector. If the market for 1992 yields a growth rate of 11 per cent, one could work on the basis of 8 per cent for 1993, 7 per cent in 1994, 5 per cent in 1995 an 3 per cent in the ensuing years. The market will first be serviced with the standard 50-litre bottles, which should soon form a viable market segment on the basis of their compact size and low price of £33. There are variable costs of £8 per gas bottle.

Discussion Problems for Petrolub

'What worries me right now is the conflict between the Czech and Slovak markets' says Mrs Smith. 'What happens if the market suddenly falls apart, as in the former USSR? The management board is not taking my warnings in this respect particularly seriously, as if this was just another of my pet theories. But I would really like to know what would happen if there were such repercussions for our firm, and what the impact on our policies would be.' Mrs Smith had already prepared a 'strategic plan', of which the following are the main questions she raised:

1 What criteria could be used to systematize the fragmenting country market? What kind of market separation would we be dealing with?
2 Will the division of Czechoslovakia inevitably be destructive? How can the positive potential of such a division be maximized?
3 Allocate Petrolub's country markets into a 4-field country portfolio, according to the criteria of market attractiveness and barriers to entry. Where are the most attractive markets now, and where will they be after a disintegration? What are the implications for business policy?
4 What impact does the division of the market have on marketing processes and strategies in the lubricant sector? To what extent will these have spillover effecs for the other country offices?
5 What consequences would the market split have for the filling station sector? Take into account the various contractual forms. Analyse the impact of losing filling stations on price policy.

Consider, in particular, the problems associated with a price rise in the Czech Republic, or of a cross-border price-equalization policy: formulate a new price-response function for the Czech Republic. What co-ordination needs would arise? What would happen if lower prices were fixed in Slovakia?

6 Describe the consequences in the liquid gas sector. What impact would the market split have on costs? Develop various scenarios with the aid of spreadsheets.

Bibliography

Ackermann, M. (1997) 'Auswirkungen auseinanderbrechender Märkte in Mittel- und Osteuropa auf das Marketing internationaler Unternehmen', Diploma thesis, Instititute for Business-to-Business Marketing, Westphalian Wilhelmian University, Münster.

Adam, B. (1993a) 'Grundstein für die Festung Europa', *Top Business*, no. 10, pp. 34–8.

Adam, B. (1993b) 'Krieg der Sterne', *Top Business*, no. 4, pp. 30–6.

Adam, D. (1996) *Planung und Entscheidung*, 4th edn, Wiesbaden.

Adolphs, B. (1997) *Stabile und effiziente Geschäftsbeziehungen. Eine Betrachtung von vertikalen Koordinationsstrukturen in der deutschen Automobilindustrie*, Lohmar.

Ahlert, D. (1996) *Distributionspolitik*, 3rd edn, Stuttgart/New York.

Albaum, G., Strandskov, J., Duerr, E. and Dowd, L. (1989) *International Marketing and Export Management*, London.

Ali, I. (1984) 'Rice in Indonesia: Price Policy and Competitive Advantage', *Bulletin of Indonesian Economic Studies* (BIES), no. 3, pp. 80–99.

Altmann, J. and Kulessa, M. E. (eds) (1998) *Internationale Wirtschaftsorganisationen*, Stuttgart.

Anonymous (1996) 'Die Giganten kehren zurück', *Manager Magazin*, Special edition, January 1996, pp. 3–22.

Anonymous. (1999) 'Porsche verlangt als erster Einheitspreise in Europa', *Frankfurter Allgemeine Zeitung*, no. 176, 2 August, p. 19.

Anonymous. (2000) 'Airbus beschließt endgültig den Bau des größten Flugzeugs der Welt', *Frankfurter Allgemeine Zeitung*, no. 296, 20 December, p. 22.

Anonymous. (2001a) 'Hersteller haben Vorbehalte gegen Arzneibestellung im Internet', *Frankfurter Allgemeine Zeitung*, no. 18, 22 January, p. 17.

Anonymous. (2001b) 'Transrapid fährt Ende 2003 in Shanghai', *Frankfurter Allgemeine Zeitung*, no. 18, 22 January, p. 15.

Anonymous (2002) *Business Korea*, 12 March, p. 20.

Appel, H. (1999) 'Fehlzündung in zwei Zylindern', *Frankfurter Allgemeine Zeitung*, no. 178, 4 August, p. 13.

Assmus, G. and Wiese, C. (1995) 'How to Address the Gray Market Threat Using Price Co-ordination', *Sloan Management Review*, Spring, pp. 31–41.

Attour, S. and Harris, G. (1999) 'How Are Three Decades of Debate about Advertising Standardization Reflected in the Practices of Multinational Companies', K. Backhaus, (ed.) *Contemporary Developments in Marketing*, Montpellier, pp. 15–30.

Ayal. I. and Zif, J. (1985) 'Competitive Market Choice Strategies in Multinational Marketing', H. V. Wortzel and L. H. Wortzel, (eds), *Strategic Management of Multinational Corporations*, New York, pp. 265–77.

Backhaus, K. (1999) Industriegütermarketing, 6th edn, Munich.

Backhaus, K., Aufderheide, D. and Späth, G.-M. (1994) *Marketing für Systemtechnologien: Entwicklung eines theoretisch -ökonomisch begründeten Geschäftstypenansatzes*, Stuttgart.

Backhaus, K., Erichson, B., Plinke, W. and Weiber, R. (2000), *Multivariate Analysemethoden*, 9th edition, Berlin.

Backhaus, K., Evers, H.-J., Büschken, J. and Fonger, M. (1992), 'Marketingstrategien für den schienengebundenen Güterfernverkehr', in H.-J. Evers (ed.), *Contributions from the Institute for Transportation Science at the Westphalian Wilhelmian University of Muenster*, no. 126, Göttingen 1992.

Backhaus, K. and Funke, S. (1996) 'Auf dem Weg zur fixkostenintensiven Unternehmung', in *Zeitschrift für betriebswirtschaftliche Forschung (ZfbF)*, no. 2, pp. 95–129.

Backhaus, K. and Meyer, M. (1986) 'Ansätze zur Beurteilung von Länderrisiken', in *Zeitschrift für betriebswirtschaftliche Forschung (ZfbF)*-Special edition 20, pp. 39–60.

Backhaus, K., Mühlfeld, K. and Schlöder, F.-E. (1999) 'Measuring the Degree of Standardization in International Advertising – a Multivariate Analysis-Based Model', in L. Hildebrandt, D. Annacker and D. Klapper (eds), *Proceedings of the 28th Conference of the European Marketing Academy*, Berlin, w. p.

Backhaus, K., Mühlfeld, K. and van Doorn, J. (2001) 'Implementing a Consumer Perspective on Standardization in International Advertising – a Multivariate Analysis-Based Approach Employing a Student Sample', *Journal of Advertising Research*, vol. 41, no. 5, pp. 53–61.

Backhaus, K. and Siepert, H.-M. (1987) *Auftragsfinanzierung im industriellen Anlagengeschäft*, Stuttgart.

Backhaus, K. and Voeth, M. (1994) 'Strategische Allianzen – Erfolgversprechender Weg zur Existenzsicherung in der Textil- und Bekleidungsindustrie?' *Schriftenreihe des Textilverbandes Nord-West*, no. 94, pp. 10–38.

Backhaus, K. and Voeth, M. (1999) 'International Price Coordination on Integrating Markets', in K. Backhaus, (ed.), *Contemporary Developments in Marketing*, Montpellier, pp. 31–44.

Backhaus, K.-H. (2000) 'Konzeption und Implementierung des Pricing Prozesses im internationalen Unternehmen – ein Pilotprojekt', in C. Belz and J. Mühlmeyer, (eds), *Internationales Preismanagement* (*International Pricing*), Vienna/Frankfurt, pp. 38–52.

Bain, J. (1956) *Barriers to New Competition: Their Character and Consequences in Manufacturing Industries*, Cambridge/Mass.

Baron, S., Bierach, B. and Thelen, F. (1997) 'Konsum ist lokal', *Wirtschaftswoche*, no. 10, 27 February, pp. 130–3.

Barrett, C. B. (1996) 'Market Analysis Methods: Are Our Enriched Toolkits Well Suited to Enlivened Markets?', *American Journal of Agricultural Economics*, vol. 78, iss 3, pp. 825–9.

Bartlett, C. A. and Ghoshal, S. (1990) *Managing Across Borders*, New York.

Bartlett, C. A. and Ghoshal, S. (2000) *Transnational Marketing – Text, Cases, and Readings in Cross-border Management*, 3rd edn, Boston.

Bassen, A., Behnam, M. and Gilbert, D. U. (2001) 'Internationalisierung des Mittelstandes. Ergebnisse einer empirischen Studie zum Internationalisierungsverhalten deutscher mittelständischer Unternehmen', *Zeitschrift für Betriebswirtschaft (ZfB)*, no. 4, pp. 413–32.

Bauer, C. L. (1982) *The Rate of Interactive Information Diffusion*, 1982.

Bauer, P. (1993) 'Die neue US-Regierung geht beim Welthandel auf Konfrontationskurs', *VDI-Nachrichten*, no. 14, p. 14.

Bavarian Metal and Electro Association (1995) *Investitionen im Ausland: Umfang, Richtung, Motive, Arbeitsplatzeffekte. Ergebnisse einer Unternehmensbefragung*, Munich.

Becker, U. (1996) *Das Überleben multinationaler Unternehmungen*, Frankfurt.

Berekoven, L. (1983) *Der Dienstleistungsmarkt in der Bundesrepublik Deutschland: Theoretische Fundierung und empirische Analyse*, Göttingen.

Berekoven, L. (1985) *Internationales Marketing*, 2nd edn, Berlin.

Berndt, R., Fantapié Altobelli, C. and Sander, M. (1997) *Internationale Marketing-Politik*, Berlin/Heidelberg.

Berndt, R., Fantapié Altobelli, C. and Sander, M. (1999) *Internationales Marketing-Management*, Berlin/Heidelberg.

Berschens, R. (1998) 'Methapher für ganz Europa', *Wirtschaftswoche*, no. 50, 3 December, pp. 50ff.

Beyer, H. (1993) *Interne Koordination und partizipatives Management*, Marburg.

Bieling, M. (1999) 'Der Internationalisierungsprozeß von Marken', Diploma thesis, Institute for Business-to-Business Marketing, Westphalian Wilhelmian University, Münster.

Bierwisch, H.-J. (1994) 'Von der Texaco zur Dea – die Geburt einer neuen Marke', *Harvard Business Manager (HBM)*, no. 2, pp. 68–74.

Blume, G. (2000) 'Wie Weihnachten nach Peking kam', *Die Zeit*, no. 52, 20 December, p. 32.

Bornfeld, A. (2000) Auf dem Weg zu einem europäischen Preis- und Konditionensystem – Das Beispiel Pritt, in C. Belz and J. Mühlmeyer (eds), *Internationales Preismanagement (International Pricing)*, Vienna/Frankfurt 2000, pp. 152–8.

Bovée, C. and Arens, W. (1986) *Contemporary Advertising*, Illinois.

Bradley, F. (1991) *International Marketing Strategy*, Cambridge.

Bradley, F. (2002) *International Marketing Strategy*, 4th edn, Cambridge.

Braehmer, U. (1983) Nachrichtendiffusion in Großunternehmen – Eine empirische Fallstudie zur kommunikativen Verbreitung von unternehmensinternen Nachrichten in einer industriellen Großorganisation, Münster.

Bridgewater, S. and Egan, C. (2002) *International Marketing Relationships*, New York.

Bucklin, L. P. (1990) *The Grey Market Threat to International Marketing*, MSI Report no. 90/116, Boston.

Bufka, J. (1998) 'Koordinationsmuster im internationalen Dienstleistungsunternehmen: Ergebnisse einer neo-kontingenztheoretischen Untersuchung', M. Kutschker (eds), *Integration in der internationalen Unternehmung*, Wiesbaden, pp. 172–205.

Burger, R., Krüger, J. and Neubert, A. (1998) 'Internet-basierter Teleservice', *Industrie Anzeiger*, no. 3, pp. 37–40.

Burgmaier, S. (1997) 'Harte Bandagen: Das Kartell der großen Kartenorganisationen in Europa zerbricht', *Wirtschaftswoche*, no. 7, 6 February, pp. 42 ff.

Büschemann, K.-H. (1999) 'Viele Preise für einen Mercedes', *Süddeutsche Zeitung*, no. 173, 30 July, p. 2.

Buzzell, R. D. (1968) 'Can You Standardize Multinational Marketing?', *Harvard Business Review (HBR)*, no. 6, pp. 102–13.

Cateora, P. R. and Graham, J. L. (1999) *International Marketing*, 10th edn, Boston.

Cecchini, P. (1988) *Europa '92: Der Vorteil des Binnenmarktes*, Baden-Baden.

Channon, D. F. and Jalland, M. (1979), *Multinational Strategic Planning*, London.

Clark, T. (1994) 'National Boundaries, Border Zones, and Marketing Strategy: A Conceptual Framework and Theoretical Model of Secondary Boundary Effects', *Journal of Marketing*, pp. 67–80.

Corral, C.-B (2002) 'Hellenic Rug Expands to India', *Home Textiles Today*, 18 March 2002, p. 8

Cournot, A. (1924) *Untersuchungen über die mathematischen Grundlagen der Theorie des Reichtums*, Jena.

Cummings, R. W. (1968) 'Effectiveness of Pricing in an Indian Wheat Market: A Case Study of Khama, Punjab', *American Journal of Agricultural Economics*, pp. 687–701.

Czepiel, J. A. (1992), *Competitive marketing strategy*, London.

Czinkota, M. and Ronkainen, I. A. (1998) *International Marketing*, 5th edn, Fort Worth, Tex.

Dähn, M. (1996) *Wettbewerbsvorteile internationaler Unternehmen: Analyse – Kritik – Modellentwicklung*, Wiesbaden.

Danzon, P. M. (1998) 'The Economics of Parallel Trade', *Pharmacoeconomics*, no. 13, pp. 293–304.

Daser, S. and Hylton, D. P. (1991) 'The European Community Single Market of 1992: European Executives Discuss Trends for Global Marketing', *International Marketing Review (IMR)*, 5th edn, pp. 44–8.

Davis, S. M. and Lawrence, P. R. (1977) *Matrix*, Reading.

Deal, T. E. and Kennedy, A. A. (1982) *Corporate Cultures: The Rites and Rituals of Corporate Life*, Reading.

Deysson, C. (1994) 'Mann fürs Grobe', *Wirtschaftswoche*, no. 9, 4 March, pp. 32–6.

Dichter, E. (1962) 'The World Consumer', *Harvard Business Review*, pp. 113–22.

Dichtl, E., Leibold, M., Beeskow, W., Köglmayr, H.-G., Müller, S. and Potucek, V. (1983) 'Die Entscheidung kleiner und mittlerer Unternehmen für die Aufnahme einer Exporttätigkeit', *Zeitschrift für Betriebswirtschaft (ZfB)*, 1983, no. 5, pp. 428–44.

Didzoleit, W. (2001) 'Eintritt versperrt', *Spiegel*, no. 2, 8 January, p. 71.

Dmoch, T. (1996) 'Die Entwicklung standardisierbarer Bilder für die erlebnisorientierte Euro-Werbung', *Planung & Analyse*, no. 4, pp. 28–33.

Doole, I. and Lowe, R. (2000) *International Marketing Strategy*, 2nd edn, London.

Droege, W. P. J., Backhaus, K. and Weiber, R. (1993) *Strategien für Investitionsgütermärkte*, Landsberg/Lech.

Duncan, R. B. (1972) 'Characteristics of Organizational and Perceived Environmental Uncertainty', *Administrative Science Quarterly*, no. 9, pp. 313–27.

Dunkel, M. and Gersemann, O. (1999) 'Maximaler Schmerz', *Wirtschaftswoche*, no. 31, 29 July, p. 30.

Durnoik, P. G. (1985) *Internationales Marketing*, Baden-Baden.

Dwyer, R. and Tanner, J. (1999) *Business Marketing – Connecting Strategy, Relationships, and Learning*, Boston, Mass.

El-Agraa, A. (1989) *International Trade*, New York.

Ellis, F., Magrath, P. and Trotter, B. (1991) *Indonesia Rice Marketing Study 1989–1991, Main Report*, Bulog.

Emerson, M. (1989) *The Economics of 1992: An Assessment of the Potential Economic Effects of Completing the Internal Market of the European Community*.

Fälschle, C. (1999) 'Markt mit Hindernissen', *Capital*, no. 7, pp. 99–102.

Forman, D. H., Lancioni, D. R. A. and Smith, M. F. (2000) 'Strategic Management Options of International Pricing', in C. Belz and J. Mühlmeyer (eds), *Internationales Preismanagement (International Pricing)*, Vienna/Frankfurt, pp. 30–7.

Frese, E. (1992) *Organisationstheorie*, 2nd edn, Wiesbaden.

Funke, S. (1995) *Fixkosten und Beschäftigungsrisiko*, Munich.

Gaul, W. and Lutz, U. (1993) 'Paneuropäische Tendenzen in der Preispolitik: Eine empirische Studie', *Der Markt*, no. 4, pp. 189–204.

Gaul, W. and Lutz, U. (1994) 'Pricing in International Marketing and Western European Economic Integration', *Management International Review*, no. 2, pp. 101–24.

Gersemann, O. (1999) 'Mit voller Wucht', *Wirtschaftswoche*, no. 4, 21 January, p. 25.

Ghemawat, P. and Spence, A. M. (1989) 'Die Modellierung des globalen Wettbewerbs', M. E. Porter (ed.), *Globaler Wettbewerb. Strategien der neuen Internationalisierung*, Wiesbaden.

Govindarajan, V. and Gupta, A.K. (1991) *Knowledge Flow Patterns, Subsidary Strategic Roles, and Strategic Control within MNCs*, Best Paper Proceedings, Academy of Management National Meetings, Miami, 1991, pp. 21ff.

Grill, B. (2001) 'Wer nicht zahlen kann, stirbt', *Die Zeit*, 29 March, p. 29.

Gutzmer, A. (2001) 'Wer kennt schon Aventis', *WamS*, no. 9, 4 March, p. 57.

Hair, J., Anderson, R., Tatham, R. and Black, W. (1998) *Multivariate Data Ananlysis*, 5th edn, Prentice Hall College Div.

Håkansson, H. and Snehota, L. (1995) *Developing Relationships in Business Networks*, London/New York.

Hakio, C. S. and Rush, M. (1989) 'Market Efficiency and Cointegration: An Application to the Sterling and Deutsche Mark Exchange Markets', *Journal of International Money and Finance*, pp. 75–88.

Handge, L. (1997) 'Fern und doch so nah – Teleservice verbessert Kundenbindung auf weit entfernt liegenden Wachstumsmärkten', *Maschinenmarkt*, no. 40, pp. 20–3.

Hatschikjan, M. A. (1995) 'Haßlieben und Spannungsgemeinschaften – Zum Verhältnis von Demokratien und Nationalismen im neuen Osteuropa', *Das Parlament*, Beilage B 39/95 (Aus Politik und Zeitgeschichte), 22 September, pp. 12–21.

Hax, H. (1965) *Die Koordination von Entscheidungen*, Cologne.

Hedlund, G. (1981) 'Autonomy of Subsidiaries and Formalization of Headquarters – Subsidiary Relationship in Swedish MNCs', L. Otterbeck (ed.), *The Management of Headquarters – Subsidiary Relationship in Multinational Corporations*, Aldershot.

Heinrichs, J. (1973) 'Die Koordination von Entscheidungen in multinationalen Unternehmungen', Dissertation, Mannheim.

Henderson, B. D. (1980), *Perspectives on Experience*, Ann Arbor, Mich.

Hennan, D. A. and Perlmutter, H. V. (1979) *Multinational Organization Development*, Reading.

Hermann, A., Ochel, W. and Wegner, M. (1990) *Bundesrepublik und Binnenmarkt '92*, Munich.

Hill, C. W. L (1996) *International Business – Competing in the Global Marketplace*, 2nd edn, New York.

Hill, J. S. and Still, R. R. (1984) 'Adapting Products to LDC Tastes', *Harvard Business Review*, (*HBR*), no. 3/4, pp. 92–101.

Hill, W., Fehlbaum, R. and Ulrich, P. (1981), *Organisationslehre*, 3rd edition, Berne/Stuttgart.

Hinrichs, W. (1989) 'Der deutsche Einzelhandel auf dem Wege zum Europäischen Binnenmarkt – Probleme des Mittelstandes', *Markenartikel*, no. 6, pp. 260–8.

Hinzdorf, T. (2001) 'Informationsbasierte Marktintegration – Entstehung integrierter Märkte im internationalen Marketing durch Informationsdiffusion', Dissertation, Ingolstadt.

Hite, R. E. and Fraser, C. (1988) 'International Advertising Strategies of Multinational Corporations', *Journal of Advertising Research*, no. 4, pp. 9–17.

Hollensen, S. (2001) *Global Marketing: A Market-responsive Approach*, 2nd edn, Prentice Hall.

Homburg, C. (1995) 'Single Sourcing, Double Sourcing, Multiple Sourcing . . .? Ein ökonomischer Erklärungsansatz', *Zeitschrift für Betriebswirtschaft* (*ZfB*), no. 8, pp. 813–34.

Hotze, H. (1999) 'Brittan bleibt bei der Banane hart', *Welt am Sonntag*, no. 6, 7 February, p. 60.

Huckemann, M. and Dinges, A. (2000) 'Die Harmonisierung der Europäischen Preise – Das Beispiel 3M', in C. Belz and J. Mühlmeyer (eds), *Internationales Preismanagement* (*International Pricing*), Vienna/Frankfurt, pp. 170–91.

Hünerberg, R. (1994) *Internationales Marketing*, Landsberg/Lech.

Institut der deutschen Wirtschaft (Cologne Institute for Business Research) (1997) 'Globalisierung im Spiegel von Theorie und Empirie', *Beiträge zur Wirtschafts- und Sozialpolitik*, no. 235, Cologne.

International Monetary Fund (2000), Schuldeninitiative für die Hochverschuldeten Armen Länder (HIPCs), Informationsblatt, 11 September.

Jacob, H. (1971) *Preispolitik*, 2nd edn, Wiesbaden.

Jarillo, J. (1988) 'On Strategic Networks', *Strategic Management Journal*, pp. 31–41.

Jeannet, J.-P. and Hennessey, H. (1998) *Global Marketing Strategies*, 4th edn, Boston, Mass.

Jensen, S. (1998) 'Der Preis ist heiß', *Manager Magazin*, no. 3, pp. 119–31.

Johnsen, R. E. and Johnsen, T. E (1999) 'Networks as a Means to Internationalisation for Small Firms: An Explanatory Case', in K. Backhaus (ed.), *Contemporary Developments in Marketing*, Montpellier, pp. 295–308.

Kaas, K. P. (1973) *Diffusion und Marketing – Das Konsumentenverhalten bei der Einführung neuer Produkte*, Stuttgart.

Kahler, R. and Kramer, R. L. (1977) *International Marketing*, Cincinnati.

Kalish, S., Mahajan, V. and Muller, E. (1995) 'Waterfall and Sprinkler: New-Product Strategies in Competitive Global Markets', *International Journal of Research in Marketing*, pp. 105–19.

Kant, M. A. L. and Borchert, M. (1995) 'Internationales Preismanagement und Preisinformationssysteme bei der Continental AG', in D. Baier and R. Decker (eds), *Marketingprobleme: innovative Lösungsansätze aus Forschung und Praxis*, Regensburg, pp. 103–12.

Kanter, R. M. (1996) 'Case Study: Using Networking for Competitive Advantage', *Strategy & Business*, no. 3, pp. 1–13.

Kapferer, J.-N. (1989) *Strategic Brand Management: New Approaches to Creating and Evaluating Brand Equity* (translation of: *Les marques, capital de l'entreprise*, 2nd edn, London.

Kappagoda, N. (1997) 'The Debt Crisis: Fifteen Years On', http://www.acdi-cida.gc.ca/xpress/dex/dex9703.htm

Karfakis, C. J. and Moschos, D. M. (1990) 'Interest Rate Linkages within the European Monetary System: A Time Series Analysis', *Journal of Money, Credit and Banking*, pp. 388–94.

Keegan, W. J. and Green, M. C. (2001) *Global Marketing Management*, 7th edn, Prentice Hall.

Keegan, W. J. and Schlegelmilch, B. B. (2001) *Global Marketing Management – A European Persepective*, London/New York, p. 376

Kieser, A. and Kubicek, H. (1992) *Organisation, 3. Auflage*, Berlin/New York.

Killough, J. (1978) 'Improved Payoffs from Transnational Advertising', *Harvard Business Review (HBR)*, no. 4, pp. 102–10.

Kläsgen, M. (2000) 'Heftige Kapriolen, *Die Zeit*, no. 1, 28 December, p. 25.

Kleinert, J., Schimmelpfennig, A., Schrader, J. and Stehn, J. (2000) *Globalisierung, Strukturwandel und Beschäftigung*, Kieler Studien 308, Tübingen.

Kobrin, S. J. (1984) *International Expertise in American Business*, New York.

Köhler, R. and Hüttemann, H. (1989) *Marktauswahl im internationalen Marketing*, in K. Marcharzina and M. K. Welge (eds), HWInt, Stuttgart, pp. 1428–40.

Kommission der Europäischen Gemeinschaften (EU Commission) (1989) 'Sich den Herausforderungen der frühen 90er Jahre stellen', *Europäische Wirtschaft*, 1989, no. 11, pp. 208ff.

Kommission der Europäischen Gemeinschaften (EU Commission) (1992) *The Economics of 1992 – An Assessment of the Potential Effects of Completing the Internal Market of the EC*, Brussels.

Krämer, L. (1985) *EWG-Verbraucherrecht*, Baden-Baden.

Kreikebaum, H. (1998) *Organisationsmanagement internationaler Unternehmen*, Wiesbaden.

Kreke, J. M. (1991) 'Strategische Maßnahmen eines Handelsunternehmens zur Vorbereitung auf den Europäischen Binnenmarkt', in A. Töpfer and R. Berger (eds), *Unternehmenserfolg im europäischen Binnenmarkt*, Landsberg/Lech 1991, pp. 397–411.

Kreutzer, R. (1989) *Global Marketing – Konzeption eines länderübergreifenden Marketing*, Wiesbaden.

Kuchar, V. (2001) 'Meat producers Mull Export Union to Stave off Dropping Demand', *Prague Business Journal*, 12 November, vol. 6, no. 45, p.13.

Kulhavy, E. (1993) *Internationales Marketing*, 5th edn, Linz.

Lamparter, D. H. (2001) 'Comeback der Verlierer', *Die Zeit*, no. 9, 22 February, p. 19.

Lampe, F. L. (1999) 'The Internet in International Marketing Management', in K. Backhaus (ed.), *Contemporary Developments in Marketing*, Montpellier, pp. 361–75.

Lampert, T. (2000) 'Die Messung der Arbitrageneigung von Nachfragern im Internationalen Marketing – ein konzeptioneller und empirischer Vergleich', Diploma thesis, Institute for Business-to-Business Marketing, Westphalian Wilhelmian University, Münster.

Landwehr, R. (1988) *Standardisierung der internationalen Werbeplanung*, Frankfurt.

Levitt, T. (1983) 'The Globalization of Markets', *Harvard Business Review* (*HBR*), no. 5, pp. 87–91.

Liedtke, A. (1992) ' "Raider heißt jetzt Twix, sonst ändert sich nix" ', *Markenartikel*, no. 9, pp. 402–15.

Lilien, G. and Kotler, P. (1983) *Marketing Decision Making: A Model Building Approach*, p. 311.

Linden, F. A. (1998) 'Global daneben', *Manager Magazin*, no. 5, pp. 54–65.

Löbler, H. (2000) 'The Impact of Exchange Rate Changes on International Pricing', in: *Operation Research Proceedings*, Berlin/Heidelberg, pp. 509–16.

Losonez, M. (1990) 'RGW- und EG-Perspektiven der künftigen Beziehungen aus ungarischer Sicht', in R. Welzmüller (ed.), *Marktaufteilung und Standortpoker in Europa*, Cologne, pp. 339–52.

Lutz, U. (1994) *Preispolitik im internationalen Marketing und westeuropäische Integration*, Frankfurt.

M+M EUROdATA (1997) Internationalisierungswelle im Lebensmittelhandel rollt an, M+M EUROdATA-Pressemitteilung, 12 November.

M+M EUROdATA (2000) Lebensmittelhandel Europa: TOP 5 mit nahezu doppeltem Marktanteil innerhalb von 10 Jahren, M+M EUROdATA-Pressemitteilung, 15 November.

Martin, H.-P. and Schumann, H. (1996) *Die Globalisierungsfalle: Der Angriff auf Demokratie und Wohlstand*, Hamburg.

Meffert, H. (1989a) 'Globalisierungsstrategien und ihre Umsetzung im internationalen Wettbewerb', in *Die Betriebswirtschaft* (*DBW*), 1989, pp. 445–63.

Meffert, H. (1990) *Marktorientierte Unternehmensführung im europäischen Binnenmarkt: Perspektiven aus der Sicht von Wissenschaft und Praxis*, Stuttgart.

Meffert, H. and Bolz, J. (1993) 'Standardization of Marketing in Europe', in C. Halliburton and R. Hünerberg (eds.), *European Marketing – Readings and Cases*, Cambridge, pp. 45–62.

Meffert, H. and Bolz, J. (1998) *Internationales Marketing-Management*, 3rd edn, Stuttgart.

Meissner, H. G. (1990) 'Marketing im Gemeinsamen Europäischen Markt', in H. Berg, H.G. Meissner and W. B. Schünemann (eds), *Märkte in Europa – Strategien für das Marketing*, Stuttgart.

Meissner, H. G. (1994) 'Internationale Markenstrategien', in M. Bruhn (ed.), *Handbuch Markenartikel*, Stuttgart, vol. 1, pp. 673–85.

Merkle, E. (1984) 'Technologiemarketing', in *Marketing ZFP*, no. 1, pp. 5–14.

Moen, Ø. (2000) 'SMEs and International Marketing: Investigating the Differences in Export Strategy Between Firms of Different Size', in *Journal of Global Marketing*, no. 4, pp. 7–28.

Moore, J. (1997) *Pharmaceutical Pricing – 1997 Edition*, London.

Mueller, B. (1991) 'Multinational Advertising: Factors Influencing the Standardized vs. Specialised Approach', *International Marketing Review*, no. 1, pp. S.7–18.

Mühlbacher, H., Dahringer, L. and Leihs, H. (1999) *International Marketing*, 2nd edn, London.

Müller, S. and Kornmeier, M. (2000) 'Mentale Eintrittsbarrieren: Subjektive Einflüsse auf Art und Weise der präferierten Markteintrittstrategie', in D. v. Oelsnitz (ed.), *Markteintritts-Management*, Stuttgart, pp. 13–42.

Münster, W. (1999) 'Verbotener Druck auf die Händler', *Süddeutsche Zeitung*, no. 173, 30 July, p. 2.

Mutimear, J. (2000) 'Parallel Wars Rage on in Europe', in *Managing Intellectual Property*, December 99/January 2000, no. 95, pp.15–18.

Nairn, G. (1997) 'Trading Places: From Purchasing to Invoicing, Business Are Linking Up', in *Financial Times*, 27 August, p. 15.

Naisbitt, J. (1984) *Megatrends*, Bayreuth.

OECD (1996a) *Market Access after the Uruguay Round*, Paris.

OECD (1996b) *Trade and Competition: frictions after the Uruguay Round*, Paris.

Ohmae, K. (1985) *Triad Power: The Coming Shape of Global Competition*, New York.

Ohmae, K. (1996) *The End of the Nation State: The Rise of Regional States*, London.

Oliver, T. (1996) *The Real Coke, the Real Story*, New York.

Onkvisit, S. and Shaw, J. (1993) *International Marketing – Analysis and Strategy, 2. Auflage*, New York.

Pay, D. de (1989) 'Kulturspezifische Determinanten der Organisation von Innovationsprozessen', *Zeitschrift für Betriebswirtschaft (ZfB)*, Ergänzungsheft 1, pp. 131–40.

Perlitz, M. (2000) *Internationales Management*, 4th edn, Stuttgart.

Perlitz, M. and Seger, F. (2000) 'Konzepte internationaler Markteintrittstrategien', in D. v. Oelsnitz (ed.), *Markteintritts-Management*, Stuttgart, pp. 89–119.

Pfeiffer, D. (2000) 'Das Ende der Airbus-Zitterpartie', in *WamS*, no. 47, 19 November, p. 71.

Picot, A., Reichwald, R. and Wiegand, R. (2001) *Die grenzenlose Unternehmung*, 4th edn, Wiesbaden.

Porter, M. (1989) 'Der Wettbewerb auf globalen Märkten: Ein RahmenKonzept', in M. Porter (ed.), *Globaler Wettbewerb. Strategien der neuen Internationalisierung*, Wiesbaden, S. 17–68.

Porter, M. E. (ed.) (1986) *Competition in Global Industries*, Boston, Mass.

Prahalad, C. K. and Doz, Y. L. (1987) *The Multinational Mission*, London.

Quack, H. (1995) *Internationales Marketing*, Munich.

Raffee and Kreutzer (1989) 'Organizational Dimensions of Global Marketing', in *European Journal of Marketing*, no. 23, pp. 43–57.

Ravallion, M. (1985) 'The Performance of Rice Markets in Bangladesh during the 1974 Famine', *Economic Journal*, vol. 95, is 377, pp. 15–29.

Ravallion, M. (1986) 'Testing Market Integration', *American Journal of Agricultural Economics*, vol. 68, pp. 102–9.

Read, R. A. (1994) 'The EC internal Banana Market: The Issues and the Dilemma', *The World Economy*, no. 17, pp. 219–35.

Reischauer, C. (1997) 'Höllisch aufpassen', *Wirtschaftswoche*, no. 37, 24 October, pp. 120–3.

Ricks, D. A. (1983) 'Products that Crashed into the Language Barrier', *Business and Society Review*, no. 1, pp. 46–50.

Ring, P. S. and van de Veen, A. H. (1992) 'Structuring Co-operative Relationships between Organizations', *Strategic Management Journal*, pp. 483–98.

Sabel, H. and Weiser, C. (1998) *Dynamik im Marketing*, 2nd edn, Wiesbaden.

Samiee, S. (1998) 'The Internet and International Marketing: Is there a Fit?', *Journal of Interactive Marketing*, no. 4, pp. 5–21.

Samli, A. C., Still, R. and Hill, J. S. (1993) *International Marketing – Planning and Practice*, New York.

Sander, M. (1997) *Internationales Preismanagement: eine Analyse preispolitischer Handlungsalternativen im internationalen Marketing unter besonderer Berücksichtigung der Preisfindung bei Marktinterdependenzen*, Heidelberg.

Schirm, S. A. (1999) 'Globalisierung – eine Chance für Entwicklungsländer?', *Informationen zur politischen Bildung*, no. 263, pp. 26–31.

Schlöder, F.-E. (1998) 'Standardisierung in der internationalen Kommunikationspolitik: Einsatzmöglichkeiten von Scoring-Modellen zur Beurteilung des Standardisierungsgrades', Diploma thesis, Institute for Business-to-Business Marketing, Westphalian Wilhelmian University, Münster.

Schneider, D. (1998) 'Die Internationalisierung des Einzelhandels: Trends und Erfolgsfaktoren', *ZfB*, no. 12, pp. 1325–39.

Schneider, D. J. G. (1984) 'Ansatzpunkte für ein internationales Investitionsgüter-Marketingkonzept', *Der Markt*, no. 3, pp. 69–77.

Schneider, D. J. G. (1995) 'Internationale Distributionspolitik', in A. Hermanns and U. K. Wißmeier (eds), *Internationales Marketing-Management*, Munich, pp. 256–80.

Schneider, D. J. G. and Müller, R. U. (1989) *Datenbankgestützte Marktselektion: Eine methodische Basis für Internationalisierungsstrategien*, Stuttgart.

Schneider, M. (1999) 'Der Masterplan des Metro-Lenkers', *Welt am Sonntag*, no. 6, 7 February, p. 55.

Schneider, M. (2001) 'Brandstifter Opel', *WamS*, no. 3, 21 January, p. 49.

Schott, J. and Oegg (2001) 'Europe or the Americas: Toward a Tafta South?', *World Economy*, June.

Siems, D. (1994) 'Lächerliche Strafen', *Wirtschaftswoche*, no. 9, 10 March, p. 34.

Silvapulle, P. and Jayasuriya, S. (1992) 'Testing for Market Integration: A Multiple Cointegration Approach, Discussion Paper 25/92, Department of Economics, La Trobe University (Australia), August.

Simon, H. (1989) 'Markteintrittsbarrieren', in K. Macharzina and M. K. Welge (eds), *Handwörterbuch Export und Internationale Unternehmung*, Stuttgart, pp. 1441–53.

Simon, H. (1992) *Preismanagement: Analyse, Strategien, Umsetzung*, 2nd edn, Wiesbaden.

Simon, H., Lauszus, D. and Kneller, M. (1998) 'Der Euro kommt: Implikationen für das europäische Preismanagement', *DBW*, no. 6, pp. 786–802.

Simon, H. and Wiese, C. (1992) 'Europäisches Preismanagement', *Marketing ZFP*, no. 4, pp. 246–56.

Stehn, J. (2000) 'Globalisierung und Beschäftigung', *Wirtschaftswissenschaftliches Studium (WiSt)*, no. 9, pp. 528–30.

Stonehouse, G., Hamill, J., Campbell, D. and Purdie, T. (2000) *Global and Transnational Business: Strategy and Management*, New York.

Tabor, S. R. (1989) *Price and Quality of Rice in Java: An Investigation into the Demand for Closely Related Goods*, Amsterdam.

Takeuchi, M. T. and Porter, M. E. (1989) 'Die Koordination globaler Fertigungsprozesse', in M. E. Porter (ed.), *Globaler Wettbewerb. Strategien der neuen Internationalisierung*, Wiesbaden, pp. 95–126.

Tempstra, V. and Sarathy, R. (1999) *International Marketing*, South-Western Publishing.

Thiesing, E.-O. (1989) 'Einzelhandel im gemeinsamen Binnenmarkt – Auswirkungen und strategische Optionen', in M. Bruhn and F. Wehrle (eds), *Europa 1992: Chancen und Risiken für das Marketing*, Münster.

Thorelli, H. B. (1990) 'Networks: The Gray Nineties in International Marketing', in H. Thorelli and S. T. Cavusgil (eds), *International Marketing Strategy*, 3rd edn., Oxford, pp. 73–85.

Timmer, P. (1974), *A Model of Rice Marketing Margins in Indonesia*, Food Research Institute Studies, no. 2, pp. 145–67.

Tödtmann, C. (1995) 'Markenschutz: Schnell anmelden', *Wirtschaftswoche*, no. 15, 6 April, pp. 94–6.

Tostmann, T. (1984) 'Möglichkeiten und Grenzen internationaler Werbekampagnen', in A. Hermanns and A. Meyer (eds), *Zukunftsorientiertes Marketing für Theorie und Praxis*, Berlin, pp. 217–34.

Tostmann, T. (1985) 'Die Globalisierung der Werbung', *Harvard Manager (HM)*, no. 2, pp. 54–60.

Trabold, H. (1999) 'Gesellschaftliche Auswirkungen internationaler Wirtschaftsbeziehungen', *Informationen zur politischen Bildung*, no. 263, pp. 31–41.

Trommsdorff, V. and Schuchardt, C. A. (1998) *Transformation osteuropäischer Unternehmen*, Wiesbaden.

Ulrich, H. (1983) 'Management – eine unverstandene gesellschaftliche Funktion', in H. Siegwart and G. Probst (eds), *Mitarbeiterführung und gesellschaftlicher Wandel: Die kritische Gesellschaft und ihre Konsequenzen für die Mitarbeiterführung*, Berne/Stuttgart.

Urban, M. (2000) 'Markteintritt von Automobilherstellern in Asien', in D. v. Oelsnitz (ed.), *Markteintritts-Management*, Stuttgart, pp. 269–86.

Usunier, J.-C. (2000) *Marketing across Cultures*, 3rd edn, London.

Vogler, S. (1998) *Arzneimittel – Vertrieb in Europa*, Vienna.

Welge, M. K. (1989) 'Koordinations- und Steuerungsinstrumente', in K. Macharzina and M. K. Welge (eds), *Handwörterbuch Export und Internationale Unternehmung*, Stuttgart, pp. 1182–91.

Went, T. (2000) *Vereinheitlichung der Werbung im Rahmen der internationalen Marktbearbeitung: eine empirische Untersuchung am Beispiel des Shampoo-Marktes*, Frankfurt.

Whitelock, J. and Chung, D. (1989) 'Cross-Cultural Advertising – An Empirical Study', *International Journal of Advertising*, pp. 291–310.

Wiechmann, U. (1974) 'Integrating Multinational Market Activities', *Columbia Journal of World Business*, Winter, pp. 32–44.

Williamson, O. (1991) 'Comparative Economic Organization: The Analysis of Discrete Structural Alternatives', *Administrative Science Quarterly*, pp. 269–96.

World Bank (1988) *World Debt Tables, External Debt of Development Countries*, Washington, DC.

WTO (World Trade Organization) (2000) *International Trade Statistics*, Geneva.

WTO (World Trade Organization) (2001) *International Trade Statistics 2001*, table II.1, p. 29.

Wyeth, J. (1992) *The Measurement of Market Integration and Applications to Food Security Policies*, Discussion Paper No. 314, Institute of Development Studies.

Young, S., Hamill, J., Wheeler, C. and Davis, J. R. (1989) *International Market Entry and Development*, Eaglewood Cliffs, NJ.

Zentes, J. and Swoboda, B. (2001) 'Bedeutungswandel des Internationalen Marketing', *Frankfurter Allgemeine Zeitung*, no. 133, 11 September, p. 33.

Zhang, S. and Schmitt, B.-H. (2001) 'Creating Local Brands in Multilingual International Markets', *Journal of Marketing Research*, vol. 38, August, pp. 313–25.

Zoeten, R. de (1993) *Technische Harmonisierung und Euro-Marketing*, Munich.

# Index

Note: f = figure; n = note; t = table; **bold** = extended discussion.